THE EVALUATION OF PSYCHIATRIC TREATMENT

Officers of the

AMERICAN PSYCHOPATHOLOGICAL ASSOCIATION

for 1962

Lauretta Bender, M.D., *President*

D. Ewen Cameron, M.D., *President-Elect*

Jerome D. Frank, M.D., *Vice-President*

Fritz A. Freyhan, M.D., *Secretary*

Bernard C. Glueck, Jr., M.D., *Treasurer*

W. Horsley Gannt, M.D., *Councillor*

Reginald S. Lourie, M.D., *Councillor*

COMMITTEE ON PROGRAM

Paul H. Hoch, M.D., *Chairman*

Joseph Zubin, Ph.D.

James P. Cattell, M.D.

THE EVALUATION OF PSYCHIATRIC TREATMENT

Edited by **PAUL H. HOCH, M. D.**

Department of Mental Hygiene, State of New York; College of Physicians and Surgeons, Columbia University, New York City.

and **JOSEPH ZUBIN, Ph. D.**

Department of Mental Hygiene, State of New York; Department of Psychology, Columbia University, New York City.

THE PROCEEDINGS OF THE FIFTY-SECOND ANNUAL MEETING OF THE AMERICAN PSYCHOPATHOLOGICAL ASSOCIATION, HELD IN NEW YORK CITY, FEBRUARY 1962.

GRUNE & STRATTON

NEW YORK • LONDON • 1964

SAMUEL W. HAMILTON AWARDS

NAME		SYMPOSIUM
Clarence P. Oberndorf, M.D.	1952	*Depression*
John C. Whitehorn, M.D.	1953	*Psychiatry and the Law*
David M. Levy, M.D.	1954	*Psychopathology of Childhood*
Stanley Cobb, M.D.	1955	*Experimental Psychopathology*
Sandor Rado, M.D.	1956	*Psychopathology of Communication*
Karl M. Bowman, M.D.	1957	*Problems of Addiction and Habituation*
Bernard Glueck, Sr., M.D.	1958	*Trends in Psychoanalysis*
Sir Aubrey Lewis, M.D.	1959	*Comparative Epidemiology in the Mental Disorders*
Franz J. Kallmann, M.D.	1960	*Psychopathology of Aging*
Nolan D. C. Lewis, M.D.	1961	*Future of Psychiatry*
Franz Alexander, M.D.	1962	*Evaluation of Therapy*

LILLIAN AND HENRY STRATTON AWARDS

Name		*Symposium*
James Birren, Ph.D.	1960	*Psychopathology of Aging*
Benjamin Pasamanick, M.D.	1961	*Future of Psychiatry*
Heinz E. Lehmann, M.D.	1962	*Evaluation of Therapy*

Library of Congress Card Number 64-22049

381 Park Avenue South, New York, N. Y.

Printed in the United States of America (K-A)

CONTENTS

Part IV: Special Problems of Evaluation

Appendix

PREFACE

EVALUATION OF THERAPY should be as important in psychiatry as auditing is in commerce, yet we have lagged considerably behind commercial practice in this regard. Few psychiatrists would tolerate in their secretaries the kind of bookkeeping which they practice in their own field; or if they did, they would soon go bankrupt. Why this state of affairs prevails in psychiatry is one of the paradoxes of our time. Practitioners of medicine often have the pathological laboratory as the final crucial testing ground for their failures as well as successes. Even pathology is not always unequivocal in its answer, but at least it provides an independent criterion. This is what is lacking in the evaluation of psychiatric therapy. As long as psychopathology does not offer the crucial tests that pathology has already developed, there is no hope of improving our evaluation. We must supply psychopathology with measuring rods which will enable us to decide in a given case, the degree of improvement obtained.

It is a great pleasure to see that in this symposium, we have ceased giving lip-service to the needs of evaluation, have ceased hiding behind such evasionary tactics as studying the "process" when outcome evades us, and have begun to develop basic instruments of evaluation which can stand the test of practice. One of the vexing problems that has emerged is the need for criteria of outcome which, on the one hand, take into consideration individual psychopathology and, on the other, consider the tolerance for deviant behavior available in the community. Apparently, improvement in today's hospitals and clinics can not depend on lifting of symptoms alone. Reintegration into the community and family is essential before even the pathology-free patient can be rehabilitated. However, studying the social aspects alone is not enough. The interaction between psychopathology and the social milieu, now the least understood link in the chain of recovery, seems to be the crucial problem for which our best efforts are needed. This is not to indicate that we now have well developed tools for evaluating individual psychopathology. We still need a good deal of work even in this area, but the social area, being the more recently developed, is in greater need of progress.

THE EDITORS

FRANZ ALEXANDER
1891 - 1964

FRANZ ALEXANDER, M. D.

Samuel W. Hamilton Award Lecturer, 1962

THE SAMUEL W. HAMILTON MEMORIAL AWARD was established in the memory of Dr. Hamilton who was President and for many years Secretary of the American Psychopathological Association. His contributions to American Psychiatry were great. The improvements of many state hospital services can be attributed to Dr. Hamilton's untiring work and efforts. His view of psychiatric progress was always broad and unprejudiced.

In this spirit this year's award is given to Dr. Franz Alexander. To give you some details of Dr. Alexander's background, he was born in Budapest, Hungary on January 22, 1891. He has had an illustrious career in Hungary, Germany, and in the United States. He finished medical school at the University of Budapest and interned at the University Hospital of Budapest from 1912 through 1913. Dr. Alexander took postgraduate training in experimental pathology at the University of Berlin, trained at the Physiological Institute of Cambridge University, and worked in the Institute of Public Health at the University of Budapest. Following 1932 he did research in psychosomatic medicine at the Psychoanalytic Institute in Chicago and it was in 1932 that he became its first Director. Since 1956 he has been Director of the Psychiatric and Psychosomatic Research Institute at Mt. Sinai Hospital in Los Angeles. He was Clinical Professor of Psychiatry at the University of Illinois from 1943 to 1956 and since 1957, Clinical Professor of Psychiatry at the University of Southern California. Dr. Alexander has published extensively and in the following we would like to mention a few of his major contributions to the fields of psychiatry and psychoanalysis. Many of his published papers from 1921 to 1961 appear in his book THE SCOPE OF PSYCHOANALYSIS: SELECTED PAPERS OF FRANZ ALEXANDER; THE WESTERN MIND IN TRANSITION, OUR AGE OF UNREASON, and PSYCHOANALYSIS: PRINCIPLES AND APPLICATION.

As Director of the Psychoanalytic Institute in Chicago he influenced American psychoanalysis to a considerable degree, and in my own and countless others' opinions, for the better. Alexander saw clearly how many of the orthodox, dogmatic theories, and clinical approaches were out of date and out of step with contemporary psychiatry.

Franz Alexander has made many, many contributions to the theories of psychoanalysis where he tried to reconcile the biological aspects with the social, and especially in psychosomatic medicine and in criminology. We consider his main contributions to be the introduction of a shorter form of psychoanalysis and psychotherapy, and the freeing of the psychoanalytic technique from much of its ritualistic methodology. His new interests are to objectivate psychoanalytic therapy, the study of its technique in the way of recordings, and the evaluation of these recordings.

All these outstanding contributions have made Dr. Franz Alexander one of the most prominent psychoanalysts in the United States and abroad and we feel that his studies in psychopathology should be recognized with the highest award we can bestow, namely, the Samuel W. Hamilton Memorial Award.

PAUL H. HOCH, M.D.

Part I: Methods of Evaluating Various Types of Psychiatric Treatments

1

THE EVALUATION OF PSYCHOTHERAPY

by LEWIS R. WOLBERG, M.D.*

WHATEVER VALUES WE PLACE ON PSYCHOTHERAPY—its fabulous history, its break with tradition, its bountiful and imaginative theories, the spectacular publicity it has received, and the power and reputation of its practitioners—these are but incidental to the supreme test of its worth in terms of its capacity to help people feel better and function better. Unfortunately, it has been extremely difficult to establish a causal relationship between the techniques and methods of any psychotherapeutic system known to us today and the changes that have been brought about through the instrumentality of this system. A number of adventitious dimensions contaminate our findings in that emotional problems seem to respond to factors other than therapeutic method, such as spontaneous remission, placebo cure, the random healing benefit of a simple relationship situation, emotional catharsis brought about by mere verbalization, and sundry rationalistic, escape and control devices. Negative adventitious elements that block treatment benefits and that often go undetected are also present in the form of insidious, unyielding resistances and therapist incompetence. It would behoove us to bring order to this phenomenalistic chaos by subjecting the events that occur during and as a result of psychotherapy to the discipline of ordered observation and experiment. However, because present-day propositions that exist in the field of psychotherapy are not of a high order of empirically-tested probability, it is difficult to demonstrate the effects of treatment by any concrete methods and operations. Attempts to apply probability theory to the events of psychotherapy are blocked by formidable difficulties involving special

*Postgraduate Center for Mental Health, New York, N. Y.

problems of the therapist, the resistances of the patient, the amorphous status of diagnosis, the prejudiced selection of the sample, the involved uses of outside judges, coders and raters, the inability to employ adequate controls, the interferences of coincidental healing factors, and the complexities inherent in psychotherapeutic process. These obstructions would seem to spell the death of any attempts at evaluation. If, however, we admit that we are unable to approach the problem completely by scientific method, this does not mean that we have to abandon all measurements and observations. Proper employment of our current instruments may lead us to more sophisticated designs and to more precise tools. The problem is that we have not been utilizing our present instruments appropriately or consistently.

What is essential is that we agree on criteria of improvement and upon necessary compromises with ideal change. Various indices of change may then be delineated including observations and reports, self-administered inventories, projective tests, dreams, physiological measurements, and the content analysis of interviews. Employing such criteria of improvement and applying the indices of change, we may then construct a practical model of evaluation, and we may devise methods that can provide us with a more solid underpinning for the worth of the psychotherapeutic process which for years has been subjected to distortion and misinterpretation.

A Practical Approach to the Evaluation of Psychotherapy

There is an oft-told story about Albert Einstein that applies to our present dilemma about evaluation. One night while being lionized at the Park Avenue home of a socialite, his hostess slipped out onto the terrace with her famous guests. She remarked enthusiastically, "Dr. Einstein, you know I, too, am interested in astronomy." Pointing to a star, she continued: "Every clear night I come out here to admire Venus, and I have done this for the past ten years." "But madame," retorted Einstein, "that star is not Venus, it is Jupiter." "Oh," exclaimed the hostess, "aren't you wonderful, Dr. Einstein, to be able to tell the sex of a star from this distance."

Unlike Einstein, we mere mortals are still too far away from both Venus and Jupiter to be able to discern their exact nature. But this does not stop us from speculating about them, and taking whatever measurements and observations are warranted by the limited instruments we have at our disposal. And we can come to some interesting and useful assumptions, realizing that as our rocketry advances to bring us close to our stellar subjects, additions and revisions will add to our present knowledge.

The fact that we are still too far away from essences of psychotherapy to deal with it by scientific method, does not mean that we must abandon the measurements and observations that are permitted by our current instruments. Indeed the use of these instruments may enable us to elaborate interesting and practical approaches. The real problem in our current lag is that we are delinquent in utilizing the means that we have at our disposal at present which can reveal much pertinent information and help bring about the development of new, more elaborate, and more discriminating methodologies.

This leads us to the question as to whether or not we are able to devise a practical plan for the evaluation of psychotherapy that takes into account the major limitations that confront us now. In research studies where expense is no object, it may be possible to set up a complicated apparatus for data collection, manipulation and interpretation that may help us reach this goal. The locus for such an experiment would probably have to be a school for the training of psychotherapists, an outpatient clinic or a hospital. Students in training could readily be induced to cooperate, but their inexperience would be a handicap introducing a variable that may be a burden to good evaluation. Unfortunately, seasoned psychotherapists are not too often interested in research. They are usually so imbedded in private practice that they have no time to devote themselves to an extensive study. The best work in evaluation would probably come out of the efforts of these trained psychotherapists if they could be induced to work on a project. This might be possible if they had at their disposal a simple, organized method of collecting data, an effective way of guaranteeing the anonymity of their patients, and a painless means of maintaining contact with them for follow-up studies.

The cooperation of patients is not too difficult to obtain. Where they can be convinced that the experimental design is part of their treatment, it may be possible to gain their collaboration without sacrifice of therapeutic benefit. They may be instructed in advance regarding the essential tests and interviews, and in this way prepared for what is to come. Where they resist, the research scheme in their particular cases may have to be abandoned. Patients attending clinics are easier to persuade than private patients, since they expect to be interviewed by more than one person. However, even private patients may be willing to participate if a rationale for a detailed study can be presented to them.

Let us assume, however, that we must adapt ourselves to the restrictions that prevail, namely, that an elaborate research plan cannot be executed for the many reasons that have already been detailed. Let us suppose also that we have access only to the data that are given us by the therapist, and that researchers are unable to interview the patients or their families. Can we under these circumstances evolve an evaluative structure that may give us reasonably accurate results?

One practical model for the assessment of results in psychotherapy is suggested by the method often used in evaluating the success of medical treatment. Let us, as an example, take the case of an individual who seeks medical aid for severe headaches. A physical examination reveals the presence of hypertension and the physician comes to a tentative conclusion that the headaches are related to a heightening of blood pressure. The first step in treatment is to establish a base-line of the present status against which one can make future comparisons. A detailed history is taken, searching for factors that may have been responsible for the hypertension, constitutional and experiential. The onset and development of the patient's complaint factor, i.e., his symptom of headache, are studied in great detail, including the effect upon other functions of the body, as well as the impact on work and social adjustment. A detailed physical examination is then executed, such as blood pressure measurements under conditions of rest and activity, blood chemistry, electrocardiography, vascular studies, fluoroscopic and x-ray surveys of the chest, as well as other explorations to establish the extent of actual damage and functional disorganization of the vital organs. An attempt is then made to define the etiological factors responsible for the hypertension, and, following this, a treatment plan is outlined. The physician may decide to give the patient an antihypertensive drug and to evaluate its effects. He has available to him instruments that enable him to assay the extent of beneficial change. For instance, he is able to gauge improvement in terms of blood pressure reduction, and restoration of alterations in the blood, urine and cardiac tracings. Amelioration of symptoms as reported by the patient, and the increase in physical and social capacities are also considered important. The patient is temporarily discharged when maximal improvement has been obtained, being enjoined to return for periodic check-ups. Follow-up studies determine the permanence of the results as well as the need for changes in medication or the institution of other therapies. In evaluating the effectiveness of the antihypertensive drug, the physician would have to consider the associated nonspecific ameliorative factors, such as the placebo element, the influence of the tension-alleviating relationship with the therapist, and the healing touches of rest and of adopting an easier philosophy toward responsibilities, which in themselves could promote improvement. Insofar as control is concerned, by the time the antihypertensive drug was released by the manufacturing drug company, a number of studies would have been completed, which would, to an extent at least, deal with the adventitious variable.

Were we to compare this model of medical evaluation with what happens in the average patient under psychiatric treatment, we would be shocked indeed at the dearth of data that were collected at the start of treatment that could act as a base-line for later comparisons. In some cases a formal history would be taken, in others not a single note would be entered other than a few items of statistical interest, such as the name, address, telephone number, age and occupation. A few dreams may later be transcribed, and occasional entries may accent major developments. Rarely would there be notations on each session, a speculation on prognosis, or a formulation of the dynamics. Generally the therapist would not take advantage of testing, both because of the expense element and because he may not have too much respect for the information that he obtains from psychological tests. Relatively few other instruments would be available to him for the objective measurement of improvement. He would depend almost entirely on the patient's subjective reports regarding his symptoms and adjustment. If he employed analytic techniques, he would also take into account changes in the dream structure and in the nature of the patient's relationship with him. Therapy would probably end when the patient felt that he had obtained as much benefit from the treatment as was consonant with his goals or when the therapist himself believed that the patient had progressed as far as he could. Rare indeed would there be a follow-up study of what happened in the years supervening after treatment. On the basis of the available information one would, to say the least, be handicapped in any attempt to study either process or outcome.

Is it possible for us to devise a better methodology by which we can observe the effects of psychotherapy? Despite its drawbacks, there may be some virtue in utilizing as a model some of the practical tactics of evaluating medical disorders. The principal problem is contriving an ordered way of collecting data. Admitting that we may not know exactly the most pertinent items on which to focus at the present time that would specifically be applicable to outcome prediction and validation, it may be possible to collect an assortment of facts that could be subjected to immediate examination, and later on to a more refined analysis by researchers. The following routines may be applied:

1. *The Taking of a Standardized History:* A surprising amount of information may be gathered from a detailed and organized history. Great gaps will exist if one waits for a spontaneous unfolding of historical material which obviously will be diluted by the current concerns of the patient and therapist. In addition to the usual statistical data, it is helpful to enter the following items into the record: (a) the chief complaint, (b) the history and development of the complaint, (c) the existence of associated and lesser complaints and symptoms, (d) the effect of the complaint factors on physical health, appetite, sleep, sexual functions, work, family life, interests, recreations, community contacts, and general interpersonal relationships, (e) attitudes of the patient toward his problem, and his theories about its nature, (f) the existence of any hereditary family illness, (g) data about parents and siblings, (h) significant events in the past history, such as neurotic disturbances in childhood; difficulties in physical growth, educational achievement, school progress, modes of resolution of dependence; and problems in sexual maturation, marriage, parenthood and social relations, (i) general attitudes toward authorities, peers and subordinates, as well as attitudes toward the self, (j) habitual modes of handling conflict (k) previous attacks of emotional illness and their consequences, including hospitalization, (l) details regarding former psychotherapeutic experiences, (m) possible precipitating factors in the present environment, (n) nature of motivations for the current therapeutic effort, and (o) level of insight. Elsewhere there have been described ways of collecting these data at the initial interview ([45]pp 207-215). There is no escape from the careful gathering of such information if one wishes to evaluate the results of treatment. Should the therapist belong to a school or adhere to a philosophy that depreciates the therapeutic value of formal history-taking, he may be comforted by the fact that his break with tradition will last for only one or two sessions, that it may give him a better understanding of the patient's problems and personality, that it will help the patient get started verbalizing freely, and that it may convince the latter of the therapist's thoroughness and in this way act in the interest of a working relationship. If the therapist is strongly against note-taking, he may avoid this by making an electrical recording of the sessions.

2. *The Filling Out of a Questionnaire by the Patient:* This may seem unnecessary where a detailed history has been taken. However, the employment of a questionnaire does give us something objective against which we can compare the patient's responses to a similar questionnaire at a later date. This is particularly helpful where the patient refuses to come in for a formal follow-up visit. A suggestion for the composition of a simple questionnaire has been offered ([45], pp 832-833) as well as for one that is more detailed.

3. *The Administration of a Personality Inventory:* As indicated previously

careful employment of a self-administered personality inventory, such as the Minnesota Multiphasic Personality Inventory may be found useful as an objective vehicle for a comparative before- and-after study. An inventory now in the process of standardization may possibly be of interest.[51]

4. *The Administration of Projective Tests:* The Rorschach, Thematic Apperception Test. Man-Woman Drawing, and a sample of handwriting may be taken for discriminative inspection and compared with similar tests obtained later during therapy and after treatment has been completed. As useful as projective tests may be in giving us objective before-and-after responses, there are some practical drawbacks, not the least of which is the fact that the patient may be unwilling or unable to go to the expense of taking a test battery. Many psychotherapists are hesitant in recommending this added item of financial burden to their patients, or in subjecting them to the testing situation itself. If expense is the objection, the therapist may easily procure Rorschach cards and, though he will not be able to administer the test as expertly, or in any way to score it, he can list the qualitative responses to the cards. Similarly he may ask the patient to draw a picture of a man and a woman, filing this with the Rorschach responses in the case record. If he is ambitious, he may expose the patient to the Thematic Apperception Test cards and either tabulate the responses in writing, or record them on a tape or plastic disc recorder. One may instruct patients to write down their reactions during a self-administered TAT test, thereby getting both the responses and a sample of handwriting. It may also be possible to arrange for, at a modest cost, the expert administration of psychological tests, delaying their scoring until after a research study has been begun, the financing of which may be able to take care of the costs.

5. *The Recording of Dreams:* Of importance also is the recording of any dreams that the patient remembers, particularly repetitive dreams. Dreams at the start of therapy are of great moment and should be noted in careful detail. Where the therapist is not analytically oriented, he may still collect dreams. which can be studied by a researcher with an analytic background.

6. *The Obtaining of a Good Physical Examination:* It goes without saying that a good physical examination is indispensable to provide a gross index of the physical health of the individual at the start of treatment. Without it we may not be able to ascertain the significance of changes in the physical status at the end of therapy. The detailed results of the examination should be filed in the patient's case record.

It is possible, that, in the future, precise instruments will be elaborated which can record the presence of subtle physiological changes in the individual. These would probably involve psychogalvanic, electromyographic, biochemical and electroencephalographic studies as well as other physiological measurements which would deal with somatic components. It is conceivable that these will give us a good index of somatic readjustments.

7. *Electrical Recording:* Electrical recording, on tape or plastic disc, is sufficiently advanced and economical to be practical as a routine. With proper preparation, patients will not object, and there will be no interference with the therapeutic process ([45], pp 686-687). It is recommended that recordings of the first few sessions be stored for future reference. It is so important to

have this material for later transcription that it constitutes an almost basic requirement.

It is recommended that all of the above base-line studies, completed at the beginning of therapy, which provide a means for comparison, be duplicated at least once a year, prior to the end of treatment. Electrical recordings may be made, however, if one desires to study process, at intervals throughout the treatment period. It would be helpful to note in the case record the techniques that are being employed in treating the patient, if these can be delineated, and the patient's reactions to them. This may enable a researcher to discern how closely the operative psychotherapeutic processes approximate the therapist's specifications of the model he is following. It may also help determine whether the patient is responding to therapeutic or to adventitious elements.

The matter of follow-up is of great consequence and regretfully almost entirely neglected in contemporary psychotherapeutic practices. Psychotherapy is presumed to equip the individual to deal consistently with the exigencies of life. If, following termination of what seems to be a successful case, the patient suffers a relapse and is unable to resolve it, we would have to revalue the optimistic estimate of the therapeutic outcome. On the other hand, we often witness termination in relatively unimproved states in patients who, after a period, begin to derive benefits from their treatment. The insights gained apparently have required the passage of time before they could influence new behavioral patterns. This delayed learning is characteristic of the reshaping of many complex conditionings. A follow-up study in the latter instances would alter our previous pessimistic evaluation of treatment outcome.

In our follow-up studies, we may, for practical reasons, have to limit ourselves to the patient's reports. It is unethical, and may be dangerous, to communicate with employers, teachers and family members, although, where the therapist has been in contact with the latter, and where they bear no ill-will toward the patient, a casual inquiry may bring out some interesting data. The report of concerned family members must always be accepted in the context of a possibly prejudiced view toward the patient and his adjustment. They may demand as a standard, rules of conduct that do not conform with good mental health, for instance, obeisance, subordination, overambitiousness, meticulousness and perfectionism. Because the patient does not come out of therapy with these traits, they may downgrade the therapeutic effort. On the other hand, due to overprotectiveness, or a fear of acknowledging faults in the patient, they may overlook the less obvious disturbed attitudes of the patient and overrate his adjustment.

It is important in follow-up for the therapist to interview the patient and, as has been indicated, to repeat the studies performed at the beginning of therapy. Patients do not resent being interviewed after termination; they even appreciate it. They may be prepared for follow-up at the time of termination by being told that it is customary to appear for a "check-up" at the end of a year and to expect a card when "check-up time" comes. At the follow-up interview, the patient may be instructed that the next "check-up time" is a year or two later. It would seem that a 5-year follow-up period should be ample to ascertain the permanency of changes.

In the event the patient refuses to come in for a personal interview, he may be willing to fill out a questionnaire indicating his ideas about how he feels, the nature of his adjustment and how he has benefited, if at all, from treatment. This is, of course, a poor substitute for an interview and the repetition of base-line studies. However, it is better than nothing and a considerable amount of information may be gathered from this kind of correspondence.

At the Postgraduate Center for Mental Health, Riess, Gundlach and Sager[66] conducted a follow-up study by mail in the form of a fact-gathering attempt to find out what patients were like some years after termination of treatment. Two hundred and one cases were randomly chosen from among patients who had at least 1 year of treatment at the Center and who had terminated their therapy at least 2 years prior to the contact with the follow-up project. Termination was defined as the cessation of treatment regardless of whether or not termination was planned or unplanned and independent of evaluation of the patient's past progress or status at the time of termination. Under the signature of the therapist, a questionnaire was mailed to patients, probing the symptomatology as recalled at the onset of treatment and at present; the current sense of being; the relationships with a number of significant fellow individuals, mates, co-workers, superiors, subordinates, friends, parents and children; the ability to function independently at work, socially and sexually; attitudes toward therapeutic experiences; and projections about the self. The final part of the study was a follow-up interview administered to a selected group of respondents by a psychiatrist with no previous contact with either the patient or the research. The evaluation studies were made by five different and independent observers, the patient, the screening psychiatrist, the therapist, the research staff and the follow-up psychiatrist. Of the 201 questionnaires mailed, a total of 108 or 53 per cent were returned with answers. Sixty-two more questionnaires were sent back with incorrect addresses. Five arrived blank and the remainder, only 16 per cent, were not returned.

Outcome evaluation of group therapy offers a few special problems, but, in general, the principles applying to individual therapy may be extended to persons in groups. Each member should be exposed to the outlined routines to establish a base-line immediately before he is placed in the group. In combined therapy, it is presumed that he will have had an initial base-line work-up at the start of his individual therapy. This is repeated upon his introduction to the group. The observation of the patient's behavior at the beginning of his group experience is important. The therapist is usually too busy to record the details, which may be the responsibility of a special observer or recorder. Better still—and this is being done at the Postgraduate Center—the process may be observed and recorded through a one-way mirror,

REFERENCES

1. Strupp, H. H.: Psychotherapists in Action. New York, Grune & Stratton, 1960.
2. Sargent, H. D.: Psychotherapy research project of the Menninger Clinic. *20:* 226-238, 1956.
3. Zax, M. and Klein, A.: Measurement of personality and behavior changes following psychotherapy. Psychol. Bull. *57:* 435-448, 1960.
4. Seeman, J. and Raskin, N. J.: Research perspectives in client-centered therapy. *In* Mowrer, O. H. (Ed.). Psychotherapy: Theory and Research. New York, Ronald, 1953, pp. 205-234.
5. Reznikoff, M. and Toomey, L. C.: Evaluation of Changes Associated with with Psychiatric Treatment. Springfield, Ill., Charles C. Thomas, 1959.
6. Zubin, J.: Evaluation of therapeutic outcome in mental disorders. J. Nerv. & Ment. Dis. *117:* 95-111, 1953.
7. Herzog, E.: Some Guide Lines for Evaluative Research. Wash., D. C., U. S. Dept. of Health, Education & Welfare, 1959, p. 62.
8. MacIver, J.: The Frog Pond. New York, George Braziller, 1961.
9. Tigani el Mahi: Personal communication.
10. Volgyesi, F. A.: "School for patients," hypnosis-therapy and psychoprophylaxia. Brit. J. Med. Hypnotism. *5:* 8-17, 1954.
11. Gliedman, L. H., Nash, E. H., Imber, S. D., Stone, A. R. and Frank, J. D.: Reduction of symptoms by pharmacologically inert substances and by short-term psychotherapy. Arch. Neurol. & Psychiat. *79:* 345-351, 1958.

12. MENNINGER, K. A.: What are the goals of psychiatric education? Bull. Menninger Clin. *16:* 156, 1952.
13. HOLT, R. R. AND LUBORSKY, L.: Personality Patterns of Psychiatrists, vol. 1. New York, Basic Books, Inc., 1958.
14. MURRAY, H. A.: Criteria for selection of psychiatrists to work in veterans hospitals. (Uunpublished manuscript)
15. RUESCH, J.: Social factors in therapy. *In* Psychiatric Treatment. Chap. VI. In Proc. Assoc. Res. Nerv. Ment. Dis., Vol. 31. Baltimore, Williams & Wilkins, 1953.
16. BINGHAM, J.: The Inside Story; Psychiatry and Everyday Life. Compiled under the direction of Fritz Redlich. New York, Knopf, 1953.
17. SHAKOW, D. et al: Recommended graduate training program in clinical psychology. Am. J. Psychol. *2:* 539-558, 1947.
18. EYSENCK, H. S.: The effects of psychotherapy: an evaluation J. Consult. Psychol. *16:* 319-324, 1952.
19. LEVITT, E. E.: The results of psychotherapy with children: an evaluation. J. Consult. Psychol. *21:* 189-196, 1957.
20. SARGENT, H. D.: Psychotherapy research project of the Menninger Clinic. II. Rationale. Bull. Menninger Clin. *20:* 226-233, 1956.
21. THORNE, F. C.: Rules of evidence in the evaluation of the effects of psychotherapy. J. Clin. Psychol. *8:* 38-41, 1952.
22. GREENSPOON, J.: The effect of two nonverbal stimuli on the frequency of members of two verbal response classes. Am. J. Psychol. *9:* 384, 1954.
23. —: The reinforcing effect of two spoken sounds on the frequency of two responses. Am. J. Psychol. *68:* 409-416, 1954.
24. GLOVER, E.: Research methods in psychoanalysis. Int. J. Psychoanal. *33:* 403, 1952.
25. BERG, I. A.: Measures before and after therapy. J. Clin. Psychol. *8:* 46-50, 1952.
26. OBERNDORF, C. P. GREENACRE, P. AND KUBIE, L.: Symposium on the evaluation of therapeutic results. Int. J. Psychoanal. *29:* 7-33, 1948.
27. WITMER, H.: The later social adjustment of problem children: a report of thirteen follow-up investigations. Smith College Studies in Social Work *5:* 1-98, 1935.
28. HUNT, J. McV. AND KOGAN, L. S.: Measuring Results in Social Casework: A Manual on Judging Movement. New York, Family Service Ass'n. of America, 1950.
29. WATTERSON, D. *J.*: Problems in the evaluation of psychotherapy. Bull. Menninger Clin. *18:* 232-241, 1954.
30. MALAMUD, D. L.: Objective measurement of clinical status in psychopathological research. Psychol. Bull. *43:* 240-258, 1946.
31. KLEIN, H. R.: A study of changes occurring in patients during and after psychoanalytic treatment. *In* Current Approaches in Psychotherapy. New York, Grune & Stratton, 1960, pp. 151-175.
32. MILES, H. H. W., BARRABEE, E. L. AND FINESINGER, J. E.: Evaluation of psychotherapy: with a follow-up study of 62 cases of anxiety neurosis. Psychosom. Med. *13*: 83-105, 1951.

33. DYMOND, R. F.: Adjustment changes in the absence of psychotherapy. J. Consult. Psychol. *19:* 103-107, 1955.
34. MILLER, J. G.: Criteria and measurement of changes during psychiatric treatment. Bull. Menninger Clin. *18:* 130-137, 1954.
35. DRESSEL, P. L.: Some approaches to evaluation. Personnel Guid. J. *31:* 284-287, 1953.
36. GORDON, T., GRUMMON, D. L., ROGERS, C. R. AND SEEMAN, J.: Developing a program of research in psychotherapy. *In* Rogers, C. R. and Dymond, R. F. (Eds.): Psychotherapy and Personality Changes. Chicago, Univ. of Chicago Press, 1954, pp. 12-34.
37. MCNEMAR, A.: Psychological Statistics, New York. Wiley, 1949.
38. FIEDLER, F. E.: A comparison of therapeutic relationships in psychoanalytic, non-directive, and Adlerian therapy. J. Consult. Psychol. *14:* 436-445, 1950.
39. —: The concept of an ideal therapeutic relationship. J. Consult. Psychol. *14:* 239-245, 1950.
40. —: Factor analyses of psychoanalytic, non-directive, and Adlerian therapeutic relationships. J. Consult. Psychol. *15:* 32-38, 1951.
41. ZUBIN, J.: Standard control groups for the evaluation of therapy. *In:* Proceedings of the Second Conference of Mental Hospital Administrators and Statisticians. Public Health Service Pub. No. 226. Wash., D. C.: Nat'l. Inst. of Ment. Health, Public Health Service, 1958, p. 63.
42. SNYDER, W. U.: The present status of psychotherapeutic counseling. Psychol. Bull. *44:* 297-386, 1947.
43. American Psychoanalytic Association; Committees at work. Bull. Am. Psychoanal. A. *6:* 17, 1950.
44. BERMAN, L.: Some problems in the evaluation of psychoanalysis as a therapeutic procedure. Psychiatry *18:* 387-390, 1955.
45. WOLBERG, L. R.: The Technique of Psychotherapy. New York. Grune & Stratton, 1954.
46. PARLOFF, M. V., KELMAN, H. C. AND FRANK, J. D.: Comfort, effectiveness and self-awareness as criteria of improvement in psychotherapy. Am. J. Psychiat. *111:* 343-351, 1954.
47. ROGERS, C. R.: Changes in the maturity of behavior as related to therapy. *In* Rogers, C. R. and Dymond, R. F. (Eds.): Psychotherapy and Personality Change. Chicago, Univ. of Chicago Press, 1954, pp. 215-237.
48. KAUFMANN, P. E.: Changes in Minnesota Multiphasic Personality Inventory as a function of psychiatric therapy. J. Consult. Psychol. *14:* 458-464, 1950.
49. SCHOFIELD, W.: Changes in responses to the MMPI following certain therapies. Psychol. Monogr. *64:* 311, 1950.
50. LEARY, T. AND HARVEY, J. S.: A methodology for measuring personality changes in psychotherapy.. J Clin. Psychol. *12:* 123-132, 1956.
51. WOLBERG, L. R., et. al.: An inventory for the evaluation of personality problems and change. To be published.
52. MURPHY, W. F.: Problems in evaluating the results of psychotherapy. Arch. Neurol. Psychiat. *66:* 653-654, 1951.
53. KUTASH, S. B.: The impact of projective techniques on basic psychological science. J. Proj. Tech. *18:* 453-469, 1954.

54. Schafer, R.: Psychological test evaluation of personality change during intensive psychotherapy. Psychiat. *18:* 175-192, 1955.

55. Piotrowski, Z. A. and Schreiber, M.: Rorschach percept-analytic measurement of personality changes during and after intensive psychoanalytically oriented psychotherapy. *In* Bychowski, C. and Despert, J. L. (Eds.): Specialized Techniques in Psychotherapy. New York, Basic Books, 1952, pp. 337-361.

56. Dymond, R. F.: Adjustment changes over therapy from Thematic Apperception Test Ratings. *In* Rogers, C. R. and Dymond, R. F. (Eds.) Psychotherapy and Personality Change. Chicago, Univ. of Chicago Press, 1954, pp. 109-120.

57. Modell, A. H.: Changes in human figure drawing by patients who recover from regressed states. Am. J. Orthopsychiat. *21:* 584-596, 1951.

58. Reznikoff, M. and Mundy, L.: Changes in human figure drawings associated with therapy: a case study. Am. J. Psychotherapy *10:* 542-549, 1956.

59. DiMascio, M. A., Boyd, R. W., Greenblatt, M. and Solomon, H. C.: The psychiatric interview (a sociophysiologic study). Dis. Nerv. Syst. *16:* 4-9, 1955.

60. Boyd, R. W. and DiMascio, M. A.: Social behavior and autonomic physiology: A sociophysiologic study. J. Nerv. & Ment. Dis. *120:* 207-212, 1954.

61. Bexenstein, V. E.: A case study of the use of palmar sweating as a measure of psychological tension. J. Abnorm. Soc. Psychol. *50:* 138-143, 1955.

62. Thetford, W. N.: The measurement of physiological responses to frustration before and after non-directive psychotherapy. *In* Mowrer, O. H. (Ed.): Psychotherapy: Theory and Research. New York, Ronald, 1952, pp. 641-656.

63. Thetford, W. N.: An objective measurement of frustration tolerance in evaluating psychotherapy. *In* Wolff, W. and Precker, J. A. (Eds.): New York, (Personality Monographs.) Grune & Stratton, pp. 26-62, 1952.

64. Shagass, C. and Malmo, R. B.: Psychodynamic themes and localized muscular tension during psychotherapy. Psychosom. Med. *16:* 295-314, 1954.

65. Mowrer, O. H. (Ed.) Psychotherapy: Theory and Research. New York, Ronald, 1952.

66. Riess, B. F., Gundlach, R. and Sager, C. J.: The uses and interpretations of a follow-up study of patients in psychoanalytic psychotherapy. J. Psychol. *53:* 219-232, 1962.

2

EVALUATION OF DRUG TREATMENTS IN PSYCHIATRY

by JONATHAN O. COLE, M.D.*

THIS IS A MOST APPROPRIATE POINT in time to discuss the evaluation of drug treatments in psychiatry. Chlorpromazine and reserpine have now been in clinical use for almost 10 years. Enough time has elapsed for the general usefulness of these drugs to be evaluated on the basis of clinical experience accumulated by many psychiatrists in many clinical settings. Many types of more detailed controlled clinical researches have also been conducted on these two drugs and many similar drugs have been tested in patients. Eight other potent phenothiazines and two other rauwolfia alkaloids are now on the market.

The effects of prolonged clinical experience on the use of the two original drugs are interesting to examine. In one large State system on December 15, 1961, chlorpromazine alone was being used in the treatment of 23,872 patients, while reserpine alone was being used on only 4,334 patients.†

These data are in general agreement with those obtained in the few[3,29,30,32,34] studies in which the utility of the two drugs in the treatment of schizophrenic patients has been directly compared. It is equally important to note that, despite the general agreement that chloropromazine is the more effective drug in the treatment of schizophrenic patients, the possibility that certain types of patients do better on reserpine than on chlorpromazine has been occasionally suggested[18] but never seriously tested. Also, though reserpine has clear biochemical effects on the central nervous system in experimental animals, no study has been reported correlating the specific biochemical effects of the drug with the degree of clinical change.

---

*Chief, Psychopharmacology Service Center, Research Grants and Fellowships Branch, National Institute of Mental Health, National Institutes of Health, Public Health Service, U. S. Department of Health, Education, and Welfare.

†These figures were provided by Mr. Robert E. Patton, Director, Statistical Services, State of New York, Department of Mental Hygiene, Albany, N. Y., and reflect data on drug use in the New York State Hospital system.

This brief statement concerning the evaluation of the two original drugs in the modern phase of clinical psychopharmacology presents, in miniature, the status of the field as a whole. Certain types of gross, practical and important clinical information have been obtained. Other types of information requiring more perceptive hypotheses, the use of more complex statistical analyses, or the application of methods from several disciplines have been slower to emerge.

On the other hand, one can be encouraged by the fact that the first 10 years of experience with insulin shock treatment produced only 60 controlled or comparative studies of that treatment's effectiveness in psychiatric patients,[10] while there have been at least 522 controlled studies of drug treatments in psychiatric patients carried out since 1952.

What has been learned over the past decade about the evaluation of drug treatments in psychiatry? What types of studies can now be done which could not have been done in 1937 or 1952? The remainder of this paper will attempt to answer these questions, drawing both upon available evidence and upon the author's reasoned opinion where evidence is lacking.

What are the schematic characteristics of drug evaluation in psychiatry? One has a drug or drugs, a group of patients, a treating physician, observers and observations of clinical status, a milieu in which the treatment occurs and, sometimes, nonclinical measures which may be relevant to the characteristics either of the drug or of the patients studied. The question most often asked in clinical psychiatric drug research is, "Does Drug A in patients of Type B at Dosage C as administered by Therapist D in Setting E produce changes in Measure F as noted by Observer G?"

It is probable that all of these factors influence the outcome of any given study. As a caricature (one which has occasionally been made almost real in the published literature), any "effective" drug like chlorpromazine can be shown to be ineffective by giving it at a low enough dose for a short enough period in chronic patients in an antitherapeutic environment on insensitive or inappropriate measuring instruments administered by unskilled or biased observers. From this it follows that any clinical drug study must be planned intelligently to answer a reasonable question in an effective manner. A recent paper by Hoffer and Osmund,[15] which argued against the double blind controlled study in psychopharmacology, was in fact, only showing that a controlled study of drug X in patient type Y will not provide conclusive proof that drug X is really effective in patient type Z and therefore was really arguing against the asking of unreasonable questions using controlled double-blind studies.

Given a reasonable hypothesis to test, does the evaluation of drug therapy in psychiatry differ substantially from the evaluation of other forms of somatotherapy or psychotherapy? Clearly the use of the drug or drugs is the major difference. If anything, drugs are more flexible than other therapies. One can ask if a single dose of a drug reduces excitement in patients with delirium tremens or alters verbal behavior during a single psychotherapy hour and one can also ask if 5 years of maintenance drug treatment alters social adjustment in the community or reduces total time spent in psychiatric hospitals. The patient populations involved range all the way from surgical patients with preoperative anxiety through schizophrenics with 20 years of hospitalization. The possible treatment settings and the possible relevant criterion measures are equally varied.

One nonpharmacological aspect of drug treatment which has a major influence on the number of controlled studies actually carried out is, basically, an economic one. Drug treatment can be administered with less expense (in terms of personnel time) than can psychotherapy or, for that matter, insulin shock treatment. Thus, the staff is freed to assess change more accurately and to undertake large controlled studies not as feasible with other therapeutic approaches.

The use of drugs also permits a flexibility of dosage difficult to achieve with psychotherapy. The individual drug, as a treatment method, gives a concrete specificity to the treatment less easily achieved with psychological treatments.

Drugs, as treatments, bring with them concerns about overdosage and over side effects which are much more obvious than with other treatments. The deficits in memory and muscular pains that occur with ECT are equivalent phenomena, but have played a less direct role in the way the treatment is assessed. It is also quite likely that psychotherapy may have its own undesirable side effects, at least in some patients, but these are more difficult to separate from the manifestations of the illness itself.

Drugs do have advantages: biochemical or electroencephalographic changes can be used as independent evidence of pharmacological effect; further, direct measurement of drug levels in blood, spinal fluid or urine are often feasible or can be readily developed, although approaches of this kind have been employed only rarely.

In addition, the continuing development of new chemicals with interesting behavioral effects in animals will continue to pose a type of question less often encountered in other types of psychiatric treatment: Is this new compound of any value in the treatment of any psychiatric symptom or syndrome? No other treatment area is likely to produce a continuing series of unknowns requiring identification of a possible area of usefulness.

Let us proceed now to a consideration of typical types of drug evaluation studies and the problems they pose.

Early Clinical Drug Evaluation

Although much has been said about the importance of controlled studies, random assignment of patients to treatment groups, the selection of appropriate criterion measures, etc., it is obvious that to design such a study one must first know enough about the drug to put forth a reasonable hypothesis for testing. To do this, one must find out at what dosage a given drug produces clinical changes in a specific symptom, syndrome or type of patient. One must also know the side effects that may complicate the study. Investigations aimed at obtaining this information, usually called early clinical drug evaluation, are exemplified by Delay and Deniker's original study with chlorpromazine[7] or Kuhn's original work with imipramine.[19] Both studies clearly stated preliminary findings that have been adequately confirmed by subsequent controlled studies. On the other hand, trying a good drug in the wrong patients can effectively prevent the development of a reasonable hypothesis. For example, early clinical investigations of iproniazid were carried out only in chronic schizophrenics[16,32] and so missed its antidepressive effect.

In the preliminary study of new agents in psychiatric patients, it is evident that the adequacy of the evaluation depends entirely upon the observational skills and clinical judgment of the investigator and his team. The need for close attention to possible untoward side effects and careful observation of the patients make any formal double blind controlled study undesirable. Careful manipulation of dosage until either clinical change or undesirable side effects appear is necessary for the adequate study of any new compound.

One major problem deserves mention here. Much of this work is currently being done in chronic schizophrenic patients with poor prognosis for recovery. This insures that a truly dramatic cure for chronic schizophrenia will not be missed. However, many of these patients are available for study because they have proved resistant to existing drugs. The amount of change to be expected on new compounds similar to existing drugs may be minimal. Furthermore, drugs with antidepressive or antianxiety actions or with new unanticipated types of psychopharmacologic activity may be difficult to detect in such a population. A drug with great specificity for the treatment of the chronic alcoholic, for example, might be most difficult to identify in chronic psychotic patients since its specific properties are difficult to anticipate, much less detect. It follows that some heterogeneity of patient population is necessary for the identification of certain types of drug action. Since all major types of psychopharmacologic agents now in general prescription use, with the possible exception of benactyzine, chlordiazepoxide and several sedatives, were first identified as having unusual and unpredicted clinically useful properties in patients, the study of new drugs in patients is both highly necessary and highly demanding of special skill. Methods for the discovery of new types of drugs cannot be stipulated or prescribed. But methods for the validation and extension of discoveries can be meaningfully discussed and the advantages and disadvantages of specific approaches to specific patient populations can be suggested. In general, the gap between initial discovery of a promising new compound and the confirmation or rejection of its value through well designed controlled clinical trials has been narrowing, but there is still far too much uncontrolled clinical assessment going on before such rigorous studies are carried out or reported.

Clinical Drug Evaluation in Chronic Schizophrenics

The logistics of the controlled clinical trial are certainly simplified in the chronic schizophrenic since such patients are readily available in moderate numbers in all State hospitals. Specific selection criteria can be stipulated and the appropriate patients can be assembled on research wards. Stratification of patients on two or three important variables can be carried out and the study completed on a predetermined schedule free from most of the vagaries accompanying any study dependent on the flow of suitable new admissions from the community. On the negative side, such chronic patients are more likely to be unable to cooperate in psychological test procedures or to be verbally underproductive and, therefore, unratable on some portions of interview-based rating scales. Many such patients are already on some drug and will require withdrawal from treatment for some period, probably at least 3 months, if a return to more florid symptomatology is desired. There is also a problem in judging improvement which may arise. Increased activity, verbal productiveness and social aggressiveness on the part of previously withdrawn and apathetic patients may be observed and measured both by psychiatrists and by nursing staff, but may be judged improvement by the former and worsening by the latter.

It is also likely that in the future the proportion of any such population resistant to drugs of presently known types will be increasing and results obtained on such patients may generalize less and less well to the efficacy of the same drugs in acute schizophrenic patients.

A special problem in the current clinical literature is the frequent observation that some patients who had been treated on one phenothiazine will do better when transferred to another phenothiazine. Such observations require more rigorous exploration than they have received to date. Is this simply due to longer phenothiazine treatment causing greater improvement? Does any change, or the extra attention accompanying change in medication always cause some degree of extra improvement? Or, do some subgroups within a heterogeneous chronic schizophrenic population clearly do best on the particular phenothiazine or a particular group of phenothiazines? The time is certainly ripe for studies that expose chronic patients to reasonably prolonged treatment periods on two or more phenothiazines with administration of each treatment on two separate occasions, using what might best be described as a double crossover design, to determine whether the superiority of one drug over another in any group of patients is really specific to the drug itself and not attributable to the other factors noted above.

It should be added that, in this particular clinical situation, crossover studies have been badly neglected while being, in my judgment, too often inappropriately employed in studies of depression or neurotic anxiety.

Clinical Drug Evaluation in Acute Schizophrenia

Reported research results on tranquilizing drugs over the past few years, including the VA's collaborative studies of drug treatments in newly admitted schizophrenic patients[5,6] as well as preliminary results from the NIMH-PSC Nine-Hospital Collaborative Study of Phenothiazine Treatment of Acute Schizophrenic Psychoses, have all amply confirmed the feasibility of controlled clinical trials of drugs in acute schizophrenia. They have also confirmed the sensitivity of a number of existing measuring instruments including the Lorr MSRPP and the newer Lorr IMPS scales as well as the Burdock Ward Behavior Rating Scales and global ratings of change in revealing true differences between active drugs and placebo. It is clear that the general effectiveness of drugs for acute schizophrenia can be adequately measured and the differences (in over-all efficacy) between similar drugs, such as chlorpromazine and promazine,[5,8,9,11] can be readily detected. Present techniques can be equally well applied to new drugs developed for use in this type of patient.

All this provides modest cause for optimism but leaves unanswered many other important questions. Much more work needs to be done on predictors of response to drugs in acute schizophrenia. Here, even such gross descriptive variables as sex, race and socioeconomic status have been inadequately studied. One must be concerned, in addition, both with general predictors of drug response or of response to all types of therapy, and with predictors that may be specific for an individual drug.

To date there is little evidence that the several highly effective phenothiazines, e.g., chlorpromazine, thioridazine, fluphenazine, trifluoperazine or perphenazine[1,6,20] differ significantly from each other in over-all clinical efficacy and questions concerning differential efficacy on specific target symptoms or patient types have scarcely received rigorous study. One possible approach to this problem is to use statistical methods, such as discriminant function, on bodies of existing data to determine whether patients responding to one phenothiazine can be discriminated from patients responding to a second, in terms of any characteristics of their psychopathology or previous psychiatric history. A second approach is the selection from existing collaborative studies of those patients with initially high levels of a particular type of psychopathology, such as paranoid projection, apathy, or motor excitement, to see whether within such relatively homogeneous groups drug differences show up more clearly.

It is equally possible to design studies in advance that select only patients with extreme types of specific psychopathology but the ebb and flow of new admissions and the difficulty in rapidly applying detailed selection criteria at intake make such studies more difficult logistically than the retrospective analysis of larger studies that have used broader selection criteria.

Clinical Drug Evaluation in Depression

Since the emergence of the monoamine oxidase inhibitors and of imipramine in 1958, there has been considerable evidence that adequately designed controlled studies utilizing clinical rating scales can detect differences between these drugs and placebo.[2,14,17,22,37,38] Comparisons between these drugs and electroconvulsive therapy have produced less clear results, although ECT has not, to date, been shown to be significantly inferior to these drugs in treatment of depressive conditions.[14,37,38] Certainly controlled comparative studies involving random assignment of depressed patients to all treatments can provide crude answers concerning over-all effectiveness.

Again, the more complex but more crucial questions have not been answered. Given three types of treatment as apparently different in mode of action as imipramine or amitriptyline, the several MAO inhibitors, and ECT, it is reasonable to ask whether different types of depression respond differently to the three treatments and whether a study of predictors of response might not bring more clarity into a thoroughly confused field. Classifying depressions crudely into "psychotic" and "neurotic" types in uncontrolled studies has produced only general impressions that psychotic depressions may respond a little better to at least imipramine and ECT than do neurotic depressions.

In depression one also has another serious problem. Spontaneous remission is usually observed in controlled studies as placebo response, since many neurotic depressions may do quite well without the specific biological treatment. Differential predictors of spontaneous improvement, as well as of response to the three available types of therapy, need to be worked out. For studies of the monoamine oxidase inhibitors, biochemical tests of level of pharmacological inhibition of the enzyme are needed to insure adequate dosage, since it is always possible that inferior clinical results from the use of any given MAO inhibitor may be due to inadequate dosage rather than to the ineffectiveness of the drug used.

In depression, in particular, there is a major need for studies of the efficacy of maintenance drug therapy in preventing recurrences of depression, since ECT is suspected of decreasing the time between depressive episodes and is certainly not effective in preventing subsequent illnesses.

The short-term, double-blind, cross-over study, comparing a drug with placebo in depression, which has had a recent vogue in the

Journal of Mental Science, does not meet these needs and is liable to the criticism that lack of relapse following a shift to placebo after 3 weeks on active drug does *not* prove that the drug was *not* responsible for any original improvement seen.

It would also be most interesting to see whether the personality and therapeutic approach of the treating physician contributes significantly to the efficacy of drug medications used in the treatment of depression. Many of the clinical investigators reporting very high improvement rates with antidepressive drugs are individuals with strong personalities and strong convictions and it is always possible that their high success rates are due to an interaction between their personality and the drug. This is at least one possible explanation for the higher improvement rates in uncontrolled studies than are usually reported in controlled clinical trials.

Clinical Drug Evaluation in Neurotic Outpatients

Probably the greatest confusion in the literature on controlled clinical trials exists in evaluation of drug response in neurotic outpatients. Meprobamate, for example, has been reported to be superior to placebo in some studies[21,28,35] and no more effective than placebo in other studies.[24,26,33] Such studies are plagued by a reasonably high rate of placebo response, which may make drug effects difficult to demonstrate, and by substantial dropout rates. If one were to assume that only those patients who felt better kept coming back to the clinic for more medication, difficulties in showing differences between drug and placebo could be anticipated when only symptomatic change in patients remaining in the study was examined.

A special study now underway under grant support at Johns Hopkins University and the University of Pennsylvania in collaboration with the Psychopharmacology Service Center comparing the effects of positive and neutral drug prescribing behavior on patient response to meprobamate and placebo, is showing a significant interaction between treatments and therapeutic behavior. Patients receiving the active agent in a setting of drug-positive physician behavior remain in treatment to a much greater extent than patients on placebo or patients receiving the active drug in a neutral setting. If the attitudes and behaviors of the treating physicians are a major determining variable in the response of neurotic outpatients to drugs, research in this field will increase in complexity, making meaningful evaluations of drugs even more difficult to obtain.

The probability of such an interaction is supported by a recent analysis of data from a VA cooperative study of drugs in neurotic outpatient[25] which showed that therapists falling into the Whitehorn and Betz category B, had much better results with neurotic outpatients than did therapists falling in their category A.

It is also interesting to note that type A physicians did better than type B physicians in the treatment of schizophrenic patients at the Phipps Clinic.[4]

It is, of course, possible that our current problems in this area of clinical evaluation stem from the relative weakness of existing drugs. If chlordiazepoxide is so much more effective than other antianxiety compounds, as the uncontrolled studies and the company's literature would indicate, perhaps its potency would make the pharmacological effect override differences in the personalities and prescribing behaviors of the physicians using the drug.

One other problem in the outpatient area is, of course, the wide differences in the types of patient studied in different outpatient settings. There are already indications that patients treated for neurotic anxiety in general medical clinics show more somatic side effects than do patients treated in a similar manner in psychiatric clinics.[27] Also, since antianxiety drugs probably have their widest use in general practice, methods need to be developed for the study of their effectiveness in the general practice situation. This is particularly necessary since patients coming to treatment in university outpatient departments, where controlled outpatient drug studies are usually conducted, have often already failed to respond to similar drug treatments in the hands of their private physicians. Thus, these patients may constitute an atypically unresponsive population which would tend to reduce the possibility of detecting true drug effects in controlled studies carried out in such clinics.

Measurement of Clinical Change

Given a potent drug to be compared with an inert placebo, adequate dosage and duration of treatment and an appropriate patient population, it is likely that any of a number of clinical rating scales which quantify a variety of discrete items of psychopathology will suffice to show the superiority of active drug using statistical tests of significance. Global ratings of severity of illness or of a major single target symptom may be almost as useful if the rating system provides a modest range of degrees of symptom severity. Even crude "improved *vs.* unimproved" classifications of the patients treated can give significant chi squares under these conditions.

It is likely that widening the range of possible scores and the use of covariance analysis to correct for differences in initial level and, where appropriate, intelligent stratifications of the sample of patients will increase the sensitivity of the clinical trial. On the other hand, as one stretches the refinements of the measuring instruments and the design and raises the number of patients studied, there arises a danger of achieving statistical significance while losing clinical significance.

Also, there is reason to believe that total morbidity scores in complex conditions like schizophrenia may run the danger of missing real drug-induced shifts in psychopathology, e.g., less apathy and withdrawal, but more anxiety and suspicion, which cancel each other out when a total morbidity score is calculated.

The availability of computer programs able to carry out principle components factor analyses with varimax rotation may give greater probable reliability and certainly give greater objectivity than simpler more approximate hand calculator approaches used in the past. Factor scores thus obtained may provide more discrete information on drug effects. Since existing and widely used scales like the Wittenborn[35] and the Lorr IMPS[23] were developed from the factor analysis of data on a large number of patients rated at a single point in time, they may be criticized for providing factor scores reflecting the association of symptoms in untreated patients, leaving the possibility that drug-induced changes may not follow this pattern, but may scatter through individual items on a variety of factor scores. The Overall-Gorham abbreviated scale[12] is derived from phenothiazine sensitive items on the older Lorr MSRPP and may therefore be a better instrument for measuring phenothiazine effects in schizophrenic patients. On the other hand, it can be argued that phenothiazine-specific items might be less sensitive than a multipurpose scale in assessing the effects of a totally new type of drug. In evaluating drug treatments in both schizophrenia and depression, it is likely that really effective treatments may cause across-the-board change in all associated types of psychopathology. However, the use of multi-item rating scales with factor or cluster scores certainly provides greater assurance that discrete drug effects or lack of effects on specific symptom areas will be detected when and if indeed they occur. They therefore appear to be worth the additional rating time and the greater complexity of data analysis. In addition, initial level scores on such scale items or factors may prove useful in the future as predictors of drug response. Their value lies in the increased detail of the information provided rather than in their major superiority to more global ratings in detecting general drug effectiveness.

There is also some question as to which type of observation by what kind of observer is "best" in drug studies. Particularly in studies on hospitalized patients the problem is real. It is a hard question to answer. A recent study by Wittenborn et. al.[36] on depressed patients in the New Jersey State Hospital system, using covariance analysis, showed physicians to be more sensitive to detailed differences between treatments than were the nurses. A preliminary analysis of the first 112 patients in the current NIMH-PSC Nine-Hospital Collaborative Study of Phenothiazine Treatments of Acute Schizophrenia has showed on covariance analysis that global ratings by both doctors and by nurses, most Lorr IMPS factors, and the Burdock Ward Behavior Scale were all highly sensitive to differences between the active drugs and placebo. A discriminant function analysis of the same data after 6 weeks of treatment showed the Burdock Ward Behavior Scale as used by the nurses to be the single measure most efficient in discriminating between the drugs and placebo, with the doctors' rating of the Lorr IMPS factor of "Apathy and Retardation" being the measure adding most to the discrimination. Since the IMPS does not have a total morbidity score it is still possible that a doctors' total morbidity score might have shown more efficiency. The fact that the nurses global rating of severity of illness was the fourth most powerful discriminating measure of the 21 studied does argue for the major contribution of nurses' ratings to this particular study. The problem clearly is far from settled and probably the sensitivity of the two types of raters will vary with the skills of the individuals involved and the specific instruments used. There is certainly no basis for discarding either type of observation.

A less frequently used type of measure, patient self-rating, deserves more attention than it has received. In the NIMH-PSC study noted above, the patients' self-ratings on the aggressiveness factor of the Clyde Mood Scale was the third measure, coming after the doctors' rating of Apathy and Retardation, on the discriminant function analysis.

Mention should be made of the place of multiple raters using the same instrument and the place of interrater reliability. Certainly, in the development of a new scale, evidence of item, as well as of factor, or of total morbidity score reliability is highly desirable. However, since the NIMH-PSC study was using established scales, we have averaged the ratings of pairs of raters without checking closely on inter-rater reliability and have achieved quite satisfactory sensitivity with a low error term. If sensitivity to drug effects with its confirmation of validity can be readily obtained, overattention to reliability may not be an absolute requirement of measuring instruments for successful controlled clinical drug trials.

Bias and the Double-Blind Method

Given potent drugs with recognizable side effects, absolute "blindness" on the part of observers, particularly ward personnel in placebo-controlled studies, may be difficult to achieve. However, as more has been learned about existing, well-studied drug treatments, the problem has shifted. Even when the general efficacy of newer drugs is studied, the crucial question is not whether the drug is more potent than placebo, but is the new drug significantly different from existing standard drugs. Since this type of study does not require a placebo group, the double-blind may be more efficient than before in reducing possible rater bias. It is worth emphasizing that the individual numbering of each patient's medication is necessary in double-blind studies, since trials continue to be carried out in which each drug treatment is coded only by group (for example, chlorpromazine capsules being called drug A and placebo capsules drug B). In the latter case, breaking the code for one patient destroys the blindness for the whole group of patients on that medication.

There is a related problem on the rating side. Raters who see the patient only to do the particular rating clearly have the least chance of being biased and the least information on which to base their ratings while raters involved in the patients' daily care have both the most information and the most possiblity for bias. At the present time when difficult discriminations between active drugs are a greater problem than simpler discriminations between drug and placebo, maximum information on which to base sensitive ratings appears more necessary than the reduction of possible bias at all costs.

Interestingly, modest bias in the absence of double-blind conditions does not necessarily influence study results. The current study of ECT, imipramine, phenelzine and isocarboxazide being carried out in the Massachusetts state hospital system began with a negative attitude toward ECT and a preference for drug therapies. Despite this, an interim report of results has shown ECT to be the most effective of the four treatments studied[14] even though the shock patients were known as such to the raters.

Computers and Drug Evaluation

The very rapid development of high speed computers with concomitant increasing ease of programming has reduced the expense and increased the ease with which data from controlled clinical trials can be subjected to detailed statistical analyses. The amount of data collected does not have to be restricted to the capacity of a single statistical clerk to run a calculator. This does not mean that tremendous amounts of data on a heterogeneous conglomeration of patients on a mess of drugs should be collected in the hope that a statistical consultant armed with a computer can arrive on the scene after the study and bring Nobel Prize-worthy findings out of chaos. It does mean that analyses of covariance can now be carried out with unequal numbers of patients in the cells of the design and that unbiased full factor analyses can be carried out to see whether clarity is added to the interrelationships of the phenomena being measured. It also means that procedures such as discriminant function can be used to answer questions not previously possible to answer.

Over and above these glittering possibilities, the availability of such help is leading investigators to seek statistical consultation when it really counts, before starting the study. This often helps to clarify the research question and to motivate investigators to quantify their observations, whether or not high speed computers are really necessary to the analysis of the findings.

It has been argued that overemphasis on statistical approaches may be replacing good clinical observation and the development of new and imaginative ideas about how drugs work. It's difficult to say whether this concern is justified. Certainly clinical studies of drug treatment not involving controls or statistics, other than early clinical studies of new drugs, have not been productive of unique and testable hypotheses about specific properties of known drugs. The fault may be in the drugs rather than in the investigators and multivariate analyses may turn out to add little to existing knowledge, but existing technological advances and new statistical methods deserve serious application to the problems of clinical drug evaluation.

Other Approaches

The difficulties currently being experienced in predicting which patients will respond to a generally potent drug on the basis of history or observable psychopathology may mean that the clinician's brain is being overloaded by too much data and that electronic computers will be more effective in ordering the available data. On the other hand, it may mean that these variables are simply not the relevant ones. The comment made by Gottlieb[13] at a research conference several years ago, to the effect that classifying paretics into a single clinical group on psychopathological grounds in the absence of knowledge of etiology would be impossible, continues to hound me. It may be that biochemical or neurophysiological abnormalities may turn out to be the crucial predictors. It's hard to tell where to begin to look for predictors, although the application of computer methods to the EEG is a reasonable place to start, since methods are now available which have not been adequately explored and there is considerable evidence that effective drugs do cause specific EEG changes.

At the other extreme, it is possible that complex interactions between the attitudes of patients and the attitudes of the treating staff may be modulating drug response to a greater degree than is now appreciated. It is certainly not too early for this type of influence to be explored in detail looking for interactions between individual patient dynamics and milieu rather than for cruder effects of milieu on the drug response of all patients in a given study.

Conclusion

Ten years of clinical research on the effectiveness of drugs in the treatment of psychiatric patients have shown that well designed controlled clinical trials are both feasible and meaningful. They have also shown that skilled clinical observation is the only good method to date for identifying new drug types. Neither type of approach has been too helpful in identifying discrete differential predictors of clinical response to any one of the several drugs available for use in any given clinical syndrome. More effective use of statistical methods, of clinical acumen and of biological approaches are called for to unravel this crucial problem.

REFERENCES

1. Adelson, D. and Epstein, L.: A study of phenothiazines with chronically ill schizophrenic patients. J. Nervous & Ment. Dis. in press.

2. Ball, J. R. B. and Kiloh, L. G.: A controlled trial of imipramine in treatment of depressive states. Brit. M. J. *2:* 1052-1055, 1959.
3. Barrett, W. W., Ellsworth, R. B., Clark, L. D. and Ennis, J.: Study of the differential behavioral effects of reserpine, chlorpromazine, and a combination of these drugs in chronic schizophrenic patients. Dis. Nervous Syst. *18:* 209-215, 1957.
4. Betz, Barbara J. and Whitehorn, J. C.: The relationship of the therapist to the outcome of therapy in schizophrenia. Psychiat. Res. Rep. *5:* 89-105, 1956.
5. Casey, J. F., Bennett, I. F. Lindley, C. J., Hollister, L. E., Gordon, M. H. and Springer, N. N.: Drug therapy in schizophrenia; a controlled study of the relative effectiveness of chlorpromazine, promazine, phenobarbital, and placebo. Arch. Gen. Psychiat. *2:* 210-220, 1960.
6. —, Lasky, J. J., Klet, C. J. and Hollister, L. E.: Treatment of schizophrenic reactions with phenothiazine derivatives; a comparative study of chlorpromazine, triflupromazine, mepazine, prochlorperazine, perphenazine, and phenobarbital. Am. J. Psychiat. *117:* 97-105, 1960.
7. Delay, Jean, Deniker, P. and Harl, J. M.: Utilisation en thérapeutique psychiatrique d'une phénothiazine d'action centrale élective (4560 RP). [Therapeutic use of a phenothiazine derivative RP 4560 (chlorpromazine) in psychiatry.] An. Méd.-Psychol. *2:* 112-117, 1952.
8. Englehardt, D. M., Freedman, N., Glick, B. S., Hankoff, L. D., Mann, D. and Margolis, R.: Prevention of psychiatric hospitalization with use of psychopharmacological agents. J. A. M. A., *173:* 147-149, 1960.
9. Fleming, B. G., Spencer, A. M. and Whitelaw, E. M.: A controlled comparative investigation of the effects of promazine, chlorpromazine, and a placebo in chronic psychosis. J. Ment. Sci. *105:* 349-358, 1959.
10. Geller, M.: The treatment of psychiatric disorders with insulin 1936-1960. A selected annotated bibliography of controlled and comparative studies. In press.
11. Gilmore, T. H. and Shatin, L.: Quantitative comparison of clinical effectiveness of chlorpromazine and promazine. J. Ment. Sci. *105:* 508-510, 1959.
12. Gorham, D. R. and Overall, J. E.: Dimensions of change in psychiatric symptomatology. Dis. Nervous Syst. *22:* 576-580, 1961.
13. Gottlieb, J.: Personal communication.
14. Greenblatt, M., Grosser, G. H. and Wechsler, H.: A comparative study of selected anti-depressant medications and electroshock therapy. Am. J. Psychiat. An: complete 1962.
15. Hoffer, A. and Osmond, H.: Double blind clinical trials. J. Neuropsychiat. *2:* 221-227, 1961.
16. Kamman, G. R., Freeman, J. G. and Lucero, R. J.: The effect of l-isonicotynl 2-isopropyl hydrazine (IIH) on the behavior of long-term mental patients. J. Nervous & Ment. Dis. *118:* 391-407, 1953.
17. Kiloh, L. G., Child, J. P. and Latner, G.: A controlled trial of iproniazid in the treatment of endogenous depression. J. Ment. Sci. *106*: 1139-1144, 1960.
18. Kline, N. S.: Use of reserpine, the newer phenothiazines and iproniazid. A. Res. Nerv. & Ment. Dis. Proc., *37:* 218-244, 1959.

19. Kuhn, R.: The treatment of depressive states with an iminodibenzyl derivative (G 22355). Schweiz. med. Wchnschr. *87:* 1135-1140, 1957.

20. Kurland, A. A., Michaux, M. H., Hanlon, T. E., Ota, K. P. and Simopoulos, A. M.: The comparative effectiveness of six phenothiazine compounds, phenobarbital and inert placebo in the treatment of acutely ill patients: personality dimensions. J. Nervous & Ment. Dis. *134:* 48-61, 1962.

21. Laties, V. G. and Weiss, B.: A critical review of the efficacy of meprobamate (Miltown, Equanil) in the treatment of anxiety. J. Chronic Dis. *7:* 500-519, 1958.

22. Leyberg, J. T. and Denmark, J. C.: The treatment of depressive states with imipramine hydrochloride (Tofranil). J. Ment. Sci. *105:* 1123-1126, 1959.

23. Lorr, M., Klett, C. J., McNair, D. M. and Lasky, J. J.: Manual, inpatient multidimensional psychiatric scale (IMPS). January 1962. Washington, Veterans Administration, *33:* 11, [4]p, 1962.

24. McNair, D. M., Weistein, G. J., Michaux, W. W. and Raskin, A.: Meprobamate and chlorphromazine in psychotherapy: Some effects on anxiety and hostility of outpatients. Arch. Gen. Psychiat. *4:* 381-389, 1961.

25. McNair, D. M., Callahan, D. M. and Lorr, M.: Outpatient studies in psychiatry: therapist "type" and patient response to psychotherapy. Prepublication Report Number 2, Aug. 1961.

26. Moriarty, J. D.: Broad spectrum treatment of the neurotic and the borderline psychotic patient in office practice. J. Neuropsychiat. *1:* 112-117, 1959.

27. Rickels, K.: Personal communication.

28. —, Clark, T. W., Ewing, J., Klingensmith, W. C., Morris, H. M. and Smock, C. D.: Evaluation of tranquilizing drugs in medical outpatients; meprobamate, prochlorperazine, amobarbital sodium, and placebo. J. Am. M. A. *171:* 1649-1656, 1959.

29. Shawver, J. R., Gorham, D. R., Leskin, L. W., Good, W. W. and Kabnick, D. E.: Comparison of chlorpromazine and reserpine in maintenance drug therapy. Dis. Nervous Syst. *20:* 452-457, 1959.

30. Shepherd, M. and Watt, D. C.: A controlled clinical study of chlorpromazine and reserpine in chronic schizophrenia. J. Neurol. Neurosurg. & Psychiat. *19:* 232-235, 1956.

31. Smith, J. A.: The use of isopropyl derivative of isonicotinylhydrazine (Marsilid) in the treatment of mental disease; a preliminary report. Am. Pract. & Digest Treat. *4:* 519-520, 1953.

32. —, Christian, D., Rutherford, A. and Hendersen, H. C.: Effects of phenothiazines in chronic psychotics refractory to previous treatment. Exhibit presented at American Psychiatric Association, Philadelphia, April 1959.

33. Uhlenhuth, E. H., Canter, A., Neustadt, J. O. Payson, H. E.: The symptomatic relief of anxiety with mephobamate, phenobarbital and placebo. Am. J. Psychiat. *115:* 905-910, 1959.

34. Wirt, R. and Simon, W.: Differential Treatment and Prognosis in Schizophrenia. Springfield, Ill., Charles C. Thomas, 1959.

35. Wittenborn, J. R.: Wittenborn psychiatric rating scales. New York, Psychological Corporation, 1955.

36. —, Plante, M. and Burgess, F.: A comparison of physicians' and nurses' symptom ratings. J. Nervous & Ment. Dis. *133:* 514-518, 1961.

37. —, — and Livermore, N.: The efficacy of electroconvulsive therapy, imipramine and placebo in the treatment of young depressed women. J. Nervous & Ment. Dis. An complete, 1962.

38. —, —, —, — and —: The efficacy of electroconvulsive therapy, iproniazid and placebo in the treatment of young depressed women. J. Nervous & Ment. Dis. *133:* 316-332. 1961.

39. Zukin, P., Arnold, De Vere G. and Kessler, C. R.: Comparative effects of phenaglycodol and meprobamate on anxiety reactions. J. Nervous & Ment. Dis. *129:* 193-195, 1959.

3

EVALUATION OF PSYCHOANALYSIS A CLINICIAN'S VIEW

by HOWARD DAVIDMAN, M.D.*

PSYCHOANALYSIS began as a medical treatment for emotionally troubled people. Today it has become a cultural force permeating the social experiences and institutions of modern civilized man. It has altered man's self-awareness and his understanding of his fellows in daily life. In medicine the understanding of the physician-patient relationship has been enriched and psychoanalysis has stimulated and moulded all modern forms of psychotherapy.

Psychoanalysts have been busy men, working in an enormously complex field characterized by frontier conditions. Perhaps this is why meticulous scientific study of psychoanalysis itself, as a treatment process, has been so delayed and rudimentary.

Individual analysts, in their clinical work, dissatisfied, and trying to improve their understanding and therapeutic effectiveness with their patients, have experimented widely with both their techniques of psychoanalytic treatment and with their theoretical formulations. Many variations of the treatment process and of treatment tactics have resulted. These have been reported in clinical essays and expressions of opinion, and have been transmitted to students of psychoanalysis in varied kinds of training institutions. The process of education has resembled the relationship of master and apprentices, and has resulted in the formation of varied schools of thought in psychoanalysis.

Traditionally, the raw, first hand data of the treatment experience has only been observable by the participant analyst himself. It could only be communicated to others through the therapists' own reports.

These accounts, written from notes taken during a session, or purely from memory, are incomplete, inaccurate, and have been subjected to both conscious and unconscious processes of selection and reorganization by the analyst. The auditor of case reports, and of studies ap-

*New York School of Psychiatry.

plying rating scales to interview reports, often remains in doubt about whether the approach and the selection does any justice to the actual experience of the therapist's and the patient's work together. He often doubts whether the explanation of the therapeutic changes resemble the forces in actual operation. Many reports, aiming to prove a theoretical point, select the data with this end in view, and inevitably leave the auditor with a distorted view of the treatment. Massive clinical reports of psychoanalyses have filled files in analytic institutes with material that is unreliable and wholly inadequate for meaningful research.

Many analysts have been concerned with this built-in barrier to the scientific study of treatment, and most have been aware of the inadequate and misleading reports of the students whose work they have supervised.

In 1928 Lasswell[8] suggested sound recording of treatment sessions and at about the same time Sullivan[10] proposed filming interview sessions in order to study nonverbal components of communication. He also used sound recordings of clinical interviews in order to study his own work, as did Zinn.[17] Leighton, Lidz, [8,9] Kubie[6] and others advocated the use of sound films in research in the 1940's.

The objections to sound recording of sessions for fear of introducing distortion of the data or of invasion of the privacy of the patient have proved invalid, now that many have made it an accustomed procedure, and its revolutionary impact and technical novelty has worn off. Today it seems evident that adequate sound film recording of entire psychoanalyses, and of the analysts immediate postsession reports, are a methodologic prerequisite for meaningful treatment process research. Shakow,[16,17] has indicated that the difficulties in the use of sound film can be overcome by appropriate research design. He predicts that in the near future, the necessity for this technique will prevail over any initial shock it may provoke in some therapists. Such data would remove the handicap under which qualified research workers in this area now labor, knowing their data to be inadequate and often misleading. It would remove the charge that treatment process research was done with poor methods, or was not open to the ordinary criteria for scientific investigation. Such data could be communicated to groups of investigators that were wholly independent of each other.

The evaluation of psychoanalysis as a treatment method would seem to require some agreement about its nature, and intrinsic procedures.

Such agreement would enable one to decide not to study some particular form of treatment because it was clearly not a psychoanalysis. But it is not yet possible to plan research on such a foundation because psychoanalysis contains contending schools of thought advocating practises of wide diversity. Diversity in theory and practice also exists between the members of any society of psychoanalysts. The attempt to define psychoanalysis itself results in controversy.

Discussions of differences easily become polemical; some analysts privately regard others as rigid, foolish, dogmatic and authoritarian, or else as radical, deviant, and corruptive of the "true" heritage of Freud. Despite the presence of so much heated feeling the startling fact remains that no scientific research seems to have been done to compare the actual practice of different contending analysts or to compare their clinical results. Convictions are based rather on careful individual work and thought, on "common sense," or on emotional allegiances.

Traditional attempts to define psychoanalysis have included such ideas as:

1. Psychoanalysis is a treatment for persons largely capable of total reconstruction.
2. Psychoanalysis requires no less than five sessions a week. (A summer vacation is usually assumed.)
3. The patient must be recumbent on a couch with the analyst seated behind him.
4. There should be no less than 300 sessions. Some require a much greater number.
5. "Free associations" are to be encouraged and gathered. "Free association" is often stated to be the method of psychoanalysis.
6. The sessions should be held as closely to 50 minutes as possible.
7. Dream interpretation is an essential part of psychoanalysis.
8. The analyst must provide as little information about himself as is humanly possible. The purpose of this "analytic incognito" is to make of the analyst a screen on which infantile fantasies can be projected. The "incognito" fosters the display of inappropriate defensive maneuvers, and aids in the re-enactment of troubled childhood relationships with significant persons. These phenomena may then all be interpreted.
9. Treatment, properly termed psychoanalytic, must be based on the formation and resolution of a "transference neurosis."
10. Some analysts claim that treatment must go through stages and that occasionally the ideal of a "complete" analysis can be attained.
11. Some feel that financial sacrifices are a necessary part of the procedure.
12. Contact with relatives and mates, the uses of information other than that emanating from the patient, is said by some analysts to be destructive and alien to psychoanalysis.

13. Analysis is not "suggestive" nor "educational" in its therapeutic action, but is based on "accurate interpretation" and emotional assimilation and "working through" of "insight."

This confused list of tactics and principles has been challenged and opposed in every detail. Many analysts accept some of the items and deviate from others. Some who subscribe to these tenets actually violate them regularly in their clinical practice, but seem only dimly aware of this discrepancy, or else regard their practise as a deviation forced on them by practical pressures or the special therapeutic need of a patient who is really "not an analytic patient," and who is "not really" being analyzed.

Other definitions of psychoanalysis emphasize the provision of a "corrective emotional experience." This concept means that the analyst consciously and actively behaves in a manner opposite to or different from the neurotogenic behavior of the parents, thus enabling the patient to correct previously automatic behavior and learn new and appropriate modes of interpersonal adaptation. Many analysts believe that the formation of a meaningful, constructively based relationship between the analyst and the patient in present reality, is the basic prerequisite for psychologic change in psychoanalysis, and that interpretations and all tactical procedures are secondary to this foundation. The regulation of the duration and frequency of sessions, the regularity of the schedule, the relative position in space of therapist and patient, the use of "outside" information, communication with people actively concerned with the patient, are all handled quite flexibly by many analysts. Many can not separate "suggestion," "education," and "interpretation" in their own thinking about their therapeutic actions. Some encourage, some discourage the formation of the "transference neurosis;" some feel free to move either way depending on their view of the patient's needs. Some are very silent, others are actively communicative. Some feel free to make judicious use of personal revelation to the patient, a few feel no great objection to social contact with their patient. These kinds of difference exist among the most intelligent, experienced, and highly trained psychoanalysts, many of whom have altered their beliefs and practices considerably since their student days. In radical contrast to the idea of "complete analysis," many psychoanalysts consider that analysis provides new and refined skills for understanding self and others, new skills for living, and that at a certain point the patient takes over full responsibility and self-direction, no longer needs the physical presence of his analyst to practise his new skill in living, and may always return for further analysis if new or old problems prove to be beyond his capacity to manage his life to his own satisfaction. This view has it that analysis never ends, but that the physical presence of the analyst becomes unnecessary. The criteria for termination of treatment are variable among psychoanalysts, and should receive special study.

Some claim that analysis is best suited to highly verbal, intelligent educated, and rather healthy people who wish to enrich their lives and increase their fulfillment. Others would apply the method under varying conditions to very disturbed and borderline patients who may lack the qualities noted above.

Some analysts consider the attempt to define psychoanalysts to be premature, because of the lack of tested knowledge based on adequate scientific observation and comparative research. Many feel that an established definition would diminish the freedom needed for experimentation with clinical techniques. All these issues thus briefly scanned in this review of definition difficulty, and many more, remain virgin territory for meticulous research. Some pressure to form rigid definitions stems, not from science, but from the conditions of private practise which require measures to maintain professional standards or to protect a means of livelihood in an area susceptible to charlatanism. The broadest definition of psychoanalysis that has been offered is that it includes any treatment based on sound psychodynamic principles performed by an adequately trained person. Evidently there are a wide variety of psychoanalytic therapies in reputable use today, and therefore the term psychoanalysis serves only as a label for many specialized forms of psychotherapy. Generally these treatments pay much more intensive attention to the patients' individuality and emotional experience than do other forms of treatment.

These treatments are also distinguished by the good intelligence, extensive training, and broad cultural background of the practitioners, who bring high levels of integrity, devotion and therapeutic skill to their work. Psychoanalysis provides the best material available today for research in intensive psychotherapy. The collection of sound film recordings of whole treatments is the urgent next step in meaningful research into the problems thus far suggested in this paper as such a film library would provide valid observational material for study. Some suspect that it might be demonstrated that fine clinical efforts and results are possible with a wide variety of techniques and theoretical formulations. However, good clinical results do not in themselves validate the particular explanatory psychodynamics the practitioner may offer from his own frame of reference.

In recent decades leaders of psychoanalytic thought may be said to tend to develop the science of psychodynamics in two contrasting ways. Many have returned to closer scrutiny of the phenomena of the treatment session, to meticulous observation and description of the patient physician interchange. Theoretical constructs are formulated to explain observational data using simple abstractions in close harmony with the data. This method respects scientific procedure and understands psychodynamics as a division of biologic science, and now requires a laboratory such as the research institute using sound film recordings being suggested here. This approach contrasts with the thinking of those who seem to feel that biology and psychodynamics are unrelated. Theoretic concepts like the libido theory, or the life and death instinct theory and similar formulations are increasingly being viewed as formerly useful and historically interesting outmoded tools. Newer constructs, amenable to validation, are developing, such as the adaptational psychodynamics taught by Rado[12,13] and the approaches seen in the work of Alexander, Masserman, Kardiner and many others. Treatments can be classified on the basis of clear motivational analysis of the patients' capacity for cooperation and growth.[13] This approach would replace any authoritarian separation of psychotherapies into psychoanalytic and nonpsychoanalytic, and replace it by descriptions of appropriate treatments aimed at individual patients' needs. Sound theory of treatment should aim to encompass all psychotherapeutic situations.

The other tendency in psychodynamics is a path of attempted reconciliation; by the expansion of old theoretic concepts that have been jarred by new observations and demands, by the creation of new subordinate abstractions in the interest of maintaining system consistency, beloved theory is preserved not from scientific need, but to meet the emotional needs of some practitioners. A loss of clarity, utility and suitability to validation results and there may develop a tendency to substitute study of abstract theory for study of patients and their therapists. It would seem that the establishment of a library of sound films of psychoanalyses would provide a most needed antidote to the pitfall of obscurantism that plagues our field. It would at least help separate mystics and cultists, whose ideas are not based on objective observations of the events of treatment, from those who tackle the difficult task of scientific evaluation.

Today, systematic observation and study is required. The differences over the definition of psychoanalyses reflect the existence of great variations. The meaning and results of these technical variations in analytic activity must be established by the comparative research that has been so long neglected. The comfortable opinion that despite theoretic differences, in private practise the real experience is much the same, is rightly suspect. Critics can rationally question the scientific soundness of a discipline whose basic performance is veiled, and whose formulations must be accepted without scientific scrutiny. In the future sound film recordings can enable us to learn much more from each other and clarify many old problems, such as:

1. Do the various methods of psychoanalysis produce equally satisfactory results?
2. Do some of the techniques produce better results with certain kinds of patients, than with others. If so, can we discover what kinds of patients will derive more benefit from which of the differing techniques?
3. Do results of qualitatively different nature stem from the analysts' particular orientation and practise?
4. Do some types of procedures produce better results for some kinds of analyst than for others?
5. Does the analyst's belief about the nature of his own clinical techniques correspond to the observations of skilled observers?
6. How do variations in techniques affect the content of analysis, the rate of therapeutic change, the levels of activity, the control of acting out, and the facilitation of reasonable decision and action by the patient?
7. How does the maturation of the analyst affect his therapeutic style? Does his maturation improve his results? Do experienced men produce different results than beginners? Wherein lie the differences in performance?
8. What are the causes of failure in psychoanalytic therapy? What are the causes and the processes through which patients prematurely terminate their psychotherapy?

In "Analysis terminable and interminable" Freud[1] emphasized the importance of the personal characteristics of the analyst as a factor influencing analytic results; he felt that the analyst should possess a high degree of mental health, and act both as model and teacher for his patient. He said that both patient and therapist must share a profound love of truth. Strupp[18] takes Freud to mean that the analyst in his own individuality must provide the patient with a model of creative existence in order to lead by his own example; and not be reduced to dependence for clinical effectiveness solely on the impact of his words. Necessarily the study of the analyst as a person has attracted more attention as time has passed. It is now widely felt that he is himself the vital factor in effecting psychotherapeutic change, and that the main tool he uses is really himself. An excellent example of research into this area, based on the use of sound film recordings of interviews, can be found in a recent book by Strupp.[19] Holt and Luborsky[2] have provided a study indicative of the growing concern with the scientific problem of finding the appropriate human being to become a good psychoanalyst. Among the many questions open for study concerning the analyst are:

1. His capacity for empathy, under what conditions may it be active or withheld; how does this influence results. How do limited or extensive emphatic capacities facilitate or impede clinical results in different kinds of patients?
2. The analysts greater or lesser interest in the patients current reality and current emotional situation as an influence on clinical results.
3. Analysts concepts of treatment goals and objectives vary. How do their variations affect the treatment process and the results?
4. The emotional maturity of the therapist varies; his emotional problems may resemble or be remote from those of his patient. What effect does this have on various patients?
5. How and to what extent does the analyst offer himself as a real focus for identification? What results ensue? What effect does his capacity for personal pleasure, social and cultural activity and love and marital success have on the conduct of psychoanalysis?
6. Is it true, as some have claimed, that the age and sex of the analyst, and his other individual characteristics, only alter the momentary content of the earlier part of the analyses but do not affect the ultimate outcome?
7. What activities can be proved to be antitherapeutic? How do patients cope with these, and perhaps correct for them?
8. Just how do radically different kinds of patients use the individuality of the analyst?
9. How does the analyst's own evaluation of his procedures, of the reasons for the statements he made, of his countertransference, and of the transference compare with the evaluations of skilled nonparticipant observers?
10. What are the effects and modes of action of accurate and inaccurate interpretation? Of "educational" elements and of "suggestion"?
11. Perhaps we may reliably discover the kind of analyst best suited for different kinds of patients. Today patients are referred intuitively, based on knowledge of a few colleagues and their availability. We might also study the problems and techniques of the referring interview.
12. Analysts using a strict "incognito" should be compared in performance and results with those who do not.
13. Variations in management of the transference neurosis from encouraging it, to attempting to limit it have been advocated. The results require study as does the correlation of this variation with the analysts' personality.

14. Criteria for mental health vary among analysts—some behavior is deemed healthful. Variations in judgment and action in this area would be of value to study.
15. How do analysts operating as evaluators of psychoanalytic therapy agree or disagree depending on similar or dissimilar academic, cultural and theoretic backgrounds? How do they vary in their acumen as observers?

The question and problems I have been raising are in no sense new. The basic methodologic problem of the material to be used has limited attempts to study them. Sound film recording in an institute dedicated to treatment research seems the satisfactory answer today and in some centers of analytic research there is evidence of progress in this direction. Participation in research projects of this type would, I believe, augment the skills of an analyst and enrich the education of those in training. Students would perhaps accept earlier in their careers, their need to develop their own individual and spontaneous treatment style as a result of such shared experience. Each analyst has, of course, been analyzed at least once. Styles of training analysts vary. Each analyst has been closely scrutinized by skilled supervisors of his clinical work and by his teachers. During this extensive professional preparation, a wealth of clinical information is gathered which is largely lost to research. Unusual scientific dedication would today be required for a group of analysts and training analysands to permit their work together to be recorded under scientific scrutiny. The growth of our profession as a scientific discipline would seem to indicate such studies; when in the past the need was great physicians have at times experimented upon themselves. The idea does not seem to me to be too outlandish to consider. Pilot groups might be found to undertake such an effort. As yet, however, we have found no reliable substitute for absolute confidentiality in the management of training analyses. The protection of our patients, who are not destined to be our colleagues, has been much less difficult.

Follow-up studies of psychoanalyses[4,10,11,14,15] would also be more fruitful if based on sound film recordings of the analysis and of the follow-up interviews. Outcome studies based on documentary reports suffer from being a study of documents and of how observers write of their therapeutic experiences, rather than first-hand study of patient performance. Sometimes it seems that this problem is dismissed or discounted. But many who have worked diligently in these difficult areas agree on being beset with methodologic difficulties. Their material has often consisted of summaries of interviews and the use of rating scales by analytic "judges." Both the limited data and the rating scales confine the effort to limited areas of judgment and limited the use of the analyst "judges" full skills as interpreters of human experience. Permanent sound film recordings would free the research teams to fulfill the goals of their research. Despite the many years during which the need for sound movie film was apparent, and although research workers were interested in this idea, neither the public nor the psychoanalysts have been sufficiently interested in such work to make more than a beginning. Years ago men like Kubie[5] called for the establishment of institutes dedicated to psychotherapy research using film recordings. However, research often remains a secondary poorly supported and conventionalized interest of analytic institutes. A proper research institute would have to be highly endowed and would require a core of full-time planners and researchers dedicated to this aim. The cooperation of other psychoanalysts to perform the treatment and to furnish full reports of their postsession impressions, and still others to act as observers would be necessary. All the personnel of such an institute would have to be highly remunerated.

The problem of the reluctance of analysts to allow themselves and their work to be the subject of research by nonparticipant observers, or to be seduced by the technique from therapeutic endeavor into exhibitionism, could be overcome by many through self-analysis, and by support from the research team. If psychoanalysis is scientific, it is subject to the laws of scientific method which suggest cooperation in this laboratory research. Patients who were able to obtain valuable treatment by cooperation in this type of work would have difficulty similar to that which they now overcome in training clinics where they act as contributors to the educational needs of the school by participating in case conferences and meetings with supervisors.

Trained men of varied disciplines could cooperate in such research efforts with fewer difficulties to overcome than in the past. Projects requiring years of work could be planned and carried out in such a research institute. The magnitude of the material would also permit studies of selected segments of it. Such a research institute could provide the technical skills for adequate sound film recordings in controlled settings. The analyses recorded would include the work of experts and beginners. The library of filmed analyses might well have uses besides those originally conceived. Freud and his contemporaries left us with a specialized view of the upper castes of his time and place, which has stimulated scholars in many nonpsychiatric fields. The film library proposed here might serve future workers similarly. A research institute would profit from affiliation with an institution for training in psychoanalysis, and also from close cooperation with the graduate facilities and scientific atmosphere of a university. In such settings, teams of investigators might most easily be available, and physiologic resources could be incorporated into the studies. Other materials could be included as the research designs suggested.

It seems to me, that the political and economic climate in our country is becoming increasingly favorable to the support of and need for such efforts, particularly in the event that we prove wise enough to ensure our survival by the establishment of a peace economy. The cost of such effort is really low when measured in the context of need and neglect in the mental health field.

Psychoanalytic treatment is such an enormous and complex sample of crude life experience that it would seem to possess artistic dimentions, as well as material for scientific analyses. The practise of medicine has traditionally been called an art because it involves the wedding of technical knowledge, and emotional human influence to help troubled people in individual efficacious ways. The self-conscious experts in the art of human therapeutic influence are the psychoanalysts. I believe that psychoanalysis will always have an artistic dimension no matter how fully understood it becomes. If this aspect were taken seriously it would be apparent that a new type of study and contribution to the field would be achieved by recording the work. This is the field comparable to the best work of art appreciation and art criticism that flourishes in the art forms. Each psychoanalyst is a unique product of his biology, his experience and his cultural setting. Each has an individual style. While at work, using his free-floating attention, he functions both as scientist and artist. The peculiarity of this art form is that only he and his patient have any chance to experience it; there is no larger audience. As an artist he is in the same situation as the performing musician, actor or dancer before their work could be recorded. At present art appreciation of psychoanalysis does flourish informally, and consists of anecdotes, gossip, and the evaluations of the writings, teachings, and personal experiences with analysts by students and former patients. This lore is filled with distortion and falsified memories, lingering adorations and resentment, and unprintable stories. No one can judge the reliability of such impressions; but how much more valuable it would be to have the work of the pioneers in the field available for observation. I think the art interest would survive even if the mystery were removed. For this reason, too, the clinical work of famous practitioners, leaders of psychoanalytic thought, if recorded, would document their personal style and skills as well as their scientific views. Any one who has read fine art criticism, such as the work of Faure[21] on painting, will realize what a valid contribution such studies make to the growth and historical understanding of any field. We would all benefit by seeing analyses conducted by Freud, although the proponents of classic techniques would no longer be able to attribute so many of their methods to him. The clinical work of Ferenczi, Adler, Rank and Jung and the work of Zilboorg, Horney, Hartman, Rado and a host of others, if recorded, might well heighten our understanding of their contributions and increase our own knowledge and effectiveness. Surely the preservation of our evanescent art for study by future professionals would contribute to their understanding, clarify their confusions, and perhaps provide them with some pleasure.

REFERENCES

1. Freud, S.: Analysis, Terminable and Interminable. Collected papers, vol. 5. London, Hogarth Press, 1950, pp. 316-357.
2. Holt, R. R. and Luborsky, L.: Personality Patterns of Psychiatrists. New York, Basic Books, 1958.
3. Kardiner, A., Karush, A. and Ovesey, L.: A Methodologic Study of Freudian Theory. (a) Basic Concepts. J. Nervous & Mental. Dis. *129:* 11-19, 1959. (b) The libido theory. J. Nervous & Ment. Dis. *129:* 133-143, 1959. (c) Narcissim, bisexuality and the dual instinct theory. J. Nervous & Ment. Dis. *129:* 207-221, 1959. (d) The structural hypothesis, the problem of anxiety, and post-Freudian ego psychology. J. Nervous & Ment. Dis. *129:* 341-356, 1959.
4. Klein, H. R.: A study of changes occurring during and after psychoanalytic treatment. *In* Current Approaches to Psychoanalysis. New York, Grune and Stratton, 1960.
5. Kubie, L. S.: Practical and Theoretical Aspects of Psychoanalysis. New York, International Univ. Press, p. 245, 1950.
6. —: Among others in problems in clinical research. Round table, 1946. Am. J. Orthopsychiat. *17:* 196-240, 1947.
7. —: Psychoanalysis and scientific method. *In* S. Hook, (Ed.) Psychoanalysis, Scientific Method and Philosophy. New York, Univ. Press, 57-77, 1959.
8. Lasswell, H. D.: The problem of adequate personality records: a proposal. Am. J. Psychiat. *85:* 1057-66, 1928.
9. Leighton, A. H. and Lidz, T.: Am. J. Psychiat. *48:* 740-744, 1942.
10. Pfeffer, A. Z.: A procedure for evaluating the results of psychoanalysis: a preliminary report. J. Am. Psychoanal. 418-44, 1959.
11. —: Follow-up study of a satisfactory analysis. J. Am. Psychoanal. A. *9:* 698-718, 1961.

12. Rado, S. and Daniels, G. (Editors): Adaptational Development of Psychoanalytic Therapy in Changing Concepts of Psychoanalytic Medicine. New York, Grune and Stratton, 1956, pp. 89-100.
13. —: Recent Advances in Psychoanalytic Therapy 1953 in Psychoanalysis of Behavior, Coll. Papers of S. Rado. New York, Grune and Stratton, 1956, pp. 251-267.
14. Sargent, H. D.: Methodologic problems of follow-up studies in psychotherapy research. Am. J. Orthopsychiat. *20:* ...., 1960.
15. —: Intrapsychic change: methodological problems in psychotherapy research—psychiatry, *24:* ...., 1961.
16. Shakow, D.: The recorded psychoanalytic interview as an objective approach to research in psychoanalysis. Psychoanalyt. Quart. *29:* 82-97, 1960.
17. —: Discussion of papers by Leary and Gill and Rogers. *In* E. A. Rubinstein and M. B. Parloff (Eds.): Research in Psychotherapy. New York, American Psychological Assoc., 1959.
18. Strupp, H.: Some comments on the future of research in psychotherapy. Behavioral Sc. *5:* ...., 1960.
19. —: Psychotherapists in Action. New York, Grune and Stratton, 1960.
20. Sullivan, H. S.: Affective experience in early schizophrenia. Am. J. Psychiat. *6:* 467-483, 1927.
21. Faure, E.: History of Art, Garden City, New York, ...

*New York City.

4

EVALUATION OF SOMATIC THERAPIES

by LOTHAR B. KALINOWSKY, M.D.*

METHODS OF EVALUATING TREATMENT RESULTS in psychiatry started with the discovery of the first somatic treatments. One of the reasons was that results could be obtained with these treatments in a predictable and relatively short period of time. Furthermore, they could be standardized better than the previously available psychotherapeutic procedures which inevitably varied from one therapist to the other. Also, the somatic treatments were primarily applied to patients in hospitals which facilitated observation of immediate as well as long-term results. It soon became apparent that despite these favorable conditions, statistical studies came to quite contradictory conclusions. It is, therefore, worthwhile to list some of these reasons for failure of such investigations, to discuss ways of preventing mistakes, to show what type of investigation has been neglected in the past, and how methodology can be improved in the future.

Evaluation became fairly well systematized during the first years of insulin-coma treatment. Later, possibilities and limitations of statistical evaluation were confirmed in convulsive therapy. Subsequent therapeutic methods such as psychosurgery and finally pharmacotherapy began to show that different yardsticks must be applied to different treatments. It also became obvious that there are handicaps in any evaluation by means of a purely statistical approach, and that clinical observation by experienced workers should not be entirely discarded as unscientific, although it should be carefully compared with statistical figures. The most obvious but often neglected requirement is that statistical methods in the evaluation of treatments in mental illness must be worked out in collaboration with a clinician experienced in the psychiatric disorders treated and the therapeutic method applied.

Statistics on insulin-coma treatment already showed that first of all the patient material must be broken down according to duration of illness. Since the effectiveness of all shock treatments is essentially

*New York City.

limited to patients with comparatively short duration of illness, reports not separating acute and chronic cases present either too favorable results because acute cases prevailed, or too unfavorable results because chiefly chronic patients had been treated. In schizophrenia a further breakdown according to subtypes and, possibly, according to type of onset is necessary in order to arrive at conclusions of practical significance. Differences in the patient material or psychiatric hospitals as, for instance, that of some psychiatric training centers compared with that of large mental institutions, explain some of the widely contrasting results obtained with these treatments. Attempts at combining the material from different hospitals has also been proved to be misleading. Apart from the type of patient admitted, criteria regarding diagnostic principles, intensity of treatment, and evaluation by the staff may differ widely from hospital to hospital.

At the present time, when double-blind studies are considered a strict requirement, it may appear strange that the most reliable statistics on insulin treatment were derived from experts who had treated the investigated patient material themselves. The Swiss survey by Müller and the German statistic by von Braunmühl have become the models for evaluation of insulin, convulsive, and combined insulin-convulsive treatment. They and some later statistics have remained the yardstick for what can be achieved with somatic treatments, when properly applied, and the resulting figures must be used to measure the value of subsequently introduced methods of treatment. Most statistics furnished by experts show a surprising accordance of the results obtained. Some workers made the distinction between "recovered," "much improved," and "unimproved," while others objected to the term "recovered," and substituted for it "full remission" since schizophrenic disease hardly ever clears up without any defect symptoms. When full remissions and variously defined social remissions were combined, most statistics agreed on results obtainable with insulin-coma treatment. For the various subtypes of schizophrenia figures for remissions were approximately twice as high as figures from the few available statistics on spontaneous remissions. Similar figures were obtained in schizophrenics for convulsive treatment with metrazol and electric shock if intensive treatment was applied. Here as well as in insulin treatment it became apparent that the most striking discordance in results stemmed from differences in the intensity of treatment. The statistician is in no position to see from his charts how the therapeutic method has been applied. Even if he counts the number of insulin comas, he does not know the depth of the coma reached in the individual applications. In convulsive therapy both metrazol and electric shock showed convincingly that most patients become symptom-free after very few treatments, but that only continuation of treatment up to 20 or more will lead to optimal results. This is not contradicted by statistical findings that patients with the largest number of treatments showed the poorest outcome; it is statistically true only because chronic and unresponsive schizophrenics are apt to receive the longest series of treatments.

The outcome of a treatment should not be judged too early as it has been done in some statistics. Many patients relapse within weeks which proves that symptoms had only been covered up by the treatment. Evaluation several weeks after termination of treatment and long-term studies showed quite uniform results, wherever the treatment had been applied adequately. Relapses in successfully treated schizophrenics are frequent, but it is unjustified to condemn a treatment because of the statistical findings that a 10-year follow-up shows little difference between treated and untreated patients. Such conclusions, made repeatedly, overlooked the fact that patients may have spent years outside of the hospital, and also that relapses can be treated again.

Long-term follow-ups of depressions are even more misleading. Most manic-depressive depressions usually last less than a year or even 6 months. It is obvious, therefore, that figures for remissions are almost identical after a year for treated and untreated patients. Yet, the time lost by a patient not treated with ECT or pharmacotherapy, his suffering, and other considerations such as the suicidal danger make such long-term statistics on these patients meaningless.

The next treatment introduced, namely, psychosurgery, demonstrated for the first time that the methods of evaluation must be modified according to the way a treatment changes the patient symptomatologically. Psychosurgery, even if successful, rarely leads to complete disappearance of the symptomatology at least in the group of schizophrenias, but it reduces symptoms and changes the emotional response of the patient to his symptoms. Personality changes due to the postoperative impairment of frontal lobe function interfere with the outcome in various degrees. The result in favorable cases is a patient who is able to live outside of a hospital, even though his ability to function is impaired by various factors. This applied to probably one third of all operated chronic schizophrenics, while another third made a better adjustment within the hospital, and the last third still remained too sick to leave the hospital. These figures, confirmed in many studies, were used for the critical statement that most treatments in psychiatry improve one third considerably, one third slightly, and left one third unimproved. In schizophrenic case material such conclusion neglected the fact that these lobotomized patients had been failures from other treatments, and that, therefore, statistics for this method have an entirely different meaning than those on previously used treatments in the same patient. It is furthermore difficult to bring out statistically that schizophrenics with a high degree of deterioration prior to the operation, show a different degree of improvement from those who had shown no signs of deterioration such as most pseudoneurotic schizophrenics and some late paranoids. The superiority of psychosurgery particularly in pseudoneurotic schizophrenics has been shown convincingly in the figures of Hoch and his co-workers, when compared with results in other types of chronic schizophrenia, where psychosurgery was largely abandoned after the introduction of pharmacotherapy. Yet, it was an interesting finding that long-term follow-ups after psychosurgery, quite contrary to other somatic treatments, show qualitatively further improving results over the years, and a recent report from the British Ministry of Health confirmed that improvements even in chronic schizophrenics, as limited as they may be, are better maintained than in most other somatic treatments in psychiatry. This is mentioned to show the intricacies of any statistical evaluation as long as they are not seen in the framework of clinical experience with all treatment procedures.

A frequently made mistake is to assume that a method applied subsequently to one under which the patient had failed, necessarily proves the superiority of the second method. A patient who relapses under convulsive therapy and responds well to insulin, has already been treated intensively, and the second treatment might have a cumulative effect. This is equally true for patients who failed under insulin but responded to subsequent convulsive treatment. If patients who failed under both, respond to psychosurgery despite some personality defects, this by no means proves the superiority of psychosurgery over the previously applied methods.

Pharmacotherapy poses a new set of problems in statistical evaluation. While methods such as double-blind and triple-blind studies had not been previously applied to treatments in psychiatry, the experience with pharmacotherapy has certainly not avoided serious mistakes in methodology. The clinical experience of the effectiveness of the neuroleptic drugs in certain groups of patients is unquestionable. It already has been convincingly established in the very first French and Swiss clinical reports on chlorpromazine and reserpine. How much has been added to this knowledge by refined statistical methods can be a matter of debate. The difficulty in measuring the therapeutic action of these drugs lies in their primarily symptomatic effect on so-called target symptoms. The final result has often been measured in discharge rates and other criteria which are easily influenced by extraneous factors. The matter is complicated by the frequent need to maintain the patient on the medication which is especially difficult in the chronic schizophrenics. The impairment of the patients' functioning by the side effects is a factor that cannot be measured easily but that weighs heavily on the over-all results with neuroleptic drugs.

Truly comparative studies between the older methods such as shock treatments and pharmacotherapy which should be done under equal conditions on matched patient material, are not available. Many efforts have been made to exclude for proper evaluation the possible psychological factor of special attention given to a patient under an active drug. To question the effect of neuroleptic drugs or other somatic treatments on grounds of suggestibility, means to overlook that in previous times many ineffective drugs were used, or, for that matter, much attention given to patients, particularly in private hospitals, without noticeable effect on the schizophrenic symptoms. These critical remarks are by no means made to discourage the most accurate methods of evaluation but to point out that the therapeutic action of new methods must be seen in the framework of all previously acquired knowledge.

The exclusive reliance on large figures in statistical evaluation led to some practices which should be strongly objected to. This includes the widespread use of reports by many individual psychiatrists who were supplied with a new drug by the drug companies, and who tabulate their results with this drug for compilation by the manufacturer. Some drugs have been exclusively launched on the basis of such information. This method is obviously open to all kinds of mistakes. Every doctor has different criteria for the diagnosis of psychiatric disorders and evaluation of therapeutic results. There is no way to determine which other medications an office patient is taking, and many patients dissatisfied with the drug, will just change doctors which eliminates unfavorable cases from the study. The preference for large statistics in contrast to studies with small but well documented patient material has led to many wrong conclusions regarding both older and newer somatic treatments. It is true that more careful methods have been designed in pharmacotherapy than in any of the older methods. Yet, the criticism must be made that methods of evaluation worked out by clinicians on the previous treatments were neglected to the detriment of many drug studies. Drug research has again shown what became equally apparent in other areas of psychiatric research, namely that statistical methods applicable to other fields of endeavor, are not necessarily applicable to psychiatric studies. This point evolved convincingly a few years ago in a symposium on epidemiological research of which this Association was one of the sponsors.

At the end of this presentation a few remarks may be permitted about investigations which would be highly significant but have never been performed, supposedly because they require a research design not suitable for quick results. It is difficult to understand why such widely used methods as insulin and convulsive treatment have hardly ever been compared in any long-term study on matched patient material within the same hospital. The same is true for other therapeutic techniques such as different modalities of electric shock methods which competed with each other based on unsubstantiated claims. The most acute present problem should be a comparison of older and newer methods. Matched groups of patients should be followed over years, but it is one of the shortcomings of present day research that few experienced clinical researchers remain in a given hospital for such longitudinal studies. As long as such studies are not available, clinical evaluation by psychiatrists with experience in all rather than one single treatment method must be used to supplement data obtained from large statistics. It is amazing that even such simple questions as the relative value of ECT and antidepressant drugs could not be solved in clearly designed parallel series of patients treated with the two methods. It is also no proof for the superiority of combined treatment with ECT and drugs if some workers claim that the combination made it possible to reduce the number of necessary electric shock treatments from 12 to 6 which many psychiatrists found a fully adequate number of ECT's without simultaneous medication. Also the *quality* of a remission should receive greater attention, when older and newer treatments are being compared. Rating scales have been of little help. There is no scientific method to measure such questions as the comparison of an insulin or electric shock remission, and a favorable pharmacotherapeutic result which must be maintained with continued medication, or to fully evaluate the subjective discomfort of otherwise symptom-free patients on a maintenance dose of certain drugs.

A promising attempt to combine the need for statistically meaningful numbers and careful investigations of small groups of patients has been made in a cooperative study which is under way in five German university hospitals. After long deliberations their research psychiatrists agreed on principles of evaluation for simultaneously conducted studies on new drugs, and to pool their results.

In conclusion it can be stated that great efforts have been made during the last 25 years to arrive at a reliable evaluation of somatic treatments in psychiatry. Many errors have been committed; yet, a wealth of material has been accumulated. Acquaintance with all the various methods of evaluation used should help us to improve our methodology and to arrive at more reliable conclusions in future studies.

Discussion

by PAUL H. HOCH, M.D.*

DR. WOLBERG CLEARLY DESCRIBES the factors which contaminate our findings in evaluating psychotherapy and calls attention to those many factors playing a role in the therapeutic process. Many scientific investigators have wondered how, when multifactorial causation is involved, the separate factors could be defined. Nevertheless, progress has been made, and even more progress would be made, if we were to experiment with different evaluation designs and give up the idea that psychotherapy cannot be evaluated because the different factors are too difficult to disentangle. We still have much more to learn about the therapeutic process before we attempt an evaluation of therapy. Admittedly, the evaluation of psychotherapy will not be fully satisfactory for a long time, but continued attempts would at least give us the ability to improve upon what we have today.

Dr. Wolberg also describes the fact that many psychiatrists have only a paucity of notes and other instruments on hand and that it is very difficult to reconstruct what actually happened from such notes. Nevertheless, we have to emphasize that notes of therapists cannot be as extensive as notes made for research projects. Notes are rarely organized in such a way that they include all factors in which different research projects are interested. Nevertheless, we fully agree with Dr. Wolberg that in order to be able to evaluate psychotherapy the basis of this should adhere to established rules of medical practice. The difficulty is that even if we have extensive records on a patient, the important versus the unimportant and the subjective biases cannot be controlled. In some instances the records may give a completely false impression as to what really occurred. However, attempts should be made to maintain some records. The same applies to tape recordings and similar devices. No doubt in the future new methods will gradually emerge as to how to sift such material.

It is also very commendable that Dr. Wolberg recognizes that subjective assessment of impressions by the patient is not necessarily an acceptable criterion for the effectiveness of psychotherapy and

*Commissioner of Mental Hygiene, State of New York; Professor of Clinical Psychiatry, College of Physicians and Surgeons, Columbia University.

more objective evaluation methods will be necessary; in our opinion the patient's own appraisal with all its subjectivity and distortions, if properly noted, is still the most important evaluation tool. The discrepancies which exist between the patient's appraisal and that of the therapist's are often conspicuous and sometimes shed light into techniques and theories of the claimed psychotherapeutic methodologies. The patient often will report what the therapist wants to hear and at other times he will often disparage successful therapeutic intervention. The patient's subjective and objective assessment of the therapeutic process brings up another important point, namely, the value and role of insight into therapy. It was assumed formerly that the development of insight would mean general improvement, whereas improvement without insight was called spurious and based upon the transference relationship. It is obvious that this formulation is not in accordance with well known facts and will not satisfy those, who while claiming that psychotherapy cannot be investigated objectively, in the same breath still want fully logical explanations explaining its *modus operandi.* Genuine improvements and even recoveries were observed in patients without any "psychodynamic" insight into their condition. On the other hand, there is a considerable number of patients who verbalize insight into their psychodynamic mechanisms without demonstrating any change. The distinction between intellectual and emotional insight expresses an awareness of this problem; unfortunately, we do not know what emotional insight is. Furthermore, the ability of having insight into supposedly causative mechanisms where the causes are not clearly understood is questionable.

Dr. Wolberg stresses the importance of follow-up studies. We are somewhat reluctant to accept the use of questionnaires if not at least combined with sample interviews to verify and clarify many of the answers to these questionnaires.

He also describes the different approaches in psychotherapy and I think solid progress could be made if we were able to compare and evaluate the different techniques. At present the claims to superiority of one method or another are often based on belief and not evidence. It would also be very important to clarify the role of short and prolonged psychotherapy and determine what kind of patient is able to benefit from one or the other.

We fully agree with Dr. Cole that systematic studies are needed in the field of evaluation and that a better methodology must be evolved. Many clinical evaluations today are done at great expense to confirm clinical factors which most clinicians dealing with drugs know without elaborate evaluations. We have a great need to organize and refine the methodology used today.

Dr. Cole touched upon the problem of individualization in the use of drugs. It is obvious no drug exists that would be best for all kinds of patients and helpful in all psychiatric conditions. For instance, chlorpromazine, in my experience, statistically speaking, is superior to reserpine because many more patients respond more favorably to chlorpromazine than to reserpine. This, of course, does not mean that there will not be individual patients where reserpine is superior. Therefore, this problem has to be approached partly on a statistical basis, but due consideration must be given to individual responses.

In his presentation Dr. Cole also discusses the relationship of insulin treatment and psychotherapy. If different treatment methods are available it is necessary to evaluate the effect comparatively. Again statistical methods and methods of individual responses are of importance.

In the discussion of drug therapies and other somatic therapies considerable time is spent in discussing their side effects. The toxicity of some of these drugs in some individuals is constantly called to the attention of the physicians treating them. For obvious reasons very little attention is paid to the side effects in nonsomatic therapies and therefore to the uninitiated it may appear that somatic therapies have side effects and the others do not. It is obvious the somatic therapies producing side effects in the body are usually quite conspicuous and therefore considered specific whereas the side effects of psychotherapy are usually in the psychic realm.

Dr. Cole also calls attention to animal experiments and to the clinical indications for use of drugs. We feel, as he does, that while animal experimentation is of great importance, drugs which influence the human psyche ultimately must be evaluated in man. No animal experimentation can substitute for such investigations. Animal experiments usually permit a more global evaluation of the drugs but it is not possible to study the ramifications of drug effects in animals on specific mental symptoms. This is also a reason why clinical evaluations must be made. Unfortunately, in clinical research two forces are coming to the fore which I believe need special attention. Many drugs are advocated—probably for commercial purposes—indicating too broadly that a drug is of value in every form and every kind of mental disorder which, of course, leads to disappointments and disillusionment if it is tried in conditions where it is ineffective. The other extreme is to advocate drugs whose chemical form and clinical actions are very similar to each other endeavoring to convince the physician that some very special and circumscribed clinical symptom will yield to the drug. For instance, a claim can be made that obsessive or paranoid behavior is very much influenced by a drug. At present there is very little evidence that drugs influence specific psychiatric symptomatologies in the sense they only effect one or two symptoms. Usually they influence a fairly broad spectrum of psychiatric symptoms. Further research may isolate how drug action on specific psychiatric symptoms occurs.

Dr. Davidman has evaluated psychoanalytic therapy from a clinician's point of view. He has stated, and we fully agree, that psychoanalysis is working in an enormously complex field characterized by frontier conditions. Here, of course, we may ask how long is it possible to claim that it is a frontier condition. We believe that the rather rudimentary attempts to evaluate psychotherapy are due more to the fact that the therapy is subjective between therapist and patient is more difficult than in those therapies which are far more impersonal. The attempt to objectivate psychoanalysis or psychotherapy is relatively new because no reliable instruments have been available or suggested to attempt such a task. The newer recording techniques (sound recording and sound film), of course, would be able to record the proceedings in a therapeutic session. However, the difficulty is that if therapeutic procedure is recorded in its entirety it could become a very laborious and very expensive procedure. There are also problems with selective recording. Total recording comprises such a mass of material that it is not easy to differentiate the important from the unimportant; it depends upon the value conflictual with judgment of the evaluators which, of course, could be what would be emphasized in selecting the so-called representative recordings from the vast total material. Dr. Davidman is also correct in stating that a great deal of discussion has gone on about the trappings of psychoanalysis and the importance or nonimportance of certain rituals, namely, the patient is treated lying down or sitting up, is treated three times a week or five times a week, and similar issues. No doubt undue emphasis has been placed upon these issues while the far more important problems have not been touched upon.

Dr. Kalinowsky correctly states that the evaluation of somatic therapies is more standardized than that of psychotherapies. However, this does not mean the evaluation of somatic therapies cannot and should not be improved considerably. Different yardsticks must be applied to different therapies; at the same time we believe the evaluation of therapeutic results should be comparable regardless of the treatment evaluated. Without this we never will be able to say which treatment is better. It is also important to stress that very often a comparison of one treatment with another is not as important as a clear definition of which patient will respond better to one form of therapy or to another.

Dr. Kalinowsky also discusses the importance of the double-blind technique against clinical appraisal. Both of these are necessary and they complement each other. Good and unbiased clinical evaluation will always be of great importance regardless of how mechanized and automatized some evaluations may become statistically. The battle between the different evaluation techniques is between the more objective and the more subjective. Both are important and should throw light on many issues. The preoccupation of some clinicians to objectify everything in psychiatry is doomed to failure. At the same time, the belief that objectification or evaluation should be applied is wrong. There are those who claim that everything is subjective and therefore cannot be approached with statistics or other methods. Instead of continuing this type of discussion, we believe it would be more fruitful to define which psychic phenomena can be evaluated today objectively and which will remain in a subjective and highly individualistic realm.

Dr. Kalinowsky correctly points out that a great deal of pessimism has been generated based upon follow-up statistics indicating that a great many schizophrenic patients who are treated will relapse. We agree with some of his appraisal; but it must be stressed that all treatments used in the major psychoses are not the last word and therefore an appraisal of research and a clinical appraisal of treatment are based on different criteria. The clinical appraisal usually stresses the failure of the available treatments whereas the research appraisal endeavors to analyze the strengths and weaknesses of a particular treatment toward the eventual goal of introducing more effective methods. Dr. Kalinowsky contrasts the evaluation of treatment that is based upon statistical techniques using a large group of patients against the evaluation of a small number of patients by a single therapist. He feels the evaluation by a large group of investigators does not contribute a great deal because they may apply different statistical criteria and even different clinical methodology as against one investigator handling a small group of patients. We feel that both approaches are important. It is true that lesser statistics are more uniform in data gathering but could be more biased than the larger ones where varied data come to the fore. It is true, of course, that the evaluation of large data is far more difficult and this is the reason why some of the conclusions based upon these studies are sometimes questioned. We may say, however, that the failure of a therapy, especially when unreasonable claims are made for its efficacy, is more often based upon smaller than larger statistics.

Dr. Kalinowsky also advocates the use of matched patient material in evaluation studies and more longitudinal studies. We fully approve of the longitudinal part of these suggestions. Nevertheless, when we consider this matching, we are far more skeptical that this can be done adequately. We have participated in many evaluation studies and are aware of how many "matched studies" are not really matched studies but equate only a few obvious features in the patient's history.

One of the most difficult problems in evaluation is to overcome the biased investigator who arrives at his conclusions by preconception using an elaborate investigation to confirm his therapeutic biases.

Part II: Technical Issues

5

QUANTITATIVE TECHNIQUES FOR THE EVALUATION OF PSYCHIATRIC TREAMENT

by EUGENE I. BURDOCK, PH.D. AND ANNE S. HARDESTY, M.S.*

SINCE THE NATURAL COURSE of mental illness may lead with almost equal probability to eventual remission, exacerbation or continuation of symptoms, efforts to assess the efficacy of any treatment are confounded by the necessity to demonstrate that the treated patients who have improved either clearly outnumber the one-third who would be expected to improve in any case or that they are drawn from among the two-thirds who would not otherwise have improved.

The first of these two possible demonstrations requires that the treated group be a representative sample of the population of patients. Failure to fulfill this requirement in studies of the efficacy of the somatic therapies[1] or of psychotherapy reflects the basic conflict between the necessary conditions for scientific investigation and the medical ethic of applying what is considered the best treatment for each individual patient. In this context some of us will recall the dramatic account of the destruction of a scientific inquiry through purely humanitarian motives in the novel *Arrowsmith* by the late Sinclair Lewis.

On the other hand, to demonstrate the efficacy of a new treatment with potential chronic or regressed patients requires identification of the future chronics either before they become ill or during the early period of their illness when the disease process is presumably still

---

*Biometrics Research, Columbia University and N. Y. State Department of Mental Hygiene.

This investigation was supported by PHS Research Grant No. 03546 from the National Institute of Mental Health.

reversible. This is an extremely difficult task. Some retrospective studies aimed at specifying background attributes prognostic of outcome have suggested that there are certain characteristics which predict outcome irrespective of therapy.[2-3] Since retrospective studies suffer from severe sampling limitations which may produce gross biases, they are at best merely propaedeutic to a scientific inquiry. A final verdict always depends on the predictive success obtained in a prospective study.

Evaluation of therapy is also seriously impeded by the lack of satisfactory criteria of outcome. While there is general agreement as to the identification of the extremes, i.e., the former patient who is an outstanding success or the chronic regressed patient who needs continual nursing care, intermediate grades of outcome are less susceptible to identification because they depend upon social norms which allow for considerable variability from what is recognized as typical or expected behavior. Efforts to develop quantitative techniques for the evaluation of psychiatric treatment[4] have therefore been focused on certain critical aspects of the course of the illness: hospital admission, response to therapy and outcome.

Four different kinds of quantitative techniques have been used in the evaluation studies that are reported in what follows: (1) Observational methods . . . (2) structured interview . . . (3) life table analysis . . . (4) Outcome Index.

TABLE 1—Analyses of Inter-Observer Agreement for Regular Duty Personnel on the Ward Behavior Inventory

Institution	No. of Patients	No. of Observers	Intraclass R	Residual Mean Square	Component of Variance Due to Observers
A	10	4	.77	56.52	77.60
B	47	2	.76	52.58	61.51
C	29	2	.79	55.23	0
D	8	2	.57	26.82	54.43
E	28	4	.65	45.57	73.94
F	24	2	.87	27.87	8.96

Note: The best results were obtained at Institution F where the observers (nurses) were highly trained.

TABLE 2—Reliability of Ward Behavior Inventory by Two-Way Intraclass Correlation in Psychopharmacology Service Center Collaborative Study of Effectiveness of Phenothiazines for Treatment of Chronic Schizophrenics (eight hospitals over four observation periods)

Hospital	Before Drug			1st Week			3rd Week			6th Week			Mean		
	N	s	R	N	s	R	N	s	R	N	s	R	N	s	R
1	—	—	—[a]	11	5.78	.817	6	3.92	.922	—	—	—[a]	8	5.196	.856
2	77	8.09	.670	76	10.08	.619	61	7.80	.777	46	6.26	.844	65	8.389	.713
3	38	3.67	.960	37	5.01	.914	32	4.64	.944	28	3.99	.934	34	4.363	.940
4	78	5.95	.860	76	6.24	.893	72	5.39	.907	57	5.40	.914	71	5.787	.894
5	36	7.15	.833	33	8.88	.746	33	7.78	.854	33	6.74	.924	34	7.673	.855
6	33	6.24	.840	32	7.21	.741	29	6.38	.829	26	5.89	.801	30	6.480	.805
7	21	8.73	.812	10	6.24	.642	14	8.74	.704	6	7.86	.858	13	8.213	.783
8	22	7.29	.840	15	7.29	.866	15	6.57	.865	16	5.50	.842	17	6.761	.853
Total	305	6.807	.827	290	7.794	.792	262	6.627	.859	212	5.816	.894	267	6.417	.859

Note: One hospital was not included in the reliability analysis because of failure to use paired observations.

[a]Omitted because less than 6 paired observations.

Observational Methods

Illustrative of the observational methods are the Ward Behavior Inventory and the Children's Behavior Inventory. The Ward Behavior Inventory[5] consists of items descriptive of the behavior of a hospitalized mental patient. The items are especially designed for dichotomous ratings by the psychiatric nurse or attendant. The reliability of the scale has been studied by analysis of inter-observer agreement and of internal consistency. Analyses of agreement among observers who are regular duty nurses or attendants are shown in table 1. Table 2 shows the reliability obtained with the Ward Behavior Inventory in a nine-hospital collaborative study undertaken by the Psychopharmacology Service Center and reported elsewhere in this volume.[6] The sensitivity of the WBI to changes brought about by treatment has been demonstrated in several studies. Results of these studies are reported in table 3.

During 1959-1960, WBI protocols were collected for 118 patients at the New York State Psychiatric Institute. None of these patients had had a previous admission to a psychiatric hospital, but at the time the ratings were made the patients had been in the hospital for various lengths of time ranging from 1 week to 6 months. All but one of the patients were of urban origin and the majority were of middle class background.

The total scores and the individual items were assessed both as predictors and as criterion measures. For these purposes each patient was followed for 2 years after his initial rating and an Outcome Index (see below) computed. A correlation of .20* was found between the total score on the WBI and the Outcome Index. As this group of patients is more similar than is the case in many institutions, and as homogeneity is known to attenuate correlations, this figure probably represents a conservative estimate of the true correlation.

Biserial correlations between the number of nights out of hospital and item scores were also computed. Approximate 95 per cent confidence limits were established by multiplying the standard error of the biserial correlation by 1.96. On inspection it became apparent that some of the items had high correlations because one or two patients with widespread pathology exhibited the corresponding behavior. Therefore, an arbitrary criterion was established that five or more patients needed to show the pathological behavior before the biserial

---

*$p < .05$

TABLE 3.—Criterion Studies with the Ward Behavior Inventory

Institution	Patients	Comparison	N	Criterion	Method	Statistic
State Hospital A	Geriatric Females	I Energizer vs. placebo	48	Change	Covariance	F = 6.50*
		II Reversal of drug and placebo groups				F = 4.69*
State Hospital B	Chronic schizophrenics	Baseline vs. Wy2445	M24 F24	Change	Covariance	F = 4.35* n. s.
State Hospital C	Chronic schizophrenics M & F	Thorazine vs. Mellaril vs. Placebo	74	Change	—	n. s.

*Significant at .05 level of confidence.

was accepted. Of the ten items which met this criterion, five are indicative of problems in verbalization and communication:

Talks, mutters and mumbles to himself.
Repeats words and phrases in a meaningless and mechanical manner.
Slurs his speech.
Either mixes up words, or repeats sounds, or makes up new words (word salad, clang associations, neologisms).
Talks and talks (pressure of speech).

One item involves both affect and communication:

Likes to talk about his family.

One item is significant of depersonalization:

Says that part or all of himself is outside of his body, or that someone else is in his body, or that part of his body does not belong to him (feelings of depersonalization).

Two items relate to memory and confusional states:

Appears helpless, perplexed and confused.
Has trouble remembering (names, etc.)

Finally, one item refers to cooperativeness:

Resists or refuses to do ordinary things expected of him (dressing, washing, etc.)

In all, for those with poor outcome a pattern of thought disorder is revealed in faulty communication, depersonalization, confusion and memory impairment together with disturbance of affect and negativism.

It is interesting that only one item indicative of uncooperativeness related to poor outcome, and that one an extreme of negativistic behavior. Here at least there is no support for the notion that a patient's release rests mainly upon his readiness to comply.

For evaluating the behavior of children a special Children's Behavior Inventory[7] has been designed. The CBI is applicable to children between the ages of 1 and 15. Initially a list of items was drawn up which clinical experience indicated were significant of varying degrees of psychopathology. Psychiatric texts and articles were scanned for behaviors characteristic of emotional disorders of childhood.[8-13] Each symptom was checked in more than one important source. Symptoms so obscure as to have only a single reference were eliminated, so that the remaining list consisted of symptoms judged significant by several of the reference sources.

The symptoms were then screened to determine the ages at which they first became significant of developmental anomaly. A number of

TABLE 4.—Comparison of Normal and Maladjusted Children on the Children's Behavior Inventory

Sample (Normals)	Sex	N	Mean Age	Mean Score	s
Nursery School	M&F	59	4	7	6.7
Public School	M&F	15	8	7	4.5
Parochial School	M&F	29	9	6	4.5
Pediatric Hospital	M&F	21	8	8	5.4
Total		124		7	5.3
Round the Clock Observations-Normals					
Summer Camp A	M	21	10	11	8.5
Summer Camp B	M	43	9	12	7.1
Total		64		11.5	7.8
Sample (Emotionally Disturbed)					
New York Research Hospital	M	27	9	15	7.5
	F	15	9	22	12.6
School for Autistic Children	M	12	6	21	4.9
	F	2	1) 4	24	—
			2) 5	21	—
School for Mental Defectives	M	17	6	17	9.8
	F	13	6	20	10.2
New Jersey Research Hospital	M	18	10	32	8.4
	F	4	11	24	8.4
New Jersey State Hospital	M	32	10	22	12.2
	F	19	11	28	13.6
Total		159		22.3	9.7

All figures are reported from field observations in which several children were observed during the same interval. With the exception of the camp boys, the results reflect observations over two working days.

sources[14,15] make reference to the ages at which certain asocial behaviors may be expected to disappear in the great majority of normal children. From other discussions extrapolations could be made though specific norms are not available for most symptoms.

The items in the inventory were grouped according to age level in 2-year intervals. This serves to simplify the observer's task, since he can ignore all items which have not yet become symptomatic.

The Children's Behavior Inventory has been employed in several pilot studies which have given encouraging evidence of its power to discriminate between normal and abnormal groups. These are summarized in table 4.

The observational techniques described above have been designed specifically to yield objective descriptions of behavior under clinical conditions and with maximum reliability. The following features are particularly noteworthy.

1. The behavior of the mental patient is recorded by a trained professional observer according to a standard procedure. In this way, the bias due to self-ratings and the excessive variability characteristic of clinical notes are both minimized.
2. The observations are limited to a prescribed time period.
3. The items call for judgments of observables rather than for inferences about dynamics.
4. The items focus attention on the appearance, deportment and verbalizations of the patient.
5. A molecular level of specificity is aimed at in contrast to the usual global description obtained from uncontrolled clinical observations or the severely limited atomic descriptions produced in laboratory studies. For example, the item, "Has tic or twitch (distorts face, turns neck, blinks, etc.)" gives a molecular description of behavior. A corresponding description at a more molar level would be, "Shows conversion symptoms." At the other extreme, an atomic description might be, "Shows contraction of facial musculature." The molecular item is small enough to retain the uniqueness of the behavior which is lost in the global description. At the same time, it is large enough to preserve the essentially pathological quality of the behavior which may be obscured in the atomic description. Finally, it is free of anecdotal features or psychodynamic inferences which are themselves refractory to quantitative treatment, and which are sources of error variance for other components of the description.
6. The items have been designed for dichotomous judgments. Although a greater number of items is required to cover the same content that can be incorporated into a few multiple-choice items, the apparent brevity of the latter type of inventory is misleading, for both speed and accuracy appear to be improved and the observer's cooperation more readily obtained with dichotomous items.

7. Reliability can be assessed by comparisons of observations made independently by two or more observers and by analyzing the total variability in a set of observations into components attributable to subjects, to observers and to residual error.
8. Validity can be studied by comparing scores with already established independent criteria of behavior and by correlating scores with outcome. Change in score as a response to a specific treatment can be used as an index of the sensitivity of the instrument.

Structured Interviews

Examples of standardized interview procedures designed to facilitate quantification are provided by the Structured Clinical Interview and the Mental Status Schedule. These instruments provide schedules of open-ended questions and statements to be used by the interviewer as standard stimulus material. Interdigitated with the schedule are the items of the inventory. The inventory represents an extension of the observational technique in that both the content of the subject's verbalization as well as the accompanying behavior are systematically described.

The Structured Clinical Interview (SCI) consists of an interview schedule and an accompanying inventory of maladaptive behaviors. The interview is intended for use by the psychologist in any context in which he is interested in securing quantitative indices of salient psychopathology. It is an appropriate tool for such purposes as community survey, psychiatric screening, classification of mental patients, measurement of response to treatment, and prognosis of outcome. It can be administered in a guidance clinic, counseling center, outpatient clinic, hospital or mental institution. The interview takes from 15 to 30 minutes and is designed to provide a uniform stimulus context so as to obtain comparability across subjects.

The inventory describes the evoked behavior of the subject, both verbalization and demeanor. The subject's verbal responses, physical appearance, and comportment are recorded on the inventory during the progress of the interview. The dichotomous items cover a wide range of psychopathological indicators.

The interview is constructed so as to direct the subject's attention toward significant areas of adaptation. However, the stimulus material is essentially neutral, making only an oblique approach to areas of potential pathology. Questions are phrased in such a way as to preclude simple "yes" or "no" responses. The interview thus resembles a projective technique in that the interviewer's statements or questions serve as ambiguous stimuli which the subject, to some extent, invests with his own meanings. But the responses are standardized by being recorded on the inventory in units of behavior. Typical questions are:

"Tell me something about yourself. What kinds of problems do you have?"
"What kind of an imagination do you have?"
"What has your social life been like?"
"How do you get along with the opposite sex?"
"How does your family treat you?"
"Tell me something that interests you in the news."

These questions are always presented in precisely these forms, but if the answer is ambiguous, the interviewer asks:

"Can you tell me more about it?"

or he may repeat the question. If the answer refers to the past, the interviewer asks:

"How much of a problem *is* this for you?"

Answers to "What kind of an imagination do you have?" vary from a noncommittal "all right" to a frank report of delusional or hallucinatory experiences. An "all right" may be belied by obvious indications of hallucinations. Significant behavior, both reported and observed, is recorded on the corresponding part of the inventory. The questions about social relations and about getting along with the opposite sex commonly provoke verbal reports of problems. Often when no verbal report is forthcoming, increased movement, evasiveness or observable discomfort make for a significant response.

Strict adherence to the interview protocol provides a standard stimulus situation which minimizes the effect of the interviewer's behavior on the subject. The procedure to be followed by the interviewer is analogous to that recommended for use in the administration of such psychological tests as the *Wechsler Adult Intelligence Scale* and the *Stanford-Binet Scale*. For the inventory to qualify as a psychometric instrument, it is essential that the interviewer should not depart from the prescribed interview procedure.

It is important that the interviewer fill out the inventory as the interview is going on in order that the information may be recorded while it is still fresh in mind.

A total score is obtained by counting the maladaptive responses. Total scores may be used to compare subjects with each other and to evaluate changes after treatment. The inventory can also be scored on the 15 subtest areas of which it is composed so as to provide a clinical profile. The subtest areas are as follows: Anxiety, Apathy, Autistic Thoughts, Conceptual Dysfunctioning, Depression, Excitement, Hostility, Irritability, Inappropriate Affect, Maladaptive Habits, Mannerisms, Perceptual Dysfunctioning, Sexual Deviance, Somatic Dysfunctioning and Suspiciousness.

The reliability of the SCI has been tested on a series of successive admissions to New York Psychiatric Institute. Simultaneous independent observations were obtained by a team of four psychologists on 28 patients. In order to obtain multiple simultaneous observations, a special interview room with one-way window and provision for amplification of sound was used. The interviewer and each observer independently filled in the inventory. Reliability was evaluated by a two-way analysis of variance, results of which are shown in table 5.

TABLE 5.—Reliability of the Structured Clinical Interview

Source	MS	df	
Patients	99.06	27	
Observers	43.39	3	$F = 6.45^{**}$
Residual	6.72	81	

$$s^2_{obs} = \frac{MS_{obs} - MS_{res}}{N} = 1.31$$

$$R_{intraclass} = \frac{MS_{pt} - MS_{res}}{MS_{pt} + 3MS_{res}} = .77$$

**p < .01

The intraclass R of .77 indicates that less than 25 per cent of the variance of a score is attributable to residual error variance. Note that there were significant differences among observers. ($F_{obs} = 6.45, p < .01$).

If we view these observers as a sample from some large pool of observers, then we can estimate the variance among observers as:

$$\frac{MS_{obs} - MS_{res}}{28} = 1.3095$$

This is about 1/5th of the residual variance. It can be reasonably inferred both that the instrument itself is reliable and that inter-observer differences are not so large as to vitiate the results.

Internal Consistency

Point biserial correlations were computed for each item in relation to total score on a sample of 75 successive admissions to the Psychiatric Institute during 1961. For this analysis the protocol by the actual interviewer of each patient was used. Although this sample reflects a restricted range of pathology because of the admission policy of the institution, 98 items showed positive correlations with total score. Of these, 46 items had 95 per cent confidence limits which excluded zero. In general, the evidence of internal consistency points to the unitary quality of this instrument as a measure of the construct of "global pathology."

Concurrent Validity

Validity was examined by correlating the total scores on the SCI with scores on the Ward Behavior Inventory, which contains items descriptive of maladaptive behaviors as observed and recorded by ward nurses and attendants. The observational range of the WBI is greater than that of the SCI, since it calls for observations of behavior over a longer span of time and includes interaction with other patients. Two studies of the correlation between the WBI and the SCI were completed. The results are summarized in table 6.

On the first study of 16 resident patients, the obtained r = .68 so that $.28 \leq p \leq .88$. The second study involved 73 of the 75 newly admitted patients reported in the internal consistency analysis. The obtained correlation here was .35 so that $.13 \leq p \leq .54$. These same 75 patients were also interviewed with an unstructured clinical interview by the psychiatric residents on the admission service. After these free interviews, the items of the SCI were filled in. The correlation obtained between the record completed after uncontrolled interviews and

TABLE 6.—Concurrent Validity of Structured Clinical Interview

			Unstructured Interview
Criterion	WBI	WBI	WBI
Subjects	Resident patients	New Admissions	New Admissions
N	16	73	73
r	.68	.35	.22
5% Confidence limits	$.28 \leq p \leq .88$	$.13 \leq p \leq .54$	$.01 \leq p \leq .43$

the WBI on this same group of patients was .22 so that $.01 \leq p \leq .43$. The correlation between the full SCI and the inventory of items from the SCI obtained in the free interview was .40, with standard error of .10.

A standard inventory of the patient's mental status at admission to hospital can provide a base point against which to assess the significance of any changes in psychiatric status. To serve this need a Mental Status Schedule has been devised in collaboration with Dr. Robert L. Spitzer, psychiatric research fellow in Biometrics Research. The MSS contains open-ended questions intended to elicit from the patient responses which will reveal the presence or absence of psychopathology. The questions have been designed so as to minimize bias due to positive or negative suggestion on the part of the interviewer and have been arranged in such an order as to provide a systematic survey of the patient's current mentation according to a definite sequence. By following the prescribed order in so far as possible the interviewer insures complete coverage. Adherence to the standard procedure makes the interviewer's task easier and at the same time enhances the usefulness of the schedule for comparisons among patients. Juxtaposed opposite each question or series of questions are statements which describe possible responses by the patient. The interviewer indicates his judgments as he proceeds with the interview while the response is still fresh in mind by circling *T* if the statement is *true, NT* if the statement is *not true*. It takes between 30 and 45 minutes to complete the MSS, depending on how loquacious the patient is. After all of the items have been completed, the interviewer may extend the interview in depth, but no judgments should be changed in the light of subsequent disclosures. The 250 items are descriptive of the content of a patient's verbalization or of the behavior he exhibits during the interview. The items cover the following areas: attention; attitude toward interviewer; physical appearance and hygiene; spontaneous physical behavior; amount and rate of speech; quality of speech, phonation; observed emotion; reported emotion; interpersonal relations; sex; antisocial impulses, action or habits; delusions; perceptual distortions; fears and phobias; hallucinations; somatic disturbances and body image; self-punitive and suicidal thoughts; disturbances of thought and obsessions; compulsions; memory; attitude toward illness; attitude toward treatment; orientation. Since each item has an adaptive and a maladaptive alternative, the sum of maladaptive responses can be used as a score for over-all severity of illness. Subscores for clinical syndromes can also be derived. Thus, some 50 items are descriptive of depression, while several others are contraindicative. Similarly, another group of items can provide a subscore for paranoid mentation, etc.

Life Table Analysis

In many situations it may not be possible to carry out controlled studies for the evaluation of treatment regimens. Administrative restrictions or urgent therapeutic needs may force introduction of new treatments on a relatively large scale before long-term clinical trials have been carried out. This has been the case notably with the new ataraxic drugs. Their immediate effects were so dramatic as to make their use widespread almost overnight. However, their long-range therapeutic benefits are still undetermined. In such instances some insight into the over-all effectiveness of a new program can be obtained by the application of actuarial and epidemiological methods of evaluation.

Life table analysis of outcome of treatment is a widely used technique for the evaluation of programs in physical medicine.[16,17] It is usually applied to studies where the natural course of the disease leads to early death. The analysis involves construction of a modified life table in which the proportion of deaths in each successive time interval is accounted for as well as the cumulative proportion by the end of the total period of follow-up, usually 5 years.

Because mortality is not a significant outcome of mental disease, it has not been customary to apply the method of the modified life table to evaluation of psychiatric programs. However, by focusing attention on the proportions of patients restored from hospital to the community in successive intervals, a modified life table can provide a significant description of the effectiveness of psychiatric programs. An instance of such an application is provided in a study of the effectiveness of an intensive treatment program applied to geriatric patients.[18]

Outcome Index

At any particular point in time the patients in a mental hospital vary with respect to length of stay, number of admissions, number of releases and time since first admission. A single index number combining these factors could provide a criterion for assessing the predictive validity of psychiatric prognoses, psychological tests and treatment regimens.

Previous attempts to describe the fates of institutionalized patients by Crandell et al.[19,20] culminated in an "immobility index" which was the ratio of number of months of hospitalization to number of admissions during the 2 years following first admission. This immobility index was found to correlate negatively with subsequent outcome.

The Outcome Index[21] represents a refinement of the earlier immobility index. The O.I. combines time out of hospital and number of admissions and releases with total time elapsed since first admission. The relative weights given to admissions and releases were determined empirically from a sample of patients ranked in order of length and frequency of hospital experience. Previous studies as well as clinical observation suggest that each successive readmission increases the expectation of subsequent admissions, but each successive release is less indicative of genuine remission. The *Outcome Index* ranges from zero for a patient with no significant releases to a hypothetical maximum of one for a patient who spends no days in the hospital.

Previous studies[22] have suggested that by the end of the second year of hospitalization the careers of mental patients have become stabilized. Therefore, 2 years have been taken as a basal follow-up period for dividing patients into homogeneous groups with respect to the *Outcome Index*.

The *Outcome Index* based on the first 2 years after admission provides a reasonably stable criterion for assessing effectiveness of treatment and for distinguishing institutional policies. Three successive samples of first-admission patients taken from a regular state mental hospital show basically similar patterns of outcome despite different diagnoses, different age groups, and the varying effects of the current trend in drug therapy. When outcome indices were subsequently recomputed for these patients to include a third year of follow-up, the 2 year index was found to be substantially unchanged. The *Outcome Index* can be used to characterize institutions as well as to describe individual patients. This latter application is illustrated by a comparison of the three state hospital samples with a sample from a psychiatric institute for teaching and research which makes selective admissions and places emphasis on long-term psychotherapy.[21]

Summary

Four quantitative techniques for assessment of mental patients are described. Studies to establish their effectiveness as predictors and as criterion measures are delineated. Certain techniques summarize the experience of groups (e.g., life table analysis); others focus on the individual patient (observational inventory, structured interview, outcome index). These methods were developed to provide objective measures of known reliability. Behavioral descriptions such as these can be used to obtain evaluations of treatment which are independent of the judgment or theoretical orientation of the therapist but correlated with the social norms for defining mental illness and remission.

REFERENCES

1. Staudt, Virginia M. and Zubin, J.: A biometric evaluation of the somatotherapies in schizophrenia. Psychol. Bull. *54:* 171-196, 1957.
2. Zubin, J., Burdock, E. I., Sutton, S. and Cheek, Frances: Epidemiological aspects of prognosis in mental illness. *In* B. Pasamanick (Ed.): Epidemiology of Mental Disorder. Wash., D. C.: AAAS, 1959, pp. 119-142.
3. —, Sutton, S., Salzinger, K., Salzinger, Suzanne, Burdock, E. I. and Peretz, D.: A biometric approach to prognosis in schizophrenia. *In* P. Hoch and J. Zubin (Eds.): Comparative Epidemiology of the Mental Disorders. New York, Grune & Stratton, 1961, pp. 143-203.
4. Burdock, E. I. and Hardesty, Anne S.: Observational inventories for the assessment of mental patients. Psychopharm. Ser. Cent. Bull. *2:* 14-16, 1962.
5. —, Hakerem, G. Hardesty, Anne S. and Zubin, J.: A. Ward Behavior Rating Scale for mental hospital patients. J. Clin. Psychol. *16:* 246-247, 1960.
6. Cole, J. O.: Evaluation of drug treatments in psychiatry. *In* P. H. Hoch and J. Zubin (Eds.): The Evaluation of Psychiatric Treatment. New York, Grune & Stratton, 1964.

7. Burdock, E. I. and Hardesty, Anne S.: A Children's Behavior Diagnostic Inventory. Ann. N. Y. Acad. Sci., in press.
8. Bender, Lauretta: Childhood schizophrenia. Am. J. Orthopsychiat. *17:* 40-56, 1947.
9. Caplan, G. (Ed.): Emotional Problems in Early Childhood. New York, Basic Books, 1955.
10. Chess, Stella: An Introduction to Child Psychiatry. New York, Grune & Stratton, 1959.
11. English, O. S. and Pearson, G. H. S.: Common Neuroses of Children and Adults. New York, W. W. Norton, 1937.
12. Kanner, L.: Child Psychiatry, 3rd ed. Springfield, Ill., Charles C Thomas, 1957.
13. Mahler, Margaret S.: On child psychosis and schizophrenia. Psychoanalyt. Stud. Child. *7:* 286-305, 1952.
14. Macfarlane, Jean, Allen, Lucille and Honzik, Marjorie P.: A Developmental Study of the Behavior Problems of Normal Children between 21 months and 14 years. Berkeley, Calif. Univ. of Calif. Press, 1954.
15. Lapouse, Rema and Monk, Mary: An epidemiological study of behavior characteristics of children. Am. J. Publ. Hlth. *48:* 1134-1144, 1958.
16. Greenwood, M.: Epidemiology: Historical and Experimental. Baltimore, Johns Hopkins, 1926.
17. Dublin, L. I. and Lotka, A. J.: Twenty-five Years of Health Progress. New York, Metropolitan Life Ins. Co., 1937.
18. Burdock, E. I., Elliott, Helen E., Hardesty, Anne S., O'Neill, F. J. and Sklar, J.: Biometric evaluation of an intensive treatment program in a state mental hospital. J. Nerv. Ment. Dis. *130:* 271-277, 1960.
19. Crandell, A., Zubin, J., Mettler, F. A. and Logan, N. D.: The prognostic value of "mobility" during the first two years of hospitalization for mental disorder. Psychiat. Quart. *28:* 185-210, 1954.
20. —, —, — and Kugelmass, N.: Mobility in chronic schizophrenia with special regard to psychosurgery. Psychiat. Quart. *30:* 96-113, 1956.
21. Burdock, E. I. and Hardesty, Anne S.: An Outcome Index for mental hospital patients. J. Abnorm. Soc. Psychol. *63:* 666-670, 1961.
22. Kramer, M., Goldstein, H., Israel, R. H. and Johnson, N. A.: A historical study of the disposition of first admissions to a state mental hospital. Experience of the Warren State Hospital during the period 1916-1950. Publ. Hlth. Monogr., 1955, No. 32 (Publ. Hlth. Serv. Publ. No. 445. Publ. concurrently w. Publ. Hlth. Rep., 1955, *70:* 1135-11363).

6

THE PLACEBO RESPONSE AND THE DOUBLE-BLIND STUDY*

by H. E. LEHMANN, M.D.†

A CURIOUS PHENOMENON occurred in 1946. The concept of the placebo and the procedure of using it which had existed in medicine for centuries is a rather subdued fashion, suddenly burst into methodological and experimental prominence with the explosive brilliance of a supernova. Probably, and not unlike the sudden brightness of such an astronomical spectacle, the extraordinary interest in the placebo which we are witnessing at present will in time recede again to more normal proportions.

Historical Development of the Placebo Concepts

The recorded use of placebos in medicine dates back to 1787 when it was defined in Quincy's Lexicon as "a commonplace method of medicine."[39] In 1945 Pepper wrote a scholarly paper on the placebo because, as he pointed out, there had never been one written about it and no mention was made of the term in the Cumulative Index at that time. However, since in the 19th and the beginning of the 20th century the placebo had been freely prescribed and the word in daily use, Pepper suggested that "the giving of a placebo seems to be a function of the physician which like certain functions of the body, is not to be mentioned in polite society."[36]

But at the Cornell Conference on Therapy in 1946, Gold[13] made a spirited case for the placebo and the double-blind control method of therapeutic agents, and almost over night the unmentionable placebo became a fashionable scientific gadget. It soon rose to the role of a status symbol of the behavioral scientist. Today, the use of single-blind

*The experimental work reported in this study was partly supported by Grant 604-5-425, from the Department of National Health and Welfare, Ottawa, Canada.

†Verdun Protestant Hospital.

and double-blind placebo controls in experimental designs tends to distinguish the sophisticated white-collar investigator from the amateurish and unskilled experimenter.

One might argue that a radical innovation had been introduced when in addition to the old clinical use of the placebo for therapeutic purposes its important role for experiment and methodology was discovered. However, as early as 1912 Hollingworth[25] took it for granted that a good investigator experimenting with drugs in human subjects employed placebos and double-blind procedures, although he did not use these terms which came into general use only after the Cornell Conference.

The meaning of the term placebo in the experimental situation is no longer that of a pleasing and comforting agent as which it had served the clinician so long in his therapeutic practice. Like the term tranquilizer which is now well established in popular and scientific usage even for many agents whose primary effect is not that of quieting the patient, we also have to accept the term placebo in many instances as a misnomer. Gaddum[18] has proposed to call a pharmacologically inert substance a dummy rather than a placebo and this term has found limited acceptance, particularly in the British literature. Wolf[44] defines the placebo effect as "any effect attributable to a pill, potion, or procedure, but not to its pharmacodynamic or specific properties" and stresses that such effects derive from the significance the whole surrounding situation has for the patient.

This modern expanded meaning of the placebo action as any unspecific or unspecified effect on human experience or behavior has led to its application well beyond the pharmacological context to certain surgical procedures, diets, baths and climatic cures. Wolf considers the mountain air treatment of tuberculosis as a placebo ritual based on undisciplined inferences.[44] Sanazaro even speaks of the placebo effect in medical education when experiments with curriculum contents and course designs replace the emphasis on the specific factor which in his opinion is really the teacher-student relationship.[34] It does not seem to be appropriate, however, to refer to some psychotherapeutic results indiscriminately as placebo effects.[26] Such results, if they occur in the course of planned psychotherapy are mediated by psychological mechanisms which unlike the psychological effects of a placebo are not unspecific but can be specified, at least theoretically.

The striking lack of specificity which characterizes the placebo effect proper was most convincingly displaced in the classic Hawthorne study by Roethlisberger and Dickson[37] when they observed that the withdrawal of better working conditions as well as their introduction led to improved work performance and increased work output. This study may be considered as the first systematic investigation of the placebo effect by experimental means.

The psychodynamic aspects of the therapeutic effect certain unspecific medical procedures may exert have been considered in a comprehensive study by Glover in 1931, when he dealt with what he thought to be the therapeutic effect of inexact interpretation.[20] He postulates that every medical prescription is implicitly an interpretation in the psychoanalytic sense. Thus the physician prescribing exercises creates artificial conversions in his patient, advice as to diet may be equated with the induction of artificial compulsions and the giving of any drugs amounts to the production of artificial paranoia. While many of his claims and theories appear rather far-fetched to a nonanalyst and while some of his conclusions drawn 30 years ago might not be acceptable to psychoanalysts today, the paper still is of interest for anyone who is working seriously in the field of unspecific treatment responses.

Placebo Effects

The effects of a placebo while being unspecific, are not unstructured; they have meaning and their meaning is dependent on the influence of impulses coming from the cerebral cortex. Consequently, it may be assumed that any organ whose function can be influenced by integrated stimuli originating in the cerebral cortex is also capable of responding to placebos. Wolf cites experimental evidence that impulses arising in the cerebral cortex may influence the functional activity of the nose, bladder, esophagus, colon, heart, blood flow through the kidneys, the stomach and the duodenum.[44]

There are numerous reports on the effectiveness of placebos in a variety of pathological conditions and Beecher found that in some 15 studies involving more than a thousand subjects 35 per cent of subjects were satisfactorily relieved by placebos.[5] The symptoms responding to pharmacologically inert substances include headache, postoperative pain, angina pain, cough, nausea and vomiting, anxiety and other mood changes as well as seasickness and the common cold. Frank observed that a group of patients suffering from a variety of psychoneurotic conditions and receiving short-term psychotherapy showed distinctly greater improvement when they were also given a placebo.[16]

All these observations leave little doubt that the placebo effect is a widespread and important clinical factor and commands careful consideration in every therapeutic situation.

Placebos will not only produce the hoped for therapeutic effect, they may also be quite "toxic."[5,45] The most frequent undesirable side-effects of placebos are inhibitory in nature and consist in drowsiness, headache and feelings of heaviness and fatigue, but dryness of mouth, palpitation, epigastric pain, diarrhea, nausea, syncope, uticaria, angioneurotic edema, miosis, even high-tone deafness,[43] eosinophilia, extrapyramidal symptoms and reduction in concentration of serum lipoproteines[44] have been reported following the administration of pharmacologically inert substances, while Cleghorn[11] demonstrated the stimulation of adrenocortical responses following saline injections, probably evoked as a secondary reaction to the anxiety aroused by the injection procedure.

Placebo Reactors

Lasagna and his co-workers[29] have tried to determine what features characterize the personalities to the 30 to 60 per cent of people who are usually found to react to placebos in any study of this kind. They found that the placebo reactor's personality can be described as an outward oriented, somewhat anxious and immature individual, who tends to be happier in the hospital than the nonreactor who in turn is less dependent and less concerned about himself than the reactor. These findings were based on interviews and Rorschach tests. Joyce[27] studied the dummy reactions of medical students and found that those students who showed the greatest response to the inactive substance scored higher on a rating scale of autonomic self-awareness, and on the Bernreuter Personality Scale appeared less self-confident, less dominant, more sociable and more extraverted than the nonreactors. These personality attributes resemble those described by Lasagna. Knowles and Lucas[28] found that theology students tended to respond more strongly to placebos than student nurses. They interpreted this finding as evidence that the cultural background—in this case the degree of sophistication in medical matters—plays an important role in a person's response to placebos. The same workers observed that there was a correlation between persons who scored high on the neuroticism scale of the Maudsley Personality Inventory and those who reported symptoms on a check list following the ingestion of a pharmacologically inert substance, but only when the questionnaire was administered in a group setting. They view this as evidence for the potentiating effect the group situation has on unspecific responses.

Joyce[27] found that he could no longer predict a person's reaction on the basis of his test performance if he had been absent from the experimental situation for some time. Wolf[44] gave 27 subjects a placebo prior to a dose of ipecac on seven occasions and observed that the distribution of placebo responses, in this case the absence of nausea and vomiting, was not better than chance over the period of the seven trials. In other words, a person might respond strongly to a placebo one day but be quite immune to its effects on another occasion soon after. Batterman[2] and Pannekoek[35] also were impressed with the fact that a reactor may easily and unpredictably turn into a nonreactor. It appears then, that it would not be possible to reliably eliminate placebo reactors from any therapeutic trial with a new drug as has been proposed by some investigators.[3] While certain personality types are probably more likely to respond to placebos on most occasions, no predictions can be made on a particular subject's response for a particular trial, since a person's placebo responsiveness is apparently a wide-range potential and not a constant factor.

Mechanisms of Placebo Responses

Why, and in which manner a placebo produces its effect in the human organism is still to considerable extent a matter of theoretical conjecture. Suggestibility is probably one of the complex factors, particularly if the patient or the experimental subject has been provided with a set of anticipated and suggested results. Such a set of instructions regarding the expected response must not necessarily be made explicit in every case. People, in general, and particularly patients in distress, are often highly responsive to nonverbal clues displayed in the experimenter's or physician's manner. Gliedman[19] reports on two groups of patients with bleeding ulcers who were given placebos. The doctor told one group that the new medicine would certainly help them to get better, while the other group was told by the nurse that they were receiving an experimental medication. In the first group 70 per cent of the patients improved greatly, while in the second group only 25 per cent showed a favorable response. Feldman[14] reported that 77 per cent of patients treated by an enthusiastic therapist improved, but only 10 per cent of the patients receiving the same drug from a therapist who believed that drugs spoiled the dynamic approach, showed similar improvement. (It should be noted, however, that the evaluation of the drug effect was undertaken by each therapist himself, which leaves this important aspect of the experimenter uncontrolled.) Fisher[15] is currently engaged in a comprehensive investigation of the interaction between a subject's psychological set and the pharmacological effects of a psychotropic drug. He has established that these two actions are not simply additive but can at times neutralize, or even reverse each other. In one of his experiments a group of college students was given a fairly large dose of dexedrine, but some of the students were told that they were receiving a hypnotic and a number of these students became drowsy and fell asleep. In order to control the influence of the anticipatory set on patients during a placebo-controlled therapeutic trial with a new drug, Clauser[10] has suggested that each drug trial should be conducted twice, once with a positive and once with a negative suggestion as to the expected therapeutic effectiveness of the drug and placebo.

Conditioning of the patient has been proposed by Gliedman et al.[19] as an important mechanism of placebo action. Such conditioning would operate through a variety of circumstances surrounding a therapeutic situation. Beecher[4,6] has observed that the strength of a person's placebo response is positively correlated with the intensity of stress to which he is exposed and this was confirmed by Knowles and Lucas[28] in their experiments. In the stressed individual there exists a state of increased cortical excitation which would supposedly render him more conditionable. At the same time, the stressed person tends to regress and become more dependent which in turn would lead to increased suggestibility.

There are certainly other mechanisms involved in the placebo action as well, mechanisms of which we have not yet developed any clear concepts. Evidence for such an assumption can be found in the fact that placebo responses frequently can be observed under conditions when the subject is not under obvious stress and neither he nor the experimenter have any notion as to the probable effects of the placebo.

It might appear strange that volunteer subjects in a stress-free and generally undifferentiated situation should show any significant change of performance in psychological tests, if the only new variable introduced is the administration of a placebo. Yet, in one double-blind controlled experiment the placebo was responsible for more deviant test performances than six psychoactive drugs.[30] Through the analysis of such placebo reactions in a neutral setting, my collaborator Knight and I were led to conclude: (1) that certain psychological functions and test procedures are more 'placebo-prone' than others, and (2) that each individual carries his own set of attitudes and expectations into a drug experiment and will respond in terms of these attitudes and expectations, even though they might not be consciously accessible to him or to the experimenter.

In general, we found that tests which involve psychological aspects of timing are more likely to be placebo-prone than tests which are based on criteria of accuracy. Furthermore, there seemed to emerge two different types of responses in placebo reactors: one type of personality tended to improve his performance when given a placebo without any explicit or implicit information as to the anticipated effects, while another personality type would react with a deterioration of performance following the administration of such a neutral placebo. While our evidence is not yet completely convincing, the trends so far indicate that persons with a low score on the neuroticism scale of the Maudsley Personality Inventory fall into the first category, i.e., they improve following unstructured placebo administration, while persons scoring high on neuroticism in the Maudsley Personality Inventory often show impaired performance on a variety of tests after placebo.[31]

The neuroticism factor had a correlation of .59 with decrement or impairment of performance. On the other hand, the average subject in our experiments revealed himself as susceptible to placebo effects as to the effects of moderate doses of psychoactive drugs, and when given a placebo in an unstructured situation tended to perform better on certain objective tests than before the placebo.

At this point, we should recall that the term placebo has assumed manifold meanings today. Originally, it referred only to a substance which unspecifically would remove existing symptoms. In an experimental context the term was extended to include emerging new subjective and objective phenomena, for instance drowsiness or muscular weakness. However, placebo effects might also consist in increased alertness or increased muscular strength. Finally, placebo effects might only be detected through their influence on special test performances. It is this latter meaning of placebo action to which we refer in our experiments which were set up to distinguish between the two different types of reactors, those who do better and those who do worse after receiving a placebo. That this difference is an important one requires no further explanation. Obviously, it would be useful to have means of predicting the direction of placebo effects in an individual.

In a recent investigation undertaken with Prescott, we have attempted to analyze the relationship between placebo and psychoactive drug effects on test performance, autonomic responsiveness, conditionability and suggestibility. A detailed description of the experiments would not be within the scope of this paper; however, some of the findings bearing on the problem under discussion will be given here.

Starting with the assumption that there were persons who were nonreactors, we further distinguished between subjects with a prevailing tendency to improve and others with a tendency to perform worse after placebo. Our data from the previously mentioned experiments related the subjects with a tendency to impaired performance to a high neuroticism score.

Our recent results suggest the existence of significant correlations between well integrated or appropriate autonomic responses and improved performance on various tests under placebo. Appropriate autonomic responding is identified by:

1. Short latency of the GSR to a noxious unconditioned stimulus (114 db tone at 900 cps).
2. Decreases in basal resistance level during pain.
3. Few nonspecific GSR fluctuations during pain.
4. Well developed discriminated conditioned GSRs.

This latter measure was obtained by taking the difference between extinction amplitude responses to the excitatory and inhibitory conditional signals. Our results are as follows:

The shorter the latency of the UCR the greater is the improvement under placebo on card 2 of the Stroop test and on tapping speed, the correlations being .47 and .41, respectively (table 1). Short latency of the UCR is related to increased discrimination of conditioned responses ($r = .39$) and increased latency of the UCR is significantly correlated with an increase of body sway under suggestion ($r = .54$). The latter finding may indicate a relationship between inappropriate autonomic responsiveness and increased suggestibility. (It should be noted that correlations which are equal to or greater than $r = .44$ are significant beyond the .05 level.)

Additional findings indicate that the frequency of nonspecific GRSs obtained during an experiment on pain tolerance is significantly and negatively correlated with an autonomically discriminating conditioned response (r = .47).

It was further determined that the frequency of these nonspecific fluctuations of the GSR is significantly correlated with impaired performance, as measured by increased time, on the track tracer under placebo (r = .46).

These findings, namely that increased frequency of nonspecifics is significantly related to impaired discrimination of a conditioned response and impaired performance on a psychomotor task under placebo are consistent with the findings of Silverman et al.[14] that an increase of nonspecifics is significantly related to decrement in human performance on a tracking task where time on target was the measure employed. This experiment was conducted under stress induced by means of a centrifuge.

Birch et al.[7,8] also have demonstrated that nonspecific GSRs are a monotonic function of arousal and that at very high levels of arousal, where disorganization in human behavior occurs, a high number of nonspecific GSRs are observable.

Another aspect of autonomic functioning, recorded under pain, that we found to relate significantly to improved performance on reaction time under placebo, is the decline of basal resistance (r = .48). Such

TABLE 1.—Correlations between Autonomic Responses and Test Performance

Unconditioned response latency & stroop test (2)	r = .47*
Unconditioned response latency & tapping speed	r = —.41
Unconditioned response latency & discriminatory conditioned response	r = —.39
Unconditioned response latency & body sway test	r = .54†
Nonspecific GSR & track-tracer time	r = .46*
Basal resistance decline & reaction time	r = —.48*
Conditioned response amplitude & time estimation reproduction	r = —.50*

*PL-05.
†PL-02.

a decrease under painful stimulation could be considered an appropriate autonomic response, whereas the high number of nonspecifics reported above could represent inappropriate autonomic responding. These measures may well reflect dimensions of well integrated vs. poorly integrated autonomic functioning, which in turn have been shown to relate significantly to human performance under placebo in other situations.

A final relationship that deserves mention is the significant negative correlation between positive conditioned responses and time estimation reproduction (reproducing a time interval of 15″, $r = .50$).

In brief, our findings may be interpreted to mean that individuals who manifest well integrated autonomic functioning will show improved performance on psychomotor, perceptual and cognitive tasks under placebo conditions. And conversely, individuals who manifest poorly integrated autonomic functioning will react with impaired test performance under placebo conditions.

It should also be noted that all our significant correlations between autonomic variables and test performance variables under placebo involve a time parameter. This is in keeping with our earlier findings that placebo responses tend to affect time components of psychological functions rather than accuracy.

Therapeutic Aspects of the Placebos

The clinician's attitude toward the placebo has undergone a peculiar change in the last 20 years. Our growing sophistication in pharmacology, psychodynamics and experimental design has all but eliminated the naive and comfortable attitude of the old physician toward this time-honored remedy. Many clinicians today seem to feel a mixture of contempt, curiosity and anxiety when confronted with placebo responses. Even some enlightened therapists would probably feel embarrassed if it were shown that they themselves had become "victims" of a placebo. But is there any rational basis for preferring the results of a barbiturate to those of an effective placebo if one is suffering from insomnia? It seems that we have not yet completely exorcised our primitive anxiety of magic practices which may be aroused whenever we employ physical means to bring psychic mechanisms into operation. Hofling[24] concluded from an analysis of questionnaires, that the average doctor likes to think of himself as ordering placebos less often than his colleagues, and that when he orders them he is more often than not in a hostile frame of mind. Wolf[44] mentions three situations in which the placebo is still frequently employed today: in the withdrawal of narcotics, as a tiding-over measure until the therapist has established a constructive relationship with the patient and as an experimental control. All these measures seem to carry some apologetic connotation about the use of the questionable placebo. Again, one cannot easily find rational objections to the clinical use of a placebo by a knowledgeable physician in any situation in which he considers it to be therapeutically indicated. However, no physician should prescribe placebos unless he feels at ease about them and is reasonably sure not to harbor any fantasies of "showing his patient up," nor should he feel the need to apologize to science, his colleagues or his own medical conscience about his prescription.

In a careful and open-minded study, Hankoff, Freedman and Engelhardt[21,22] have recently shown that the absence of a placebo response is correlated with treatment failure in chronic ambulatory schizophrenics. Those patients who responded to placebos, also tended to use denial as a defense mechanism and had a better prognosis. Their therapists conceived of the placebo as a nonverbal communication between doctor and patient which operates within the framework of a concrete relationship and may under certain conditions be more therapeutic than the ambiguous situation of the psychiatric interview.

Methodological Principles of Experimental Control

The determination of cause-effect relationships does not require any control if the effects of the independent variable one is studying, are introduced into a *stable* system. It requires no controls if one draws the conclusion that the movement of a heavy curling stone across the ice is the result of the push imparted to it by the curler (fig. 1).

If the system in which the action takes place is *unstable* and undergoing changes in time, the determination of the effects of other agents on such a system calls for controls. In the case of a physical unstable system a non-treatment control would be needed. (To return to our previous example, if one wanted to be sure that sweeping in front of the moving curling stone really changes its movement in the desired direction, one would have to observe control curling stones with identical, initial velocity, on an identical surface but not subjected to the "treatment" of the broom in front of it.)

If the system one is investigating is more complex and possesses the property of being behaviorally *responsive* to stimuli rather than merely physically reactive, the control needed is an unspecific stimulus, a placebo, as in an experimental situation where conditioning responses of animals are observed under various drug treatments.

Finally, if the system is of a still higher order of complexity and of a nature which allows for *transactional* processes to develop, a double-blind control is required in order to eliminate the bias that might be introduced through feed-back mechanisms between the observer and the observed. The double-blind placebo study would therefore, appear to be at first glance, an essential component of any well designed therapeutic trial with psychoactive drugs.

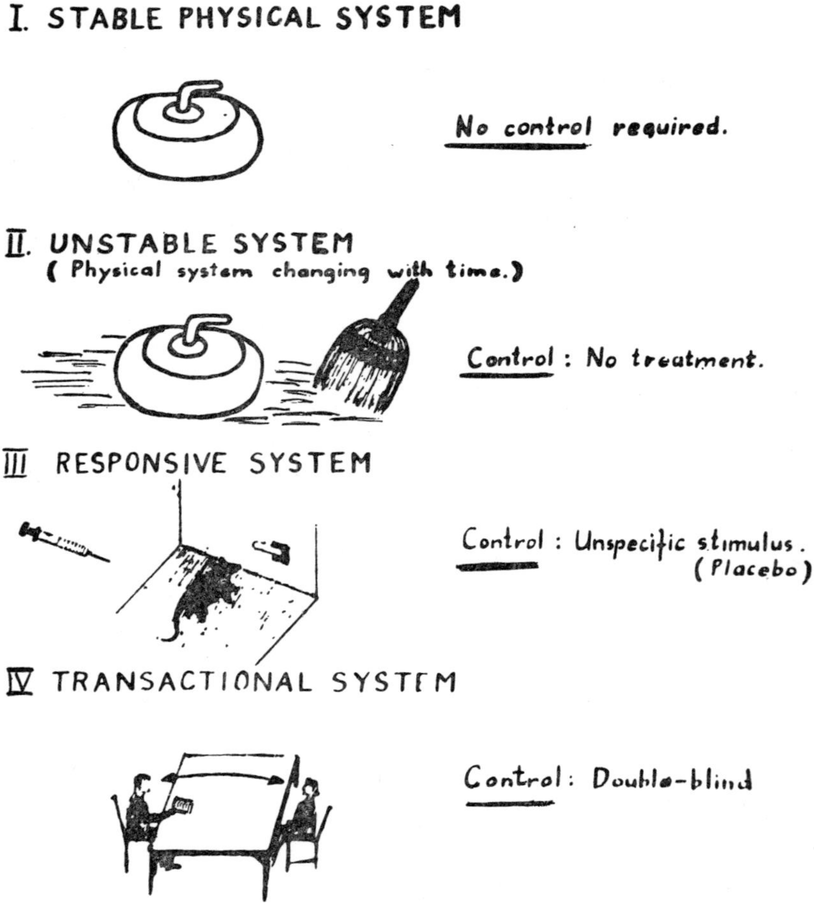

FIG. 1.—Different controls required in different systems

Complex Problems of the Double-Blind Control

Clinical experiments in the field soon reveal serious limitations of this method which theoretically appears to be so elegant and foolproof. In the double-blind study neither the experimental subject nor the experimenter know which individual drug or placebo the subject is receiving until the code is broken at the end of the experiment.

However, an obvious difficulty lies in the fact that drugs often have characteristic secondary effects which can be identified by many persons. Such effects may be behavioral or clinical manifestations, e.g., restlessness, drowsiness, tachycardia, nausea, excessive salivation or extrapyramidal symptoms, and in this case might be recognized by the nursing and medical staff as well as by the patient himself. Or the specific drug effects may only be accessible to the patient, e.g., a characteristic change of one's awareness of his bodily functions or the identification of a distinctive type of drowsiness. (Many people are capable of differentiating between the kinds of drowsiness induced by excessive fatigue or by barbiturates or by chlorpromazine.) In order to protect the double-blind design it has been proposed to employ so-called "active placebos," e.g., phenobarbital to mimic the effects of certain tranquilizers on the arousal system or atropine to imitate the autonomic effects of some psychotropic drugs. The validity of such an expedient may be questioned on two grounds: first, to introduce similar but not identical secondary effects is experimentally unsound and might be compared to employing blue placebos because that is the closest one can come to equating a green test drug, in the hope that most patients would not notice the difference in hue; second, because there always remains the possibility that the secondary effect of the active placebo may contaminate the evaluation of the experimental variable.

As Modell and Houde[34] have pointed out, the double-blind control can not compensate for other shortcomings in the experimental design, e.g., inadequate matching, failure to randomize, poor criteria for evalution and faulty statistical analysis of data. Modell describes an instructive experiment: when patients were asked to prepare daily reports on the analgesic properties of aspirin and placebo in a double-blind trial, no difference appeared, but when data were collected immediately by a physician at the bedside, a double-blind study did reveal significant differences between the same active drug and the placebo. The adherence to an impressive double-blind design may trick the experimenter into a feeling of false security and cause him to neglect other important though less sophisticated aspects of the experimental situation, e.g., his method of collecting data.

While conducting double-blind trials Batterman and Grossman[1] observed the curious phenomenon of the placebo consistently producing such a high percentage of therapeutic results that no significant difference between placebo and experimental drug could be detected. Such a difference appeared, however, when they switched to single-blind placebo trials; the placebo would then be less effective while the active drug would increase its efficacy. They refer to this as a "levelling-off" effect of the double-blind method. It appears likely that their differences in placebo response were due to the unwitting transmission of clues to the patients whenever the experimenters knew which was the drug and which the placebo. In some way, however, the double-blind method seemed to obscure the presence of an actually existing pharmacotherapeutic property of the drug.

A startling result of a double-blind study with phenobarbital, meprobamate and placebo was reported by Uhlenhuth et al.[42] Of two physicians not aware of the nature of the agents they prescribed, one obtained significant differences between the two sedatives and the placebo; the other physician's data showed no significant difference between active drugs and placebo. As one would expect, the therapist who obtained positive results had great confidence in pharmacotherapy, while the therapist whose results were negative was characterized by considerable scepticism regarding the therapeutic use of drugs. It is, nevertheless, surprising that the therapist's attitudes so strongly and deceptively broke through the very barrier which had been assumed to be foolproof protection against attitudinal contamination, namely, the double-blind control.

Hoffer and Osmond[23] argue persuasively that the double-blind method when applied in the conventional manner may obscure the presence of significant differences when the sample under study is not really homogeneous. A group of psychiatric patients can hardly ever be expected to represent a homogeneous sample today because our methods of classifying and grouping psychological phenomena are still rather crude and we do not yet dispose of many unequivocal criteria of psychopathology. The same authors seriously question the ethics of using double-blind designs if patients might be temporarily deprived of the benefit they would receive through the use of drugs known to be therapeutically effective. To circumvent these objections they propose certain modifications which they call the two-phase and the ethical double-blind.

Tuteur[41] warns the clinicians of the pitfalls hidden in the double-blind method and also expresses concern about ethical problems associated with such experimental designs. He points out that in addition to possibly preventing patients from obtaining benefit from drugs with well established therapeutic properties, the morale of the nursing staff is sometimes lowered when they see that a group of patients is kept on a certain drug (placebo) although they are not getting better and might, in contrast to other patients who are improving, appear to deteriorate.

While this kind of argument may arouse little sympathy and understanding in the strictly experiment-oriented researcher, it does have serious implications for the clinical investigator, no matter how sophisticated he is regarding experimental designs because he carries the ultimate responsibility for a therapeutic trial. Legal and political aspects must always be considered in the sense that administrative complications or issues should be prevented, at all costs, for once they have arisen it is usually too late to deal with them effectively.

There is one other point that requires careful thought before one decides on double-blind experiments, namely, the growing difficulty of finding a sufficient number of fairly well matched psychiatric patients for therapeutic trials. Because the use of drugs is so widespread nowadays and so many psychopharmacological investigations are going on simultaneously, it sometimes takes a long time before one can assemble even a small representative sample of fresh cases. This time would be doubled if one insists on a placebo-controlled design.

Finally, as more and more double-blind studies are conducted the medical and nursing staff in some places have tended to become test wise and weary. Some intriguing experiments have been carried on for many months during which the whole medical staff of a hospital had to be successfully deceived by one or two informed experimenters as to the nature of the substances the physicians were asked to prescribe. They were told that some of the pills were energizers, some tranquilizers and some placebos while in reality all were placebos. The study showed that physicians and nurses can be influenced to produce placebo results according to their expectations (this was more true for "tranquilizing" expectations than for "energizing"), but one would venture to guess that such double intelligence infiltration of a hospital staff has also caused some conscious or unconscious resentment and consequently some lowering of staff morale when the final denouement was made public.

We may sometimes accept the stimulation of paranoid fantasies and attitudes in our staff in the interest of science, or accept any and all of the other problematic aspects of the double-blind design just described, provided the gain of the method is so great that it cannot be equalled by other available procedures. This would be difficult to prove for most experimental drug therapy controls. Such controls are not foolproof. Cole and Clyde[12] reviewed the literature on chlorpromazine in 1960 and found that 37 controlled clinical trials of the drug showed it to be unequivocally superior to the comparison treatment, while 16 controlled trials showed unequivocally the opposite. Is one to conclude that the majority of results rather than the quality of the experiment constitutes the decisive factor?

Clinical Competence and Experimental Sophistication

The real issue is not whether a study followed a designed control but whether or not it was supervised and carried through by investigators whose clinical competence would at least be equal to their experimental sophistication. If Loranger et. al.,[32] reject the argument that many of the most valuable drugs were discovered by clinicians without the use of experimentally controlled trials and counter that for each drug that will be confirmed in future clinical experience there are half a dozen which never make the grade, they would still have to bring evidence that those who were deceived by ineffective drugs were as competent clinicians as those who favored the effective ones. Freyhan[17] has repeatedly challenged the rigid insistence on experimental controls and has stressed the need for more careful and systematic clinical investigation which too often is neglected in our instrumentalized era of protocoled research. Martini,[33] after thorough discussion of the subject comes to the conclusion that double-blind designs should not be used routinely and that repeated clinical trials will often give more reliable results than a single well controlled study, while Chassan[9] favors intensive models based on long-term observations of individual patients.

It must be admitted that for an investigator who lacks clinical experience, a placebo-controlled double-blind study is more likely to eliminate false positive findings. In this case he is also more likely to come up with false negative results which Hoffer and Osmond[23] have proposed to call "Obecalp" responses ('placebo' spelled backwards.)

While the absence of placebo controls in a therapeutic trial might reflect the investigator's lack of experimental sophistication, it might also be the result of the investigator's better-than-average clinical ability. By the same token, the use of placebo controls might be the result of knowledgeable planning on the part of the investigator or might reflect a feeling of inadequacy in the clinical sphere.

The field of psychiatry is charged with more complexities than any other area of research. More than any other type of investigation, psychiatry makes demands on the judgment of those conducting research in this field. The choice of method for each individual therapeutic trial should depend on the considered judgment of a clinically competent and experimentally sophisticated investigator. He might choose a careful clinical trial without experimental controls or he might follow a rigidly controlled double-blind design, but his choice will neither be determined by vague clinical impressionism nor by sterile methodological ritual.

REFERENCES

1. Batterman, R. G. and Grossman, A. J.: Effectiveness of salicylamide as analgesic and antirheumatic agent: Evaluation of double blindfold technique for studying analgesic drugs. J.A.M.A. *159:* 1619-1622, 1955.
2. —: Placebo and non-reactors to analgesics. Fed. Proc. *16:* 280, 1957.
3. Beecher, H. K., Keats, A. S., Mosteller, F. and Lasagna, L.: The effectiveness of oral analgesics (morphine, codeine, acetylsalicylic acid) and the problem of placebo "reactors" and "non-reactors." J. Pharmacol. *109:* 393-400, 1953.
4. —: Evidence for increased effectiveness of placebos with increased stress. Am. J. Physiol. *187:* 163-169, 1956.
5. —: Measurement of Subjective Responses. New York, Oxford University Press, 1959.
6. —: Increased stress and effectiveness of placebos and "active" drugs. Science *132:* 91-2, 1960.
7. Burch, N. R. and Greiner, T. H.: Drugs and human fatigue: GRS parameters. J. Psychol. *45:* 3-10, 1958.
8. — and —: A bioelectric scale of human alertness: Concurrent recordings of the EEG and GSR. Psychiatric Research Reports 12, Amer. Psychiatric Association. 183-193, January 1960.
9. Chassan, J. B.: Statistical inference and the single case in clinical design. Psychiatry *23:* 173-184, 1960.
10. Clauser, G.: Zur Kritik des sogenannten doppelten Blindversuchs in der Arzneimittelprüfung. Med. Klin. *51:* 1403-1404, 1956.
11. Cleghorn, R. A., Graham, B. F., Campbell, R. B., Rublee, N. K., Elliott, F. H. and Saffran, M.: Anxiety states: their response to ACTH and to isotonic saline. Proc. first clin. ACTH Conf. Blakiston, Philadelphia, pp. 561-565, 1950.

12. COLE, J. O. AND CLYDE, D. J.: Analysis of clearly significant and clearly non-significant controlled studies of chlorpromazine in which the chlorpromazine-treated group was compared with inert placebo, no treatment, or presumably ineffective medication (barbiturates or benactyzine). Information supplied by Psychopharmacology Service Center, N.I.M.H. Washington, 1960.

13. Cornell Conference on Therapy: The use of placebos in therapy. N. Y. State Med. *46:* 1718, 1946.

14. FELDMAN, P. E.: The personal element in psychiatric research. Am. J. Psychiat. *113:* 52-54, 1956.

15. FISHER, S.: George Washington University. Personal communication.

16. FRANK, J. D.: Problems of controls in psychotherapy as exemplified by the psychotherapy research project of the Phipps Psychiatric Clinic. *In:* Research in Psychotherapy Proceedings of a Conference, Washington, D. C., April 9-12, 1958.

17. FREYHAN, F. A.: Psychopharmacology and the controversial clinician. Drugs and Behavior. Uhr and Miller (Eds.): *In* An: Publisher 1960, pp. 184-198.

18. GADDUM, J. H.: Clinical pharmacology. Walter Ernest Dixon Memorial Lecture. Proc. Roy. Soc. Med. *47:* 195, 1954.

19. GLIEDMAN, L. H., GANTT, W. H. AND TEITELBAUM, H. A.: Some implications of conditional reflex studies for placebo research. Am. J. Psychiat. *113:* 1103-1107, 1957.

20. GLOVER, E.: The therapeutic effect of inexact interpretation. Internat. J. Psychoanal. *12:* 131, 397.

21. HANKOFF, L. D. FREEDMAN, N. AND ENGLEHARDT, D. M.: The prognostic value of placebo response. Am. J. Psychiat. *115:* 549-550, 1958.

22. —, ENGELHARDT, D. M. AND FREEDMAN, N.: Placebo response in schizophrenic outpatients. Arch. Gen. Psychiat. *2:* 33-42, 1960.

23. HOFFER, A. AND OSMOND, H.: Double-blind clinical trials. J. Neuropsychiat. *2:* 221-227, 1961.

24. HOFLING, C. K.: The place of placebos in medical practice. Gen. Practice *11:* 103-107, 1955.

25. HOLLINGWORTH, H. L.: The influence of caffeine on mental and motor efficiency. Arch. Psychol. *3:* 1-166, 1912.

26. HOLLISTER, L.: Placebology: sense and nonsense. Curr. Ther. Res. *2:* 477-83, 1960.

27. JOYCE, C. R.: Consistent differences in individual reactions to drugs and dummies. Brit. J. Pharmacol. *14:* 512-21, 1959.

28. KNOWLES, J. B. AND LUCAS, C. J.: Experimental studies of the placebo response. J. Ment. Sci. *106:* 231-240, 1960.

29. LASAGNA, L., MOSTELLER, F., VON FELSINGER, J. M. AND BEECHER, H. K.: A study of the placebo response. Am. J. Med. *16:* 770-779, 1954.

30. LEHMANN, H. E. AND KNIGHT, D. A.: Placebo-resistance of different psychological functions. Psychiat. Quart. pp. 1-12, 1960.

31. —: Measurement of changes in human behavior under the effects of psychotropic drugs. Neuro-Psychopharmacol. *2:* 291-303, 1961.

32. LORANGER, A. W., PROUT, C. T. AND WHITE, M. A.: The placebo effect in psychiatric drug research. J.A.M.A. *176:* 920-925, 1961.

33. MARTINI, P.: Die unwissentliche Versuchsanordnung und der sogenannte doppelte Blindversuch. Dtsch. Med. Wnschr. *82:* 597-602, 1957.
34. MODELL, W. AND HOUDE, R. W.: Factors influencing clinical evaluation of drugs, with special reference to the double-blind technique. J. A. M. A. *167:* 2190-2199, 1958.
35. PANNEKOEK, J. H.: Critical evaluation of the efficacy of new drugs. Postgrad. Med. J. *33:* 396, 1957.
36. PEPPER, O. H. P.: Note on placebo. Am. J. Pharm. *117:* 409-412, 1945.
37. ROETHLISBERGER, F. J. AND DICKSON, W. J.: Management and the worker, Cambridge, Mass., Harvard Univ. Press, 1939.
38. SANAZARO, P. J.: The placebo effect in medical education. J. Med. Educ. *35:* 416-20, 1960.
39. SHAPIRO, A. K.: The placebo effect in the history of medical treatment. Implications for psychiatry. Am. J. Psychiat. *116:* 4, 298-304, 1959.
40. SILVERMAN, A. J., COHEN, S. I. AND SHMAVONIAN, B. M.: Investigation of psychophysiologic relationships with skin resistance measures. J. Psychosomat. Res. *4:* 65-87, 1959.
41. TUTEUR, W.: The double-blind method: Its pitfalls and fallacies. Am. J. Psychiat. *114:* 921-922, 1958.
42. UHLENHUTH, E. H., CANTER, A., NEUSTADT, J. O. AND PAYSON, H. E.: The symptomatic relief of anxiety with meprobamate, phenobarbital and placebo. Am. J. Psychiat. *115:* 905-10, 1959.
43. WOLFF, H. G.: The use of placebos in therapy. Conference on Therapy. N. Y. State J. Med. *46:* 1718, 1946.
44. WOLF, S.: The pharmacology of placebos. Pharmacol. Rev. *11:* 689-704, 1959.
45. — AND PINSKY, R. H.: Effects of placebo administration and occurrence of toxic reactions. J.A.M.A. *155:* 339-341, 1954.

7

PRINCIPLES IN THE EVALUATION OF THERAPIES FOR MENTAL DISORDERS

by SAMUEL W. GREENHOUSE, PH.D.*

I AM IMPRESSED with the number of meetings, symposia and conferences held in the last few years on what I suppose could be called the formal aspects of doing research in the evaluation of therapies in mental illness. There was the Conference on the Evaluation of Pharmacotherapy in Mental Illness in September 1956. There was a conference on Research in Psychotherapy in April 1958, a good portion of which was devoted to methodological problems in evaluating psychotherapy. In May of 1959, a conference was held on Approaches to Research in Mental Retardation in which the major emphasis was on problems in research methodology in general. The committee on research of the Group for the Advancement of Psychiatry has been meeting several times a year in the consideration of more specific problem areas in research. I have no doubt that during this time span of 5 to 6 years, there were many more similar gatherings assembled for the same purpose. In short, it seems to be the fashion these days to talk about principles and methods. As a result, I feel certain that many in this audience have previously heard and seen in print, probably more than once, the so-called common sense principles of doing research in general and of evaluating therapies in particular. It would appear that some high authority suddenly became familiar with that tenet of good experimental design, namely, the necessity of having replication, and is applying this important principle to psychiatrists, clinical psychologists and others performing research in the mental disorders. Doubtlessly, this high authority takes the shape of committees responsible for the planning of programs.

I will therefore try to avoid belaboring you too much with either statistical or logical generalities and will rather emphasize problems specific to psychotherapy. These problems are not selected because

*National Institute of Mental Health.

they appear in the literature or in academic discussions as major sore spots in evaluating therapy. They have been singled out for discussion because I have been confronted with them in day-to-day consultations with research psychiatrists and clinical psychologists. However, since this paper is supposed to be on principles, let us briefly identify and review what these are.

Principles

In the history of medicine, many procedures have been employed to produce an evaluation of a therapy. Many of these come from clinicians who try a new therapy on a certain number of their patients having a given disease, or more precisely, having certain symptoms and then compare their results of improvement with either the results on their own patients on other therapies or with results appearing in the literature. Research investigators in general are agreed in disregarding such evaluations as nonscientific and brush them aside with a shrug and mumble which sounds like "clinical impression." Although I agree generally with such a view, I sometimes suspect that some research psychiatrists do not understand why such evaluations are not acceptable. Thus, for example, one finds psychiatrists criticizing an evaluation of some psychotherapy such as psychoanalysis because there were no controls and yet will argue against the need for controls or the need for a random selection of subjects in their own drug studies on the basis that they are very familiar with the course of, say, schizophrenia.

It should be made clear that the following discussion does not pertain to such evaluative procedures. It will refer only to evaluations which take the form of experiments. Indeed, if there is anything here which can at all be stated as a first principle it is that an evaluation of a therapy should be an experiment. It seems to me this is basic and holds whether one is evaluating a new therapy, an old therapy with modifications or several different therapies. What is also basic and elementary, perhaps, and should be mentioned at this point, is that very rarely can the experimental evaluation be carried out on the basis of one case. Variation between individuals with a disorder require many subjects to represent treated and untreated groups.

Obviously, those many therapists, interested in evaluating their therapeutic techniques, who do not accept this principle, will probably find the remarks here of little value to them. These investigators consciously prefer, for a variety of reasons, to evaluate therapies based on so-called "naturalistic" observations rather than on experiments. Unfortunately, the use of this phrase has tended to cause some confusion with the use of a similar expression describing a research procedure often used in epidemiological studies. Most of the principles can be applied to the latter although they appear to be irrelevant and do not apply to the procedure as practiced by the therapists referred to. However, I should like to return to this point later.

It is convenient to consider the various issues under the following four main groupings.

(a) The preliminary thinking related to the decision to evaluate some therapy.
(b) The design of the experiment.
(c) The execution of the experiment.
(d) The analysis of the data, conclusions drawn, the inference that can be made and reporting of results.

I include the last for the sake of being exhaustive but will have very little to say in this area since it is inappropriate to the subject of this meeting.

(a) *Preliminary thinking:* The elements that need to be considered in this area are:

1. The purpose or goal of the therapy to be evaluated.
2. The criteria by which the therapy will be assessed. Will the major criterion be the number of subjects cured or the extent of improvement shown.
3. The choice of measurement instruments to measure the disease status of the patients.
4. The determination and definition of the population of patients with the disorder to be represented in the experiment: acute or chronic, with short or long hospital duration, male or female or both, etc.
5. A familiarity with the degree of effectiveness of other, older therapies used on the same type of patients.
6. Whether the evaluation is to be primarily of the treatment of human subjects per se or is it to be of the effect of the therapy on the disease process.
7. The postulation of one or more precise questions which are to be answered by the evaluation. A question of the type, "Will this therapy produce at least 10 per cent greater improvement than a certain therapy averaging 25 per cent in similar patients?"—such a question is necessary if the investigator will want to know how many subjects to use.
8. How long a time will the evaluation take? Will it be a small or large scale study?

(b) *Design of the experiment:*

1. There should be a planned comparison or control group to the treated group. The type of control group can vary: either a separate group or

a matched group or a design chosen such that each person is his own control.

2. The subjects should be selected at random from the defined population.
3. A decision whether a subject should be accepted for the experiment must be made prior to the knowledge of which group he will be in.
4. Subjects should be randomly assigned to the treated and control groups. If the controls are to be matched then for each pair of subjects similar with respect to the set of matching characteristics, one member should be assigned at random to a group and the other subject assigned to the other group. If subjects are to be their own controls then they should be randomly assigned to the possible orders, such as the order of administration of therapy and placebo.

(c) *Execution of the experiment:*

1. Certain parts of the experiment should in so far as possible be done in the blind. In evaluating a drug, the investigator assessing clinical change should not know the group to which the subject belongs. Note that this principle by itself requires the use of a control group, although there are other, more important justifications for control.
2. If the therapist is to be considered a part of the therapy, an independent observer should do the evaluation.
3. Withdrawal of patients from the study should be carefully checked in order to determine that the factors correlated with the loss of subjects are operating equally in the two groups.
4. A principle which I feel comes as close to being universally held as any possibly can is that all observations should be unbiased.

With respect to (d), analysis and reporting of data, there is one comment that should be made and it has to do with the reporting of results. Some studies publish a minimum of data, usually in a derived form. Some just indicate that groups did or did not differ significantly on a given rating scale without indicating the scores achieved. I have seen many published papers, in which the analysis of variance is the method of analysis, present a complete analysis of variance table showing the mean squares, F and significance level values for main effects, such as age, social class and severity of disease and for their interactions, yet nowhere present the mean values for the various subgroups of these characteristics. On the other hand, there are some who urge that as complete data as possible be presented for each subject in the study although the demands of editors to conserve space in journals weigh heavily against this. This seems a rather trivial point relative to more major issues here. But, if communication of one's findings to colleagues is necessary to the advance of a science, it only seems natural that one ask that published results should communicate.

The foregoing is a mere statement of elements and principles to be considered in the evaluation of a therapy which is in the form of an experiment. It will be observed that under the headings of experimental design and execution the statements are given as principles whereas under preliminary thinking the statements present the kinds of things that ought to be considered. The latter only reflects the fact that we do not presume to give principles on how to think.

Problem Areas

Goals of Research in Therapy

Whitehorn[1] recently stated the goal of therapy to be "health." He then discussed the difficulties surrounding this concept in a rather thorough and significant discussion of the aims of the therapist. One of the points made by Whitehorn was the distinction between the therapist's efforts directed against a pathogenic process and his need to treat the patient. Whether this distinction is a real one or whether it is peculiar only to clinicians in psychiatry are interesting questions in their own right. However, of greater concern to us is the effect of this distinction on research in therapy. It appears that there is a reluctance on the part of psychiatrists to do research on the evaluation of therapies with respect to mere outcome. What seems to be favored is the study of therapy in order to assess the process or to obtain evidence with regard to a theory of personality ([1], p. 276),

I think it is important to understand the view here and I therefore would like to state the position as I understand it. The therapist is doing something in a psychotherapeutic complex involving an interaction between a patient with a mental disorder and himself. Whether the therapist is treating a process or the patient, it seems clear that he is attempting to effect a cure at best or an alleviation from symptoms at worst. Sometimes the word "change" is used, that is the therapist desires to bring about a change in the patient's condition. Someone now becomes interested in studying this psychotherapeutic complex. He decides not to study whether the therapist is accomplishing his aim of applying an effective treatment. This is too prosaic a kind of research; it is applied and practical. Also in studying outcome of therapy he will become associated with a research area where ([1], p. 278) "the quality of research—has been impressively inadequate—treated by the loosest impressionistic reporting of individual successes and by the most superficial and unsophisticated research attempts." Furthermore, why should he devote his efforts to outcome studies when he is convinced that ([1], p. 278) "the effectiveness of psychotherapy has long since been established and need not be investigated further." Thus our researcher, having rejected to do research on the aim of therapy, goes after bigger game. He will study not what the therapist accomplishes but what he does—the so-called "process" of interaction between the patient and the therapist. Presumably the research attempts here are more sophisticated. But most important, the research here is on a much higher level having in view the construction of a theory of personality.

In order to start at a common point of criticism, let us assume something extreme. Let us assume that psychotherapy is not and has not been effective (in the sense that the patient shows no change) in treating patients with mental disorders. Then I trust we will all agree that the study of the process and any theory based on it are useless. For if what the therapist does is not related to the patient's mental, emotional or behavioral status, since the patient is unaffected by the experience, knowledge of this particular process cannot lead to meaningful understanding of the personality of the patient or his disorder. But our assumption was extreme. Let us now assume that psychotherapy is effective sometimes and not effective other times. Now in order to study the process our researcher must observe a specific situation, that is, he will study the interaction between a given therapist and a given patient. If the therapy is effective and the outcome proves favorable, our investigator is fortunate. For what he has observed is related to the change. (That the change is specific to the interaction is of course an assumption.) On the other hand, if the therapy is ineffective and no change occurs, our investigator is unfortunate, and what he has studied and any theory based on it are useless. If the investigator does not measure outcome, how can he know which situation he is in?

It should be emphasized that no argument is being made here against the study of process. What is being argued is that the study of process must be accompanied with that of outcome. Furthermore, principles of good research apply just as much to the study of process as they do to research in outcome.[2]

In the study of outcome in evaluating therapy, a problem with respect to goals arises in the wide definition encompassed by the meaning of therapy. Thus, for instance Cohen[3] has stated: "It seems almost a truism that in attempting therapy with a person suffering from mental illness, all aspects of his functioning—his life in his environment, his physical being, and his mental attitudes—must be taken into account intellectually and must be dealt with therapeutically." Goals of therapy stated in this manner are obviously all encompassing, requiring a measurement of a therapeutic effect on almost every aspect of living. Clearly such wide goals make research difficult in so far as objective and sensitive measurement instruments may be lacking.

Heterogeneity of Patients with Mental Disorders Even Within a Given Diagnostic Category

It is universally recognized that response to treatment whether it be in the biological and behavioral sciences, in the physical sciences or in industry varies with the individual being treated. Even if the treatment effect were constant for all individuals, the observed measurements vary from subject to subject primarily because individuals differ in the characteristic being measured without the treatment. In many different disease situations, subjects with the disease, show greater variation of a trait related to the disease than do normal controls. This is particularly true with respect to the variation of certain behavioral variables in persons with mental disorders. In schizophrenia, in particular, several investigators in drug therapy have indicated a differential response to pharmacological agents, i.e., the drug effect varies from subject to subject and cannot be considered constant.

As a consequence of these observations, we note that the greater the variation between subjects, the larger must the effect of therapy be in order to be detected as significant. This means either using larger numbers of subjects in treated and control groups or introducing various devices to reduce the variation. There are three procedures I should like to mention, the second and third being commonly favored in research in the behavioral sciences.

If a listing of the population of individuals is available and if information is available on each individual with respect to those characteristics believed to cause the greater variability, then clearly one should stratify the population on the basis of these traits and sample at random from the resulting subgroups. Thus, for example, several studies with schizophrenics have stratified a hospital population on the basis of sex, diagnostic category such as catatonics, affectives, etc., length of stay in hospital and other relevant variables. This procedure is probably the most familiar and most commonly used method for controlling variation. It will be noted that the selected factors are controlled experimentally. In some instances, where a factor was not controlled before the experiment but where measurements were made on the factor during the study, it is possible to introduce statistical control on this factor through the analysis of covariance.

Another technique to reduce the variation needed to serve as an error is to use a patient as his own control. In this type of design, subjects serve as "random blocks" in analysis of variance terminology. If the order in which the control and various treatments are to be given to subjects is to be randomly determined, one must be on guard against the possibility of an order effect. Many studies in drug therapy have used this procedure where it was assumed that the effect of drug A had worn off by the time drug B was given. A serious problem arising with the use of a subject as his own control is related to the length of time over which therapy is necessary. An observation on the mental status of a subject on therapy for 1 year raises the question what would have been the observation on the same subject if there were no therapy.

A partial answer to this last question is given by a third procedure often used in behavioral science research. This is the matched pairs technique. Here two subjects are matched on factors believed to increase variation between subjects such as age, sex, diagnoses, duration of illness, etc. Then one of the pair is randomly assigned to therapy and the other held as a control. Both members are observed over the period of therapy. At the end of treatment, the difference between the two as measured by some criterion variable including clinical assessment is taken as an estimate of the effect of the therapy. This obviously must be repeated with many pairs. Obviously the matching is an attempt to yield the difference between the subject with therapy and, as nearly as possible, the same subject without therapy over the same time period. At the same time, the variation between the individual pair estimates of treatment effect does not contain variation between subjects on the response variable. Clearly the validity of this technique depends upon, first, the extent to which matching is complete so that the two individuals are as alike as possible with respect to the characteristics affecting the response variable, and second, the extent to which the course of the disease over the time period would have been the same for both members of each pair.

A problem in assessing therapies for the mental disorders, particularly in the attempt to confirm a previously reported successful therapy, is the type of patients selected for the study. When these are not the same kind of patients as used in the original research, conflicting and ambiguous results may follow. It should be recalled that Delay's original observations on the tranquilizing effect of chlorpromazine were made on agitated, hyperactive schizophrenics. It is perhaps too obvious and unnecessary to point out that the investigators who selected depressives and other types of schizophrenics were not evaluating the original observation but were in fact breaking new ground, investigating new uses of the drug. Negative results with depressives have no bearing on whether chlorpromazine reduces agitated and hyperactive behavior.

Controls

Some references have already been made to the kinds of controls that can be used in an evaluation. Much has been written on this subject by both methodologists and experimentors. One excellent document, worthy of mention, is that put out by the research committee of the Group for the Advancement of Psychiatry.[4] There thus remains little to be said on controls that has not already been stated many times.

I should like to make one comment that does not appear in the literature. As mentioned earlier, there are many clinicians who believe controls are not necessary in evaluating a therapy or in performing some other kind of research. Conferences on methodology in psychiatric research invariably reflect the controversy between "naturalistic" studies and scientific experiments or between noncontrolled and controlled studies. Speaking very precisely, I would contend there is no such issue, simply because there is really no such thing as a noncontrolled study, particularly in therapy evaluation. Consider the psychotherapist who determines that 50 per cent of his patients show improvement after 1 year of therapy. As a clinician he may be satisfied with this figure and with this figure alone. He may have no concern with results that other therapies produce. But as one interested in *evaluating* his therapeutic procedure, his result of 50 per cent cannot stand alone. He must compare this with some other number. He may find this comparison number in the literature or even in his own past experience with other subjects. Thus, the investigator, requiring a control value with which to compare his result, selects a value obtained outside of his study, thereby subjecting his comparison and his inference to the hazards of additional variation and of possible bias due to changing conditions over them.

In summary, then, the issue is not between controlled and noncontrolled studies. The issue is rather between controls that are explicitly planned for as an integral part of the research and those that are not.

Randomization

Randomization together with appropriate controls constitute the two major conditions of optimium research. If we confine our attention to the evaluation of a therapy or to a clinical trial exploring the difference between two therapies, the principle of randomization states that there be a random allocation of subjects to each of the two groups. By so doing, it is hoped to accomplish two things: (1) eliminate any bias that may result from a subjective and haphazard assignment of patients to the groups, and (2) convert uncontrolled variation arising from a large number of experimentally uncontrolled factors, known or unknown, into completely random variation so that the appropriate random error for assessing group effects can be measured. ([2], Chapter 5 and [5], p. 245.)

It should be pointed out that the two principles of randomization and controls had encountered considerable opposition in the past from clinicians in therapy research in many parts of medicine. Due to the admirable efforts of the Medical Research Council in the United Kingdom and of various groups in biostatistics and public health in the United States, much of this opposition has been overcome. In England, for example, it is now rare for a clinical trial of a pharmacological agent for any disease to be carried out without controls and randomization.

Interestingly enough, the basic reason for opposing control groups and randomization in therapy research in fatal diseases such as tuberculosis, namely, the ethical problem, should not be a problem in psychiatry. That is, it is assumed that no one randomly assigned to a control group in a psychopharmacological study or in a group psychotherapy study lasting 6 months to 1 year will die or deteriorate appreciably.

Concluding Remarks

May I now conclude with some general remarks on methodology. As mentioned in my opening remarks, investigators in the behavioral sciences generally and in psychiatry particularly have been subjected in the last decade to an avalanche of discussion on methodology. As one could have predicted, a reaction is beginning to set in, and sometimes in a highly articulate manner. Thus, for example, Festinger ([6], p. 358) stated:

"I do not think that problems in methodology are usually of prime importance in doing research. The refinement of methodology, while a good thing in and of itself, should be secondary to the discovery of relationships and the development of understanding."

More recently, Strupp, in his article on psychotherapy in the 1962 Annual Review of Psychology, reviews two publications by D. Rapaport. Strupp writes: "Furthermore, (It is Rapaport's contention) many researchers implicitly or explicitly subscribe to the erroneous belief that the pacemaker of scientific advance is methodology. There is a grave danger that we may become the prisoner of our methods, and that a slavish adherence to empty formulas of hypothesis testing tends to stifle naturalistic observation, genuine curiosity, and speculation."

It may be that both Festinger and Rapaport are referring to specific psychometric and statistical methods with which some psychologists and psychiatrists become perhaps overly associated, such as factor analysis, significance testing, etc. Or they both may be referring to the very obvious tendency of many behavioral scientists, trained as psychologists and sociologists, to devote a good portion of their productive careers to concern with methodology rather than to actual subject matter problems. However, I hope their criticism and their words of caution are not related to that aspect of methodology which is identified with those procedures that embody statistical and logical principles and a mode of reasoning governing the validity of conclusions and the generalizability of inferences based upon empirical data. No scientific discipline as a whole can, it seems to me, ever place too much emphasis on such methodology. For this constitutes the very essence of the Scientific Method.

I suppose that there will be investigators with perfect designs and execution producing trivia, adding little to the progress of a given field. But trivia are always found out and quickly too. On the other hand, a so-called major finding which is based on an invalid inference can lead to a great deal of harm in a discipline by fortifying a poor theory, by attracting large numbers of investigators and by requiring a great deal of time to correct. This is particularly true in the evaluation of therapies not only for the mental disorders but also for any disease.

REFERENCES

1. Rubinstein, E. A. and Parloff, M. B. (Editors): Research in psychiatry. *In:* Proceedings of a Conference. Washington, D. C., American Psychological Association, 1958.
2. Cox, D.: Planning of Experiments. New York, John Wiley & Sons, 1958.
3. Cohen, Mabel Blake (Editor): Advances in Psychiatry. New York, W. W. Norton & Co., 1959.
4. Committee on Research, Group for the Advancement of Psychiatry, Report No. 42, New York, 1959.
5. Cornfield, J.: Principles of research. Proceedings of the 1959 Woods School Conference on Approaches to Research in Mental Retardation. Am. J. Ment. Def. *64:* 2, 1959.
6. Festinger, L.: Sampling and related problems in research methodology, Proceedings of the 1959 Woods School Conference on Approaches to Research in Mental Retardation. Am. J. Ment. Def. *64:* 2, 1959.

8

PSYCHOPATHOLOGICAL ISSUES IN JUDGING OUTCOME OF PSYCHIATRIC TREATMENT

by FRITZ A. FREYHAN, M.D.*

THE PLEASURE I FELT when I was invited to participate in this symposium was mixed with apprehension after I saw what task had been assigned to me. Is there another topic in psychiatry which has caused as much confusion, controversy and hard-boiled avoidance? Only an idealist could walk into the halls of psychiatry expecting to find a climate of vigorous fascination with ultimate therapeutic results. I dare not probe too deeply into the motivational complexes which have so effectively suppressed any widespread desire to take issue with the question of therapeutic outcome. What I will attempt is to examine some of the barriers which have kept back the flow of informative data on therapeutic re-evaluations.

That there is a "here," a point in time at which a person becomes a patient is generally conceded to be the all important event. Next comes the exploration of the patient's past, the "before," in search for the roots of his difficulties. On logical grounds the "after," which is really the patient's future, cannot be dissociated from the urgent diagnostic and therapeutic issues in psychiatry which still wait for clarification and confirmation. The conventional designation "follow-up" is undoubtedly a prosaic misnomer for what should really be an immensely challenging study of psychological and social developments. One can understand the disenchantment with a census type of follow-up based on such medical models as may be used for cancer, tuberculosis or rheumatoid arthritis. That such models cannot be applied to psychiatric disorders is evident if one only contemplates the many basic disagreements on concept and definition of mental illness. If a schizophrenic psychosis is understood as a biological process by one group, but as a state of social maladaptation by another, questions of onset, treatment and outcome must carry vastly different implications.

*National Institute of Mental Health.

The title of this presentation may be taken as an affirmation that we have instruments for measuring the permanency of therapeutic results. As you will see shortly, I do not believe this to be the case. The evaluation is furthermore complicated by the absence of an agreement on the nature of the illnesses for which the patient is treated to recover. What all therapies have in common is some rationale which promises an attack of some kind on what are assumed to be the pathogenetic determinants. Somatic treatments are expected to correct or abolish biological dysfunctions. Psychotherapy has been defined as "the science and art of influencing behavior so as to make it (a) more efficient and satisfactory to the individual, and (b) more compatible with social norms."[1] The question of the fulfillment of these goals is therefore inseparable from the nature of the therapeutic process and furthermore from the therapist's conscience.

How relevant are comparisons of therapeutic responses on discharge and on the 5 and 10 year level? Do we know which illnesses are chronic? What reasons prompt us to believe that the treatments effect those factors which determine the prolonged or chronic course of the illness? That schizophrenic disorders are a primary object in this discussion is suggested by the phrasing of the title.

But in approaching the long-term evaluations of schizophrenics, we meet head-on that old but ever imposing barrier: unitary psychosis or group of schizophrenias. And here I am reminded of a statement attributed to Gruhle[2] when he, over 30 years ago, summed up the status of scientific knowledge on schizophrenia: "if one compares the years 1800 to 1850 with the years 1900 to 1930, it is discouraging to see that the arguments with which the opposing scientists are concerned have not become better nor have the opponents become wiser." When Eugen Bleuler introduced his concept of schizophrenia, he defined the illness as follows: "By the term dementia praecox or schizophrenia we designate a group of psychoses whose course is at times chronic, at times marked by intermittent attacks, and which can stop or retrograde at any stage, but does not permit a full restitutio ad integrum.—One comes closest to reality if one makes it clear that merely the general direction of the course of this disease is toward a schizophrenic deterioration, but that in each individual case, the disease may take a course that is both qualitatively and temporally rather irregular." I cannot be persuaded to believe that we have advanced very far beyond this factual definition. The question whether or not schizophrenia is a unitary psychosis has remained unanswered. But everyone continues nonchalantly to treat schizophrenia as an illness as witnessed by a multitude of books and articles which report the results of the treatment of "schizophrenia." Various qualitative and quantitative evaluations of therapeutic responses have been associated with schizophrenia, with the tacit assertion that by virtue of being a chronic illness a reported improvement reflects on the efficacy of the treatment.

The problem of clinical determinations of prognostic differentials is still in its infancy.

We owe decisive advances to the work of Zubin whose comprehensive analyses of prognostic factors has paved the way for systematic validation studies.

Since the element of time, time in relation to pathology and treatment, is our major concern in this discussion, I wish to present some schizophrenics from whose life we can gather the kind of information which is only seldom available.

Some Facts of Life of the Schizophrenias

Shown in figures 1, 2 and 3 are the catamnestic profiles of patients who had in common admittance to the same psychiatric hospital (the Delaware State Hospital) where they were diagnosed to have schizophrenic psychoses. As one looks at these profiles, the patients remain anonymous inasfar as individual personality and clinical symptomatology are concerned. But they assume a measure of identity in terms of their capacity for psychosocial adaptation. What is indicated for each patient from left to right is the age on admission, the duration of the initial hospitalization and the subsequent developments with

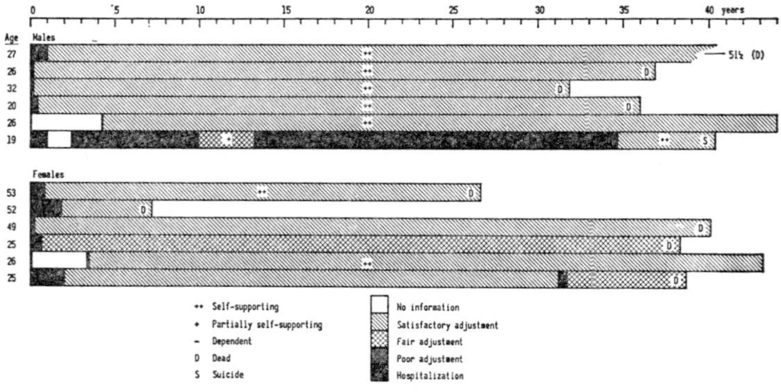

Fig. 1.

regards to the status of self-support (++), partial self-support (+) and economic dependency (—). We also notice whether the general level of social relationships was satisfactory, fair or poor. Readmission to the hospital is specified in terms of its duration. Lastly, natural death (D) and suicide (S) are reported.

As is evident, each patient returns after the initial hospitalization to his or her life, some to work and be self-supporting and to enter into social relationships which, to the people in their environment, seemed free from manifestations of mental illness. Others were less successful or failed completely in achieving self-support or were reported to have shown, with varying severity, psychological and social peculiarities of schizophrenia. Important are the differences in the capacity to sustain adaptational levels. There are many with no further hospitalization while others had one or several readmissions. However, none of them remained in the hospital; after each hospitalization they returned to their lives, functioning once again at various levels of

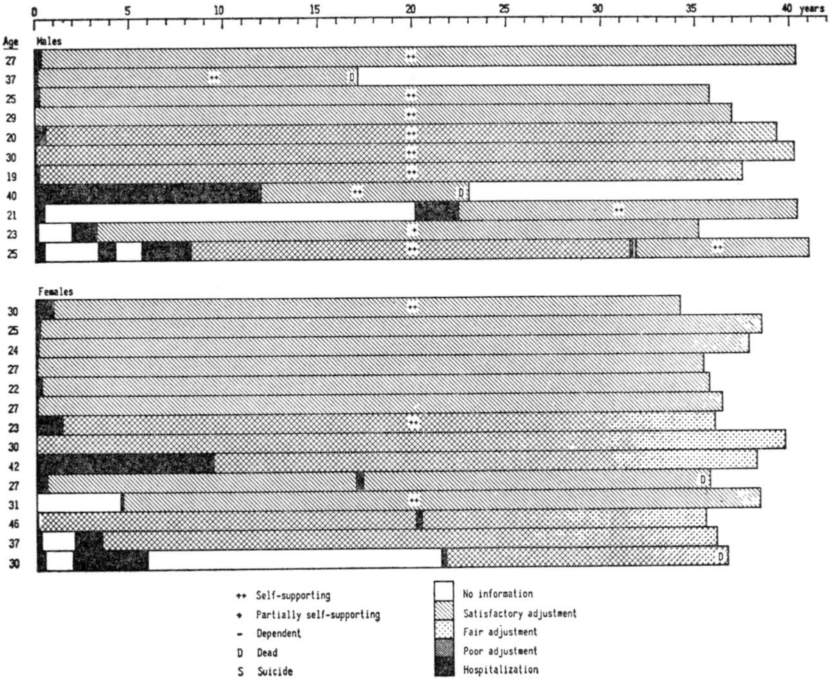

FIG. 2.

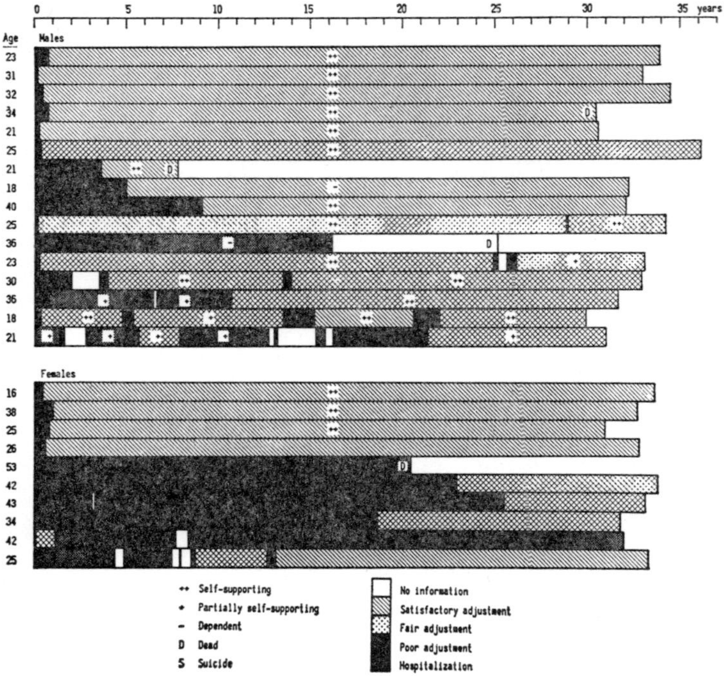

Fig. 3.

achievement and normalcy. All patients represent consecutive admissions to the same hospital. Left out are those schizophrenics who remained continuously hospitalized, either from the first or a subsequent admission; who died in the hospital or immediately after discharge; or who vanished after discharge so that no further contact could be made.

Of interest is that of those schizophrenics, not shown in these figures, who following readmission remained continuously hospitalized, 50 per cent and over had their fateful readmission within 3 years after discharge; between 60 and 70 per cent within 5 years after discharge and between 80 and nearly 90 per cent within 10 years after discharge. Evidently then, the malignant pattern of chronicity emerges early. These schizophrenics neither adapted to their life situations after discharge nor responded to hospitalization once readmitted, but drifted into stagnant chronicity. For the patients shown in figure 1, 75 per cent, in figure 2, 62 per cent and in figure 3, 82 per cent had their first readmissions within 5 years after discharge. The remainder was readmitted after intervals of 20 years and longer.

What is the significance of these data? Since in the literature long-term catamnestic studies of schizophrenic patients are conspicuous by their absence, the profiles of these 63 patients, men and women, covering a life-span of between 3 and 5 decades after the initial hospitalization provide a deeper insight into the schizophrenic problem in terms of time unlimited. The information concerning each patient was obtained by the research department at the Delaware State Hospital, then under my direction, in the years from 1957 to 1960. Sources of references were (1) the relocated patient, (2) relatives and community agencies. For the majority, the sources of information were multiple rather than single. The research social worker kept detailed protocols on her contacts with the former patient, the family and other sources of information. Inasfar as the accuracy of diagnosis is concerned, I can only say that every effort was made to eliminate those patients who, because of inadequate information or descriptions more indicative of other mental disorders, were considered ineligible. These patients belong to the cohorts admitted between 1900 and 1930: Table 1 (1900-1915), Table 2 (1916-1923), Table 3 (1924-1931).

The significance of this period will not escape you since we find ourselves in the so-called pretreatment era. These patients did not have what we now consider the benefits of major somatic and psychological therapies. Thus we may accept the evidence that schizophrenics do not conform to the concept of a process psychosis. And there is furthermore the suggestion that schizophrenics recover by their own devices. In this connection, we remember the endless arguments whether it is justified and proper to talk about natural or spontaneous courses of schizophrenia. Perhaps we can avoid this controversy by referring to *the facts of life of the schizophrenias*. These facts are most valuable for the generation of psychiatrists, psychologists and sociologists who entered the arena since modern therapeutic procedures had gained their foothold. It is true that the sociologically oriented investigators may appreciate more than the clinicians those therapeutic elements which preceded and coexist with modern methods of treatment. It is clearly difficult or impossible to differentiate hospitalized patients into treated and nontreated groups since the multitude of potential therapeutic influences is not limited to modern therapeutic procedures. Nevertheless, there remains the possibility that the circumstance of hospitalization regardless of the quality of its milieu may be

TABLE 1.—1900-15

	Age on Admission	Hospital yrs.	Hospital mos.	Out yrs.	Out mos.	Hospital yrs.	Hospital mos.	Out yrs.	Out mos.	Hospital yrs.	Hospital mos.	Out yrs.	Out mos.	Hospital yrs.	Hospital mos.	Out yrs.	Out mos.	Hospital yrs.	Hospital mos.	Out yrs.	Out mos.
Males	27	1	—	50	7 (D)																
	26		2	36	8 (D)																
	32		2	31	5 (D)																
	20		5	35	7 (D)																
	26		½	4	2		1	40	—												
	19	1	—	1	5	7	6	3	4	21	5	5	8 (S)								
Females	53		10	25	10 (D)																
	52	1	10	5	4 (D)																
	49		3	39	8 (D)																
	25		7½	37	8 (D)																
	26		1	3	3		2	39	8												
	25	2	—	29	2		6	7	— (D)												

TABLE 2.—1916-23

	Age on Admission	Hospital		Out		Hospital		Out		Hospital		Out		Hospital		Out		Hospital		Out	
		yrs.	mos.	yrs.	mos.	yrs.	mos.	yrs.	mos.	yrs.	mos.	yrs.	mos.	yrs.	mos.	yrs.	mos.	yrs.	mos.	yrs.	mos.
Males	27		4½	40																	
	37		2	17	(D)																
	25		3	35	6																
	29		1	36	10																
	20		7	38	9																
	30		¾	40	2																
	19		3	37	3																
	40	12	—	11	(D)																
	21		6	19	8	2	3	18													
	23		1¾	1	9	1	4	31	11												
	25		6	2	10		11	1	5	2	7	23	3		2		1		1	9	2
Females	30		11½	33	2																
	25		3	38	2																
	24		2	37	7																
	27		1¼	35	3																
	22		3¾	35	4																
	27		1	36	3																
	23	1	5	34	6																
	30		¼	39	7																
	42	9	5	28	9																
	27		7	16	4		5	18	8 (D)												
	31		¼	4	5		1¾	33	9												
	46		1	20	—		4	14	1												
	37		3	1	9	1	6	32	6												
	30		4¾	1	6	4	—	15	6		4	14	10 (D)								

TABLE 3.—1924-31*

	Age on Admission	Hospital		Out		Hospital		Out		Hospital		Out		Hospital		Out		Hospital		Out	
		yrs.	mos.	yrs.	mos.	yrs.	mos.	yrs.	mos.	yrs.	mos.	yrs.	mos.	yrs.	mos.	yrs.	mos.	yrs.	mos.	yrs.	mos.
Males	23		9	33	2																
	31		2	32	10																
	32		5	34	2																
	34		9	29	9 (D)																
	21		3	30	4																
	25		4	35	10																
	21	3	7	4	2 (D)																
	18	5	—	27	3																
	40	9	1	23	—																
	25		2	28	9		1	4	11												
	36	6	8	7	4	2	2	9	— (D)												
	23		3	24	8		3		6		6	6	11								
	30	2	—	1	6		5	9	7		5	19	—								
	36		10	5	1		6		2		1	3	4		7	21	1				
	18		4	4	5		7	8	2	1	8	5	5	1	5	7	11				
	21		1	1	3		3	1	2		2	2	5		3	2	3		3	4	—
			7		4		2	2	1		6		5	5	2	9	8				
Females	16		5	33	2																
	38	1	—	32	7																
	25		9	30	2																
	26		7	32	2																
	53		7	19	10 (D)																
	42	16	10	4	6	1	7	11	10												
	43	3	1		2	22	3	7	7												
	34		2	2	5		5	7	6	8	1	13	2								
	42		1	1	—		1	6	2		4		8		5	11	9		5	11	—
	25		4	3	6		6		6		6	1	11		2		5		1		7
			2	3	11		6	20	2												

*Incomplete

entirely coincidental to improvement. For reasons of methodological purity, little would be gained if the clinician's belief in his treatment, often rumored to be based on faith and conviction, be copied by the sociologist's belief in the therapeutic powers of the milieu, equally based on faith and conviction. Too many question marks remain whenever we face the riddle of the dissimilarity of responses to treatment and the unpredictable events which follow in the course of time.

The cyclothymic patient with periodical depressions presents an even harder task if the effects of the treatment are to be assessed in terms of time. Among the more specific aims for a given treatment are the reduction of the duration of the psychotic cycle as well as the lengthening of the symptom-free interval. A quick glance at the catamnestic profiles of 16 patients will illustrate the phenomena of variation and variability (figure 4). These patients had in common, aside from the diagnosis of cyclic depressions, 4 or more admissions to the same hospital (Delaware State Hospital), returning for their latest admission during the period of treatment with antidepressant drugs. Listed are in terms of months, duration of hospitalization (H) and interval (I) for each depression. Also shown are what somatic treatment, if any, the patient received during each period of hospitalization. One of the obvious conclusions to be drawn from these findings is the apparent impossibility to appraise any effect of treatment on the future course of the disorder.

I have dwelt on the importance of catamnestic profiles in order to have an appropriate background for the appraisal of the therapeutic impact in terms of the permanency of the results. If, as appears to be the case, the course of the schizophrenias is so dissimilar that the assumption of an on-going psychopathological process, manifested by recognizable disturbances, is a matter of doubt, then there is no clear-cut premise for attributing the events in later years to the effects of the treatment. The literature on the treatment of schizophrenic and affective disorders reveals what amounts to a land-slide majority in favor of the immediate effectiveness of most of the modern methods of treatment. Mueller[3] in his recent review of the reported therapeutic results of schizophrenia comments on the marked differences of opinion about immediate and late results and concludes that the data for treated and untreated patients approximate each other with the passage of time. This has long been the contention of Bleuler[4] who maintains that only patients with favorable prognoses respond to the

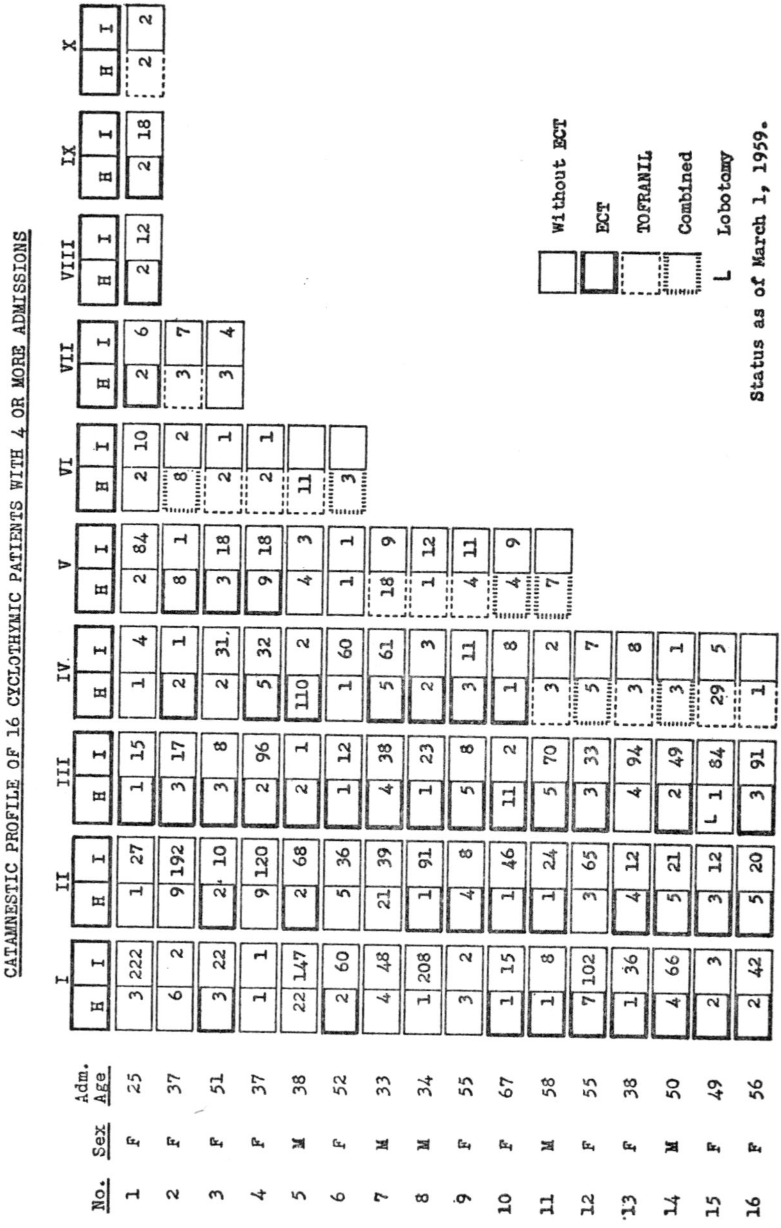
CATAMNESTIC PROFILE OF 16 CYCLOTHYMIC PATIENTS WITH 4 OR MORE ADMISSIONS
No.
Sex
Adm. Age
I
II
III
IV
V
VI
VII
VIII
IX
X
H
I
Without ECT
ECT
TOFRANIL
Combined
L Lobotomy
Status as of March 1, 1959.

FIG. 4.

various treatments in the first place. His argument is not necessarily weakened by the common observation that all treatments seem to be most effective if given during the first 6 to 12 months, i.e., at a time when one cannot yet distinguish between the more favorable or unfavorable trends. Zubin[5] reported that on 5-year follow-up studies of schizophrenic patients, "none of the therapies do better than the custodial care afforded in the 1930's." In contrast to Bleuler, however, Zubin does not accept these results as proof that the various somatic therapies merely hasten the process of recovery since, as he stresses, the treatments were given on a trial-and-error basis, producing average results but providing no information on differential responses.

My investigations of schizophrenic cohorts in Delaware, covering the years 1900-1958, in accord with results of similar investigations, show an increase of initial discharges from 35 per cent in 1915 to 90 per cent in 1958. But I also found much support for the existence of identifiable groups with radically different prognoses in each cohort.

What Do Treatments Treat

The question what do the treatments treat appears to be, curiously enough, rarely asked when it comes to long-term evaluations of therapeutic results. A critical review of knowledge of the modus operandi of various treatments and the rationale for their application brings out some strange inconsistencies. One would expect anticipations of permanent therapeutic results to be based on the evidence of permanently produced changes of functional systems. In the case of lobotomy, for example, this requirement appears to be met. A similar claim can be made for reconstructive psychotherapy. In the first instance, a structural change modifies affective and inhibitory functions. In the second instance, therapy proceeds on the premise that the patient can acquire a reality-oriented attitude to internal problems and social aspirations. But what about the convulsive and insulin coma treatments? The assertion of permanently induced changes was not only not made, but was vigorously refuted. This leaves no legitimate basis for the expectation of long-term results, unless one adheres to unproved theories of causes which these treatments are supposed to have successfully eliminated.

The advance of modern pharmacotherapy introduced new therapeutic principles. Drug-induced improvement, once achieved, can be sustained by means of continuous medication. A basis for compensatory, corrective treatment of prolonged or chronic disorders has therefore been established. The proof of such expectations depends not only on the measurements of therapeutic responses but also on the distinction of clinical populations according to prognostic differences. If the present trend to place all schizophrenics on maintenance drug treatment persists, it will be difficult or impossible to separate the patients who benefit from this treatment from those who do not.

As I already stated, the premise of the reconstruction of the personality through psychotherapy permits the expectation of permanent changes. One is, therefore, surprised and disappointed to find very few studies to document the results and prove the basic premise. The common practice to limit evaluations to the time of the termination of the treatment, constitutes a serious shortcoming. A welcome exception is the comprehensive study of Mueller[6] about the psychotherapy of schizophrenics at the University Clinic at Zurich. With Madame Sechehaye and Benedetti as principal therapists and investigators, a psychotherapeutic program was initiated in 1952. Ninety-four patients were treated who represent the material for Mueller's study. Covering a post-treatment span of from 1 to 5 years, Mueller evaluates the results on the basis of personal examination of the patients, meetings with relatives and discussions with the former therapist. This study is exemplary inasfar as the range of informative data are concerned. In 15 tables, the material is broken down according to symptomatology and its changes, duration of illness, duration of hospitalization before and after treatment, number of therapeutic hours, method and personality of therapists, etc. One methodological drawback may be seen in the fact that the greater majority of the patients also had various somatic therapies before, during and after psychotherapy. Most of the patients were re-examined more than 5 years after termination of treatment. The results were as follows: 24 of the 94 patients were free from evidence of schizophrenic symptoms; 26 patients showed residual symptoms but were able to work. The rest manifested no significant changes. In terms of insight, 16 patients attributed their recovery to the treatment, while 21 praised the therapist rather than the treatment as such. Mueller concludes that despite many questions which remain unanswered, psychotherapy can effectively change every major manifestation of the psychosis. On theoretical grounds, however, Mueller refrains from equating favorable results with cures. His reservation is influenced by the fact that it is still impossible to separate spontaneous developments from therapeutically induced changes.

A thoughtful study by Stone, Frank[7] and others explores the very question whether or not follow-up studies are at all pertinent to psychotherapeutic results. Based on an intensive 5-year follow-up of treated psychiatric outpatients, diagnosed as having a psychoneurosis or personality disorder, interest was focused on the long-term course of the illness as well as on the effects of psychotherapy. The following very interesting interpretation of the findings is offered by the authors: "It has been generally assumed that the evaluation of the effectiveness of different forms of psychotherapy depends ultimately upon follow-up studies. The findings of this study raise serious questions as to the validity of this premise. The cumulative effect of the life experiences of psychiatric patients after the termination of treatment, coupled with the impossibility of determining what part of these experiences should be attributed to changes in the patients' behavior resulting from therapy, would make it well-nigh impossible to determine what features of the end state can be attributed to a course of treatment years before." Stating further that the immediate amelioration of the patient's symptoms is sufficient justification for psychotherapy, they propose that evaluation of different forms of psychotherapy should be primarily in terms of their immediate results. What makes this view particularly significant is its departure from the premise of reconstructing the personality.

The Outlook

What, then, is the outlook? Are there ways and means which promise a more enlightened approach to both concept and method of evaluating ultimate results? In the light of past performances, the evaluator of long-term therapeutic results can be compared to Don Quixote fighting the windmills. One moment he is confronted with a reality, the next moment with a projected image. The reality may be conceived as an interaction of a chronic disorder with the sustained effects of a treatment. The projection represents the imagined interaction between an illness no longer manifest with a treatment which has long ceased to exert an effect. The historical association of a given diagnosis with a given treatment has not and cannot conceivably shed light on the intricate matters of the therapeutic prognosis. The uncertainty regarding the adequacy of the nosological classifications is not likely to be resolved in the near future. Are there other approaches which can circumvent these obstacles and barriers?

I submit that the diagnostic deadlock can be broken by switching investigative interest from standard diagnoses to psychopathological syndromes. I am not for a moment proposing to abandon the system of diagnostic classification, but I suggest that the diagnosis be qualified in terms of a detailed index of symptoms and whatever other individuality differentials lend themselves to identification. Clinical psychopathology as Weitbrecht[8] reminds us, is by no means at an end but on the contrary, in its beginning. Its real future lies in its contribution to a penetrating understanding of therapeutic activities.

I furthermore submit that the therapeutic deadlock can be broken by substituting symptom characterizing criteria for disease-oriented indications. The compelling need for evaluating therapeutic modes of action on the basis of changes in the psychopathological profile became quite apparent to me in my earlier work with the neuroleptic drugs. Not what we conceive as illnesses, but symptoms as manifestations of particular dysfunctions, serve as targets for pharmacological treatment. Most diagnostic entities comprise widely dissimilar spectra of symptoms and behavior which make the idea of disease-oriented therapy an unreasonable undertaking on empirical and theoretical grounds as well.

I consider it a reflection of the modern psychiatrist's scientific discipline that he approach the question of treatment by elaborating his assumptions of the anticipated effects on psychopathological phenomena. Only by committing himself to concrete predictions can he place himself and his confreres from the behavioral disciplines in the position to test the validity of the hypothesis which serves as his rationale for the treatment. This will pave the way for precise measurements of duration and modification of those dysfunctions which, when present, impress as the main characteristics of the illness, and when diminished or absent, suggest improvement or recovery.

Such a shift to functional evaluations of nature and duration of therapeutic effects would seem to find theoretical support in Ey's[9] organo-dynamic concept of causality in psychiatry.

In his view, the difference between the various psychiatric disorders can be understood in terms of different levels of disorganizations. In the case of the acute psychoses, the pathology expresses itself in the field of consciousness, whereas the chronic psychoses and neuroses indicate pathology in the permanent structure of the personality. Whatever reservations one may have to this modern version of Jackson's system of functional integration, it seems to me that Ey's concept comes like a breath of fresh air to those of us who, tired of the cliches of the past, wish to bring the evaluation of treatment in line with the most advanced concepts of the functional totality of man.

ACKNOWLEDGMENT

I wish to acknowledge the valuable contribution made by Miss Cecelia Herstein, Research Social Worker. Miss Herstein worked prodigiously to relocate patients, visit them in their homes and evaluate their life situations with great skill and competence of judgment.

REFERENCES

1. MASSERMAN, J.: Principles of Dynamic Psychiatry, 2nd Ed. Philadelphia, W. B. Saunders Co., 1961.
2. GRUHLE, H. W.: Quoted in Jakob Wyrsch: Klinik der Schizophrenie, Psychiatrie der Gegenwart. Klin. Psychiat. *2:* 3, 1960.
3. MUELLER, M.: Die Therapie der Schizophrenien, Psychiatrie der Gegenwart. Klin. Psychiat. *2:* 1960.
4. BLEULER, M.: Das Wesen der Schizophrenieremission nach Schockbehandlung. Ztochr. Neurol. *173:* 553-597, 1941.
5. ZUBIN, J.: Role of Prognostic Indicators in the Evaluation of Therapy, Psychopharmacology: Problems in Evaluation, National Academy of Sciences, National Research Council, publication 583, 343-355, 1959.
6. MUELLER, VON C.: Die Psychotherapie Schizophrener an der Zurcher Klinik, Versuch einer vorlaufigen katamnestischen Ubersicht, Der Nervenarzt, Heft 8, Jahrgang *32:* 354-368, 1961.
7. STONE, A. AND FRANK, J.: An intensive five-year follow-up study of treated psychiatric outpatients. J. Nervous & Ment. Dis. *133:* 410-422, 1961.
8. WEITBRECHT, H. J.: Das Syndrom in der psychiatrischen Diagnose. Fortschr. Neurol. Psychiat. ur. Genzg. *1:* 27, 1959.
9. EY, H.: Hughlings Jackson's principles and the organo-dynamic concept of psychiatry. Am. J. Psychiat. *118:* 673-682, 1962.

Discussion

by JOSEPH ZUBIN, Ph.D.*

THIS SESSION HAS DEALT with the following issues of a technical nature: (1) the preparation of instruments for detecting changes in the behavior of mental patients, during and after treatment; (2) the development of designs for placebo and double-blind studies; (3) a consideration of the importance of immediate discharge versus status 5 or 10 years later; and (4) the development of statistical methods for the evaluation of therapeutic results.

It is interesting to note that each of these developments indicates that the resistance to the introduction of scientific methods in the evaluation of therapeutic outcome is decreasing. This was not the case 10 years ago when I read a paper on these topics before the Association for Research in Nervous and Mental Disease. Our present chairman, Dr. Cameron, then indicated his disagreement with such approaches by the following statement: "I should also like to comment on Dr. Zubin's paper because it is in some sense a very key matter of this whole question of experimental design . . . I am going to say very frankly, that I do feel, as far as Dr. Zubin's paper is concerned, that what one sees here is an attempt, a valiant attempt, no doubt, but an attempt to transfer to our field the system of experimental design, designed experimentation, shall we say a philosophy of science, which really has its applicability in other fields altogether. I don't think we have frankly accepted the fact that our data are intensely variable and that we are dealing with emergent situations and not static situations. We are trying, therefore, to say this is how something *should* be in our field rather than how something *is* in our field in research."

I am glad to see that both Dr. Cameron and I have shifted positions with regard to this issue. I am not as vehement about introducing the most rigorous exacting methods and he has come a good step forward in accepting methods of control which are workable.

The first paper in this session, from Biometrics Research by Dr. Burdock and Mrs. Hardesty presents one of the fruits of the endeavor to develop tools for the objective evaluation of the behavior of the mental patient from the time he enters the hospital, during the course

*Biometrics Research, Department of Mental Hygiene, State of New York.

of therapy, and on follow-up. These tools are in no way intended to displace psychiatric judgment and evaluation. Their purpose is to provide concrete reference points which can be used from time to time to determine what objective evidence exists for any changes in behavior. Interpretation of these data, of course, will depend upon many other factors which the clinician has to bear in mind. However, in studying groups of patients for the effects of certain treatments, it is quite clear that these instruments may either support or contradict global intuitive clinical judgments, as in fact has already become evident in several studies. It is interesting to note that psychological tests have not been very useful for the measurement of changes under the various therapies. Apparently the underlying dimensions of personality or the behavioral trends which these tests tap are not as crucial to the detection of changes in behavior as are specific observational techniques such as those provided by observational inventories. By the same token the global psychiatric categories also are not as useful and unless they are couched in behavioral terms, may not give indications of changes in the behavior of patients after the various treatments.

In order to cope with the new release policies that now seem to be developing in all the state hospitals, it is necessary to develop special techniques for measuring outcome. In previous years, before the revolution in management and treatment had occurred, the proportion of patients released from the hospital was a sufficient index of the efficacy of a therapy. Now with our revolving door policy in which patients go out and come back again, there is need for a more appropriate measure, such as the Outcome Index that Dr. Burdock has proposed which incorporates all movements in and out of the hospital through the course of the follow-up period.

In his scholarly review of the literature of placebo techniques Dr. Lehmann has made only one omission that I could detect, and that is Jellinek's classic study of the effect of the placebo reactor on comparisons of the efficacy of drugs. It is interesting to inquire why it is that in so many studies about 30 per cent of the patients usually react to placebos. If the effect is truly random, why should it be 30 per cent? Dr. Lehmann's conclusion that individuals who manifest well integrated autonomic functioning show improved performance on psychomotor, perceptual and cognitive tasks under placebo conditions and conversely individuals who manifest poorly integrated autonomic functioning react with impaired test performance under placebo conditions, deserves further discussion, particularly as the correlation between autonomic variables and test performance involves a time parameter. I would like to suggest in the light of a variety of experimental results that the taking of a placebo induces an emotional response. If the emotional response is euphoric, involving expectancy of improvement, then the placebo will partake of the nature of an effective agent. On the other hand, should the emotion generated be either neutral or dysphoric, the placebo effect will not be there. It is well known that an emotional response has to represent the integration of both physiological components as well as conceptual components. While an emotion-like state can be engendered by injecting adrenaline, it is not a true emotional state unless the individual himself supplies a conceptual component (based on previous experience) for making it into an emotional state. By the same token the effect of a conceptual component can be reduced by blocking the physiological component of the response. This was done by Schacter et al., in a study in which in one group the conceptual component of euphoria and humor was prevented from interacting with physiological activation by injecting chlorpromazine to reduce the physiological arousal, and in another group the physiological component was facilitated by giving epinephrine to enhance the arousal. The epinephrine group, of course, laughed heartily at the funny film which was exhibited but the chlorpromazine group did not. The placebo apparently will be successful to the extent that it is accompanied by an expectation, conscious or unconscious, of improvement. A negative attitude, on the other hand, will lead to opposite effect. This is the reason why improvement occurs in variables which involve measurement of time since practice under influence of a beneficent mood will improve speed. Accuracy, since it is more dependent upon ability, may not benefit to the same extent.

In dealing with therapeutic results one is often faced with the problem of the adequacy of the clinical judgment of improvement. In several studies it has been found that although the clinician failed to see any significant signs of recovery, objective records of the behavior of the patient before and after treatment indicated definite results in favor of an active agent over and above a placebo. It must be borne in mind that better recording of observations by clinicians may turn up information which is now lost in the global approach towards evaluation.

The question of ethics, which is always raised in connection with control groups and placebo groups, seems to be a spurious one since if we knew the efficacy of the drug we would not be engaged in its investigation in the first place. Only drugs whose efficacy is in doubt are brought into a clinical trial and for them there is no other alternative. While it is true that most of the discoveries of the past, both new drugs as well as new methods of treatment, have come through serendipity, at least in pharmacology the day seems to be dawning when new drugs will not be discovered by accident alone, but will be developed according to specific models laid down by prior knowledge. Therapeutic techniques too will be discovered and evaluated in a more rational way. While we must not kill the goose that lays the golden egg by requiring rigorous evaluation the very day a new therapy is born, once it has passed the preliminary stages it ought to be subjected to as rigorous an evaluation as science can permit. Probably the selection of patients for the therapeutic trial and the evaluation of outcome are the two tasks which require both a high level of clinical acumen as well as methodical scientific inquiry. For the latter, the research worker is absolutely essential.

Dr. Freyhan's plea for a more objective way of evaluating therapy, coming as it does from *bedside* rather than *outside* psychiatry, is a welcome relief from the contentions of clinicians who declare that objective evaluation is impossible in psychiatry. Instead of focusing on disease categories, he proposes to focus on symptoms or patterns of symptoms (syndromes) as targets for therapy. Since there is greater agreement on symptoms than on diagnostic labels, such a procedure makes it possible to take evaluation out of the domain of the private judgment of the therapist and into the area of public scrutiny. This would be especially true if such techniques as the behavior inventories discussed by Dr. Burdock in this session were used to buttress the clinical records now in use. From this point of view, arguments about the relative merits of studies of immediate outcome vs. studies of long-term outcome become trivial. From objective information on the pre-morbid as well as on the morbid characteristics of patients, predictions as to immediate outcome can be made, and if objective records of the course of the illness during treatment are collected, eventual outcome can also be predicted, and these two prognoses need not necessarily be the same.

A focus on target symptoms is not limited to the types of therapies which Dr. Freyhan discusses—somatotherapy (including drugs) and psychotherapy. It is also the basis for the newly rediscovered behavior therapies in which methods derived from learning theory constitute the therapeutic approach. It is significant that objective criteria in therapy must at the present time be based on relief of symptoms rather than on cure of disease. Perhaps a combination of behavior therapy with somatic therapy may prove more efficacious for some types of patients than either method alone. While it is possible that in the final outcome life experience may play a more important role than therapy, perhaps prognosis of ultimate outcome could contain predictions for a benign milieu as well as for a malign milieu, each specified for the individual patient as a conditional probability. Such studies would require considerable effort and time, since we do not yet know all the pertinent variables, but there are signs of a gradually developing recognition of the relevant factors.

In view of Dr. Freyhan's hardheaded attitude at the end of his paper, it is a little surprising on rereading his introduction to see that he was far more critical of follow-up studies than he probably intended to be. There is no reason why follow-up studies cannot be developed to follow a biological model as well as a psychogenic model of the etiology of schizophrenia. In follow-up studies based on the biological model, stress would be placed on genetic, biochemical and developmental-maturational factors, while in follow-up studies based on the psychogenic model, early infantile environment and social-cultural factors would be stressed. Both types of follow-up can be carried out with, of course, different results for different diseases. Perhaps a combination of the two models into an epidemiological model might be superior to testing each model separately, but this remains a matter of strategy rather than of basic differences.

I have often wondered why the practical clinician has such a strong distaste for evaluative studies. I suppose it is based on the same aversion we have for auditors or tax collectors. But there may be an even deeper reason which I seem to sense even in some of the better clinicians. This has something to do with giving the patient the benefit of the doubt even in the face of statistical improbability. It is poor medicine to diagnose the patient as suffering from the most malignant state which the symptoms entitle him to, especially if it is a hopeless diagnosis. Instead, good clinical practice dictates the assumption that perhaps a less malignant process is at work so that there is some hope of saving the patient. Since there is always some chance of improvement even in diseases of very high mortality, the clinician may very well assume that he is treating the exceptional case with good prognosis. Conversely, it is fool-hardy after the autopsy to continue believing in the benign nature of the illness which has already killed the patient. We must separate clinical from scientific strategy. While it is true, that therapeutic optimism may bias the clinical practitioner, he should prove adamant against such bias when he evaluates outcome. This may prove too much for some clinical investigators, but they perhaps ought not to engage in evaluation. When clinical strategy is separated from scientific strategy a more objective approach such as Dr. Freyhan proposes becomes possible.

Dr. Greenhouse's paper is a model of clarity and precision and should become "required" reading for all clinicians (as well as nonclinicians) engaged in evaluation. The principles he has laid down bear no exceptions. One should, however, remember that these principles apply only to actual experimental studies—in the preliminary browsing type of research, these rigors can be relaxed. Perhaps it is the rigorous application of these principles to even preliminary hypothesis searching that the clinician (Rapoport, for example) objects to.

While I agree heartily with Dr. Greenhouse's critique of the "flight into process" when evaluation becomes difficult, I do not share his feelings about the worthlessness of investigating "process" for its own sake. The process of interaction between patient and therapist is worthy of study in its own right, but it should not masquerade as evaluation of therapy. By studying this interactive process we can learn much about the behavior of patient and therapist and it may even throw light indirectly on evaluation.

The ubiquitous variability which characterizes mental patients, is one of the most disturbing stumbling blocks which interferes with evaluation. While Dr. Greenhouse points the way to reducing this variability, he does not pay enough attention to the possibility for eliminating it by finding homogeneous subgroups within the population under study. Perhaps increasing the magnitude of the effect of therapy as a way of overcoming variability may not serve this end. Suppose the group consists of two subgroups in each of whom the therapy goes in opposite directions. Increasing the effect may only serve to increase variability, unless the group is subdivided into its natural subgroups. The techniques for finding the natural lines of cleavage in a given population are not yet fully developed and are greatly in need of further study. While randomization and controls serve a good purpose, a sample made up of portions drawn from different populations in which contrary trends in relationships between variables is found, can rarely yield significant results.

It is notable, however, that this symposium on Evaluation of Psychiatric Treatment stands out in bold relief against the symposia of yesteryear. Slow, but steady, progress is being made both in the types of goals that are set for evaluation and in the methods used for attaining these goals as well as in the technique for objectifying clinical change.

9

A TWENTY-FIVE YEAR VIEW OF THERAPEUTIC RESULTS*

by LAURETTA BENDER, M.D.

THE LONGITUDINAL VIEW of personality development is best presented by the gifted novelist. For this purpose there is none better than Thomas Mann. *The Holy Sinner* by Thomas Mann, I see as an allegory of schizophrenia, a prototype of a composite case history. Schizophrenic fantasies and dream life are intertwined story-wise with life experiences in depicting the genesis and evolution of a schizophrenic throughout his life as he might appear to us and as he experiences his inner life and reality.

This is the story of the origin and life of Pope Gregory retold "by the incarnate spirit of story telling," (p. 8),† a Benedictine monk, in language which is schizophrenic in rhythm, in the use of neologistic symbolism and "many tongues that run all together and become one, in other words, language" (p. 10).

You must read this to get all the beauty, the many nuances, and the significant meaning. I can only point to the highlights in the personality evolution of schizophrenics.

A babe is born in a dukedom in Flanders, of incestuous relations between twin brother and sister, conceived on the night the Duke, their father, died. These parent-twins are also described as we see schizophrenics—they were born with "the unusual foreign yvorie pallor . . . clearly an inheritance from distant forebears" (p. 19), "A way of looking sidelong out of one corner as though they were listening and waiting for something" (p. 20), "But we want to be little always on earth"—they said—"We have made it up like that, when we cozy together we shall then easier become angels in hefen" (p. 21), "For us two, no one is worthy neither of you nor of me,

---

*Presidential Address

†Page reference here and those that follow refer to Thomas Mann: The Holy Sinner. New York, Alfred A. Knopf, Inc., 1951. Permission for reproduction granted by publisher.

since we are wholly exceptional children" (p. 27). Thus they justified their incestuous relationship.

The penalty was that the father twin, being trained in knighthood, went off to the Holy Lands and died. His twin sister was left to reign the dukedom. After the infant was born, it was returned to God as the product of sin—placed in a casket with an ivory tablet upon which the mother had written the case history with her anguish and guilt.

In the casket he was put out to sea and was born again into the hands of a fisherman. An observant Abbot took guardianship, baptizing the infant in his own name, Gregory, and taking over the ivory tablet.

The fish-wife foster mother nursed him with her own infant and raised him with her family of eight, but he always seemed so different from the rest and was little understood by them. The fragile, beautiful, what I have called "embryologically plastic" infant was poetically described as made of "foam and sweet air." Maturation was rapid. "At five years he shot up tall and slender-limbed, varying more and more from the young rascals, his foster brothers. . . . Even so early he held his head leant to one shoulder and his arm bent to the other one, the eyes, hidden under the dark lashes, looking down sidewise into a dream" (p. 108).

At age 6 he became a scholar in Abbot Gregory's cloister and learned reading, numbers, science, philosophy rapidly. His progress was winged. When the Abbot tested him at age 11, he was amazed. By the time he was 15 years, he had mastered law and divinity. But also he had "feelings and mental images, which sometime even spoiled his taste for monkish learning and for books, in that it seemed to him not only that he was different from his kind in fabric and pattern but also that he did not fit with the monks and his fellow pupils either—that he was secretly a stranger here as there" (p. 110).

He heard talking about him and it sounded like a reproach "as though things were not quite right with him." He was dreaming of knighthood, of being one of Arthur's knights, felling terrible giants and receiving favors from the grateful and gracious widow. He was sure he could sit a horse better than the best knight. In his imagination he practiced knighthood in every detail.

Meanwhile, when they were 15 years old, his foster brother was brought to great jealousy and provoked him into a fight in which he could not help his "vital powers gathering themselves together so extraordinarily" (p. 118). He overwhelmed his foster brother by smashing his nose. As a result, the enraged foster mother revealed his founding origin. The details, together with the ivory tablet (his case history), were given to him reluctantly by the Abbot. He cast himself again upon the mercy of the sea to expiate his sinful origin. He was washed upon a shore of a dukedom ruled by a Duchess who was fighting off all comers who wanted to force her into marriage. Gregory was confident that given a horse he could win over any enemy, because of his supreme inborn gifts as a knight and because he had practiced so thoroughly in his dreams. He did, and within a year he won the Duchess in marriage. Of course, this was his own mother, so the incestuous theme recurred. Later she found the tablet and realized who he was, and in anguish they separated. He was now 17 years old.

He turned his back on everything and retreated to a bare rock in a lake, isolated himself, regressed to sucking pap from the mother earth during the second 17 years of his life, until he became as small as a hedgehog—"a prickly, bristly, moss-grown nature-thing. It knew time no more" (p. 251). Thus he spent 17 years in a catatonic regression. But prophesy came true. He was sought out to be the Pope. From the least he became the greatest. Through him, his mother was raised to become a saint, having become the lowest of sinners through him.

Such is the course of schizophrenia—inborn special traits and capacities, unique developmental features, a "different" childhood, quick learning of verbal material, around puberty fanciful day dreams, violent outbursts and pseudopsychopathic behavior in midadolescence, anxiety and guilt passing into a regressive psychotic withdrawal for the second 17 years, and return to the highest level, taking his mother with him. Remissions and quiescent periods interchanged with violence and withdrawal. This is without therapeutic intervention as we know it. Since we are endeavoring to understand the therapeutic process it is well to be aware of this natural course.

I offer the *Holy Sinner* as the control for my observations.

At Bellevue between 1938 and 1942, 43 children, age 6 to 14 were subjected to treatment with Metrazol convulsions, modified by erythroidin. This treatment was justified on the basis of the severity of the psychopathology in these children, the inadequate personality maturation, the failure to respond to more conservative treatment and the apparent hopeless future. The diagnosis was not always clear; although schizophrenia was the most common problem, in some instances organic brain disorders and psychopathic features were clearly dominant.

This group of patients have been the subject of many studies. They were included in an intensive follow-up study in 1949-52 (NIMH).* Thirteen articles have been published about them.[1-13] The current study has derived from my present position in the New York State mental hospital system.†

The early difficulty with the differential diagnosis has become clarified with the passage of time. Twenty-five males are considered schizophrenic because the childhood episode that sent them to Bellevue was clearly schizophrenic and the course through the 20 to 28 years that they have been followed has been the course of chronic schizophrenia.

Significantly each case history seems to involve all the factors leading to the definition of childhood schizophrenia as a maturational lag in all behavior areas integrated by the central nervous system, with familial genetic history, an organic or physiological crisis precipitating the schizophrenic episode, and anxiety with secondary neurotic, psychopathic or psychotic defenses.

It was exactly this group of patients, and others like them, from which this definition was formulated.

Following the course of these patients, furthermore, led to the concept that schizophrenia is a lifetime process, with occasional psychotic episodes as decompensatory processes precipitated by various organic, physiological, or psychological experiential events especially at certain critical periods in life. The course can be predicted with characteristic features at specific epochs in the life period. This includes periods of spontaneous remissions. These features will be demonstrated in this group of 25 followed from boyhood to the present time. The effect of the Metrazol convulsive therapy in modifying the predictable course will also be indicated.

These 25 boys were born between October 1925 and June 1932. Their present age is from 29 to 36 years. They were all treated with Metrazol at Bellevue Hospital between the fall of 1938 and the spring of 1942. Thereafter electric-induced convulsion replaced Metrazol. Their age range at that time was 8 to 14 years. They were known to us at Bellevue Hospital for variable periods before they received treatment.

The present follow-up located the current whereabouts of 19 men,

---

*National Institute of Mental Health Project No. MH-171-C1.

†The follow-up studies on these cases was possible only because of the unstinting work of Alvin Eldridge Grugett, Jr. and the cooperation of the Directors of the several institutions where these patients are or have been treated. Where possible they were personally interviewed and re-examined.

two others are known dead, four have not been located for the last 8 to 10 years. Of the 19 men who have been located, 10 are in a state institution or recently out on convalescence and aftercare. Nine are in the community, more or less dependent upon parents and siblings. Three are adequately employed. This does not account for the 4 not recently located. One of these, last heard from 10 years ago, was then in the Navy for his fifth year, married and had a child—the only marriage in this group of 25 men.

These 25 case histories have been reclassified into three groups, determined by the period of onset of disturbed behavior and the characteristic course. The first group of six boys had shown deviate development and behavior, more or less autistic, from infancy. They have run a chronic course without dramatic changes.

The second group of nine boys showed some degree of normal development, including speech, in infancy and early childhood and after some precipitating event presented a typical schizophrenic episode late in childhood prepuberty with a remission in early puberty and a variety of subsequent courses.

The third group of 10 boys were first psychotic after puberty or in early adolescence (11 to 13 years). All have had a chronic course with variable periods at home, where they were more or less dependent.

Early Autistic Development

These six boys were characterized by their atypical development in infancy, the inadequacy of the mental and personality development, especially of language, the generalized immaturity, the emphasis on organic disorders, the chronicity of their course, and their temporary response to therapeutic endeavors whether psychological, environmental, pharmaceutical or physiological.

In two, the family history was not remarkable; one had an epileptic aunt, the other a nervous anxious mother (as she had a right to be). But in four, the family history was heavily laden. For example, a father and his mother were pathologically symbiotic, the father abandoned his home, a maternal aunt was in a mental hospital, and the patient's only brother became psychotic and was hospitalized at 19. In each of the other families there was a psychotic hospitalized member.

The early organic factors were even more striking:

S. B. The pregnancy (third of three) was stormy; the mother was sick and miserable, due in part to the family situation; she used abortives. There was an instrumental delivery of a weak and puny infant who cried continuously. He was colicky, had diarrhea, did not gain, had calcium tetany 6 months to 2 and a half years. The pediatrician called the child "defective."

H. J's mother had a stormy pregnancy following two abortions, abortives were tried. She bled at 2 months and the last 3 weeks of pregnancy. The infant was jaundiced the first week; at 9 months he had pneumonia and was in hospital and convalescent home for 3 months.

H. S. Weighed 10 pounds at birth. Development was slow. At 9 years he was diagnosed dwarfism, Lorraine type, pleuriglandular syndrome, and dyschondroplasia (two bone cysts removed from humerus and tibia).

The early development of these boys was characterized by a sickly infancy, poor physical and motor development, dependency on the mother, slow development of speech and of socialization, mutism, fears and phobias, anxieties, temper tantrums, sibling jealousies, refusal to go to school and no relationship or play with other children.

They were seen at early ages, from 4 to 7 years, in child guidance or mental hygiene clinics and were referred to Bellevue at 9 to 14 years, after continuous school failure.

At Bellevue their behavior was described as:

S. B., age 9, not eating, compulsively chewing food and spitting it out, passive to tube feeding, anxious, clinging, cataleptic, echolalic, jingling neologisms, symbol formations, dissociated pain sensations, whirling postural responses, electroencephalogram and pneumoencephalogram within normal limits; I. Q. 49, undersized and thin.

H. J., age 11, negativistic, tense, resistive, mostly mute, inhibited. He did not enter group activities, depressed. Masturbation was excessive. He refused to eat (cooked his own food at home). His drawings were inferior and primitive, his I.Q. was 71. There were whirling postural responses. He was undersized, thin, pale, and had cyanotic hands.

H. S., age 14, was inactive, withdrawn, resistive, stayed in bed, mute, drooling, refused to eat. He stood in catatonic postures, stared at the sun. He was terrified of the external environment and internal hallucinations. He was small, immature, thin, pale.

On the ward these boys all had an intensive therapeutic program including an activity and school program, individual art and dance therapy, psychotherapy with a physician, tube feeding as indicated, sodium amytal for interviews and as a sedative and benzedrine for stimulation. Two had glandular treatment for immaturity.

They all had Metrazol with b-erythroidin, the number of treatments ranging from four to 26 convulsions. Two 14 year old boys, H.S. and W.P., also had insulin treatment for 18 and 55 days, respectively.

All of these patients responded to Metrazol. Three who were not eating, started to eat after the third or fourth injection. Two who were too disturbed to be on the children's ward, could be sent there after the second or third treatment. All were more cooperative to the activity program and their habit training became adequate. They were less anxious, less compulsive (masturbating, etc.) and somewhat euphoric. With continuing support in therapy they were all sent home in partial remission.

Two stayed home only a few months and efforts at special school placement failed. They returned to Bellevue for state hospitalization.

The case history of one of these boys can now be reviewed with the knowledge that he died suddenly at 30 years of age in a state mental hospital where he had been for 14 years. The autopsy revealed that death was due to acute left-sided heart failure with cardiac aplasia.

He was born with a cord around his neck and was cyanotic. He was typically an autistic schizophrenic infant and child with a psychotic break at puberty. Signs of hypopituitarism and hypothyroidism suggested treatment with thyroid and Antuitrin "S" with some apparent improvement. From 12 to 14 years he was maintained at home on conservative treatment. When accessible his I.Q. scored at the dull normal level.

Increased psychotic behavior at age 14 remitted promptly but insufficiently with 26 Metrazol injections, followed by 55 insulin treatments. Spinal x-rays, three electrocardiograms and an electroencephalogram showed no ill side effects. He spent another year at home and school before hospitalization at 16 years. At 30 he died of cardiac aplasia.

The current status of the other five patients is as follows:

One patient died at 22 years by drowning, in an attempted escape from a state hospital where he had been since 15 years in a regressed, negativistic, hebephrenic state.

Two have been continuously in state institutions since adolescence. One who has always been mute, except as he could communicate with his mother, has been variously treated with electric shock, amytal injections, testosterone and estrogen, and thorazine without effect. The other, who has always rated defective, is in a state school for defectives. His language is autistic, echolalic, repetitive. He is often disturbed. With the introduction of thorazine his behavior improved to the point of making his ward management favorable. He had two convulsions, however with anticonvulsant drugs and meprobamates, he has a more comfortable life in the institution.

The mother of the fifth insisted on having him at home, with visits to the clinic, after he received 11 Metrazol injections at 11 years of age, with very little apparent effect. He was kept in special classes at school until 18, achieving third grade work. He was withdrawn, lived in a world of his own, occasionally doing odd jobs. However, two older brothers are also at home, unmarried, but employed adequately to support the family.

Summary: This group with a genetic background and early paranatal organic disturbances were autistic from the beginning. Severe behavior disorders appearing late in childhood and early adolescence could be controlled best with physiological therapy, but the chronic course was not changed. A mixture of schizophrenic and organic features dominated the clinical picture throughout.

Childhood Schizophrenia with Puberty Remissions

A second group of nine boys had a history of essentially adequate early development until childhood when hospital care was required because of behavioral and psychological disturbance characterized as childhood schizophrenia.

The early life for this group was stormy because (in 8 cases) of the pathology in the immediate family. Four mothers were defective and promiscuous, at least having many children by different men, the children subjected to many traumatic experiences. In three of these another sibling was hospitalized for schizophrenia and others were known delinquents. In four, the boys lived with nonhospitalized but psychotic or disturbed parents. Only one had no family history of mental illness.

There was nearly always a severe organic and/or psychological trauma which seemed to precipitate or exacerbate the problem.

One boy had recurring otitis media, mastoiditis and mastoidectomy. Acute psychosis followed major surgery at 8 years, which has run a chronic schizophrenic course. Three boys had severe head injuries, one at 18 months when a vicious stepfather beat him unconscious and he was hospitalized with convulsions; at age 5, when he was struck by a car and was unconscious a half hour, and at age 10 struck by a car, was unconscious and bled from the nose and mouth. Another boy had numerous early illnesses, whooping cough at 3 years followed by probable rheumatic fever with a heart murmur and chorea and tonsillitis, a tonsillectomy at 4 years and severe pinworms and hookworms from 4 years until 11 years when he was hospitalized with schizophrenia.

The predisposing psychological factors were always associated with a death of a parent. One boy's adoptive mother died when he was 4 years, followed by 17 placements before he was 12 years.

Two other boys' fathers died and the home situation was otherwise badly disturbed; their depressive reaction passed into a schizophrenic episode.

Unlike the autistic boys, there was only one history of a deviate pregnancy and birth.

None was retarded in speech development. Intellectually, these boys were not retarded. Their IQ's on standardized tests ranged from 78 to 110, the mean IQ being 96.

P. A., age 9 years and 9 months, came to Bellevue after a radical mastoidectomy. His symptoms were auditory hallucinations, incoherent speech, ape-like climbing, hiding in bed or in corners to talk to voices, compulsive movements to guard off danger, fears of dying, anxiety and depression or euphoria. He showed postural whirling and neurological signs of right-sided motor weakness. The right ventricle was dilated and the electroencephalogram was diffusely dysrhythmic.

J. C., age 11. His mother was psychotic, always hated him and wished him dead. He had pneumonia at age 8, and a head injury with unconsciousness and bleeding from nose and mouth at age 10. He was withdrawn, impulsive, made sudden vicious attacks on children. He said a jack hammer was pounding in his heart and head, telling him to "kill, kill." He was rigid, cataleptic, resisted whirling. He experienced a great variety of visual, auditory, somatic (vibratory) sensations and introjected objects that directed his impulses. He had a rich fantasy life. At times he was shy, charming, appealing for help. He was oversized and strong. He was constantly struggling to control himself. He was bitter against his mother, saying she was "crazy" and one of them would kill the other.

M. P., age 6, refused to eat, undress, go to bed, or use the toilet. He was fearful, often mute, screamed at night, used bizarre language. He made no contact with children. He resisted all routine. He whirled spontaneously. He clung to adults fearfully and was bewildered and panicky.

The therapeutic program for these boys was hospitalization away from home, attempts to involve them in the activity program, school and hospital routine, special art, play, puppet and dance therapy, and psychotherapy with an individual psychiatrist. Benzedrine and barbiturates were used as indicated.

The Metrazol shock treatment will be discussed in terms of its immediate effect and the subsequent course of the patient.

The following three boys showed considerable improvement ascribed to the Metrazol:

M. P., first came to the hospital at age 6 in a bizarre, panicky psychosis (see above). He improved considerably with psychotherapy but in school he was withdrawn, bemused, vague. His school work was poor. He was overdependent on his mother and sister. At 10 years he was readmitted and had 20

Metrazol convulsive treatments and was much more active and independent (also sustained two vertebral fractures without symptoms). He has remained at home, finished high school and employed himself as a door-to-door salesman. He might be described as a pseudoneurotic ambulatory schizophrenic, still dependent on his first psychiatrist. Remission occurred at puberty; he had no pseudopsychopathic features.

F. D., was first seen at Bellevue at 8 years of age in a mute, anxious, withdrawn, negativistic behavior. He was in and out of home and hospital until 12 years—a depressed mute. After Metrazol with four convulsions, he was much improved. He was placed in a residential home to be away from his mother. At age 15, he became delinquent, he ran away, was stealing, quarrelsome, made a poor school adjustment. He was sent to a training school. He continued this pseudopsychopathic behavior from ages 15 to 17. He then joined the Navy, was married, had a son and stayed in the Navy as a career.

P. S., came to Bellevue at age 8 in a frank psychosis, anxious, fearful, withdrawn, negativistic but was given 8 months at home with clinic supervision, and at 9 years had seven Metrazol convulsions. He had been morose, withdrawn, asocial. He improved somewhat but at home regressed and returned at 10 years for electric convulsive treatment. Because of antagonism to his mother, he was placed in a residential home where he stayed until age 16 and then returned home and sought employment. He has not been heard from since age 18.

Two other boys received Metrazol at age 12½. Both made a great effort to control their impulses for running away or aggressive outbursts but were too readily overwhelmed by anxiety. They were sent to state hospitals at age 13, where they were diagnosed not schizophrenic, but primary behavior problems and within a year they were discharged. One developed pseudopsychopathic features; stealing, losing jobs. The other was dependent, depressive and pseudoneurotic. In a stressful situation he threatened suicide at age 29 and was briefly in Bellevue.

Three boys showed no apparent result from the Metrazol treatment at 10 years, but all these boys had a spontaneous remission between 11½ and 12 years of age, at which time they were at home and attending school satisfactorily and behaving like normal boys. This was maintained briefly by one boy (E. G.) before he started to show psychopathic behavior, living with homosexuals and stealing. He had a psychotic episode at which time he was paranoid, hallucinated and suicidal and was hospitalized for a year at 15 to 16. Thereafter he has remained in the community living with a man friend and employed. His brother has been hospitalized chronically with schizophrenia. P. A. did well at home, school and community until age 15, when he became delinquent (pseudopsychopathic), leaving school and home, associating with a homosexual and breaking into an apartment. Under arrest he became psychotic, was hospitalized, where he has remained with ten releases on convalescence. He was out once for 6 years, dependent, marginally employed. He received electric shock treatment twice and insulin twice. After 1956 he had several of the tranquilizers and antidepressants with partial improvement. He is currently on convalescent release.

H. R. was removed from the hospital by his mother, who interrupted Metrazol after four injections (his father had died that year in a state hospital). She sought clinic help. A year later he was better and placed in special classes at school. He finished a vocational high school at age 17 and remained home in a regressed psychotic condition. At age 19 he had 6 months treatment with insulin and psychotherapy at a sanitarium, but continued in bed, unkempt, at home. Suddenly in July 1961, at 30 years, he took and passed a civil service examination for the New York City Department of Parks and has been employed regularly since.

Summary: For these boys who had a frank psychotic episode in latency following a disorganizing organic event or severe environmental stress, remissions occurred at puberty. If Metrazol therapy coincided with puberty, it seemed to facilitate remission, especially where the symptoms were depressive. When Metrazol was given a year or more before puberty, it appeared to have little or no effect. The predictable puberty remission occurred at the usual time. Most boys in mid-adolescence developed some degree of pseudopsychopathic or pseudoneurotic disturbances, during which time all but two required some type of institutional care for a period. But the majority have been able to live a favorable, if dependent life, most of the time out of hospital.

Puberty Psychoses

Ten boys had relatively normal development in infancy and childhood; a change in personality or onset of disturbed behavior and symptoms occurring at puberty from 11 to 13½ years and hospitalization following at once or within the year. A recognizable precipitating event was rare. However, one boy (I.E.) had scarlet fever at 11-2 years with bizarre hypochondriacal complaints marking the onset of an obsessive compulsive, paranoid episode.

In four others there were earlier illness or organic disorders followed by a normal latent period until puberty.

I.W. had croup, mastoiditis, double pneumonia and a head injury before 6 years, but was normal during the school years until age 11½.

The family histories were very pathological. In all but one the father was grossly disturbed, in two families only the father was disturbed, in all other families there were siblings, grandparents or collateral relatives known to be mentally ill or disturbed. Pathology in the mothers in this group was minimal. They maintained the home and are still doing so.

In four of these families the father was in a dependent relationship to his mother, who was variously described as "tyrant," "crazy," paranoid, and who also overwhelmed her other male children (uncles to the patients). At the present follow-up, all of these fathers have abandoned the family and are wanderers, having been considered neurotic, shiftless or psychotic by agencies and the staff at Bellevue. In these five families, besides the boy who is the subject of this study, each had a brother and two had two brothers, making six brothers. Only one of these matured successfully. Four were dull, retarded in school, continuing dependent on the mother to this day as adults, none married or are fully employed. Two sisters are reported to be normal, out of the maternal home, married.

One boy (L.L.) came from a home where the father, paternal grandfather and uncle were queer, wanderers, with periods of mutism, paranoia, or autism, and abandoned the family early.

The puberty psychoses of these boys were usually acute and dramatic and seemed to show a tendency to remission as a result of treatment. For example:

J. C. C., an 11 year old Protestant Negro boy, felt something bad in his mouth and spit, refused to swallow and became mute, resistive, negative. In hospital he participated in activity therapy, Amytal interviews. He wrote bizarre fantasies but remained mute. He had nine Metrazol convulsions and started to talk after the second. He then related that he had a fellatio experience which started his symptoms. He had transference psychotherapy and left the ward a normal boy at 12 years and returned to school. At age 17, again mute, withdrawn, negativistic, he entered a state hospital where he has remained permanently.

B. G. lived with a tyrannical paranoid paternal grandmother who dominated the father. Scarlet fever at 11 years started bizarre preoccupations with eyes and urine. He displayed compulsive touching and spitting. He expressed phobias for an old lady who lived in the same house. He was preoccupied with fantasies about a witch who poisoned his mother's milk when nursing him and his food at that time. He then refused to eat. He was bewildered, whirling, cataleptic. Metrazol (ten injections) with psychotherapy was given at 12½ years. He was home for 8 months. He did well at school but was antagonistic at home. He was sent to a state hospital for 4 months at 14 years. Then he was at home until he was 26 years old, and thereafter hospitalized chronically. Another boy (L. L.) in an acute regressive, catatonic state at 12 years, with compulsive masturbation and explosive obscenities, improved immediately after Metrazol so that he was able to return home and to school for several months, but then became disturbed again and has been hospitalized since. He was a "backward" patient, mute, inaccessible, resistive, often belligerent, unclean, smearing, etc., until 1956 when tranquilizers became available. Now in interviews he speaks freely of his home visits, and current events which he learns about over the television. He has retained schizophrenic mannerisms in gestures, motility and speech. However, ideation and fantasies are not psychotic but realistic, sensitive and well informed.

Two boys, with Metrazol, started eating again, in good contact and able to enter into hospital routine on the children's ward but they could not leave the hospital. Two boys who were depressed, anxious, withdrawn and fearful, became euphoric, hypomanic, superficially alert and went home but not to school and soon returned to hospital. Shock therapy was often looked upon as an excuse for another try at home. One boy became too panicky and excited with Metrazol to be cared for at Bellevue and went directly to a state hospital but later was released in a few months.

Although some partial remissions were experienced which appeared to be related to the treatment regime, all these psychoses have run a chronic course. Three individuals have remained in the hospital continuously since they were admitted at 13, 17, and 17 years. Three have improved in hospital management on tranquilizing drugs after previous "deterioration" and now have ground privileges and frequent home visits. Another who has been in the hospital since age 13, has had a great deal of pharmacotherapy and seven trial periods at home with increasing frequency and duration. Still another has been out of the hospital since 1958 on drugs controlled in aftercare clinics, living at home and employed.

Two others have been out of the hospital since 1953 and 1954 (before drugs were introduced) and are in a dependent situation in the home. The ninth was hospitalized three times between 12 and 16 years. Since then he has had an erratic life, wandering through three states, with homosexual attachments and dancing in night clubs.

Finally, the tenth has never been in a hospital other than Bellevue, at 13 years. He has a high IQ (116). Besides high school, he had 2 years in an art college, has studied printing, photography and has had considerable employment in these areas. He is essentially an ambulatory pseudoneurotic schizophrenic.

Summary: Thus this group of ten patients shows a complete range of chronic schizophrenia from a bright pseudoneurotic never hospitalized, to an inaccessible patient chronically hospitalized for 20 years.

Physiological therapy in the form of Metrazol-induced convulsions given in the course of a puberty schizophrenic psychosis, has been helpful to some by making them more accessible for the total treatment program in the hospital or by raising their margin of tolerance sufficiently so that they could live at home and attend public schools at least for a time and at best, indefinitely.

Several of the most regressed, deteriorated patients in state hospitals for many years, have been brought back to some level of meaningful living again by the current drug therapy program, and are still improving.

Now we have not determined who the sinner may be. There are

many who will believe that the mother is always the sinner; is she not schizophrenogenic? There are others who will believe that the individual himself is the sinner since, after all, is he not the one whose behavior and fantasies are schizophrenic? However, there will be many of you attending this Fifty-Second Annual Meeting of the American Psychopathological Association, who will judge the speaker to be the sinner, for have I not given you this wealth of clinical material without charts, graphs, or statistical evaluation?

REFERENCES

1. Bender, L.: Art and therapy in mental disturbances of children. J. Nerv. & Ment. Dis. *86:* 249-263, 1937. Reprinted with follow-up in Bender, L.: Child Psychiatric Techniques. Springfield, Ill. Charles C Thomas, 1952, chapt. 13, pp. 206-220.
2. —: Anxiety in disturbed children. *In* Hoch, P. H. and Zubin, J. (Eds.): Anxiety. New York, Grune and Stratton, 1950, chap. 7, pp. 119-139. Reprinted (with illustrations) in Bender, L.: Aggression, Hostility and Anxiety in Children. Springfield, Ill., Charles C Thomas, 1954, chapt. 7, pp. 151-170.
3. —: The concept of pseudopsychopathic schizophrenia in adolescents. Am. J. Orthopsychiat. *29:* 491-512, 1959.
4. —: Childhood schizophrenia and convulsive states. *In* Recent Advances in Biological Psychiatry. New York, Grune and Stratton, 1961, vol. 3, pp. 96-103.
5. — and Cottington, F.: The use of amphetamine sulphate (benzedrine) in child psychiatry. Am. J. Psychiat. *99:* 116-121, 1942.
6. —, Freedman, A. M., Grugett, A. E. Jr. and Helme, W.: Schizophrenia in childhood—a confirmation of the diagnosis. Transact. Am. Neurol. A. *77:* 67-73, 1952.
7. — and Helme, W. H.: A quantitative test of theory and diagnostic indicators of childhood schizophrenia. Arch. Neurol. & Psychiat. *70:* 413-427, 1953.
8. — and Schilder, P.: Mannerisms as organic motility syndrome. Confinia Neurol. *3:* 321-330, 1941.
9. Cottington, F.: The treatment of childhood schizophrenia by Metrazol shock, modified by B-erythroidin. Am. J. Psychiat. *98:* 397-400, 1941.
10. —: Treatment of schizophrenia in childhood. Nervous Child *1:* 172-187, 1942.
11. Freedman, A. M. and Bender, L.: When the childhood schizophrenic grows up. Am. .J Orthopyschiat. *27:* 553-565, 1957.
12. Rapaport, J.: The therapeutic process in a case of childhood schizophrenia. Nervous Child, *1:* 180-198, 1942.
13. —: Phantasy objects in children. Psychoanalyt. Rev. *31:* 1-6, 1944. Reprinted in Bender, L.: A Dynamic Psychopathology of Childhood. Springfield, Ill. Charles C Thomas, 1954, chapt. 4, pp. 80-91.

Part III: Special Factors in Evaluation

10

PROGNOSTIC FACTORS IN THE EVALUATION OF THERAPY*

by DAVID PERETZ, M.D.,† MURRAY ALPERT, M.S. and ARNOLD FRIEDHOFF, M.D.‡

THE STUDY OF PROGNOSIS holds an important position historically as well as currently in clinical psychiatry. The serious efforts to study outcome from psychosis in the early decades of this century still serve as a part of the descriptive base of psychiatry. Though they represent genuinely valuable early attempts at organizing observations, interpretations of these studies should be guarded when applied to the contemporary scene. When Kraepelin[1] studied five hundred cases of dementia praecox, he did so within an institutional setting which itself could have affected the observations he made. Finding at that time that neither pathology nor biochemistry could fulfill his hopes for understanding mental illness, he turned toward the study of the course of illness and its outcome. In collecting life histories, he attempted to discover common, salient features in the various conditions which would contribute to the establishment of descriptive diagnosis and the assessment of prognosis. His follow-up studies, the critical step in any attempt at evaluation of outcome, were in significant measure anecdotal, based on other than direct contact with those patients who had left the hospital.

Bleuler's work,[2] by its excellence, seemed to many to make further efforts at delineation of the onset, clinical picture, course and termination of the schizophrenias unnecessary. Influenced by the psychoanalytic and psychological models of his day, he revised this group of

*This research was supported by U.S.P.H. Grant #MYP4669.

†New York State Psychiatric Institute.

‡Recipient of U.S.P.H. Research Career Development Award #MSF14024; New York University School of Medicine.

diseases to include a far wider range of pathology, from the mildest in degree to those cases more closely akin to the Kraepelinian description. The Bleulerian conceptualisation carried implicit in it a different framework of prognosis with a wider range of possible outcomes. More recently the adaptational and interpersonal schools have broadened the base still further diagnostically, and consequently prognostically.

The increase in the range of psychopathology which is now subsumed under the rubric of schizophrenia has raised problems for the evaluation of psychiatric treatment. These problems may interfere with the understanding of treatment effects. If there is a diversity of syndromes that are referred to as schizophrenia and reflect points of view or theoretical considerations rather than common causation, it would seem unreasonable to expect a unitary treatment process to effect changes across such a group. We may be expecting specific treatments to be effective in nonspecific conditions. A further problem occurs when proponents of a type of treatment also have their own criteria for diagnosis. It would be difficult, under such circumstances, to know whether the relative success of a therapeutic procedure should be attributed to the efficacy of the method or to the differences in prognosis implicitly attached to the diagnostic criteria.

We have had a particular purpose in mind in exploring the area of prognosis in relation to the evaluation of therapies. Many controlled therapeutic studies are currently constructed with samples of 20 to 40 patients divided between treatment and control groups. Because of these small samples the chance of unequally distributing patients possessing good or poor prognosis is a real one. That is to say, there may be a weighting of patients who begin with good or poor prognosis in one or another of the groups. As a consequence of this, we may find differences between the groups which are not attributable to the treatment. Ineffective treatments may appear effective or effective treatments may be masked. Perhaps there are better variables for matching patients than age, sex and diagnosis. If we were able to discover valid, reliable factors predictive of outcome, we could use these in studies for the evaluation of therapies as added controls between the groups.

One of our purposes has been to see if we could include prognosis in experimental design in this particular way. To do so we must rely on information that can be obtained within a short time after the patient comes into the hospital, before he is placed in a treatment or control group. The patient himself is the chief source of this kind of information. In a small sample study, groups could then be matched for prognosis. A prognostic scale or index would have to predict change in condition on a short-term follow-up, since this is the period used in many drug studies.

During the past several years, one of us (D.P.), in association with Dr. Joseph Zubin, has been involved in a comprehensive review of the literature on prognosis in schizophrenia.[3] Some 800 references were screened, of which 550 appropriate studies were carefully examined. It was found that the material could be divided into three general categories. One type of report contained statements of clinical experience and impressionistic viewpoints; a second was made up of studies of factors related to favorable and unfavorable outcome from the specific therapies; and finally, there were those which were actual attempts to study prognosis, with specified populations and parameters. Only about 10 per cent of the studies fell into the latter category and even among these, the data presented were often too sparse for adequate comparison. Frequently, one would find a study designating sample size, age, diagnosis and duration of hospitalization, but making no reference to type of onset, duration of illness, marital status, etc. Another might include several different characteristics. The great majority of these studies were retrospective without direct follow-up. Despite these problems in the data, certain factors appeared again and again to be predictive with consistency of direction. It seems likely that a body of prognostic impressions has become established in the literature, some as a result of sound clinical experience and some perpetuated because of a lack of controlled study.

A particular prognosis may contribute in a number of ways to outcome in the form of a "self-fulfilling prophecy." The prognosis may modify the nature and extent of the treatment to be offered. The implication of a chronic course structures certain vital commitments not only for the patient but also for the family and community as well. For these reasons and for their value as an experimental control, carefully documented prognostic criteria would provide a tool for investigative purposes for the expansion of our understanding of this disease and possibly as an aid in planning management and therapy for the patient. Zubin has extensively studied prognosis in schizophrenia using a biometric approach. He reported some of these findings at these meetings 3 years ago.[4] The report indicated that there might be significant predictive factors in the background, onset, course of illness and symptomatology of schizophrenic patients. Our study was directed toward testing these factors.

Procedures

Subjects were selected for the study from among those patients admitted to the adult services of Bellevue Hospital, Psychiatric Division, with an admission diagnosis of schizophrenic reaction, regardless of type. Between January and May of 1958, 63 patients were interviewed. Of these, two dropped from the study because the initial diagnosis was changed by the ward psychiatrist. When compared with the Bellevue Psychiatric population from which our sample was drawn, systematic selective factors do not appear to have operated to bias our sample except for a slight weighting toward females in our population.

Each patient was rated on a prognostic index at the time of interview for the presence or absence of particular characteristics being investigated. One hundred twenty-five items had been selected and categorized as background factors, factors related to onset and course of illness, and characteristics at the time of admission (signs and symptoms). These items had been selected during the literature study as those which were most frequently and consistently reported. Working definitions were framed for each prognostic item based on the usage in the literature. These were adhered to closely in the rating of each patient.

During September of 1958 we initiated a follow-up program. Our goal was to reinterview each patient between 6 and 12 months after the initial contact. Through state hospital visits, after-care clinic appointments and office visits with discharged patients, 51 patients were seen and evaluated by the investigator who had conducted the initial interviews. One patient had been transferred to a California state hospital and request for complete information as to her status was made with reference to our scale of outcome. Three patients were contacted by phone or through close family members though not seen face to face. In the latter four cases it was believed that there was sufficient information to clearly place the patient on our scale of outcome without distorting our findings. Five patients who could not be reached after repeated attempts are not included in the data analysis presented today, although we hope to contact them in future follow-ups.

Our criteria of outcome were organized to obtain a picture of overall functioning. For a patient to be rated as improved, a demonstration of a fair degree of effectiveness in interpersonal relationships, vocational, social and marital adjustment, absence of active symptomatology and presence of some affective resources was necessary. Each subject was placed on a three point scale of outcome (unimproved, slightly improved or improved). Of the 55 patients seen on follow-up, 30 were rated as unimproved, six as slightly improved and 19 as improved.

The category of slight improvement is represented by six patients who remained in the hospital, showing some improvement in their day-to-day function, interpersonal relationships, environmental contact, and emotional regulation. We could not classify them with the unimproved nor with the improved groups. They represent too small a group to be dealt with separately and will not be discussed further. It will be interesting to see if they become more like one or the other of the outcome groups on 3 year follow-up.

Results

Table 1 contains a description of the 49 patients rated either unimproved or improved at the time of follow-up. Neither age, sex, diagnosis nor length of follow-up was related to outcome. It is interesting that these are the factors usually most carefully matched in experimental work.

Table 1.—Age, Sex and Diagnosis of the Sample Population

Age	Mdn. 29.7	Range 18 - 54
Sex	Males 19	Females 30
Diagnosis	Paranoid 17	
	Catatonic 8	
	Simple 4	
	Undifferentiated 20	

An item-by-item correlation with outcome has been done. Contingency tables were set up for each prognostic factor: Chi square or Fisher's Exact Test[6] were used where appropriate. Differences which could be rejected at 5 per cent confidence levels will be reported.

Single Factor Treatment

The prognostic factors to be studied in relation to outcome were divided into background factors, factors associated with the onset and course of illness, and signs and symptoms. As we have mentioned before, all factors that we investigated had been reported by others as related to outcome.

Background Factors: Among the background factors the following were not significantly related to outcome in our sample:

TABLE 2.—Background Factors *Not* Significantly Related to Psychiatric Outcome

1. Sex	6. Life situation
2. Religion	7. Environmental demands
3. Heredity	8. Alcoholism
4. Level of social development	9. Physical health
5. Work history	

The factors in table 2 are to a large extent self-explanatory. It may be noted that the ease of measurement of the factors varies considerably. While sex and religion are, essentially, vital statistics, the evaluation of work history or environmental demands requires judgmental intervention on the part of the investigator.

We might also mention the infrequent report of any history of mental illness in the family. Only three of the 49 patients gave such a history for any member of their family. This may reflect guardedness or limits in reporting or selective factors in our population.

The background factors significantly related to outcome will be discussed.

TABLE 3A.—Background Factors Significantly Related to Psychiatric Outcome

Marital Status	Unimproved	Improved
Married	4	11
Single	22	7
		$p < .01$
Other	4	1

In table 3a we note that marital status is significantly related to outcome. Five patients who were divorced or separated were not included in this analysis. The direction of our finding, married patients faring better and single patients poorer, agrees with a number of reports in the literature.

In table 3b the relation between prepsychotic personality and outcome is presented. Patients were rated as introverted if they demonstrated a long history of fundamental lack of interest in or inability to form relationships. The direction of our finding is consistent with that most frequently reported in the literature.

TABLE 3B.—Background Factors Significantly Related to Psychiatric Outcome

Prepsychotic Personality	Unimproved	Improved
Introverted prepsychotic	26	9
Other than introverted prepsychotic	4	10
		$p < .01$

TABLE 3C.—Background Factors Significantly Related to Psychiatric Outcome

Premorbid Adjustment	Unimproved	Improved
Poor premorbid adjustment	29	13
Other than poor adjustment	1	6
		$p < .02$

In table 3c the relationship between premorbid adjustment and outcome is presented. Poor premorbid adjustment was defined by a history prior to the determinable onset of illness characterized by conflict with the self and others, difficulties in relationships and lack of productivity. In contrast with the rating of introverted prepsychotic personality, poor premorbid adjustment emphasized conflict in relationships and lack of goal orientation, while introversion emphasized tendencies toward isolation. Thirty-five patients were rated as having introverted prepsychotic personality and 42 patients as having poor premorbid adjustment. Only four patients were rated as unclassifiable as to premorbid adjustment while ten could not be classified as to prepsychotic personality. All patients who were rated as having either extroverted prepsychotic personality or good premorbid adjustment were among the improved.

TABLE 3D.—Background Factors Significantly Related to Psychiatric Outcome

Social History		
	Unimproved	Improved
Good social history	2	8
Other than good social history	28	11
		$p < .01$

Good social history is characterized by a history of effective function in educational, employment and social situations within the context of the roles attempted. In contrast, the factor of level of social development reported in table 2 as not significantly related to outcome referred to a history of achievement of socioeconomic position without there necessarily having been good function within that role. This might account for the difference in relation between these factors and outcome. Good social history is significantly related to favorable outcome in our sample and this, too, supports literature findings.

Factors in Onset and Course of Illness: Among the factors in the onset and course of illness, those not significantly related to outcome were the following:

TABLE 4.—Factors in Onset and Course Not Found Significantly Related to Psychiatric Outcome

1. Age at admission
2. Diagnostic category
3. Seclusiveness at onset
4. Treatment

While age at admission bears no significant relation to outcome, age at onset, if dichotomized into that below and that above age twenty, does. Those with onset prior to age 20 have a poorer outcome.

TABLE 5A.—Onset and Course Factors Significantly Related to Psychiatric Outcome

Age at Onset		
	Unimproved	Improved
Less than 20 years	12	3
20 years and older	16	16
		$p < .05$
Indeterminate	2	0

We must interpret the relation given in table 5a with caution. The cutting point at 20 years was selected arbitrarily so as to maximize the difference between groups. Inspection of the original data suggests that the association between age at onset and outcome may not be linear. Unfortunately, the data are not sufficient to permit tests of curvilinearity. However, the association between early onset and unfavorable outcome is in agreement with reports in the literature.

TABLE 5B.—Factors in Onset and Course Significantly Related to Psychiatric Outcome

Precipitating Factors		
	Unimproved	Improved
Conspicuous precipitating factors	0	6
Absent precipitating factors	25	8
		$p < .001$
Indeterminate	5	5

Conspicuous precipitating factors at the time of onset of illness are significantly associated with favorable outcome. This supports a number of literature reports. For precipitating factors to be judged conspicuous by the examiner they would need be of a magnitude stressful to almost anyone. Although as with many of the other factors, this one required subjective evaluation, we tended to err on the side of the conservative and only six patients were so classified, all of whom turned up among the improved.

TABLE 5C.—Factors in Onset and Course Significantly Related to Psychiatric Outcome

Duration of Illness		
	Unimproved	Improved
Duration $<$ 2 years	5	11
Duration $>$ 2 years	23	8
		$p < .01$
Indeterminate	2	0

Duration of illness was significantly related to outcome with those patients ill less than 2 years having a more favorable outcome than those ill for a period greater than 2 years. This supports a frequent finding in the literature.

TABLE 5D.—Factors in Onset and Course Significantly Related to Psychiatric Outcome

Type of Onset		
	Unimproved	Improved
Sudden	5	11
Gradual	24	6
		$p < .001$
Indeterminate	1	2

Sudden onset was associated significantly with favorable outcome, while gradual onset was associated with unfavorable outcome in our sample. This supports what is perhaps the most frequently and consistently described prognostic item in the literature. It should be mentioned that onset is a difficult thing to determine, making this consistent finding all the more striking. We attempted to describe the type of onset historically at the judged time of onset. Objective criteria of this factor would be most useful.

TABLE 5E.—Factors in Onset and Course Significantly Related to Psychiatric Outcome

Reactive Features		
	Unimproved	Improved
Reactive	1	9
Other than reactive	29	10
		$p < .001$

Reactive features in the onset of illness, where symptoms appear as a protective response to threats perceived by the patient in the environment, are generally associated with an acute onset and the presence of precipitating factors. For a patient to be rated on this factor, the criteria for precipitating factors were not as rigid as that in our previous category. Reactive features appear to be significantly related to favorable outcome in our sample.

TABLE 5F.—Factors in Onset and Course Significantly Related to Psychiatric Outcome

Lucidity		
	Unimproved	Improved
Lucid and coherent	10	0
Some disorganization	20	19
		$p < .01$

Lucidity and coherence at onset of illness appear to be associated with a distinctly poor prognosis in our sample.

TABLE 5G.—Factors in Onset and Course Significantly Related to to Psychiatric Outcome

First Attack, Previous Remissions or Chronic Course

	Unimproved	Improved	
First attack	3	10	
Chronic without remissions	21	2	
			$p < .001$
Previous remissions	6	7	
Chronic without remissions	21	2	
			$p < .01$
First attack	3	10	
Previous remissions	6	7	
			$.30 > p > .20$

Both first attack and previous remission have a significantly more favorable outcome when compared with a chronic course. This supports a number of reports in the literature. There is no significant difference between those patients having a first attack and those with a history of previous remission.

Symptoms and Signs: Approximately 75 symptoms and signs were rated at the time of admission. Space does not permit a discussion of those factors which were not found to be significantly related to outcome. Suffice it to say that we included all those which make up a comprehensive mental status examination. It is interesting to note that all four symptoms related to outcome in our sample are in a sense associated with the expression of affect. The presence of externally directed aggression, hostility and irritability were all significantly related to unfavorable outcome. Good preserved affect was significantly related to favorable outcome with diminished or constricted affect related to unfavorable outcome. These findings again support trends described in the literature, though hostility and irritability as such have not been reported on frequently.

Combining the Factors

The results presented thus far have been based on the relationship between single factors and outcome. It is also of interest that the total

TABLE 6.—Symptoms and Signs Significantly Related to Psychiatric Outcome

		Unimproved	Improved
A.	Externally directed aggression	20	6
	No externally directed aggression	10	13
			$p < .05$
B.	Hostility	21	4
	No hostility	9	15
			$p < .001$
C.	Irritability	13	1
	No irritability	17	18
			$p < .01$
D.	Good affect	1	5
	Diminished or constricted affect	28	12
			$p < .01$

number of favorable factors scored by the median individual in the improved group is eight with a range of 2 to 13. In the unimproved group the median individual has one favorable factor and the group range is from zero to 6.

In figure 1 these data are presented in a histogram. The height of each bar reflects the percentage of the group possessing the number of favorable factors indicated on the abscissa.

It is not surprising that there is a clear separation between the two groups since the individual factors were selected on the basis of just such a separation. However, because of the overlap between the definitions of the different factors it did not appear necessary to assume that the different items were measuring different characteristics. The findings of increased separation between the groups when the separate factors are combined suggests that the individual items are in fact somewhat different.

It may also be noted in figure 1 that the unimproved group is more closely clustered than is the improved group. This might be taken to indicate that it is easier to predict lack of improvement than to pre-

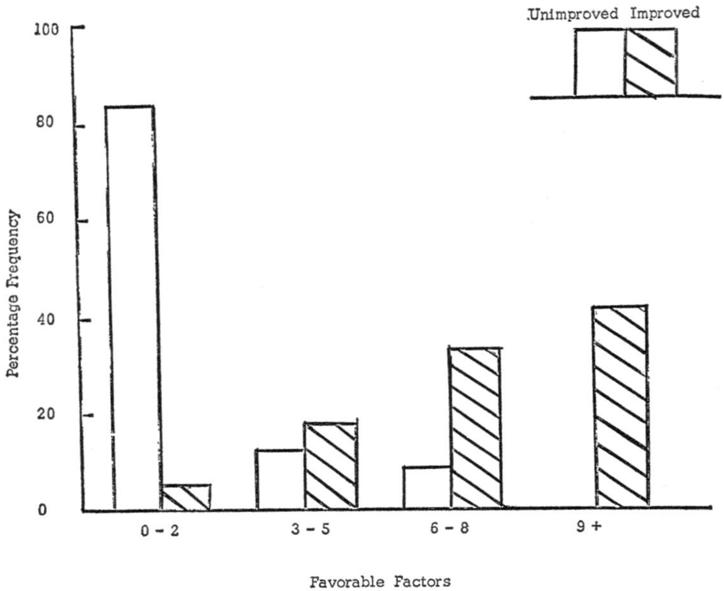

FIG. 1.—Comparison of the percentage of unimproved and improved groups showing different numbers of favorable factors.

dict improvement. Other indicators in our data also support this impression. For example, the average percentage of false positives was lower for the unfavorable factors than for the favorable factors.

Why unfavorable outcome should be easier to predict than favorable outcome is not immediately obvious at this point. Of course, the fact that there are more patients in the unimproved group would explain a large part of the difference. An unfavorable prediction would be correct for over 60 per cent of our sample.

However, more than the difference in the frequency in each of the outcome groups appears to be involved. Not only do the unfavorable factors tend to detect a lower percentage of false positives but they also tend to detect a higher percentage of the unimproved group. Some possible interpretations of this will be offered at a later point in this paper.

Comparison of Criteria of Outcome

A final point that we would like to present at this time is concerned with a comparison between the psychiatric criteria for outcome, improved v.s. unimproved, as opposed to one based on hospitalization status, whether the subject is in or out of a mental hospital. If the latter correlates highly with the former it would certainly make it easier to do follow-up studies.

In table 7 the contingency table for psychiatric status and hospitalization status is presented. The Chi square based on this table is significantly different from chance association ($p < .01$). The contingency coefficient for the data in table 7 is $C = .425$. In interpreting this figure one should remember that the upper limit for C in a two-by-two table is .707. However, the association is less than we might hope for, if we wish to use hospitalization status as a criteria for outcome.

TABLE 7.—Comparison Between Psychiatric Evaluation and Hospitalization Status

		Hospitalization Status	
		Out	In
Psychiatric status	Unimproved	A 10	B 20
	Improved	C 17	D 2
		p (Chi square) < .01	

We would anticipate that the correlation would be somewhat higher on longer follow-up. Especially in cell D containing improved patients still in the hospital could we expect change. The patients in this cell were at various points in the proces of being discharged. We would guess that these patients would soon be found in the more appropriate out-improved category (cell C).

The ten unimproved patients who are out of the hospital (cell A) present the greatest problem for those who wish to use in-out status as criteria. In an earlier paper[5] we discussed a comparison of the out-unimproved patients with the out-improved patients. Suffice it to say at this point that some of the background factors that are not related to psychiatric outcome (i.e., cultural, socio-economic, religious, work role) are related to the in-out unimproved dichotomy. We would like to emphasize that items may be related to in-out status without being predictive of psychiatric outcome.

Discussion

The results that we have presented represent an attempt to study prognosis in schizophrenia with a prospective method. They are both pilot and preliminary in the sense of sample size and short-term follow-up. A 3 year follow-up is presently nearing completion and from inspection of the data there appear to be no dramatic changes in the significance of what we have presented herein.

We are in a position currently, where our neurochemists, neurophysiologists and pharmacologists have some of the tools at their disposal necessary to provide important statements of biological functioning in mental health and illness. Their efforts are in part dependent upon the clinician's ability to make meaningful delineation between patients and patient groups which would hopefully be related to fundamental factors in the illness. Similarly, meaningful application of new therapeutic procedures requires such delineation. Prognostic factors could provide a technique for division of patients into groups. We have found some 25 factors which were significantly related to outcome in the group of patients we studied. Almost all had previously been described in the literature in the same direction of outcome that we found applying to our sample. However, over one-hundred factors which had been described as significantly related to outcome in the literature showed no relation to outcome in our sample.

These were largely symptoms and signs, though the effect of such factors as age, sex, religion, diagnostic subgroup and heredity was not apparent in this study. There are several possible sources which might explain the difference between our findings and those reported in the literature. First, we should consider the nature of the population from which our sample was drawn and recognize that it may be somewhat different from those in which these factors were found predictive. Interaction between selective factors in the population and the specific prognostic items may act in subtle ways to alter the significance of the findings. We may also note that patients were seen shortly after admission and for only several hours.

In retrospective studies a longitudinal accumulation of observations may yield a different weighting to signs and symptoms. It was our purpose in designing the study in this way to test the feasibility of cross-sectional data collection. With these results, we are encouraged to attempt to utilize prognostic factors as experimental controls while at the same time refining and cross-validating this method of study.

Our findings suggest that those factors associated with favorable outcome reflect a history of moderately effective adaptation prior to the onset of illness. Thus, marriage, extroversion, a good social history and good premorbid adjustment were the background factors associated with favorable outcome. Associated with onset and course of illness, sudden onset, demonstrable precipitating factors, a duration of illness less than 2 years, and the first attack or a history of previous remission were related to favorable outcome. Among the many symptoms studied, only the presence of good affect was related to favorable outcome in our sample. It is of interest to note how much more frequently the background factors and factors associated with onset and course of illness appear significantly related to outcome than do symptoms and signs.

The significant morbid indicators are those reflecting a long history of lack of genuine affective relationships, isolation, conflict and lack of productivity. As specifically described for background factors they refer to unmarried, introverted, poor premorbid adjustment and poor social history. Among the factors associated with onset and course of illness pointing toward unfavorable outcome were onset prior to age 20, gradual onset, lucidity and coherence at the onset, absence of precipitating factors, chronic course and a duration greater than 2 years. Unfavorable symptoms include hostility, irritability, externally directed aggression and constricted or diminished affect.

If one considered the sense of the items associated with favorable outcome, namely, suddenness of onset with precipitating factors in patients who had previously demonstrated relatively effective adaptation and possessed good affect, one might be impressed with the relationship between these findings and the concept of a reactive-type of illness. This would contrast with a gradual, insidious onset, absence of precipitating stresses, a chronic course and a history of poor adaptation in patients with constricted or diminished affect, all of which might be associated with the concept of a nuclear or process schizophrenia.

We should note that we have combined items, as described in figure 1, and find that patients frequently do not present one or the other of these patterns in pure form. Thus we may find patients presenting several of the unfavorable background factors at the same time that they show a number of favorable factors associated with the onset and course of illness. Even patients who show one or the other of the patterns in relatively pure form may diverge from the outcome characteristic of that pattern. For example, one patient demonstrated all of the unfavorable background, onset and course factors and yet appeared among the improved. We are currently preparing a discussion of characteristics of patients who diverge from prognosis.

One of our findings has been that nine of 19 improved patients presented four or more unfavorable background factors. Six of these nine patients, however, presented a large number of favorable factors associated with the onset, course and symptomatology of their illness. A further analysis of patterns is planned to study the interaction between factors.

If we refer back to figure 1 we see that over 80 per cent of the unimproved patients possessed less than three favorable factors. The improved patients were distributed much more widely in terms of the number of favorable factors they possessed. It would seem less difficult to predict an unfavorable outcome on the basis of our prognostic indicators.

Although this may at first appear paradoxical, it may be that it is easier to specify the presence of pathology than its absence.

Conclusion

In order to make a precise statement about the efficacy of a therapy, we must be able to evaluate outcome with confidence that we are measuring relevant and sufficient dimensions. Ideally, a knowledge of the course and outcome to be expected if no treatment is administered should serve as the baseline against which a therapy can be measured. In clinical psychiatry we are faced with a difficult task in defining natural history of disease. Prerequisite is the ability to identify the disease reliably. We are aware of the lack of agreement upon criteria for diagnosis of the mental illnesses.

We have been working with prognosis in an attempt to contribute to the delineation of disease patterns and possibly to provide an added control in evaluating therapy. In attempting, for our purposes, to evaluate outcome, we have been sensitized to several related problems. The first of these is related to method of follow-up and determination of outcome. Here we have noted that many studies have simply used in-out status at the time of follow-up as the measure of outcome. It may be, though evidence is far from abundant on this point, that in a 5-year follow-up an in-out measure would approximate a clinical, face-to-face judgment. We have demonstrated in our study that on a short term follow-up this is not the case. Of our group of schizophrenic patients, it was found that a number who had shown genuine improvement at the time of follow-up, nonetheless remained in the hospital awaiting the establishment of a suitable post-hospital environment.

There was another even larger group of patients who were out of the hospital but could best be described as sheltered psychotics. Only the support and tolerance of their environment permitted them to be outside the hospital. In another paper we have discussed some of the social factors which, while not predictive of psychiatric outcome, appear to contribute to in-out status. A mere statement of in-out status on follow-up would have obscured these groups, and by so doing would have distorted that which was being studied—prognostic factors in our study or methods of therapy in another.

In conclusion, our findings, within the limitations previously noted, suggest that there are verifiable factors which appear to be significantly related to outcome in the background, onset, course of illness and symptomatology of schizophrenic patients. Further work is necessary to delineate, cross-validate and better objectify these factors.

Among the reasons for presenting our data at this time is the hope that other investigators will apply similar techniques to populations which may differ in some way from ours. Only with increased knowledge of course of illness and outcome can we evaluate therapy with the confidence that our improving techniques of therapy appear to deserve.

REFERENCES

1. Kraepelin, E.: Dementia Praecox. Chicago, Chicago Medical Book Co., 1919.
2. Bleuler, E.: Dementia Praecox or the Group of Schizophrenias. New York, International Universities Press, 1950.
3. Zubin, J. and Peretz, D.: Psychiatric variables in the prognosis of schizophrenia. In preparation.
4. —, Sutton, S., Salzinger, K., Salzinger, S., Burdock, E. I. and Peretz, D.: A biometric approach to prognosis in schizophrenia. *In:* Comparative Epidemiology of the Mental Disorders. New York, Grune and Stratton, 1961, pp. 143-203.
5. Friedhoff, A. J. and Peretz, D.: Some sociological factors affecting recovery from mental illness. Presented at the International Congress of Mental Health, Paris, August, 1961.
6. Siegel, S.: Nonparametric Statistics. New York, McGraw-Hill, 1956.

11

ORGANIC FACTORS

by JOSEPH WORTIS, M.D.* and EUGENE JACKIM, M.S.

OUR ASSIGNMENT is the discussion of organic factors in the evaluation of therapies—but the truth of the matter is that there are no organic factors with which we can now evaluate therapies of psychoses. Psychotic disorders or diseases are still essentially clinical categories: the treatments nowadays employed are largely empirical. We are thus treating conditions the nature of which we do not know with methods of treatment which we do not understand. We are forced to judge the efficacy of the treatment by a more or less vague and subjective measure of clinical results while we use more precise chemical or physiological methods to detect toxicity and side effects to avoid harming our patients.

If we actually had measurable organic factors to register improvement or cure, we would, of course, at the same time have both a diagnostic tool and a possible indicator of the cause of the disease. In a few relatively uncommon psychiatric disorders—cretinism, phenylketonuria, general paresis, certain toxic or symptomatic psychoses such as those associated with pernicious anemia, lead poisoning, barbiturism and the like we have some fairly reliable indicators of the course and progress of the illness, but in the major psychoses despite decades of research, no such specific factors have yet been established. But a great deal of interest and importance has been learned in the process and there are some indications that a breakthrough may come soon.

For reasons of brevity we shall speak mostly of schizophrenia where the most active research is going on. In the past few decades various workers have claimed to find scores of measurable physiological changes associated with schizophrenia, many of which were said to vary concurrently with the course of the illness. These claims generally involve several different kinds of abnormality, quantitatively or qualitatively: (1) abnormal chemical constituents of the body fluids, (2) abnormal excretory products, (3) toxic effects of certain body fluids,

*Jewish Hospital of Brooklyn.

(4) abnormal immunological reactions, (5) abnormalities in psychophysiological functions, and (6) deviations in response to stress, loading, or functional testing. All this literature has been very ably reviewed in recent years by the McGeers,[21,22] by McFarland and Goldstein,[20] Richter,[26] Himwich,[16] Kety[19] and others, and there is no need for us to repeat their excellent work. Most of these claims have been based on small samples, inadequate controls, statistically shaky compilations, questionable procedures, or could not be confirmed. A great deal of the work is vitiated by what we regard as the false assumption that schizophrenia represents a specific disease entity rather than a syndrome, and by a failure to take into consideration probable differences in the pathophysiology of acute cases of florid active symptomatology and chronic burnt out cases that probably represent residual states. On the other hand, we would think a reasonable assumption upon which to base an interpretation of these data would be the belief that any schizophrenic population would contain a substantial number of individuals whose condition has some common cause—a number probably large enough to produce significant statistical differences from control populations. It may be too much to expect to find specific etiologic factors at this stage of our knowledge, but we can certainly seek significant or suggestive trends that may point in the direction of a solution. When these studies are viewed in the aggregate they strongly suggest that there may yet be a measurable pathophysiology of schizophrenia that can help us in our work.

Some of the earliest work on correlated physiological change, and in some respects the most satisfactory, is that of Gjessing,[11] who over 20 years ago demonstrated by extremely careful methods that recurrent catatonia was characterized by changes in nitrogen balance and that these changes often preceded the psychotic episode by longer or shorter intervals. This work has since been confirmed by several others. Of particular interest to us is his demonstration that effective treatment with thyroid hormone not only aborts or relieves the psychosis but at the same time corrects the nitrogen imbalance. Unfortunately this demonstration has been limited to a special group of rather rare cases—periodic catatonia. We are not aware of any comparable work done in other types of schizophrenia. Other reports converge on evidence that there is an abnormal serum protein fraction in schizophrenia that can be shown to be toxic in various biologic tests. A number of recent experiments suggest that there is a humoral toxic factor which impairs behavior and neural integration when injected into test animals, and that the growth of tissues, cell colonies or tadpoles is hampered in its presence. The work of Heath and Leach,[15] Akerfeld,[1] and Frohman and Gottlieb,[8] is all no doubt well known to you. Hoagland[17] in a recent critical appraisal of this literature concludes that it is quite likely that an unusual plasma globulin, possibly combined with a small molecule, is intimately involved in schizophrenia.

Some older reports strongly suggest that many schizophrenics show abnormalities in indole excretion. The McGreers[21,22] in some recent studies at first reinforced the claim repeatedly made that there is a quantitatively and qualitatively abnormal urinary excretion of aromatic amines in schizophrenia, but soon afterwards cast some doubts on their own conclusions. Other work would indicate that the abnormal physiology alters or impairs glucose metabolism, phosphorylation and pyruvate-lactate ratios. There is a real possibility that the abnormal protein if confirmed is linked to the abnormality of glucose metabolism. The work of the Lafayette Clinic in Detroit has perhaps come closest to actually isolating the abnormal protein fraction implicated in these metabolic changes. To all of these may be added the evidence presented by Malis[23] in his recently translated book, "Etiology of Schizophrenia" that a number of different immunological tests confirm the presence of an abnormal protein factor in schizophrenic blood. Of particular interest to us now is the apparent demonstration by Malis that the presence of this substance correlates closely with the severity and course of the disease. It should be noted that the work of our recent American investigators was not known to Malis, nor his work to them.

In work of our own done over the years we too have found (in confirmation of the reports of Hackfield,[13] Freeman and Zaborenke,[7] Proctor,[25] Henneman, Meduna[24] and others) a tendency to impaired glucose tolerance in schizophrenic subjects (possibly due to impaired absorption) with improvement in their tolerance curves after successful treatment, as well as a tendency in a certain group of cases to low brain tissue carbon dioxide values as reflected in internal jugular blood samples, with a restoration to normal values after insulin treatment. In confirmation of the work of several other investigators[4,7] we too have found a tendency to impaired insulin tolerance in schizophrenic subjects with a greater sensitivity to insulin after successful treatment. Those of you with experience in the administration of insulin shock treatment will recognize that insulin sensitivity tends to increase as patients move toward recovery, and that conversely insulin resistance tends to be associated with chronic recalcitrant patients, in many of whom it is impossible to induce insulin coma. In confirmation of the work of others we too have found a preponderance of low basal metabolic rates in schizophrenic subjects with perhaps a tendency to more normal values after successful treatment. We too have found that inorganic serum phosphorous levels tend to be high in schizophrenic subjects, and that these levels tend to move toward the normal range after successful insulin treatment. It may also be mentioned that Altschuler[2] has shown that the generally poor utilization of keto acids by schizophrenic subjects often tends to correlate with the clinical condition of the patient.

A different series of experiments pertain to the reactivity of the organism in various stress reactions or in certain functional systems. In general all of this work adds up to the conclusion that the schizophrenic organism displays an impaired reactivity. This is shown in the older schizophrenic patient's diminished adrenal response to stress as reflected in corticosteroid excretion, poor glucose mobilization under stress, diminished autonomic responsiveness as in the Funkenstein[9] tests, diminished respiratory response to CO^2 inhalation and diminished wheal formation in response to histamine injection.

In addition to these promising or suggestive lines of chemical study, mention should be made of another class of measurable physiological variants that has been studied in schizophrenia and which may help

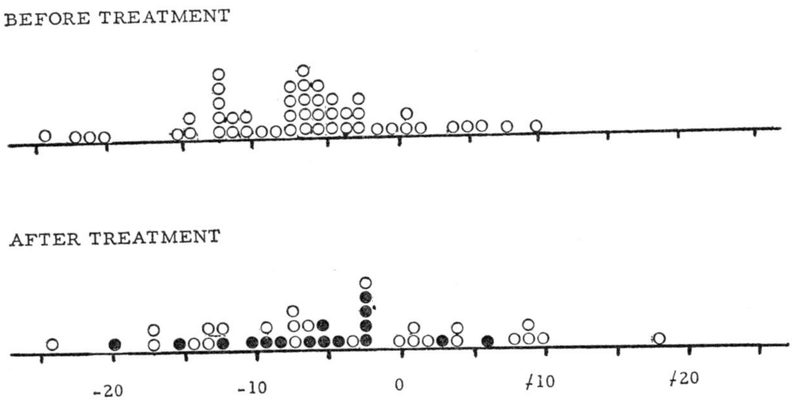

Fig. 1.—Basal metabolic rates in schizophrenic subjects before and after insulin treatment. Each circle represents an average of three determinations; the black dots represent cases that failed to respond to treatment.

us to evaluate treatment objectively. We mean the measurement of certain psychophysiological functions that can be studied and measured with Pavlovian techniques. The resemblance of schizophrenia and of schizophrenic thinking to sleep and dreams had already been emphasized on clinical grounds decades ago by Jung and others. But it was Pavlov who created an experimental basis for viewing schizophrenia as a state of partial inhibition of cortical function. This concept does not conflict but on the contrary coincides nicely with the view that toxic factors may operate in this condition. Moreover some of the physiological abnormalities such as reduced adrenocortical responsiveness, weak erythematous responses to nicotinic acid or to ultraviolet light, or diminished immunological responses, may well be related to disturbances in central regulation. The direct measurement of inhibition is possible by the use of stimulus-response tests, use of chronaxie and of operant conditioning techniques, all of which have been employed in the attempt to objectively record the presence and severity of the disease process. Soviet authors have been particularly interested in this aspect of the problem. Tatarenko,[28] for example, believes that the pupillary reaction to adventitious stimuli (the so-called orienting reflex) is an especially good indicator of the inhibitory states. Among the more recent examples of this approach may be mentioned the work of Bridger[5] who could relate the inhibitory effect of mescaline to its psychotogenic action. Skinner's operant conditioning techniques involving the behavioral recording of animals in free choice situations have been applied to man by several workers including O. R. Lindsley at Harvard. Significant aspects of behavioral response can be recorded in this way and the modification of behavior in response to therapy can thus be objectively validated. The recording of behavior can be conveniently extended to the measurement of sleep, since sleep disturbances not infrequently correlate closely with change or progress in psychotic states. Adolf Meyer's hospital charts always made provision for the graphic indication of the duration and quality of sleep, based on nurses' observations. Soviet workers[3] have made ingenious use of actograms for recording motility while asleep, since both sleep and wakefulness display characteristic motility patterns. Gjessing[12] made similar use of actograms to record motility changes in his recurrent catatonic cases. More recently the EEG has been employed to record sleep patterns, though it is inconvenient because of the necessity of electrode leads.

Among the possible objective measures of the presence and progress of the disease mention should be made of the EEG. Numerous investigators including Jasper,[18] Gibbs,[10] Hoagland,[17] the Davises[6] and more recently Heath[15] agree on the high frequency of abnormal EEG's in schizophrenia but they find no specificity or consistency in the picture, and their data again strongly suggest that we are not dealing with a homogeneous entity.

What we would all like, of course, is to have some specific test like the Wasserman, or the antigen titers of the immunologists to guide us in our work, but taraxein, ceruloplasmin and the other proposed pathognomonic tests are far from satisfying our needs. Winters and Flataker[29] seemed to have the answer when they found that mice injected with schizophrenic serum could not climb a rope successfully, but their results, though probably significant, could not always be confirmed, and the method certainly can not be used as a diagnostic tool or index of progress.

Some recent commentators have drawn pessimistic conclusions from this state of affairs. Strict experimental methods, adequate safeguards and controls, statistical analysis and the other paraphernalia of the basic sciences are relatively new to psychiatry, and our younger colleagues quite correctly criticize much of the older and some of the recent literature for its faults; but new insights and bold ideas must not be discarded because the perfect experiment has not yet been found to verify their claims. Some of the sweeping criticisms levelled against all this work seem to us extreme. We strongly suspect that already in the literature on schizophrenia one could find the basic answers to etiology and treatment, perhaps buried in some bungled report that lacked adequate controls or hidden in some tenuous statistic with a p value of only 0. 05. We even believe that the breakdown of the supposed entity schizophrenia into some component parts would split the problem wide open and allow some quick advances to be made. Adolf Meyer used to remind us that after the syphilitic origin of general paresis was discovered the diagnosis of G. P. was cut in half in Kraepelin's clinic. Can we expect something similar in schizophrenia? In a recent address by one of the leaders in our field I came across the following quotation: ". . . Most of these theories have not yet had the opportunity and advantage of testing and validation by the accepted methods of science and I doubt whether they will eventually turn out to be the most complete or valid explanation. . . . But to whatever extent these theories will be substantiated, modified or refuted by scientific evidence which is now beginning to be acquired, their contribution to psychiatry will remain a permanent and substantial one." We believe this quotation represents a fair estimate of the state of physiological knowledge in psychiatry. It is a quotation (slightly adapted) from a recent paper by Kety,[19] a distinguished physiologist and psychiatrist. But this quotation of his unfortunately referred to psychoanalysis and not to physiology. Being a physiologist, he is much harsher in his estimate of current physiological research, and goes so far as to suggest that the biological difference between a schizophrenic and a normal subject may be about the same as the biological difference between a Republican and a Democrat. I am not a physiologist and prefer to take a more hopeful and optimistic view of the physiologist's contribution.

Meanwhile I think more of these objective tests should be used on large populations in the course of treatment. They may not give us all the answers, but they can disclose significant trends, teach us a great deal about our treatment methods, and bring us closer to the day when we can understand the nature of the group of schizophrenias, what Bleuler called "Die Gruppe der Schizophrenien."

REFERENCES

1. Akerfeld, S.: Oxidation of N, N-Dimethyl-p-phenylenediamine by serum from patients with mental disease. Science *125:* 117, 1957.
2. Altschule, M. D.: Significance of changes in carbohydrate metabolism in schizophrenia. *In* J. Folch-Pi (Ed.) Chemical Pathology of the Nervous System. New York, Pergamon Press, 1961, p. 589.
3. Andreev, B. V.: Sleep Therapy in the Neuroses. Trans. B. Haigh. New York, Consultants Bureau, 1960.
4. Braceland, F. J., Meduna, L. J. and Vaichulis, J. A.: Delayed action of insulin in schizophrenia. Am. J. Psychiat. *102:* 108-110, 1946-46.
5. Bridger, W.: Neurophysiological basis of schizophrenia. Presented at the 3rd World Congress of Psychiatry. Montreal, June 7, 1961.
6. Davis, H. and Davis, P. A.: The electrical activity of the brain. Its relation to physiological states and to states of impaired consciousness. A Res. Nerv. & Ment. Dis. Proc. *19:* 50-58, 1939.
7. Freeman, H. and Zaborenke, R. N.: Relation to changes in carbohydrate metabolism to psychotic states. Arch. Neurol. Psychiat. *61:* 569, 1949.
8. Frohman, C. F., Goodman, M., Beckett, P. G. S., Latham, L. K., Senf, R. and Gottlieb, J. S.: The isolation of an active factor from serum of schizophrenic patients. Ann. N. Y. Acad. Sci. *96:* 438-437, 1962.
9. Funkenstein, D. H., Greenblatt, M. and Solomon, H. C.: Autonomic changes paralleling psychologic changes in mentally ill patients. J. Nerv. & Ment. Dis. *114:* 1, 1951.
10. Gibbs, F. A.: Cortical frequency spectra of schizophrenic epileptic and normal individuals: Tr. Am. Neurol. A. *65:* 141-144, 1939a.

11. GJESSING, R.: Disturbances of somatic functions in catatonia with a periodic course, and their compensation. J. Ment. Sci. *84:* 608-621, 1938.

12. GJESSING, L., BERNHARDSEN, A. AND FROSHANG, H.: Investigation of amino acids in a periodic catatonic patient. J. Ment. Sci. *104:* 188, 1958.

13. HACKFIELD, A. W.: Are physiologic disturbances related to the acute psychotic process in the mentally ill? Arch. Neurol. Psychiat. *28:* 883, 1932.

14. HEATH, R. G.: Clinical studies with taraxein. *In:* Neuropharmacology Transactions, 4th Conference. H. A. Abramson (Ed.) New York, Madison Printing Co., Inc., 1959, pp. 37-148.

15. —, AND LEACH, B. E.: Brain recordings with schizophrenic behavior: some metabolic factors responsible for physiological alterations. Ann. N. Y. Acad. Sci. *96:* 425-437, 1962.

16. HIMWICH, H. E.: Carbohydrate metabolism in mental disease. *In* J. Folch-Pi (Ed.): Chemical Pathology of the Nervous System. New York, Pergamon Press, 1961, p. 470.

17. HOAGLAND, H., PENNELL, R. B., BERGEN, J. R., SARAVIS, C. A., FREEMAN, H. AND KOELLA, W.: Studies in plasma protein factors that may be involved in psychoses, Chap. 29. *In:* J. Wortis (Ed.) Recent Advances in Biological Psychiatry. New York, Plenum Press, 1962.

18. JASPER, H. H.: Electrocardiograms in man. EEG Clin. Neurophysiol. Supp. *2:* 16-29, 1949a.

19. KETY, S. S.: An examination of current biochemical theories of schizophrenia. *In:* J. Folch-Pi (Ed.) Chemical Pathology of the Nervous System. New York, Pergamon Press, 1961, p. 684.

20. MCFARLAND, R. A. AND GOLDSTEIN, H.: The biochemistry of manic depressive psychosis. Am. J. Pyschiat. *96:* 21-58, 1939.

21. MCGEER, P. L. AND MCGEER, E. G.: Physiological effects of schizophrenic body fluids. J. Ment. Sci. *105:* 1-18, 1959.

22. — AND —: Aromatic urinary excretion in schizophrenics. *In:* J. Folch-Pi (Ed.) Chemical Pathology of the Nervous System. New York, Pergamon Press, 1961, p. 589.

23. MALIS, G. Y.: Research on the Etiology of Schizophrenia. Trans. B. Haigh New York, Consultants Bureau, 1961.

24. MEDUNA, L. J.: Oneirophrenia—The Confusional State. Chicago, University of Illinois Press, 1950.

25. PROCTOR, L. D., DEWAN, J. G. AND MCNEEL, B. H.: Variations in the glucose tolerance observations in schizophrenia before and after shock treatment. Am. J. Psychiat. *100:* 652-658, 1933-44.

26. RICHTER, D.: Protein and amino acid metabolism in mental disease. *In* J. Folch-Pi (Ed.): Chemical Pathology of the Nervous System. New York, Pergamon Press, 1961, p. 505.

27. STOKES, A. B.: Problems of schizophrenia: the metabolic and physiological survey of a case of periodic catatonia from illness to recovery. Folia Psychiat. Neurol. Neurochirurg. Nederlandica *61:* 252-257, 1958.

28. TATARENKO, N. P.: Principles and methods of evaluation of results in the treatment of schizophrenia. Zh. Nevr. Psikh. *58:* 722, 1958.

29. WINTERS, C. A. AND FLATAKER, L.: Effects of biological fluids from psychotic patients and normal subjects on the performance of trained rats. *In* M. Rinkel (Ed.): Chemical Concepts of Psychosis. New York, McDowell, Obolensky, 1958, p. 238.

Discussion

by BENJAMIN PASAMANICK, M.D.*

As an indication of the perversity of all evaluators, whether of papers or therapy, which I will demonstrate more fully later, I shall begin with the last paper and proceed backwards to some unknown and equivocal goal. I begin then with Dr. Wortis' valuable and provocative review of the investigations and findings of organic factors in the schizophrenias or schizophrenia.

A review of this excellent survey would be gratuitous. However, I would like to pick up Dr. Wortis' opening theme and use it to discuss what has appeared as one of the major themes and variations in this meeting, that is, the respective roles of the clinician and the research methodologist. Dr. Wortis has exerted his prerogative as a commentator to express his belief in the existence of a number of disparate entities which are included under the rubric of schizophrenia. Few of us would challenge the statement that included amongst those cases listed as schizophrenic from most hospitals and clinics are a varying number of cases which to many of us are not schizophrenia at all. But this is not the fault of the category schizophrenia but rather that of the undiscriminating clinician. One of the most flagrant examples of this has been the frequent inclusion in childhood schizophrenia (and to my thinking, probably making up a majority so diagnosed) of children who are very obvious chronic organic brain syndromes, some of them overtly defective, cerebrally palsied individuals. Presumably they were included under schizophrenia because they had certain symptoms in common. This is not surprising if we make the assumption that "true" schizophrenia is an organic disorder. Most organic psychiatric disorders have common symptoms and are sometimes difficult to differentiate, e.g., porphyria and schizophrenia. However, with adequate history, examination and laboratory investigation many, if not most, of the organic disorders can be differentiated. To fail to do so is a disservice to clinical psychiatry and is of no help to research.

The preceding remarks do not eliminate the possibility that more than one distinct entity with differing etiology is included under the

*Columbus Psychiatric Institute and Hospital.

diagnosis schizophrenia. There is fairly good evidence for both camps. I lean towards the position that ultimately there will be found one major condition which will be called schizophrenia, but that there may be a few contaminating heterogenous disorders which we have been mislabeling. We may even find that conditions which have not been thought to be schizophrenic have the same etiology. The category pseudoneurotic I think will almost certainly fall into this group. However, I would like to point out that it is unnecessary to fix one's faith on either position but it is sufficient to remember in all investigations on schizophrenia that either is possible. The investigation and analysis of the data can be so designed to take either possibility into account. It merely increases the complexity of studies. By the way, fixation on either belief is equally dangerous. The danger of including heterogenous conditions under one category is that we will so dilute the specific differences contributed by the condition in which we are interested, that no differences will be found between the experimental and control groups. This can at times be partially remedied by increasing the number of the experimental group. The danger on the other side is that, if we fragment the condition under investigation, some cases truly of that entity will fall into the comparison or control groups with the similar danger of wiping out differences which exist.

We have no recourse under these conditions but to proceed in the old and tried methods of going back and forth, making the dependent variables at one time the independent variables and vice versa to clean up our categories. For instance, if we have some evidence or rationale to believe that some reliable and valid objective, measurable variable, biochemical, physiological, psychological or other, differentiates schizophrenia from nonschizophrenia, it might be possible to determine those clinical, behavioral items which are significantly associated with the objective variable and then in a second study, concentrate on those clinical variables, choosing samples which vary widely on these items, to determine whether or not these truly predict the objective variable. In other words choose criterion groups. But this presupposes that clinicians systematically record in reliable fashion their clinical data, or that they are sufficiently clinically sophisticated so they can make the differentiating clinical observations. Here is where we clinicians have frequently failed the methodologists.

As a clinician, I am tempted to offer the psychodynamic of rationalization for this failure in order to explain the somewhat intemperate attacks upon statisticians and research methodologists made at this meeting. We tend to forget that while, paradoxically, it is the clinician who has made the most important discoveries in medicine, he did it despite and not because of his lack of sophistication in research methodology. We must remember that over the course of the centuries we have made hundreds, indeed thousands, of discoveries, the great majority of which we are very happy to forget. Indeed to resort to facetiation, in view of the incontrovertable datum that less than 5 per cent of our discoveries are not stillbirths or abortions one might state that our discoveries are made by chance. In fact, this is so often true that we have made a virtue of it and called it serendipity. However, so many clinicians have to stumble over a fact before it is discovered that I am tempted to believe that even the serendipitous event is a chance occurrence.

We clinicians tend to forget that it is we who obtain all the prestige and awards for these discoveries and that it is the research methodologist who gets little, if he avoids abuse, for his attempts to clean up after the clinicians. I have informed many a representative of pharmaceutical houses who has come to us after releasing drugs on the market after the usual clinical evaluation of the anomalous position in which we would find ourselves we were to accede to his requests. If, after the usual long, painful, costly and prosaic investigation, we were to find that the drug was of little or no efficacy, there would be no thanks. It would require a number of additional studies to confirm this, and after a few years a half dozen new drugs would be on the market, the failure of the preceding ones as well as the work necessary to force them into desuetude forgotten. If, on the other hand, after the same difficulties, we demonstrate significant efficacy, the usual and disconcerting response, by the clinician, is, "Why did you have to bother, we knew it all the time?"

We clinicians possess a ready and disconcerting facility to forget medical history and our origin. We tend to forget such matters as the centuries of phlebotomy and the rivers of blood drawn by excellent clinicians who knew that their observations were valid and true. It is interesting to contemplate what would have happened had a research methodologist performed a controlled study or two. It may very well have led to the substitution of another equally useful therapeutic medium, but it might not have been as harmful.

Another frequent target in the last 2 days has been statistics and, largely by implication, controls. I think that we clinicians forget that we use statistics all the time, that we are constantly making intercorrelations, summing patients and symptoms, and, indeed, doing everything the statistician does, except that we frequently use fatally small numbers and that grossly imperfect computer, the human brain, which is plagued by such non-mechanical psychodynamic factors as rationalization, self-interest, stubbornness, etc. We also use controls all the time since we make our judgments on the basis of clinical comparison, but like the computer, they are frequently poor controls.

The final comment on the discussion occurring in the last 2 days which I would like to make is that raised by Dr. Greenhouse, i.e., that it is essential to demonstrate efficacy of therapy before we can be much concerned with process. I too thought it self-evident before I attended the American Psychological Association conference on the evaluation of psychotherapy to which Dr. Greenhouse refers, and was shocked to learn that not only was this belief not universally held, but also that a number of individuals present stated quite unconcernedly that they were not interested in outcome. I was still further surprised to hear that Dr. Greenhouse's view was not completely supported here.

Apropos of this I have a seventeenth century volume devoted wholly to process in phlebotomy with beautiful woodcuts illustrating and discussing the various methods and locations for cutting into different veins for different symptoms and diseases. Indeed the debate and rebuttal on process in venesection had accumulated an enormous literature before it was finally replaced in the nineteenth century by equally useful measures such as homeopathy, counterirritants, etc.

It might also be indicated here lest it be interpreted as a possible sign of research sophistication, that more than one of the psychotherapists giving or discussing papers pointed to the inordinately large, and to their thinking, impossibly numerous, variables which they believed had to be controlled in experimental studies of the efficacy of psychotherapy. It should be pointed out that the number of variables is large in almost any clinical investigation of therapy, psychiatric or otherwise, that there are methods such as randomization and stratification which, with sufficiently large numbers, can cover these objections. An observer from outside our field might very well state, "that the last recourse of the psychotherapist is asking impossible questions."

I must digress from the defence of biometricians and research methodologists (instead of attacking them we should be extremely grateful for their help) and, returning to the papers under discussion, indicate another reason why evaluators and discussors are driven to distraction.

This brings us to the first paper by workers from the biometrics research group in the New York State Department of Mental Hygiene which is one of the very important series of studies of prognostic indices began by Dr. Zubin. I should begin by indicating that one of the dangers for presenters of papers offering data is that design, analysis and conclusions are laid bare to other evaluators.

This important paper deserves extensive discussion. However, I will limit my comments to two points. First, the paper offers no material on outcome criteria. Having had our own difficulties in this sphere, I would have liked to have known theirs. This is of particular importance in this validation study of prognostic indices since it is important to determine how they avoided the circularity of using the same indices, specifically the clinical ones of signs and symptoms, contaminatingly in the judgment of outcome. My guess would be, knowing the sophistication of these investigators, that they used as their major criteria indices other than the clinical ones for judgment of outcome.

Secondly, as to the factors themselves, I should think that it might have been better to call these variables or items and reserve the term factor for the usual technical, dimensional usage. The implication given at a few points in this paper is that these items are all independent. With the lack of tests of interrelationship, which are surprisingly absent, I am at liberty to let my fancy float freely. I would again guess that, if dimensional analysis were done, all these variables would fall into one, or possibly two, chief factors which would be labeled depth and duration of illness. It is unnecessary to go through all the items singly, but I should think that such items as marital status, premorbid personality and adjustment, social history, age at onset, duration, precipitating factors, gradualness of onset, nonreactivity, chronicity, and so on, are all highly interrelated. By implication at least the authors are well aware of this.

None of this discussion invalidates the central point of the paper, however, i.e., the need to control for prognostic variables in evaluation. It only makes it simpler since, if the process of randomization has not taken care of this matter, we can then take one, two, or possibly three, of the best predictors and control only for these instead of for all of them. The variables would, however, be most useful for stratification of samples in the evaluation of therapy, should this be desired.

It has already been noted, when this meeting is contrasted to the ARNMD conference on the same subject held some 10 years ago, that, except in drug studies, surprisingly little progress has been made in the last decade in the evaluation of psychiatric therapy. It might be added that surprisingly little evaluation of therapy has been done. However, I would predict that, if we continue with the progress exemplified in the last paper, a decade from now there will be significant achievements to report.

12

EVALUATION OF PSYCHOTHERAPY*

by FRANZ ALEXANDER, M.D.

One can hardly think of a more challenging and at the same time more frustrating question than that of the evaluation of psychotherapy. Questions which stubbornly defy an answer often turn out to be the wrong questions. It has been repeatedly stated that to ask the right questions is one of the main attributes of the good scientists. To ask the right questions is, however, not sufficient; to find the appropriate method to answer them is equally essential. Operational philosophy is based precisely on this tenet: to ask only questions which can be answered by available information and problem-solving devices. One cannot, of course, forbid humanity to ask questions about the vital problems of existence. The big questions of philosophy: what is man? what is his place in the universe? where is he going? what is happiness? have been asked since man as a self-reflecting being has existed. None of the answers has been verified—they only reflected the wishes, the temperament and the emotional security needs of the questioners. For the stoic, happiness and health consist in self-restraint, control and endurance; for the hedonist it means the pleasure derived from self-fulfillment. The evaluation of psychotherapy appears to belong to the category of nonoperational questions, because mental health and happiness—both global concepts—seem closely related.

The fallacy of this argument comes from equating the somewhat more concrete term "mental health" with the vaguer more philosophical concept of happiness. Nothing bears out the difference between these two concepts more clearly than Freud's saying that the effect of psychoanalysis consists in converting neurotic unhappiness into the common garden variety of unhappiness. The deeper meaning of this aphoristic statement of an empirical truth is that the world is not constructed precisely for our comfort and satisfaction, that adjustment to the hard facts of reality entails a certain amount of renunciation which is related, if not identical, with unhappiness. Adaptation to the unavoid-

*Samuel W. Hamilton Memorial Award Lecture.

able limitations of gratifications without disabling symptoms, without impairment of ego functions, without inordinate mental anguish, appears a somewhat more satisfactory definition of mental health than its equation with happiness. In this, operational formulation of the Aristotelian dichotomy—happiness versus unhappiness—is replaced by a continuum: from more to less unhappiness, more to less dissatisfaction and tension. To make the best possible deal between self-expression and its unalterable biological and social limitations, is then the meaning of mental health. Self-expression refers not only to biological urges, but also those moral and altruistic social attitudes which became thoroughly integrated as essential constituents of the personality and which may have the same or even more compelling force than instinctual trends. Moral aspirations in psychoanalytic theory erroneously were considered as necessarily limiting factors. The psychoanalytic concept of the superego as a dynamic center opposing the basic instincts was derived from the study of neurotics. This was misleading when applied to the healthy personality because one central feature of neurosis consists precisely in the failure to integrate successfully without inner conflict into the ego, the internalized social values. Genetically, the concept of the superego is valid. It is superimposed upon the original amoral personality from the social environment. However, in the course of normal development these values become thoroughly integrated into the ego similarly as foreign proteins become transformed into the organism's own proteins. The feud between the ego and superego is probably the most constant and significant feature of the neurotic personality. To achieve a harmonious union between the two is one of the goals of psychoanalysis. Ideally, in the mentally healthy person the superego should cease to remain a foreign body embedded in the total personality.

Psychotherapy attempts the assimilation of social values not in the form of a superego, which remains a foreign body, but as fully organized parts of the ego. After this goal is successfully accomplished, the unified ego contains biological and social motivations which are no longer in conflict with each other. This is what we call the adaptation of a person to his environment. Speaking psychologically of adaptation, one usually means changes within the personality. This definition of adaptation is taken over from biology. When the concept of adaptation is applied to human psychology it should include not only adaptive changes in the personality but also the process by which man creatively changes the environment to fit his personality. In this creative sense adaptation is indeed the most human faculty, since man more than any other organism is capable of changing reality according to his needs. Cultural change consists precisely in such creative performances—the creation of an environment which satisfies the subjective needs of the individual. Alteration of the environment, of course, has its limitations. In free societies the possibilities for such active changes are greater than in primitive static slowly moving societies, and greater than in totalitarian states. They are rendered possible by freedom of thought, by social mobility, by the free choice of vocation and marital partner, by the philosophy that man has a say-so about his own destiny. From this perspective, self-expression or self-realization will be different from culture to culture, and in western free societies even from person to person.

The ideally adjusted or mentally healthy person in a collectivistic authoritarian society identifies himself so thoroughly with the society as a whole, and with its ruling codes, that abandonment of highly personal idiosyncratic strivings do not appear to him as a sacrifice. His ego assimilated entirely the principle of complete subordination of the self to the society, so that no conflict remains. Of course, the question whether or not such an ideally adjusted collective personality really exists is another matter.

Psychoanalytic therapy is based on Western cultural philosophy, which tries to find for each individual his own idiosyncratic formula. This amounts to an optimal ratio between self-realization and its limitations, varying from person to person. Self-realization in the extreme case of a totalitarian society may be equivalent to denial of all individual and unique strivings. Kropotkin's anarchistic social philosophy represents the opposite extreme. Mental health—theoretically at least—is possible in both types of societies. The desirable quotient between self-expression and its limitations, however, will be radically different in these societies.

After having clarified the goal of psychotherapy as the achievement of a culturally and individually determined optimal equilibrium between self-realization and its limitation, can we turn to our main topic: to find an operational approach to the evaluation of psychotherapy. According to the prevailing trend of our time our first inclination was to turn to the most fashionable model which proved its excellence both in the basic sciences and to some degree also in medicine: the statistical approach. Because of the extreme number of variables involved, this is by no means an easy task.

The more general a question is, that is to say, the more heterogeneous the phenomena are to which it pertains, the less likely it is to find generally valid answers by means of statistics. Let me illustrate this with another example: the statistical evaluation of medicine. Medicine comprehends many different procedures. Some of them are definitely effective to restore the health in specific disorders. Others are less effective and some others may even be harmful. The statistical mean —indicating the relationship between all successes and failures—in all fields of medicine would be a rather uninteresting figure, uninteresting at least for the medical specialist. It may have value for the historian who asks, to what degree has medicine improved its capacity to restore the health of the people during the last 100, 1,000 or 5,000 years. But these figures, if at all obtainable, would be ambiguous because they are based on a tacit assumption that the genetically determined sturdiness of the race remained constant during the whole period. If the sturdiness of the race, due to genetic factors increased, increased health could not be credited entirely to improved medical procedures.

Psychotherapy belongs to the most elusive and diffuse area of medicine, and the evaluation of its merits is even less suitable for a statistical approach. Psychotherapy comprehends a most diversified array of procedures, ranging from magic suggestion, hypnosis, persuasion, consolation, reassurance, to systematic rational procedures based on advanced psychodynamic knowledge. It includes individual and group therapies, purely psychological procedures and their combination with drugs. Equally heterogeneous is the total set of the targets including transient psychopathological symptoms and reactions to extreme traumatic events, but also chronic personality dysfunctions, behavior disturbances and chronic and transient forms of psychosis. Only to increase the complexity of the problem the instruments of psychotherapy include not only the above enumerated technical procedures but also the personality of the therapist. According to our own studies, this may turn out to be one of the most significant therapeutic variables. There is strong indication that the outcome of the same procedure, be it magical incantation or standard psychoanalysis, to a large degree depends upon the idiosyncratic qualities of the therapist or magician. This factor is even more elusive because the effectiveness of the psychotherapist seems to depend largely upon a lucky combination of his and the patient's idiosyncratic qualities. It requires indeed a methodological naivete of the first order to expect meaningful answers in this field to come from statistical figures. The number of the independent pertinent variables determines the number of categories in which the whole sample has to be broken down and the greater the number of these categories, the greater is the required size of the total sample. In the case of psychotherapy this may reach astronomical dimensions. The correlations between this multiplicity of variables could be statistically handled only by computers. But meaningful coding of these variables can be hardly visualized. Coding requires disregarding certain differences between the coded variables. Without understanding the therapeutic process the probability of neglecting important differences is too great.

There is no field where there is greater need for the separate evaluation of each individual treatment. No one would consider it illuminating to establish the effectiveness of automobile repair work statistically. Each case must be evaluated on its own merits. The nature of the damage, the condition of the material and the skill of the technician determine the outcome. This simile may appear inappropriate because in automobile repair there is no complex interaction between two persons and also because psychotherapy our knowledge is not as accurate and the number of variables is much greater. We possess, however, an impressive knowledge of psychodynamics which theoretically would allow to account for the sequence of events during the therapeutic procedure. The greatest impediment against the full understanding of the therapeutic process lies not so much in lack of precise knowledge of psychodynamics, but in the lack of adequate observation of the therapeutic process. This consists in a complex transaction between two personalities, which cannot be fully described by the therapist alone. As a participant observer, he is only partially aware of his own participation in the process. A step by step account of the psychodynamic events is the only reliable method to evaluate how changes attributable to the therapeutic transactions come about. At present most of our theoretical assumptions about therapeutic factors are derived from the therapist's evaluation of the process. There is every indication that recording of the process and its observation by trained persons will greatly contribute to a more precise understanding of psychotherapy, including psychoanalysis.

After having discussed the methodological difficulties and inadequacies of the statistical approach to this problem, I do not think it necessary to go into a detailed survey of existing statistical studies. Briefly, however, I will refer to two examples—one by Fiedler[10] and one by Heine[13]—who compared the Adlerian, Freudian and nondirective therapies. Heine found no significant difference between the outcomes of the three types of psychotherapy. Fiedler, too, concluded that "The desirable therapeutic relationship is a function of the expertness of the therapist, rather than his theoretical orientation or therapeutic technique."

These statistical findings allow different interpretations: (1) That the three types of techniques are therapeutically equally effective. (2) It may indicate that the most powerful therapeutic factor consists in the lucky combination of the therapist's and the patient's idiosyncratic qualities. In other words, success is achieved whenever the patient and therapist are well matched. If the probability of such lucky combinations is the same in all three samples and are independent from the theoretical persuasion of the therapist and the technique he uses, the therapeutic results should be equal. (3) The patient's faith in the treatment and therapist may be the most influential therapeutic factor. According to Frank,[11] the patient's faith depends largely on the therapist's confidence in his system. If this should turn out the most decisive factor, and it is equally distributed among therapists belonging to different schools, their therapeutic results should be equal.

Statistical figures in themselves do not mean much without understanding the psychological processes by which therapeutic changes are achieved. The end results are due to a combination of factors, some of which are nonspecific, such as a lucky combination of the therapist's and the patient's personalities and the patient's faith in the method and in the therapist. Some others may be due to the specific nature of the procedure. These specific factors themselves consist again of the combination of therapeutically useful, indifferent, and antitherapeutic factors. I believe that the potential effectiveness of psychoanalysis because of its psychodynamic soundness could be substantially increased if certain traditional nontherapeutic and antitherapeutic elements would be eliminated from it. I do not believe that the same is true for the other forms of psychotherapy. Improving the treatment procedures, of course, is of much greater significance than are attempts to evaluate the relative value of different psychotherapies as they are practiced today. This is indeed a field in which adherence to the status quo is highly contraindicated. None of the procedures are so satisfactory that one should try to standardize them. Rational psychotherapy is a young field in great need of further development. This can only come from the precise understanding of the therapeutic process itself. These considerations, as well as the obvious unsuitability of this field for statistical research, convinced me of the need for developing appropriate methods for the study of the therapeutic process. It is encouraging that in recent years the interest has turned from statistical to process studies.

It required the stark disillusionment which followed a number of more or less ingenious statistical studies, to look for other methods which are more appropriate to this field.

A step by step psychodynamic analysis of only two or three therapeutic sessions gives more information about the workings of the therapeutic factors than a gross evaluation of outcome. Outcome is determined outside of the predictable intentionally used therapeutic factors, by a host of chance variables which are not under the therapist's control. Chance events in life when they occur at the right time may substantially contribute to the therapeutic success. We, as therapists, naturally are inclined to attribute success to our own efforts and easily overlook chance events, without which we could not have achieved our goal. We are more inclined, of course, to blame such outside events for our failures.

In the course of years I became more and more interested in certain unrecognized traditionally accepted nontherapeutic and antitherapeutic components hidden in the standard psychoanalytic procedure. This interest was the result of my trust in the soundness and validity of its theoretical foundation. Our theory is much better than are the practical results. Looking with critical eyes upon the procedure which I myself had practiced over many years, I came to suspect that the standard procedure contains a number of nontherapeutic and antitherapeutic features, which are traditionally accepted but theoretically are not essential or not even sound. I became aware of certain inconsistencies between basic theoretical postulates and therapeutic practice. These suspicions and impressions have been strongly reinforced by our own study of the therapeutic process in the Mount Sinai Hospital in Los Angeles. Certain of these suspicions now developed into convictions. I shall not try in the time at my disposal to substantiate in detail my conclusions, and shall only state them pragmatically, fully realizing that these statements must be followed up by concrete demonstration of their validity.

One of the most important contradictions between theory and practice consists in what might be called the overestimation of the relative value of cognitive insight as compared with those emotional experiences which the patient undergoes during treatment. This contradiction is derived from the fact that Freud's theory of treatment after he gave up the use of cathartic hypnosis underwent different phases. In cathartic hypnosis the abreaction of repressed emotions was paramount. The genetic insight which cathartic hypnosis yielded was, of course, gratifying for the therapist. The patient profited, however, only from the discharge of pent-up affects. After mere abreaction had proved unsatisfactory, Freud recognized that the conscious ego, in order to deal with them, must be exposed to these emotionally significant events of the past. In hypnosis this was not possible because its essence is the elimination of the ego's cognitive and critical faculties. Precisely, this elimination permits the free expression of painful and ego-alien emotional tensions. Consequently, Freud looked now for a method of reawakening these memories in the waking state. First he tried this by direct suggestion, reassurance and urging, and later by the method of free association. Free association in a sense was a mitigated form of hypnosis, inasmuch as during free association the critical and controlling functions of the ego are intentionally reduced, but not to the same degree as in hypnosis. The method of free association allowed a quasi-simultaneous appearance of repressed material and its immediate confrontation with the conscious ego. Interpretations actively helped this integrative process. The emphasis in this early phase of psychoanalysis has shifted more and more to intellectual insight as the main therapeutic agent. The next phase in the history of the treatment can be dated with the discovery of the transference phenomenon. Freud recognized that while patient and therapist were engaged in their puzzle-solving endeavor to reconstruct past pathogenic events, the patient relived—both re-experienced and re-enacted—these early emotional situations in relationship to the therapist. This introduced a new emotional and no longer primarily cognitive therapeutic factor. The crucial question of the relationship of these two factors—remembering and re-experiencing—however, was not asked by Freud, but by Ferenczi and Rank.[9] They asked: "is the recollection of the pathogenic events necessary, or is it sufficient to relive them in the therapeutic situation?" The inadequate nature of the transference emotions will become evident to the patient because they are directed toward the therapist, to whom the patient attaches feelings which are not founded on the actual relationship between the two. They were similar to conditioned responses to old cues which have been changed in the meantime. Ferenczi and Rank maintained that therapeutic results can be achieved merely by recognizing the inappropriateness of the transference reactions, even if their origin is not remembered. There can be no doubt, however, that if the original situations in which these emotions arose can be recollected, the recognition of the discrepancy between the actual therapeutic situation and the past-determined transference reactions will become more impressive. Although the genetic origin of the transference reactions often becomes—at least in general terms—conscious during analysis, there were strong indications—which I have proposed in my writings[1-4]—that recovery of distinct repressed memories appears only after the patient's ego became permeable to those ego-alien emotions which necessitated their repression. In other words, repressed memories appear after certain changes in the ego already had taken place. These changes which precede the recovery of memories are the results of the patient's emotional experiences toward the therapist, because the latter does not respond to the patient's transference manifestations in the same way as the original dramatis personae did to the patient's early expression of his emotions.

All this can be briefly summarized in saying that the emotional transactions between the patient and the therapist produce the changes in the patient's reaction patterns. These changes sometimes, but not always, are followed by the recovery of pathogenic memories. The latter gives the patient a postfactum cognitive insight into what he already discovered intuitively during the prolonged emotional interaction with the therapist. Intellectual insight only reinforces and consolidates the newly acquired reaction patterns which fit to the actual therapeutic situation, and at the same time to the patient's present life situation. This experimental process is what I called "corrective emotional experience."

The inconsistency which I am trying to elucidate should now be clear. The emotional re-experiencing of past patterns in a new framework, to which they do not fit, appears in this light as the main therapeutic agent. And yet, the official theory still insists that the specific therapeutic property of psychoanalysis consists in cognitive insight. Without denying its therapeutic effect as a consolidating factor, it is no longer possible to consider it as a primary therapeutic agent, as Bibring does when he states: "In psychoanalysis proper, all therapeutic principles are employed to a varying degree, in a technical, as well as in a curative sense, but they form a hierarchical structure in that insight through interpretation is the principal agent and all others are—theoretically and practically—subordinate to it." Finally, he states: "Be this as it may, the increasing tendency among certain groups of psychotherapists to rely on manipulative principles in combination with or in place of insight makes a theory of experimental manipulation for its proponents a very urgent task."[8] I agree with this but add to it that the exponents of the primacy of intellectual insight have the same obligation to demonstrate the effectiveness of their procedure.

This inconsistency in the psychoanalytic theory between the recognition of the transference experience as the dynamic agent of the treatment and the insistence upon the primacy of cognitive insight, can be easily understood from the history of psychoanalytic thought. Freud's early emphasis on reconstruction of the past, and his later discovery about the significance of the reliving of the past during therapy, have not been fully reconciled. The two principles, insight through remembering and re-experiencing old patterns in the transference, became juxtaposed but not sufficiently connected. The present theory reflects both these phases in Freud's thought development similar to two geological layers which belong to different epochs.

The practical consequences of the continued emphasis on intellectual insight are momentous. The search for forgotten links in the patient's history became an aim in itself. Reconstruction of the past history became equivalent to the goal of the therapy. Several authors have pointed out that both the re-enacting and remembering of the past should be subordinated to the patient's understanding and modification of his present behavior patterns. French,[7] Rado[17] and I[7] repeatedly required that the emphasis in the therapy should be on the present and future, and the revival and understanding of the past should be subordinated to the latter. It was emphasized by these authors that interpretations of the past must always return to the present and to its significance for the patient's future.[7,17] The search for the recovery of memories and for a complete reconstruction of the patient's past development is largely responsible for the unnecessary prolongation of the treatment, which can be substantially abbreviated if the experiential factors are emphasized and purposefully cultivated.

I turn now to a second inconsistency between theory and practice. The theory explicitly states that in order to reconstruct the patient's personality patterns it is necessary that he should regress, that is to say, relive his past patterns in the transference. The theory also states, however, that eventually this regressive dependent child-parent relationship must be terminated and the patient's ego must take over control so that at termination the regressive reliance on the therapist should become unnecessary. The inconsistency lies in the fact that the therapist who follows the traditional procedure never makes any real effort to make himself dispensable. He only speaks about this when he insists that the transference must be analyzed. The "analysis of the transference," however, is an ambiguous concept. The emphasis is on the cognitive recognition of the dependent transference relationship and not on the experiencing and practicing of a state of independence. The therapy goes on over years, preferably without significant interruptions, and yet it is expected that the patient merely through intellectual understanding and experiencing his dependent needs one day will get up from the couch free of this emotional residue of his childhood. Impressed by this discrepancy, Rado called the standard treatment a parentifying procedure, which he proposed to replace with his adaptational technique.[18] With the term "parentifying procedure" he refers obviously to the actual practice of psychoanalysis and not to the theory of the treatment because the theory recognizes the significance of the resolution of the transference. In practice, however, the standard procedure does not recommend any effective measures to achieve this goal, how to terminate the patient's dependent transference attitude. Essentially, Rado's adaptational technique consists in supplying the missing link, emphasizing that the patient must learn how to live in his present world, not by theory but by practice. Emphasis on the here and now, on the patient's self-reliant attitude toward the therapist, and toward his own actual life situation, is the essence of his therapeutic recommendations.

This discrepancy between theory and practice, just as the first described one, results from the same source, from the underestimation of actual experience and practice versus an overestimation of verbal cognitive formulations.

After 20 years of experimentation I have proposed a procedure which I found most effective to implement the therapeutic goal, that the patient gradually should take over his own management and become able to dispense with his reliance on the therapist. At present we have no reliable predictive methods to determine the optimal time for the termination of the treatment. The only way to find the right time is by empirical evidence, that is to say, by experimentation. I found that shorter or longer interruptions at times when they appear propitious are not only helpful to test the patient's capacity to be on his own, but they also force the patient to experience more profoundly his dependency needs and at the same time to recognize that he is able to function without the therapist's aid. The same can be achieved by the less radical method of changing the frequency of the interviews. This procedure often tremendously reduces the total number of interviews, if not the total length of the treatment. For further details I have to refer to my publications on this subject.[1,4-7]

The question of interruptions and termination leads us to another shortcoming of the standard procedure. Briefly stated, this consists in a tendency to underestimate the spontaneous recuperative faculty of the ego. In the primitive phases of medicine the main emphasis was on the medicine man's activities, just as in our field our emphasis is on the physician's activities. He is the one who expels the evil spirits. He is the one who excises the diseased parts and introduces the healing agent. He is the one who restores mental health with his interpretations. Beginning with Hippocrates, physicians increasingly recognized that healing is contingent upon the native recuperative faculties of the organism. The surgeon cannot heal the wound which he inflicted in order to cure. He only can create favorable conditions for the wound surfaces to grow together. With most of our drugs we stimulate or inhibit physiological processes, thus rendering the biochemical situations favorable for the natural healing process. In active immunization we only stimulate the organism's faculty to fabricate antibodies. In a vague fashion also, in psychotherapy, the ego's contribution to the healing process is recognized. We speak of sufficient motivation as a prerequisite for successful treatment. With our interpretations we support the existing integrative faculties of the ego. With our passive technique we try to stimulate the patient to find the solution through his own intellectual activities. And yet, we insist that most of the curative process should take place on the couch. Interruptions of treatment are looked upon as a necessary evil because we doubt that the patient's ego can accomplish anything on its own without our presence. This inclination introduces the danger of overtreatment. Informally one often hears of overtreated patients, but little is found about this in the literature.

Christian Reil, who in 1830 published the first systematic treatise on psychotherapy, insisted that mental disease is a psychological phenomenon which requires psychological methods of treatment. He wrote, "It is not since long that one began to apply psychic methods to the cure of mental disease and one recognized that the latter must be cured by such means."[19] He required that psychotherapy should become an integral part of the whole science of medicine. At the same time he sensed the significance of the self-curative powers of the personality. He showed an intuitive grasp of these powers when he discussed the rationale of his experiments with psychodrama. The patient, exposed to a drama, becomes involved in the plot. This makes him a psychologically active participant. Reil believed that this stimulates the patient's self-awareness and induces him to the proper mental activity. Viewing a theatrical performance, the patient has to struggle against imaginary dangers depicted in the drama. This stimulates his intellect and his feelings and forces him to find ways and means to rescue himself from the dangers dramatized in the play.

Heinroth, who in the first part of the past century followed Reil's psychological orientation, was even more explicit in his emphasis on the self-curative powers of the mind.[14] In giving full credit to the natural healing powers he was thoroughly Hippocratic. He believed in the curative power of time, and as early as in 1818 warned against trying to give too much treatment. He, perhaps more than modern psychoanalysts, was aware of the dangers of overtreatment.

In view of our knowledge of the universality of the regressive trend, both in normal subjects and patients, we should not forget the seductive power of the transference situation. In our Los Angeles study of the therapeutic process one of the therapists intentionally interrupted the treatment several times, only to observe the strange phenomenon that during the interruptions the patient became symptom-free and felt healthy and self-reliant. Each time the patient returned to treatment he redeveloped all of his symptoms. The transference situation triggered off a regressive process and he became again and again involved in his not yet fully resolved emotional conflicts. Then he got better, but before every interruption he again produced his symptoms as a means to prove that he still needed treatment. These repeated interruptions demonstrated the fact that the patient was capable of functioning without symptoms, and that being on his own stimulated his integrative faculties. Eventually, after 98 interviews, the treatment terminated and was followed up in the ensuing 3 years. It turned out that right after the termination he had a hard time and some of his symptoms returned. The subsequent follow-up visits showed, however, amazing advances both in his insight and general feeling and in his professional and sexual performances. The advances which he made after termination were greater than the changes which occurred during the treatment, and the last follow-up interview was most impressive in this respect. According to customary standards, this treatment was prematurely terminated. The term "premature," however, changes its meaning if one considers the goal of therapy to bring the patient to a point from at which his ego is freed for further spontaneous growth, and not to work through the whole psychogenesis of the neurosis on the couch. As stated before, we have no means to determine precisely the crucial point when the patient's ego can take over. Consequently, only experimental interruptions, tentative terminations, can help us to determine the right time. I believe that many of the so-called rapid transference cures which are not followed by relapses are based on this same principle. The naive and dogmatic belief that after a short but liberating transference experience no real personality change can take place is based on the conviction that a neurotic patient's ego has no capacity for further growth without our continued active help. The undue prolongation of the treatment beyond the crucial point when the patient's ego could take over—even though with struggles and relapses—is not only nontherapeutic but also antitherapeutic. Continuation of intensive treatment after this point demoralizes the patient. It undermines, to use Rado's term, "his self-reliant potentialities."

The question of how much treatment a patient needs leads us to the large and problematic area of indication. In acute neuroses which follow extremely traumatic experiences of physical or interpersonal nature, often so-called supportive measures are sufficient. In such cases the ego's otherwise considerable integrative powers are only temporarily impaired under the influence of excessive emotional tensions. In such cases reduction of paralyzing anxiety by drugs and support, by temporary gratification of the patient's dependency needs which become intensified through his defeats in self-administration suffice to give the traumatized ego a respite to fully regain its temporarily impaired faculties.

There is a dynamic equation between a person's native integrative powers and the tasks with which his ego is confronted. Neurosis develops—to follow the conceptual scheme of French[12]—when the integrative task exceeds the integrative capacity. The form of psychotherapy, its length and intensity, depend to a large degree upon this equation which varies from individual to individual, and which also varies during the course of the same person's life history. In critical life situations even patients who have been discharged as "cured" may relapse. Even thorough psychoanalytic treatment does not assure the patient that he will remain well under all circumstances. Patients may benefit in such instances from a limited number of supportive interviews.

It is erroneous to assume that the uncovering type of therapies, particularly psychoanalysis, are based entirely on insight and on emotional re-experiencing of past conflict situations under the favorable conditions of the treatment situation. The powerful supportive components inherent in psychoanalysis are largely underrated. The dependent transference situation because of its regressive nature does not only give the patient opportunity to revisit his past and try to deal with it anew, but also at the same time relieves the ego from the immediate need to meet his current life situation. The prospect for a long treatment, during which the patient is advised not to make important decisions, is a kind of moratorium. In some respects psychologically it has the same effect as seclusion in a sanitorium, which as we know sometimes suffices to restore emotional equilibrium. Of course, intensive uncovering psychotherapy is more than such a restful sejour in seclusion. I cannot sufficiently stress, however, the significance of correctly estimating the amount of help to be given and of the time when this help should be tapered off or entirely withdrawn. I came to the conclusion that missing the right time of termination does not amount simply to wasted time, money and energy, but may have a retarding or deleterious effect upon the healing process. On the other hand, it is equally undesirable to attempt to help merely with supportive measures a patient suffering from a chronic neurosis with a great deal of impairment of his basic ego functions. Such attempts must fail and undermine the patient's confidence in psychiatry. Since the advent of psychoanalysis, the psychiatric world became more and more cognizant of this danger. The opposite kind of misjudgment, however, entails its own dangers. These are of newer origin; they did not exist to the same degree before uncovering treatment methods had dveloped. I do not believe in the thesis that everybody can use some psychoanalysis, particularly if we restrict the term to the traditional procedure. If not indicated, it is not only uneconomical, but it might deprive the patient of a spontaneous impetus for further ego development. In a person's life 3, 4 or 5 years wastefully spent for treatment cannot be lightly discarded as insignificant.

On other occasions I have called attention to the therapeutic significance of differentiating between two kinds of regressions. Both have been described by Freud. He first described regressions to a period of ego development, in which the patient still was happy, that is to say, functioned well. Later he described regressions to traumatic experiences. He explained them as the ego's attempts for subsequent mastery. During psychoanalytic therapy both kinds of regression occur. Regression to preconflictual or pretraumatic periods often is mistaken as therapeutically valuable, when really it is only one form of resistance, an evasion to face the pathogenic events. The therapist's research interest in this early phase of ego development is easily sensed by the patient. Both he and his therapist delude themselves that they are making progress in reconstructing the history of the patient's neurosis. This type of resistance, if not detected, may be most time-consuming and may absorb the major part of the treatment. The second type of regression, that to pathogenic situations is, on the other hand, highly therapeutic. Not differentiating between the two may cost not only months but years. The research value of such delving into preconflictual periods of life may be, of course, considerable.

In a presentation which tries to evaluate the scope of psychotherapy and its place in medical practice, at least brief consideration should be given to the relationship of psychotherapy to drug therapy, a problem which recently has been receiving more and more attention.

According to one school of thought, which was lucidly exposed by Hoch,[15] the rationale of the administration of drugs during psychotherapy consists in creating an emotional state favorable to psychotherapy. He, as some other authors, such as Ostow and Kline,[16] considered the two procedures as complementary. Whether through reduction of excessive anxiety or reduction of the compelling intensity of drives, drugs may favorably shift the equilibrium between impulses and the ego's integrative capacity. Neither of these authors accept the thesis that simultaneous administration of psychomimetic drugs is incompatible with psychoanalysis. The other school of thought has much higher expectations for chemotherapy and anticipates that eventually the latter will largely replace the arduous and time-consuming psychoanalytic procedure. The philosophical fallacy of this expectation becomes obvious if one recognizes the essential similarity between psychotherapy and learning. The process which results in neurotic behavior—feeling- and thought-patterns—can be well described as an interrupted or faulty learning process. A person can be helped in his study of a foreign language by stimulants, such as coffee or dexedrine, which keep him awake and allow him to study. No drug, however, will spare him that psychological process we call learning. Drug therapy can only fulfill a similar function in the cure of chronic psychopathological conditions which result from the cumulative effect of previous interpersonal experiences. Drug therapy may make the patient more approachable to that complex emotional and cognitive relearning process we call psychotherapy. In itself, drug therapy is incapable of remedying psychopathological ego deformities which underlie the overwhelming majority of mental disturbances.

After having touched briefly on some major problems which confront us at present in the field of psychotherapy, I should like to highlight my main conclusions. My first point was that the statistical approach to the field of psychotherapy is not promising because of the great diversity of the variables involved and the difficulty in coding them meaningfully. In fact, for meaningful results only concrete individual treatments can be evaluated. My second point was that even if it were possible to evaluate statistically the relative merits of the different procedures as they are practiced today, in the present state of our knowledge this is less important than a better understanding of the actual psychodynamic processes which take place during treatment, and result in symptom relief and personality changes. Only such process studies will enable us to improve our different kinds of psychotherapeutic efforts. My third point was that psychoanalytic treatment with all its shortcomings because of its sound psychodynamic foundations has the greatest possibilities for further development. By recording of the interviews and by their observation by others than the therapist alone, the shortcomings of the procedure can be detected and the method of treatment improved. I see the main shortcomings of the standard psychoanalytic procedure in the overestimation of cognitive insight versus learning from emotional experience and practice as well as in the underestimation of the natural integrative powers of the ego. This manifests itself in an overemphasis upon the therapist's uninterrupted activities, invoking the dangers of overtreatment.

REFERENCES

1. Alexander, F.: The problem of psychoanalytic technique. Psychoanalyt. Quart., 1935.
2. —: Zur Genese des Kastrationskomplexes. Internat. Ztschr. Psychoanal. *16:* 1930; Concerning the genesis of the castration complex. Psychoanalyt. Rev. *22:* ???, 1935 (Translated by C. F. Menninger, M.D.).
3. —: Psychoanalysis (revised). Reprinted from: Psychoanalyt. Quart. *9:* 1940. 1940.
4. —: The quantitative aspects of technique. Am. Psychoanalyt. *2:* 4, 1954.

5. —: Analysis of the therapeutic factors in psychoanalytic treatment. Psychoanalyt. Quart. *19:* 4, 1954.
6. —: Psychoanalysis and Psychotherapy. New York, W. W.. Norton & Co., Inc., 1956.
7. — AND FRENCH, T. M.: Psychoanalytic Therapy. New York, Ronald Press Co., 1946.
8. BIBRING, E.: Psychoanalysis and the dynamic psychotherapies. Am. Psychoanalyt. A. *2:* ???, 1954.
9. FERENCZI, S. AND RANK, O.: Developmental goals of psychoanalysis. *In:* The Development of Psychoanalysis. New York, Nervous and Mental Disease Pub. Co., 1925. (Translated by Caroline Newton from "Entwicklungsziele der Psychoanalyse." *Internationaler Psychoanalytischer Verlag,* Wien, 1924.)
10. FIEDLER, F. E.: Factor analyses of psychoanalytic, non-directive and Adlerian therapeutic relationships. J. Consult. Psychol. *15:* 32, 1951.
11. FRANK, J. D.: The dynamics of the psychotherapeutic relationship. Psychiatry vol. & p. no., 1959.
12. FRENCH, T. M.: Integration of Behavior, vols. 1[1], 3, Chicago. The Univ. of Chicago Press, ???.
13. HEINE, R. W.: A comparison of patients' reports on psychotherapeutic experiences with psychoanalytic, non-directive or Adlerian therapists. Am. J. Psychotherap. *7:* 16, 1953.
14. HEINROTH, J. C. A.: Lehrbuch der Stoerungen des Sellenlebens. Leipzig, 1818.
15. HOCH, P. H.: Drugs and psychotherapy. *In:* Progress in Psychotherapy, vol. 5. New York, Grune & Stratton, 1960.
16. OSTOW, M. AND KLINE, N. S.: The Psychic Action of Reserpine and Chorpromazine. Psychopharmacology Frontiers. Boston-Toronto, Little Brown and Co., 1959.
17. RADO, S.: Collected Papers of Sandor Rado. New York-London, Grune & Stratton, 1956.
18. —: Adaptational development of psychoanalytic therapy, psychoanalysis and behavior. *In:* Collected Papers of Sandor Rado. New York-London, Grune & Stratton, 1956.
19. REIL, J. C.: Rhapsodien ueber die Anwendung der psychischen Cru-Methoden auf Geisteszerruettungen. Halle, 1803.

Part IV: Special Problems of Evaluation

13

AN EVALUATION OF PSYCHOSOMATIC PATIENTS: A PROPOSED METHODOLOGICAL APPROACH

by JOHN F. O'CONNOR, M.D., GEORGE E. DANIELS, M.D., CHARLES FLOOD, M.D., AARON KARUSH, M.D., MICHAEL LEPORE, M.D. and LEON MOSES, M.D.

IN THE DEVELOPMENT of psychosomatic medicine there have been essentially two phases. During the earlier phase a somatic illness was causally related to specific psychological conflict or a specific personality pattern. This direct application of psychological theory unfortunately led to oversimplification, and attempts at explaining somatic disturbances exclusively in terms of emotional etiology. However, in recent years attention has been directed more to the physiological and biochemical aspects of these illnesses. The resulting hypotheses developed are necessarily of a different order from those developed earlier. Concern has been less with the specificity of conflict, and more with exploring the mechanisms that lie between the emotional conflict experienced, and the physical expression of it. This has led to a re-evaluation of the mechanisms and effects of psychotherapy in terms of these more sophisticated concepts.

Early publications on the effects of psychotherapy in the treatment of psychosomatic disorders were generally limited to individual case reports. Although such reports facilitated the development of new hypotheses, very few of the hypotheses have been verified. For example, the theory that, suppression of anger produces striated muscular activity, leading to increased pressure on the joints, and over a period

---

From the Department of Psychiatry, The Department of Medicine and the Psychoanalytic Clinic for Training and Research, Columbia-Presbyterian Medical Center, New York.

of time, to the development of rheumatoid arthritis, suffers as a result of its oversimplification. Rheumatoid arthritis is a generalized and not a localized disease. It involves many areas other than the joints. Myographic testing has revealed no difference in muscle tonus between the rheumatoid patient and the normal.

Psychosomatic disease which, by definition, entails both physiological and psychological components, presents an excellent area for evaluating the results of psychotherapy. Unlike the neuroses and psychoses, the psychophysiological disorders allow for the direct measurement of change in an involved organ as a means of determining the effects of such treatment. The remainder of this paper will be devoted to describing such a study, and to elucidating some of the difficulties encountered in performing it.

Approximately 6 years ago an evaluation of the effects of psychotherapy* on the course of ulcerative colitis in 57 patients, was begun. The study team consisted of four members of the Department of Psychiatry and two members of the Department of Medicine. Three of the psychiatrists evaluated the psychological data. The fourth interviewed the patients and served as coordinator of the project. The two internists examined the patients, reviewed and evaluated the medical course. As the study got underway and as data began to accumulate, it became apparent that the methodological problems were extremely complicated.. In order to obtain meaningful results, many factors previously not taken into account, had to be considered.

Problems Related to the Nature of the Illness

One such problem was the variation in the natural history of the disease. This must be thoroughly understood before evaluating the results of any form of treatment, be it steroids, surgery or psychotherapy. In general, the psychophysiological disorders are diseases which tend toward remission and exacerbation with or without treatment. Though a certain percentage of these patients remain chronically ill, it is the rule rather than the exception that following an exacerbation a remission does occur. Changes can be coincident with, or independent of stressful situations, and chronologically coincident with or independent of psychotherapy. It is therefore impossible to

*The term "psychotherapy," as used in this presentation refers to a range of treatment from brief supportive psychotherapy to long term psychoanalysis. The majority of patients were seen for approximately seventy to one hundred sessions over a year's period of time. Only six patients were analyzed.

evaluate the results of treatment on the basis of the response of an individual patient. This necessitated then, either studies of a large number of patients or carefully controlled smaller groups.

It is important to determine the length of an adequate follow up, since in ulcerative colitis remissions of 2 to 5 years are not uncommon. One of the psychotherapeutically treated patients had a remission of 25 years before a recurrence of activity. The average follow-up in the study group was 15 years. No patient had been followed for less than 5 years.

Some patients who were doing well symptomatically, with a decrease in bowel movements, blood and pain, showed progression of the disease process on proctoscopic and x-ray examination. This raises a fundamental question in any evaluation of therapy; just what are the factors to be evaluated, symptoms or process? If we evaluate the symptoms, the patient has evidently improved; if we examine the colon, the disease has progressed. What is the mechanism of action of psychotherapy in such a patient? Is it that the patient's attitude toward his disease changed, resulting in a more realistic handling of it? Or has the symptom pattern changed without concommitant alteration in the disease process?

Since different types of medical and surgical treatment are used, they also have to be taken into account. Patients are frequently begun on steroids during the course of psychotherapy. When such a patient with active disease has a remission the problem of determining the actual cause of the remission arises. In individual case reports it is difficult, if not impossible, to separate out the main factors contributing to a remission.

The severity of the disease in itself is an important variable in the evaluation of either somatic therapy or psychotherapy. For instance, patients with proctitis respond favorably to any form of treatment. On the other hand, patients with total colitis do not have a good prognosis. Cessation of the disease process in the individual with severe involvement of the total colon, as a result of psychotherapy, would be much more impressive than in the patients with mild colonic involvement. If one's sample were drawn from a group of clinic patients, who had not been hospitalized, in contrast to patients who required hospitalization, the results of treatment would seem to be more favorable.

The age of onset seemed also to influence the course of the illness. In general the younger the patient, the worse the prognosis, the older the more favorable the prognosis. The prognosis of a female with ulcerative colitis is not as good as that of a male.

So that in setting up a study the group has to be defined not only on the basis of diagnosis, but also on the basis of many other factors. Therefore, the psychotherapeutically treated patients were matched with a nontreated group on the basis of four variables: age of onset, severity of the illness, sex, and the use of steroids. A control group is a necessity in psychosomatic research. It is of greatest importance in this type of study, since it is unusual for these patients to be subject to only one modality of treatment at a given time.

Problems of Data Evaluation

After dealing with problems intrinsic to the disease, difficulties specific to gathering data had to be faced. In the study there was a direct correlation between the patients' report of improvement and their positive feelings toward their therapist. This subjective evaluation proved to be inaccurate on many occasions. Similarly, in some of the cases the impression of the treating internist or psychiatrist left much to be desired. For example, two psychiatrists, both of whom were quite familiar with the disease, were rather surprised when they were able to observe the recorded data. It was the opinion of one psychiatrist that, not only had the patient responded well emotionally to psychotherapy, but also that there was a definite decrease in the severity of the disease process. On separate interview the patient concurred with her psychiatrist in this evaluation. Actually on the basis of repeated examinations of the colon, the disease had become more severe. A second patient and her psychiatrist concurred that her response to treatment was quite good. However, it was the psychiatrist's feeling that the patient had suffered from a rather mild form of colitis. While the patient had indeed improved, more important, the recorded data indicated that she had extremely severe colitis. Such incidents as these were by no means unusual.

Had the results been dependent either on the patient's or the physician's subjective evaluations, or memory, many of the conclusions would have been invalid. Retrospective data were not used. The most usable data came from the descriptions of the symptomatology and the routine proctoscopic examination recorded over the years. Many of the original hypotheses were invalidated when faced with the records of direct observation of the involved organ. For example, it was assumed that the degree of favorable response to psychotherapy would be directly proportional to the intensity and type of treatment: brief psychotherapy, long-term psychotherapy or psychoanalysis. Such was not the case. There was no observable difference in the physiological response of those patients who had been seen for 50 hours as compared to those who had been seen for 500 or more hours, although the degree of psychological improvement was directly related to the time in psychotherapy.

Method

The yearly colonic activity taken from the gastroenterologists follow-up records and the psychological functioning were both charted according to the methods described in figure 1.

The symptomatic activity of the disease was measured in terms of severity of bowel symptoms (see "symptomatic course" in fig. 1). In general, the amount of diarrhea reflects the severity of the clinical picture, if one excludes such factors as arthritis and skin infection.

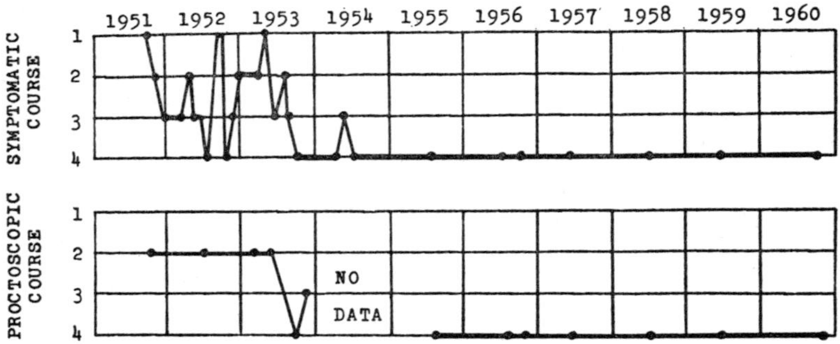

HOSPITALIZATION

11/51 7/52 3/53

PSYCHOTHERAPY

3/53 1/54 134 SESSIONS

SIGNIFICANT ENVIRONMENTAL CHANGES

• ENTERED OWN BUSINESS

EMOTIONAL RESPONSE TO PSYCHOTHERAPY:

RATINGS	BEFORE	AFTER
CAREER	2	5
SEXUAL & MARITAL	2	4
FAMILY	2	3
SELF-ESTEEM	2	5
OBSERVER		4

STEROIDS: NONE

PSYCHIATRIC DIAGNOSIS: PERSONALITY DISORDER - PARANOID PERSONALITY

Fig. 1.

These are added indications of severity of the disease process. The criteria used in the Ulcerative Colitis Clinic were as follows:

1. Incapacitating symptoms including diarrhea with stools averaging more than 10 per day.
2. Moderate symptoms with 6-10 stools per day.
3. Mild diarrhea with up to 5 stools per day, or the presence of rectal bleeding.
4. Formed stools without bleeding.

   Proctoscopic findings (see "proctoscopic course" in fig. 1) were graded on the basis of inflammatory changes in the rectum: "2" indicated active inflammation, "3" minimal or equivocal change, and "4," absence of activity. Hospitalizations were recorded. The period of psychotherapy and the number of sessions were included on the card as were any major environmental changes. These were all related in time to the course of the individual's disease.

The severity of the psychiatric condition was determined by the diagnosis. An initial evaluation was used as a base line for measurement of later psychological improvement. In an attempt to refine an evaluative approach, a method developed by Dr. H. R. Klein for the appraisal of changes in psychoanalytic patients, was used in the following manner.

Four areas of life-functioning were compared before and after psy-

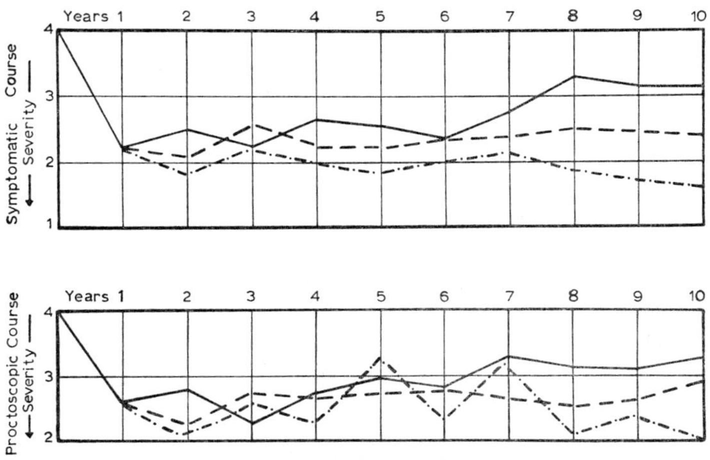

FIG. 2.—This chart is used for illustration. Although it is based on the findings gathered to date, minor variations can be expected when all the data are compiled.

chiatric treatment: career (or social), sexual and marital, family, and self-esteem. The level of function in each area was rated on a 1-5 scale, 5 indicating normal functioning and 1, poorest functioning (see "emotional response to psychotherapy" in fig. 1). An illustration is the following rating scheme for the area "career" (these measurements are exclusive of inability resulting from any impairment due directly to the severity of the colitis): "1 indicates incapable of any work; 2, unable to work more than half time, with minimal pleasure or gratification; 3, works much of the time, fairly effectively, possibly below level of training, but with limited pleasure and gratification; 4, works steadily, effectively, minor periods of dysfunction, periods of reduced pleasure; and 5, able to enjoy sustained, consistently satisfactory and harmonious work adjustment; a high degree of gratification and pleasure." The bottom right box (fig. 1) indicates whether or not the patient had been on steroids, and the psychiatric diagnosis according to the American Psychiatric Association's classification.

Figure 2 illustrates the 10 year course of the treated group, the control group and those treated patients diagnosed as schizophrenic. In averaging the ratings of these 114 patients the curve necessarily is flattened as compared to that of an individual case (fig. 1). It does, however, allow one to observe the differences in response among the treated, untreated and schizophrenic group during the period of observation. The study concentrated not on the observation of the results of psychotherapy at a single point in time, but rather on a continuous follow-up. In compiling the results in a given year it is apparent that they differ from other years, even in a large number of patients. This can be misleading and one could assume on the basis of a single year that psychotherapy has no effect (sixth year), is detrimental to the patient (third year) or is quite effective (8th year). This problem can only be overcome by taking into account the long-term course of the disease. In figue 2, at certain times, all groups show the same amount of pathology, either symptomatically or proctoscopically, but over the total time period the psychotherapeutically treated patients show a definite improvement.

Another advantage of such an approach is that many other factors can be evaluated on the basis of the recorded data. As illustrated (fig. 2) the course of these patients diagnosed as schizophrenic, even though they received psychotherapy, is worse than that of either the treated group or the control group. One can separate out other groups of patients and compare them, i.e., those who have total colitis as compared to proctitis, those who have had favorable environmental changes, etc. These individual groups can then be contrasted to the course of the study group and the control group.

Summary

The psychophysiological disorders present an area where the effects of psychotherapy can be measured in terms of physiological change. In any such study many variables are present which tend to confuse the results and necessitate a carefully controlled study. The following factors were most important.

1. A means of measuring the physiological disease process; ulcerative colitis not only allowed for symptomatic rating but also for direct observation of change in the organ involved.
2. The nature of these illnesses tends toward remission and exacerbation. This makes a long-term follow-up and a control group, basic prerequisites.
3. The use of steroids changes the pattern of an exacerbation. Little is known of the effects of long-term steroid therapy in ulcerative colitis. This necessitates matching each psychotherapeutically treated patient who received steroids, to a nontreated patient who received steroids.
4. The severity of the disease process and the type of colonic involvement —total, segmental, partial, or proctitis are important prognostic factors and have to be considered in determining the effects of any form of treatment in this illness.
5. The age of onset and the sex of the patient were factors that had to be matched in the control group. The later the onset the less severe the disease. In general the course of the disease tends to be more severe in women than in men.
6. Recording of symptoms and proctoscopic observation done at the time of the occurrence of symptoms, or on a routine visit, was necessary. The possibility of retrospective falsification on the part of the patient or treating physician was eliminated. It enabled the study of the effects of psychotherapy continuously over a period of years, rather than having data limited to a single year.

The purpose of the study was to determine the effect of psychotherapy on a medical illness. Measurements of psychological and physiological improvement were made. Each study patient was matched to a control on the basis of four variables, severity of the disease, age of onset, sex, and use of steroids. The physiological improvement was further measured in terms of symptomatic improvement and organ improvement. Conclusions as to response to psychotherapy were established on a base of symptomatic improvement and organ improvement.

14

EVALUATION OF PSYCHIATRIC THERAPIES IN CHILDREN*

by BARBARA FISH, M.D.†

THE SIMPLE FACT THAT THE CHILD is a growing organism complicates every aspect of the evaluation of psychiatric treatment in this age group. One must detect changes produced by therapy in an organism that is already in the process of change. The younger the child, the more rapid is the normal rate of growth, and the larger are the errors introduced by differences in chronological age.

Whether a particular bit of behavior is normal or abnormal frequently depends upon the age of the child involved. Behavior that is appropriate to one age may appear immature or markedly deviate if it occurs in an older child. Hyperactivity, dependency and many fears occur normally in the preschool child, but they may indicate disturbance if they persist. Furthermore, there appear to be critical periods of development for certain behaviors. After a certain age, a relative lag in development may become an absolute and irreversible deficit in function, as in the absence of communicative speech by the age of 5.[8] Therefore, in order to measure psychopathology in children, one must compare the findings with the expected behavior for children at every age.

A corollary of the rapid rate of development in early childhood is that all functions, physical and psychological, are more vulnerable in the earlier months and years of life. Either biologic or environmental insults may distort the functioning of a growing child far more than they affect the adult. Witness the effects of organic brain disorders and total deprivation in the first year of life.[7,18] Thus measures of intelligence are more sensitive indicators of disorder in children than they are in adult patients.[5]

---

*This work was supported in part by Grant No. MYP-4665 from the National Institutes of Health, U. S. Public Health Service, Bethesda, Maryland.

†Associate Professor of Psychiatry New York University School of Medicine: Psychiatrist-in-Charge, Children's Service, Bellevue Hospital, Psychiatric Division.

However, the plasticity of childhood may also lead to greater recoverability. In the absence of catastrophic damage, the striving of the young organism to achieve normal patterning and adaptive functioning is so strong that if one can eliminate the most serious obstacles to further growth, the child can frequently regain his momentum and reorganize in a normal direction.[7] This is one of the chief satisfactions in treating young children. One can frequently obtain improvement with rather economical means by using brief therapy of various sorts, and by manipulating the environment.[10,15] However, this extreme responsiveness makes it more difficult to weigh the effect of any particular aspect of treatment on the final result.

On the Children's Psychiatric Service at Bellevue, we have approached these problems by using a developmental frame of reference in evaluating psychopathology and the changes following treatment. The foundations of this approach were laid over the past 25 years by Schilder, Bender, Wechsler and their co-workers on the Bellevue Children's Service. These workers observed the normal maturational sequences of the neurological examination, the Bender Gestalt Test, the human figure drawing and the Wechsler Intelligence Scale for Children. They related these phenomena to the development of the child's spontaneous motility and play, his fantasies and social relationships. In investigating neuropsychiatric disorders, they studied the same functions in children with various neuropsychiatric disorders to determine the impact of the illness on the normal developmental patterns.[1,2,4,23] The problem child was viewed as a "problem in maturation in one or all areas of functioning biological, intellectual, emotional, educational and social."[5]

The author adopted this approach and followed the progress of neurological and psychological maturation in studying the natural history of normal and disturbed children, from infancy onward. The Gesell Development Examination[17] was adapted to yield a profile of the individual infant's capacities and handicaps in each area, and an estimate of whether development was progressing evenly or irregularly.

This analysis of development made it possible to distinguish mild neurological defects, and the fluctuating and erratic development associated with childhood schizophrenia, as well as minor variations associated with lesser personality difficulties.[11-13] There appeared to be a spectrum of development disorders. Severely disordered development occurred in organic brain disease and early schizophrenia. Milder degrees of retardation, acceleration or poor integration appeared merely to add a flavor of individuality to the developing personality.[16]

As an outgrowth of the infant studies, a similar spectrum of developmental disorders was used in evaluating the pathology of young children seen in psychiatric treatment. The diagnostic categories were divided into groups with similar patterns of assets and handicaps. Severity of pathology was defined in terms of specific impairments of function.[14] In treating disturbed children, these deviations from normal psychomotor development become the "target symptoms;" one aims to help each child achieve as normal a development as possible.

TABLE 1.—Outline of Development

1. *Motor development*
   - A. Developmental age level of posture and locomotion.[17]
   - B. Marked awkwardness (—) or agility (+).
   - C. Activity level:
     - Marked hypoactivity (—).
     - Marked hyperactivity (+).
     - All intermediate grades = normal activity (O).

2. *Fine coordination and visual-motor performance*
   - A. Developmental age level of "adaptive performance."[17]
   - A′ Or "performance" score on Wechsler Intelligence Scale for Children.
   - B. Bender Gestalt Test: age level, distortions, and "organic" difficulties.
   - C. Fine coordination, right-left dominance, apraxia.

3. *Language development*
   - A. Developmental level.[17]
   - A′ Or "verbal" score on the Wechsler Intelligence Scale for Children.
   - B. Educational tests.
   - C. School reports of academic performance.

4. *Social development*
   - A. Quality of relationships with parents, siblings, peers, teachers, therapist: patterns appropriate for age level, or problem areas.
   - B. Withdrawn (—), clinging-demanding (+), or aggressive (+) behavior.

The degree to which dysfunctions in key areas of behavior can be altered to approach the "norms" for the child's chronological age is a measure of the effectiveness of the treatment.

Problems of Matching the Pretreatment State: In child psychiatry, as in adult psychiatry, patients must be matched for diagnosis if the results of various treatments are to be compared. Diagnostic categories embody basic differences in natural history that affect the response to treatment. However, patients within a diagnostic group may have widely different spontaneous outcomes and responses to treatments. We have therefore subdivided the major diagnostic groups into categories with different types of developmental disturbance, which appear to be related to later outcome. A profile is obtained on each child which rates the past and current functioning in the various areas as to retardation, precocity or irregularity of development (see table 1).

In an earlier study of a population of middle and upper class children, the diagnostic categories of schizophrenia, organic brain disease and "primary" behavior disorders were subdivided, first on the basis of intellectual functioning, and second, according to motor activity.[14] These children come from families with a higher average intelligence and educational background than the usual clinic groups. The I.Q.'s in this group were therefore less subject to hereditary limitation or environmental deprivation and were assumed to reflect the severity of the psychiatric disorders. Such an assumption cannot, of

TABLE 2.—Spectrum of Diagnostic Groups

I. *Organic brain disorders*
- A. I.Q. under 70 — } severe to mild behavior disorders
- B. I.Q. over 70 — }

II. *Schizophrenia*
- A. I.Q. under 70 — early infantile autism, mute, echolalic.
- B. I.Q. over 70 — withdrawn, dereistic to paranoid, excited.

III. *"Primary" behavior disorders*
- A. *Hyperactive* — morbid fears and fantasies; aggressive and impulsive.
- B. *Normal activity* — neurotic anxiety, inhibition, obsessions, etc.

TABLE 3.—Distribution of I.Q.'s in Each Diagnostic Group

I.Q.:	Under 70	70 - 90	Over 90	Total
Organic brain disease	3	2	1	6
Schizophrenia	11	9	8	28
Behavior disorder	0	0	51	51

course, be made regarding other populations. In rating deviations of motor activity, hyperactivity and impulsivity in school-age children are deviations in the direction of immaturity. Hypoactivity is considered a still more serious deviation based on earlier observations of very young schizophrenic children.[13]

These subgroups were arranged in a spectrum of psychopathology ranging from major to minor disturbances of development. (see table 2).

The children with organic brain disorders had the most severe disturbances of development, and the children with "primary" behavior disorders had the least. The schizophrenic children had disturbances between these two extremes, those with mental deficiency most closely resembling the children with organic brain disease. Depressed I.Q., "scatter" on the WISC, and deviations in early motor development all occurred more frequently in the children with organic brain disease and schizophrenia.[16] In general, more severe deviations of early motor development occurred in children with I.Q.'s under 70 (see tables 3, 4 and 5).

Extremes of motor activity were also associated with more severe

TABLE 4.—Incidence of "Scatter" between Verbal and Performance Scores

	Scatter (10 points or more)	No Scatter	Total
Organic brain disease	6	0	6
Schizophrenia	24	4	28
Behavior disorder	23	28	51

TABLE 5.—Distribution of Deviations in Motor Development in Infancy

	Major Deviations	Minor or no Deviations	Total
Organic brain disease	3	3	6
Schizophrenia			
I.Q. under 70	6	5	11
I.Q. over 70	2	15	17
Behavior disorder	1	50	51

psychopathology. Hypoactivity occurred in over half of the schizophrenic children with I.Q.'s under 70, and in only one-sixth of those with I.Q.'s over 70. In the children with behavior disorders, those with hyperactivity had a high incidence of reading disabilities and "scatter" in intellectual functioning, compared to those with a normal activity pattern[14] (see table 6).

On this spectrum of psychopathology, based on developmental deviations, severity is roughly correlated with poor prognosis. Children with organic brain disease or schizophrenia who have severe mental retardation show a poor response to therapy. Children with the mildest behavior disorders, with a neurotic picture and no hyperactivity, show a high incidence of improvement with little or no therapy.[4,7-9,21,22] We have found that there is also a correlation between the severity of the developmental disorder and the potency of the drug required to produce a response.[14]

In children, the more severe, unchanging deficits in function have the same prognostic significance as long duration and chronicity of

TABLE 6.—Subgroups of Children with "Primary" Behavior Disorders

	No with Scatter over 10 points	No. Reading Disabilities No. over 6 years	Total
Hyperactive	17	12/18	26
Normal activity	6	3/24	25

symptoms in adult patients. Whenever possible, matching of treatment and control groups should be based on subdivisions of the diagnostic categories which have a similar prognosis.

Matching different treatment groups according to age is important in comparing adult patients, but it is of crucial significance in dealing with children. Differences in age increase in importance, the younger the child. A difference in age of 1 year in a preschool child or 3 years in a school-age child may be as significant as one or two decades in adult patients. Not only the absolute number of years is significant in children, but also particular ages when critical biological and psychological changes occur.

Our inpatient program separates the childen under 6 years in the nursery from the school-age children over 6 years. Actually, this represents a compromise for matching treatment groups, since 7 years of age represents a critical turning point. After age 7, many functions normally become more organized and stable. Hyperactivity, spontaneous whirling activity, and poor angulation on the Bender Gestalt test should be replaced by more mature motor and visual-motor patterns.[1,2,4] A school-age child in our culture normally learns to channel fear and rage in socially acceptable outlets, just as he controls his motility, and he learns to function in the absence of his parents. If preschool motor, perceptual or social patterns persist after the age of 7, it indicates some degree of immaturity. Such primitive patterns become highly significant of pathology in a child over 10 years.

Sometimes further subdivisions by age are indicated by the problem being studied. In studying the effect of treatment on autistic nursery school children, we use the developmental level of language function as a measure of severity. The longer the child remains mute, the worse his prognosis. Therefore, some attempt is made to equalize the number of mute children under and over 3½ years in the various treatment groups.

We have found that the responses to certain drugs change after the age of 10,[14] and it has been widely noted that psychiatric manifestations in children change after this age also. The fantasies of introjection of early childhood schizophrenia change to hallucinations and other projective mechanisms similar to those seen in adult patients. Manic-depressive psychosis may occur after 10 years of age, and neurotic manifestations begin to resemble their adult counterparts. We, therefore, believe that 10 years is another critical dividing line, and match our groups accordingly.

Measure of Change: The decision as to which aspects of change are pertinent to a particular study and what criteria should be used for improvement rests on factors similar to those discussed for adult psychiatry. Our approach to these problems has been essentially a clinical one. We have taken the clinician's judgment as to whether or not a particular child is better as the starting point for all other evaluations, and as our standard for determining whether or not scales make sense.

The goal of treatment is to make each child's development approach the normal for his age as closely as is possible. The "target symptoms" must be spelled out before treatment is begun, and will consist of those areas of development on the initial profile which were found to be deviate. When symptoms are only partly relieved, improvements are considered to be marked only if they include a significant improvement in critical developmental areas such as language, learning and social relatedness. For instance, in a nonverbal, autistic child, increase in alertness to the environment and increase in social responsiveness would be recorded as improvements; however, only the onset of communicative speech would be considered a critical change for the better, since experience has shown that long range outcome depends upon this.[8] Similarly, the loss of hallucinations in a paranoid child would be an improvement, but the change could not be considered significant if the patient remained so negative, hostile and excitable that there was no significant improvement in social relatedness.

We use objective rating scales as a way of making these clinical observations and judgments as explicit as possible, so that patients can be more readily compared, one with the other. We view such ratings as a way of examining the clinician's assumptions as to what changes constitute improvement, what factors influence prognosis, and so on. Rating scales will fall short of a global clinical judgment when they narrow the focus of observation, or distort the importance of clinical events. Such shortcomings must be recognized and corrected whenever possible. To some extent such errors are probably inherent in any rating method.

The global *severity rating* which we use *for children ages six to twelve* is a 10-point scale whose focus is the degree of organization or disturbance in integration in gross adaptive functioning, as observed by the psychiatrist on interview. We believe that integrative capacity and disorganization can be compared from one disturbed individual to another, although specific symptoms may not be the same. The relatively undifferentiated nature of most psychiatric disorders in childhood lends itself to this approach.

Severe, moderate and mild disturbance is spelled out for activity, anxiety, frustration tolerance, lability of affect, organization of thought and social behavior (see table 7).

This scale was designed for the somewhat heterogeneous population of school age which is admitted to the inpatient service. The psychotic

TABLE 7.—Severity Rating for Children Ages 6 to 12

A. *Severe:* (7-8-9)	Children whose behavior is permeated by unintergrated activity which expresses itself in severe hyper- or hypoactivity and/or extreme anxiety, with low frustration tolerance and lability or blunting of effect, with little external provocation. Thought processes as reflected in speech are unelaborative, explosive, disjointed, or dominated by unreal fantasies. Adaptive behavior is poorly patterned and characterized by negativism, aggressivity, passive clinging and/or erratic other-directed behavior.
B. *Moderate:* (4-5-6)	Children whose behavior is marked by a significant degree of unintegrated activity expressing itself in moderate or intermittent hyperactivity, irritability or apathy with some capacity for tolerating frustration and anxiety so that contact is not completely avoided: frequent spontaneous irritability and multiple problem areas. Thought processes as reflected by speech tend to be unspontaneous and restricted or explosive, with tendency toward uncommunicativeness or are moderately contaminated by fantasy and affect lability. Adaptive behavior indicates an awareness of social demands but is intruded on by aggressive, manipulative or phobic trends.
C. *Minimal:* (1-2-3)	Children whose behavior is marked by slight impairment of their activity pattern by bouts of hyperactivity or tendency toward apathy or some evidence of anxiety. Their ability to tolerate frustration and delay is impaired only in specific settings, and these are responded to with aggression or withdrawal which is short-lived and usually responsive to help. Thought processes as reflected in speech are contaminated infrequently with fantasy orientation, or there is a mild tendency toward explosive, or unelaborative responsiveness. Adaptive behavior either toward peers or authorities may be slightly impaired, but in general there is a capacity for sustained relationship with minimal suspiciousness, caution or passive magical expectations or lability.

children fall in the severe group. Those with severe neurotic character or conduct disorders fall in the "moderate" group, as do children with borderline psychotic manifestations.

We found that even when psychiatrists disagreed about the diagnostic classification of the children, they still rated them in the same category of severity. This type of scale, developed for a particular population, seems useful when used by observers who have already defined the grades of severity in terms of particular children with whom they are all familiar. However, the terms are too general to be useful in comparing data between two institutions. For this purpose, more detailed and specific scales must be developed.

The *severity rating* which we use *for children aged 2 to 6 years of age,* had to be related to developmental norms, since in this age group, the significance of symptoms is most dependent on chronological age. This scale covers the spectrum of severe psychiatric disorders which come to our inpatient nursery. Severely anxious and disorganized children, who have very severe neurotic or behavior disorders, or pseudoneurotic schizophrenia, fall in the "mild" category of this scale; children with florid schizophrenic psychoses fall in the "moderate" category and the most retarded autistic schizophrenic children fall in the "severe" category.

Follow-up experience indicates that the long-term prognosis in this last group is related to the presence of communicative speech.[8] Therefore the over-all severity is gauged by the severity of the disturbance of language development. This is modified only one point in either direction, depending on the ratings of social awareness, affect and motility. Minimal speech is defined in developmental terms, as less than 30 per cent of what is expected for the chronological age, and is spelled out for each age. When we checked the specificity of these behavioral definitions, we found that naive observers, such as first-year medical students, agreed with the ratings of the experienced psychiatrists (see table 8).

A more detailed *symptom rating scale* was needed for the school-age children, since we wished to dissect out differences in psychopathology between the children, and to follow the changes in different functions with treatment. The scales already in existence did not meet these needs. Some scales rated social behavior, but omitted most of the phenomena we wished to examine. Some relied on overly interpretive statements concerning ego function and libido organization. Other scales consisted of lists of symptoms and rated severity accord-

TABLE 8.—Severity Rating for Children Ages 2 to 6

A. *Language*

Severe:

6. Nonspeaking and nonresponding to encouragement. (Ignores directions and social approaches.)
5. Possibly few words in or out of context, or few simple comprehensions in context.
   If speech is present it should represent less than 30 per cent of that expected for the chronological age:
   for a 3 year old: no words; few simple comprehensions.
   for a 4 year old: less than 4 words.
   for a 5 year old: less than 10 words and 2-word combinations.
   for a 6 year old: less than 20 words and 3-word sentences.

Moderate:

4. Speech present, but predominantly noncommunicative and inappropriate; intermittently productive.
3. Speech present as above but predominantly communicative or more even production compared to "4."

Minimal:

2. Speech and comprehension usually appropriate to age expectation, but can be varyingly affected by many typical disorganizing signs (marked fantasy, word play to excess, frequent blocking, etc.)
1. Speech and comprehension predominantly up to age expectation in most areas, but may show "subclinical" signs of disturbance.

B. *Social Awareness*

Severe:

6. Totally evasive; apparent total disinterest in environment, avoiding all approaches.
5. Minimal response, but generally nonuseful.

Moderate:

4. Signs of awareness of essential daily routines and expectations, but limited response dominated by fear, withdrawal, active rejection of contact.
3. Signs (as above) but some initiative toward significant adults.

Minimal:

2. More often than not, appropriate handling of situations but unpredictable in variation. Usually makes contact with both adults and children with uneven success.
1. Usually appropriate response to situations, but vulnerable to certain (expected) stresses. Contact with adults and children to some satisfaction most of the time.

C. *Mood and Motility*

Severe:

6. Either extreme apathy /or/ extreme irritability; totally disorganized activity. Marked bizarre change in motility /or/ affect.

5. Any interruption in uniformity of extremes as seen in "6."

Moderate: 4. Predominant apathy /or/ irritability, which at times can be to some degree modified by examiner /or/ child himself. Disorganized motility and affect with high variability, but toward a degree of satisfaction.

3. Marked apathy /or/ irritability most of the time, but modification possible (with difficulty) about half of time.

Minimal: 2. Apathy /or/ irritability under a degree of control at most times. Changes in motility /and/or/ affect under stress are observable but relatively mild.

1. Unusual signs of apathy /or/ irritability rarely evident and then usually responsive to help. Motility /and/or/ affect rarely disorganized without understandable cause.

---

ing to the number of items present. We consider the latter an atomistic approach which does not reflect clinical reality. The number of separate adjectives which can be assigned to a child's state does not give a true estimate of the gravity of his difficulties. This is especially so if such items as nail-biting and hallucinations are treated in an additive fashion, without any weight given to their psychopathological significance.

We were primarily interested in the disturbances of integration at all levels of central nervous system functioning which characterize the schizophrenic state. Some of these may also occur in organic brain disorders and in severe neurotic disturbance. We therefore listed these major disturbances of integration as they are observed by the psychiatrist in each area of the Mental Status examination. The assumption is that the psychiatrist judges severity of illness on the basis of certain formal disturbances which can be compared from patient to patient, even though the content of symptoms varies enormously.

The symptom rating scale had to allow for particular modes of expressing psychiatric disturbances which are characteristic of children. The young child's manner of relating physically as well as verbally to the examiner is important, and he more readily shows disorders of motility than does the adult. The organization and content of his play activity must be analyzed in the same manner as the organization and content of language and thought. The abnormal thought content found in adult patients is rarely found in disturbed children under ten years. We therefore included those items which are typical of younger schizophrenic children (preoccupation with space, time, movement, flying, introjected voices, etc.). (See table 9 for outline; subheadings in parentheses.)

TABLE 9.—Symptom Rating Scale

I. *Reaction to Examiner*

a) Defective contact in interview or play situation; preoccupied to withdrawn.
b) Negative responses to examiner; reluctant to hostile refusal to respond verbally or to interact in reciprocal play.
c) Excessive clinging to examiner.

II. *Motor Activity*

a) Mannerisms: posturing, grimacing, flapping, athetoid movements; (vocal mannerisms independent of form or content).
b) Retarded or underactivity (reduced body tone; posture flaccid; motor compliance: "melting;" speech slowed, reduced in amount and volume).
c) Overactive (perseverated gross rhythmic activity: spontaneous whirling, jumping, etc.; speech rapid, increased in amount and volume).
d) Rigid, tense postures (hypertonic, stiff, jerky locomotion; tremors, twitches, tics; stereotyped rhythmic activity of body parts: rocking, head-banging, head-rolling, hitting self, etc.; speech tension: stuttering or stammering).

111. *Vaso-vegetative Function*

a) Doughy consistency of muscles of forearm and hands on palpation.
b) Circumoral pallor or cyanosis.
c) Mottled or cyanotic extremities; red to blue.
d) Constricted pupils.
e) Dilated pupils.
f) Moist, clammy palms, waxy skin.

IV. *Abnormal Emotional Reaction and Mood*

a) Inappropriate affect; excessive delay, displacement, to bizarre.
b) Underresponsive, flat affect; (no feelings of satisfaction: bored to depersonalized).
c) Excessively labile emotion; unpredictable, poorly modulated; (feels at the mercy of own affective storms).
d) Low threshold for anxiety; excessive responses to minimal stimuli whether irritability, anxiety, tension, anger, panic:
    +++ Majority of the time, frequently with little external provocation.
    ++ Frequent spontaneous irritability; multiple problem areas.
    + Related only to specific situations, but showing greater than "normal" response.
    (Feels bad-tempered, moody, oversensitive)
e) Appears distrustful, suspicious (feels wronged; from mild suspiciousness to delusions).

f) Appears angry (reports that feels anger, contempt, hatred).
g) Appears tense, apprehensive (feels tense, worried, scared).
h) Appears unhappy, sad, crying (feels unhappy, hopeless, suicidal).

V. *Abnormal Language and Thought*

a) Autistic vocabulary; nonsense words or speech at the level of jargon or below.
b) Confused, incoherent, disconnected or echolalic speech.
c) Irrelevant, tangential, rambling speech.
d) Excessively fluid shifts of thought or perseveration; short attention span, to primary process.

VI. *Abnormal Play*

a) Autistic use of objects with disregard for usual function.
b) Disjointed or stereotyped sequences or fragments of play.
c) Aimless sequences without organizing goal idea.
d) Excessive shifts of goal idea, or stereotyped perseveration of a sequence; short attention span to evidence of primary process.

VII. *Abnormal Thought Content*

a) Preoccupation with movement, space, time, lights, sounds, openings, heights, electricity, water.
b) Patient's conviction that he has magical powers, is able to fly, etc. (Rate "1" for some insight, "2" for no insight, and "3" if preoccupied with such fantasies without insight.)
c) Introjected voices or bodies. (Rate as in "b".)
d) Excessive concern over physical functions and body integrity. (Rate as in "b".)
e) Hallucinations. (Rate as in "b".)
f) Feelings of persecution or ideas of reference. (Rate as in "b".)

VIII. *Disturbance in Sensorium*

a) Decreased awareness of the environment.
b) Short attention span, high distractibility.
c) Disoriented for person; confused about age, family relationships, positions and roles.
d) Disoriented for place. (Rate "1," "2," or "3" if 1, 2, or 3 of following is incorrect:
city: name of hospital; home address.)
e) Disoriented for time. (Rate "1," "2," or "3" if 1, 2, or 3 of following is incorrect:
day of the week: calendar year: season or month.)
f) Obsessive concern with identifying persons.
g) Apparent unconcern with body boundaries—secretions, hair, clothing.
h) Impaired memory, recall.

IX. *Defective Insight into Symptoms and Need for Help*

The items were constructed as a unipolar scale, since disorders at opposite extremes (for example, hyper- and hypoactivity) may occur in the same child. Eventually the items will be weighted so as to reflect clinical experience as to which symptoms indicate the worst prognosis. In general, distorted and fragmented functioning has the worst outlook, rigidly limited or depressed functioning the next, and excessive functioning the least grave prognosis. (In areas I through VI, items are listed in this order.) For example, the spectrum of severe to mild disorder of affect goes from inappropriate and bizarre affect to underresponsive flat affect, to excessively labile, poorly modulated affect.

Behavior-adjustment ratings in children must provide for changing social expectations with age. The "social" scale of the Gesell examination[17] and the Vineland Maturity Scale provide useful measures of the child's ability to help himself and have been standardized for different ages. The expectation of a child's dependence, independence and reciprocity in his relation to adults and peers varies with age.

The child's adjustment to school and his ability to learn is as crucial for his over-all functioning as the adult's ability to work and maintain a home. Educational achievement changes slowly and is difficult to correlate with psychiatric treatment. However, more rapid changes may occur in attention span, distractibility, frustration toler-

TABLE 10.—Behavior Rating Scale

(Informant: Aide/Teacher ________________)

Ratings: 0 = not present 1 = mild, infrequent
2 = moderate, intermittent 3 = severe, frequent
(If all adjectives do not apply, circle most appropriate.)

I. *General Behavior*

A. *Motor behavior*
(*all 0 = no disturbance*)
1. Underactive-slow or infrequent activity.
2. Overactive-fast, restless, or bursts of activity
3. Poor large motor cordination: (run climb, throw).
4. Poor fine motor coordination: (tying, writing, sewing).
5. Peculiar grimacing, posturing or gestures.

B. *Emotional symptoms* (*all* 0 = *no disturbance*)
1. Indifferent, apathetic, withdrawn.
2. Sad, unhappy, weepy.
3. Shy, fearful, panicky.

4. "Touchy" or tense, irritable, excitable.
5. Moody, sullen, angry.

C. *Attention and perseverance in activities*
1. Inertia, disinterested, or refuses to try.
   (*0 = initiative and spontaneity*)
2. Absent-minded, daydreams (0 = alert).
3. Restless, short attention span.
   (*0 = concentrates, attentive*)
4. Poor frustration tolerance, gives up readily.
   (*0 = perseveres*)

D. *Language*
1. Speech "mixed up," unreal, not sensible.
2. Speech one-track, limited content or amount.

II. *Social Behavior*

A. *Relation to individual children.*
(*all 0 = positive relationships*)
(*+ = helpful to individual children*)
1. Unresponsive verbally, withdrawn.
2. Ingratiating, submissive, victimized.
3. Provocative, aggressive, assaultive.

B. *Relation to group activities.*
(*all 0 = participates*)
(*+ = leader*)
1. Reluctant to participate, withdrawn.
2. Excessively competitive, disrupting, aggressive.

C. *Group's acceptance of child.*
(*all 0 = accepted*)
1. Rejected as too peculiar, infantile, aggressive.
2. Victimized, teased.
3. Tolerated, ignored, protected.

D. *Relation to adults.*
(*all 0 = positive, friendly*)
1. Unresponsive verbally, withdrawn.
2. Clinging, demanding, infantile.
3. Negative, stubborn, defiant.

E. *Response to routines, directions, discipline.*
(*all 0 = follows directions and routines without urging or special attention*)
(*+ = "trusty"*)
1. Needs special attention, urging, help in dressing, washing, toileting (on 1, 2 or all).

ance, and the child's ability to tolerate the classroom and learning situations. The effect of these changes on the child's learning ability can be studied. The relationship between parallel measures of change is an important aspect of any evaluation of psychiatric treatment. Accordingly, we have kept these ratings of ward and school behavior separate from the psychiatrist's clinical evaluations (see table 10).

Whether a patient remains in or out of the hospital is a gross measure of adaptive functioning which can be applied to very disturbed children who are followed into adult life. It is far less applicable to studies of the prepuberty child. In this age period, a severely psychotic child may be kept protected in the community if adequate support and treatment are given. A child with less severe psychopathology may be hospitalized because his behavior is not tolerated by the community, or because his family is unable to give him the care he needs and the community provides no other alternatives.[5] Hospitalization in the face of behavioral recovery only points up the unmet needs for community services and the importance of social factors essential to recovery.

Problems of Relating Changes to Treatment: In evaluating the significance of short-term changes following treatment, and their relationship to the treatment given, the chief difference that children present from adult patients is their greater degree of spontaneous variability. Children also tend to be more dependent upon and more responsive to changes in their environment and particularly to the significant adults who care for them. The use of a placebo-treated group measures the gross effectiveness of the nonspecific measures in any treatment situation. However, in order to understand the effect of the hospital environment on an individual child, we allow a 2-week period of observation on placebo before instituting specific therapy. This period might have to be extended in other situations. Any change following treatment must be significantly greater than the earlier spontaneous fluctuations, for it to be considered an effect of treatment.

When evaluating the effects of treatment on children who are living with their families, one must have an intimate knowledge of the events at home and at school, as well as the changes in parental tension, the parents' attitudes towards the child and the therapist.[15]

Since children's symptoms change so rapidly with age, methods which use a child as his own control require even greater caution than is necessary with adult patients. These are most appropriate for short-term evaluations and for patients whose symptoms are severe and unremitting and who relapse when effective treatment is stopped.

In evaluating long-term effects of treatment in children, it is essential to identify improvements which are merely the result of growing up. This is easier to do when dealing with functions which can be corrected for age. For instance, one can see whether the rate of maturation changed significantly after treatment in following language development or intellectual and academic functioning. One could thus avoid an unwarranted sense of satisfaction in the acquisition of a few words by a retarded child, or a one-year gain in reading skill in a child who has been treated for 4 years by psychotherapy.

There is also a natural evolution of symptoms in disturbed children, since they face different problems as they grow older and develop different channels of expression. This was illustrated richly and eloquently last night by Dr. Bender. One must be aware of the critical ages at which certain symptoms spontaneously change or disappear. For example, hyperactivity frequently declines at puberty;[14,20] and florid schizophrenic symptomology may be converted at the same age into a psychopathic picture.[6] These changes occur spontaneously and may be falsely attributed to treatment which is given at this time.

More long-term follow-ups are needed, like the historic studies of Bender and Kanner,[3,19] to establish the natural history of childhood psychiatric disorders. The effectiveness of psychiatric treatments can be judged only against this background. However, it seems to us that there is still some justification for short-term evaluations in the treatment of children, perhaps more than there is in adults. Even if treatment only shortens the period of institutionalization, and so prolongs the time during which the child benefits from family, schooling and community life, one can hope that this richer experience during his formative years may give the child additional resources if illness recurs later on.

Acknowledgment

The author gratefully acknowledges the collaboration on the current studies of members of the Children's Psychopharmacology Unit, especially A. Friedhoff, M.D., M. Alpert, M.S., T. Shapiro, M.D. and J. Danziger, B.S., R.N.

REFERENCES

1. Bender, L.: Childhood schizophrenia: clinical studies of 100 schizophrenic children. Am. J. Orthopsychiat. *17:* 40-56, 1947.
2. —: Child Psychiatric Techniques. Springfield, Ill., Charles C Thomas, 1952.
3. —: Childhood schizophrenia. Psychiat. Quart. *26:* 663-681, 1953.

4. —: Psychopathology of children with organic brain disorders. Springfield, Ill., Charles C Thomas, 1956.
5. —: Emerging patterns in child psychiatry. Bull. N. Y. Acad. Med. *34:* 794-810, 1958.
6. —: Diagnostic and therapeutic aspects of childhood schizophrenia. *In* Bowman, P. and Mautner, H. (Eds.): Mental Retardation. New York, Grune & Stratton, 1960.
7. —: The brain and child behavior. Arch. Gen. Psychiat. *4:* 531-547, 1961.
8. EISENBERG, L.: The autistic child in adolescence. Am. J. Psychiat. *112:* 607-612, 1956.
9. —: The course of childhood schizophrenia. Arch. Neurol. & Psychiat. *78:* 69-83, 1957.
10. —: The strategic deployment of the child psychiatrist in preventive psychiatry. J. Child Psychol. & Psychiat. *2:* 229-241, 1961.
11. FISH, B.: The detection of schizophrenia in infancy. J. Nerv. & Ment. Dis. *125:* 1-24, 1957.
12. —: Longitudinal observations of biological deviations in a schizophrenic infant. Am. J. Psychiat. *116:* 25-31, 1959.
13. —: Involvement of the central nervous system in infants with schizophrenia. Arch. Neurol. *2:* 115-121, 1960.
14. —: Drug therapy in child psychiatry: pharmacological aspects. Comp. Psychiat. *1:* 212-227, 1960.
15. —: Drug therapy in child psychiatry: psychological aspects. Comp. Psychiat. *1:* 55-61, 1960.
16. —: The study of motor development in infancy and its relationship to psychological functioning. Am. J. Psychiat. *117:* 1113-1118, 1961.
17. GESELL, A.: Developmental Diagnosis, 2nd Ed. New York, P. Hoeber, 1947.
18. GOLDFARB, W.: Emotional and intellectual consequences of psychological deprivation in infancy: a reevaluation. *In* Hoch and Zubin (Eds.): Psychopathology of Childhood. New York, Grune & Stratton, 1955.
19. KANNER, L. AND EISENBERG, L.: Notes on the follow-up studies of autistic children. *In* Hoch and Zubin, (Eds.): Psychopathology of Childhood. New York, Grune & Stratton, 1955.
20. LAUFER, M.: Hyperkinetic behavior syndrome in children. J. Pediat. *50:* 463-474, 1957.
21. LEVITT, H. E.: The results of psychotherapy with children: an evaluation J. Consult. Psychol. *21:* 189, 1957.
22. O'NEAL, P.: The relation of childhood behavior problems to adult psychiatric status: a 30-year follow-up study of 150 subjects. Am. J. Psychiat. *114:* 961-969, 1958.
23. WECHSLER, D.: Wechsler Intelligence Scale for Children. New York, Psychological Corp., 1949.

15

THE CHILDHOOD SCHIZOPHRENIC'S RESPONSE TO SCHOOLING IN A RESIDENTIAL TREATMENT CENTER

by WILLIAM GOLDFARB, PH.D., M.D.* and
RUTH C. POLLACK, M.A.†

CURRENT STUDY AND MANAGEMENT of childhood schizophrenia has been enhanced by a climate of therapeutic conviction and optimism. The response of the childhood schizophrenic to psychiatric treatment, however, still awaits systematic, detailed evaluation. Although there is widespread acceptance that schizophrenic children may improve when treated, little can be stated with confidence concerning levels and rates of improvement and individual differences. One of the fundamental aspects of a global therapeutic design on their behalf is the school. To what extent are schizophrenic children responsive to schooling? Are they doomed to permanent impairment? If not, what is their range of educability? What factors influence their educability?

These questions are of major importance since, more than anything else, the adjustment of the schizophrenic child to school determines whether or not he will remain in his family and the community or be subjected to a drastic separation from them. When the ordinary school in the community cannot cope with him because of his disordered behavior, the psychiatric consultant is more likely to advise institutional placement and a plan involving 24 hour therapeutic management. At this point, too, the family of the schizophrenic child is more likely to accept a plan for placement of the child away from home. Similarly, when the institutionalized schizophrenic child can again adapt to a public school, his return to the community and his family

*Director—Henry Ittleson Center for Child Research, Assistant Clinical Professor of Psychiatry, Columbia University, Psychoanalytic Clinic for Training and Research.

†Research Associate—Henry Ittleson Center for Child Research.

becomes more feasible.* Although there are only a very small number of centers genuinely dominated by therapeutic objectives and possessing clinical resources for detailed design of a therapeutic community for children, these treatment centers have been able to create a professional climate of therapeutic optimism. This seems to be encouraging the public school's acceptance of deviant children and the development of special day programs for schizophrenic children living at home.

Within the residential treatment center, the school is an essential constituent of the therapeutic milieu. Not only is it located physically in the institution, but it fits its educational objectives and its conduct to the more general therapeutic goals of the treatment center. Highly individualized educational plans to suit the clinical needs of each child are worked out cooperatively with clinical and therapeutic staffs. Efforts are made to enrich the child's social and affective capabilities. With these capabilities as an integrating force, the child's abilities to orient himself to his environment and to manipulate it can be favorably affected. The teacher consciously makes herself available to the schizophrenic child as the latter puts out fearful feelers toward the teacher. In this manner the child is given a direct constructive experience in relationship with an adult person. Typically the child moves from early omnipotent absorption of the teacher to a position of separateness, combined with hope and trust in human subjects. At this point, the child's range of pleasure is expanded from the trusted adult to include the data of nature; and then learning in traditional school terms begins. This shift towards the interest in and assimilation of school facts such as reading and arithmetic thus presumes the development or improvement of some very crucial ego capacities, whose importance goes far beyond the specific requirements of education. These changes in ego competence include:

1. The attainment of more normal hedonic reactions (pain and pleasure) and their derivative emotions of pride, sympathy, group identity, etc., as the driving and binding forces in learning.
2. The improvement of informational intake through the attainment of a more rounded receptor behavior in which all sensory modalities, and particularly the distance receptors (looking and listening), are employed.
3. The attainment of a more effective self-awareness (personal identity) with clear and distinct consciousness of inner and outer processes.
4. The diminution of anxiety secondary to the serious deficiences in self-awareness of the schizophrenic child.

*It is apparent that the tolerance of the school in the community for the schizophrenic child in itself influences the therapeutic decision to place him in a hospital as much as the child's symptoms.

This report does not include a comprehensive elaboration of the ego functions that must reach a threshold of competence before schooling can be initiated. Four areas of changes in ego have been listed above to bring into relief the observation that when a child begins to give signs of being able to learn subjects like reading and arithmetic, this will have been preceded by growth in emotional organization, receptor behavior and orientation. This point is of particular relevance in a program for the evaluation of change in schizophrenic children. Clinical experience supports the observation that progress in school achievement is paralleled by progress in ego organization. It may thus be presumed that a study of longitudinal changes in educational attainment will reveal the schizophrenic child's more general maturation in self-regulation and self-direction.

In view of the practical and therapeutic value of school progress to the schizophrenic child, there is patent and immediate profit in the estimation of his growth in educational achievement while in psychiatric treatment. In addition, such assay of his educational progress recommends itself as a particularly apt device where one is seeking more generally methods for the systematic description of behavioral changes of schizophrenic children.

Effective evaluation methods are as difficult to develop or to find as they are essential. A number of questions suggest themselves. For example, what changes represent genuine and significant alterations in ego organization? In turn, what appraisal techniques reflect such meaningful shifts in a sensitive and reliable fashion? Two obvious approaches may be used. One approach is to note the presence or absence of behavioral traits which characterize all normal children from early infancy. In this instance, the absence of the trait in question would always represent a qualitative aberration from normal. Illustrations of such deviancy in an early school age childhood schizophrenic are many; for example, characteristics such as spontaneous whirling, avoidance of auditory or visual stimuli, absence of pain and defective pleasure with people or objects. The second evaluation approach exploits the fact that childhood is intrinsically a period of growth in many ego functions. Provided the child possesses normal potentiality and is given favorable environmental opportunity, the child may then be expected to show a smooth and rising curve of growth in these functions. In this instance, norms of growth can be established and a normal curve derived from the data. Growth curves of special groups can then be compared with the normal population.

In addition, individual curves of growth can be examined for gross deviancy or sudden change in direction or tempo (acceleration or deceleration). An unusual shift in curve trend serves as a signal reminding the investigator to search for relevant factors in very much the same way that an industrial analyst analyzes curves of production for purposes of control. The second approach is exemplified in the evaluation of educational attainment, which normally rises in a smooth, curvilinear fashion throughout childhood. (Normal curves of competence in reading and arithmetic, derived from standardization data in the Metropolitan Achievement Tests are shown in figures 1 and 3.)

The longitudinal evaluation of change in a child while in residence in a treatment center represents a unique form of appraisal. It represents the estimation of changes in a child while he is in treatment. The method is uniquely possible in a small, intensive treatment center able to treat children for long periods; and is in sharp contrast to evaluation approaches at varying intervals following completion of the treatment.

The educational growth of schizophrenic children in residential treatment at the Ittleson Center for Child Research has been studied systematically since 1956. This study of the educability of schizophrenic children is part of a larger design for the investigation of longitudinal changes of schizophrenic children, utilizing clinical and experimental procedures. The study was initiated at a point in the development of the Center when an acceptable therapeutic climate and program had been achieved. The school, for example, had been stabilized. All children were in attendance at the school. The teachers had achieved a desirable level of assurance and were consciously and competently participating in a treatment effort. In addition to the stabilization of treatment atmosphere and school, the Center was in process of constructing a descriptive and experimental basis for subdividing the schizophrenic children along dimensions other than educational. This makes it practicable first to discover factors which correlate with educational and clinical progress and then ultimately to proceed to a prediction and prospective study of such progress in a new group of schizophrenic children.

It needs to be pointed out that methodologic considerations have influenced the selection of schizophrenic children for admission and, therefore, for study.* Thus, for example, because of our desire to

*Selective factors are equally operative in other studies of schizophrenic children, though these factors may vary with the research setting.

study psychosocial and familial influences in childhood schizophrenia, the Center restricts admission of schizophrenic children to those from intact homes and whose parents and siblings are available for study and treatment. The psychodynamic development and structure of such schizophrenic children may well be quite divergent from that of schizophrenic children from broken homes and reared in situations of manifest neglect. It has seemed probable that the exclusion of schizophrenic children from homes with manifest neglect and the requirement of familial intactness have brought the most extremely impaired schizophrenic children to the Ittleson Center. The age of admission to treatment and study and the age range of the group were also arbitrarily controlled. The conviction determining the age of the group was that it would be more feasible to attain specialized therapeutic and investigative skills if the complicating parameter of age could be controlled. Thus the population was limited to the age range of 6 to 11 years of age. Because the Center has been more interested in the longitudinal study of a small group of children than in the cross-sectional study of larger samples of children, the children have been admitted to the Center at the lower end of the desired age range to permit sufficiently prolonged periods of treatment and study. Further, since this is a situation where one views the developmental effects of age as well as the clinical phenomena of interest, it seemed advisable to control the age factor as much as possible by increasing the homogeneity of the group studied with reference to age. The children have thus been admitted between 6 and 7 years of age. Of course, this has brought the children into the Center at an age when formal schooling is ordinarily initiated.

The age requirements of a treatment center for children influences the average age of onset of the children's disorders. Although the Center staff has ordinarily found it impossible to ascertain precisely the age of onset of the schizophrenic child's disordered behavior, a review of the onset histories of the children in the present study who were admitted at 6 to 7 years of age, indicates an insidious onset with disordered growth in ego virtually from birth in all the children.

There remains to discuss a methodologic issue of primary importance in any investigation of childhood schizophrenia. A recent series of investigations have confirmed that the classification of childhood schizophrenia is a nonspecific designation subsuming a group of children with a broad diversity of disorders. (1) Certainly, treating the children as a single group, even though they are actually heterogeneous in background, symptoms, ego predispositions and potentialities for change, may be expected to confound the search for cause and the study of treatment change. In the data that follow, therefore, an effort will be made to implement the conviction that the ego disorders of childhood schizophrenia reflect multiple factors, oftimes in combination. As will become clear in the data to be presented, subdividing the children who are usually included under the umbrella classification of childhood schizophrenia brings certain trends into relief which are beclouded when the children are treated as a single group. The Ittleson Center has been employing two subclassifications, each to be regarded as a broad category of behavioral disorder. Utilizing independent neurological judgment, based on examination and history, and a dimensional approach to such judgment of neurological adequacy, one group of children emerges with evidence of neurological impairment. For convenience these children are termed "organic." The remainder of the children, who are judged by the neurologist to be free of neurological impairment, are termed "nonorganic." These subclasses within the childhood schizophrenia group have been shown to differ in cognitive and psychomotor abilities, with the "nonorganic" group consistently superior to the "organic." There are family differences too. The families of the "organic" children are similar to normal families in psychosocial adequacy, in measures of central tendency and variability, while the families of the "nonorganic" children are always below the average of normal control families in psychosocial adequacy.[1,2] Recently, it has been demonstrated that there is a higher incidence of psychosis among the parents of the "nonorganic" children than those of the "organic" children.[3] In the educational data to be presented, therefore, the findings of "organic" and "nonorganic" subgroups will be separated.

The educational curves to be presented are derived from the longitudinal study of educational growth of 37 schizophrenic children, treated psychiatrically while in residence at the Ittleson Center. These children constitute all the schizophrenic children who have been under residential care over the past 5 years for periods of more than 18 months. The group contains 27 boys and 10 girls. There are 25 children (19 boys and 6 girls) in the "organic" subcluster and 12 children (8 boys, 4 girls) in the "nonorganic" subcluster. The "organic" children were admitted at a mean age of 7 years and the "nonorganic" children at a mean age of 6 years and 9 months.

Every 6 months the children were administered the Metropolitan

Achievement Tests which include the basic skill subjects that were of most interest, that is reading and arithmetic. This test series is an unusually comprehensive one, containing five batteries covering the entire elementary grades, including Primary I (grades 1, 2), Primary II (grades 2, 3), Elementary (grades 3, 4), Intermediate (grades 5, 6, 7) and Advanced (grades 7, 8, 9). For each child, the appropriate battery was employed in accord with his educational level. In the present group, Primary Batteries I and II and the Elementary Battery were chiefly necessary. Alternative test forms of the various batteries are available and were actually employed to avoid the contaminating disadvantages of repeating the same test with a given child. Because different test forms as well as batteries were administered to the children, their performance in each test is best described in terms of a unit of measurement that is a variant of the standard score.* The use of the standard score enables one to move from one battery and form to another and thus to record longitudinal curves of educational growth for the individual children and for groupings of the children.

As the child grows older, his skill in reading and arithmetic is assayed for a somewhat changing variety of subtests, appropriate for the given level. Thus, for example, while number concepts are stressed in the Primary I battery, arithmetic reasoning and arithmetic fundamentals are tested in the higher batteries. The score used in this study is the average of subtest scores.

In figures 1-4, curves for reading and arithmetic are presented separately for boys and girls in the "organic" and "nonorganic" subclusters. The curves are drawn on semi-longarithmic paper to clarify rate of change as well as level of performance as read from the altitude of the curves. The vertical axis represents educational attainment in standard score units. Duration of schooling, represented in the horizontal axis, may be expressed either in terms of the age of the child when tested or the duration of psychiatric treatment. Since the children have been tested at intervals of 6 months, i.e., at the middle and end of the school years, group medians have been computed at half year intervals. To smooth the curve, the method of moving averages was used, based on the mean average of three medians. When

*"The standard scores in the Metropolitan Tests are normalized scaled scores based upon the distribution of raw scores for a selected precisely defined population. This population was the modal age group at grade 6. The mean was arbitrarily set at 200 and the standard deviation at 20 points."[4]

a child could not attain any score in the reading test, he was assigned a score of 65. If unable to obtain any score in arithmetic, he was assigned a score of 105.

Six children (4 boys, 2 girls), all from the "organic" subcluster, showed no educational attainment throughout treatment. These children, who showed no educational response at all, were excluded from the group medians which were computed from the remaining 31 children, all of whom showed some degree of educability. Since the six uneducable children, whose educational curves showed zero slope, all came from the "organic" subcluster, their exclusion tended to reduce differences to be noted between "organic" and "nonorganic" subclusters of the schizophrenic children.

The educational curves of the standardization population can only be included in the age curves (fig. 1 and 3). For comparison with standardization population, therefore, these curves which relate achieve-

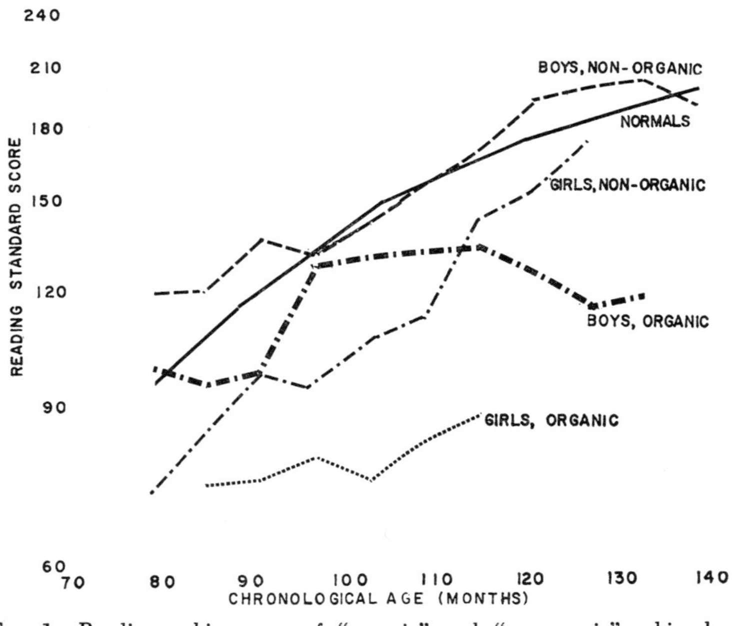

FIG. 1.—Reading achievement of "organic" and "nonorganic" schizophrenic children: by median standard scores of boys and girls at 6 months intervals of age. (Curve smoothed by 18 month moving averages. A score of 65 was assigned as the test score when a child could not attain any score on the test. If the child never attained a score on any of the tests he was completely excluded from the data.)

ment to age of child need to be employed. Obviously, there cannot be any curves for normal children which relate achievement to duration of psychiatric treatment. However, it will be noted that the curves of educational attainment by duration of treatment are smoother than the curves by age of child and more clearly differentiated the sub-clusters among the schizophrenic children (fig. 2 and 4). This difference is comprehensible because not all the children in treatment are admitted and discharged from the Center at precisely the same age, so that age increment and duration of treatment are not perfectly correlated. The curves of educational attainment by duration of treatment are the best expressions of change in treatment since these curves reflect most distinctly the results of treatment and schooling as well as the changes to be expected on the basis of increasing age and maturation.

The curves of reading achievement by age (fig. 1) permit a compari-

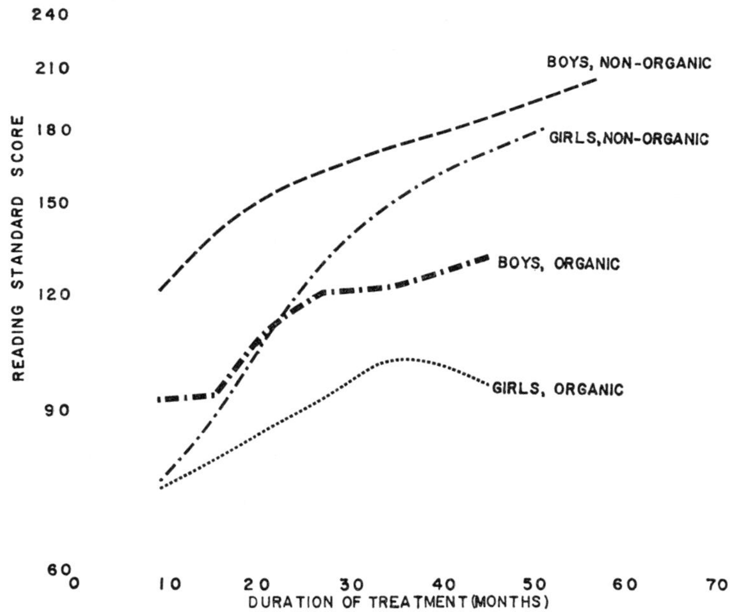

FIG. 2.—Reading achievement of "organic" and "nonorganic" schizophrenic children: by median standard scores of boys and girls at 6 months intervals of residential treatment. (Curve smoothed by 18 month moving averages. A score of 65 was assigned as the test score when a child could not attain any score on the test. If the child never attained a score on any of the tests he was completely excluded from the data.)

son of the schizophrenic subclusters and the normal standardization population. The curves of the "nonorganic" boys and girls and "organic" boys begin at 78 months, approximately 6 months beyond the average of the entering first grade child. The curve of the "organic" girls begins at 85 months, about 13 months above the average age of the entering first grade child. The "nonorganic" boys start above normal and generally maintain this position by a normal rate of increment, except for a slight dip in reading to normal levels between 97 and 127 months. The "nonorganic" girls start below normal; and although remaining below normal in the age interval covered by the curve, tend to move closer to the normal curve because of a rate of increment slightly above normal. The "organic" boys show an abrupt and rapid rise in reading accomplishment at 91 months to reach a peak achievement 6 months later, followed by a plateau in learning

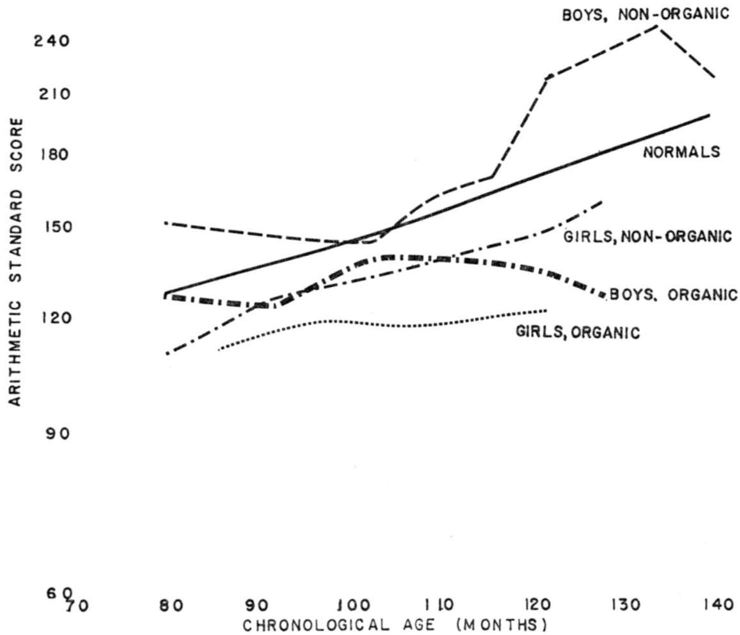

FIG. 3.—Arithmetic achievement of "organic" and "nonorganic" schizophrenic children: by median standard scores of boys and girls at 6 months intervals of age. (Curve smoothed by 18 month moving averages. A score of 105 was assigned as the test score when a child could not attain any score on the test. If the child never attained a score on any of the tests he was completely excluded from the data.)

with increasing gap relative to the learning curve of the normal child, who continues to improve in reading. The curve of the "organic" girls starts at the lowest level and shows slowest rate of increment.

Re-examination of the curves of reading accomplishment against duration of treatment (fig. 2) offers the clearest differentiation among the schizophrenic subclusters. These curves begin after the children have had 9 months of treatment at the Center. The curves may be ranked in order of altitude as follows:

1. "Nonorganic" boys—Their curve starts at the highest level and maintains its superiority.
2. "Nonorganic" girls—Their curve starts considerably lower than that of the "nonorganic" boys. Because of a faster rate of learning, however, the "nonorganic" girls eventually begin to approximate the boys in accomplishment.
3. "Organic" boys—Their curve shows a consistent rise until about 30 months of treatment, when the rate of learning increment begins to diminish sharply.

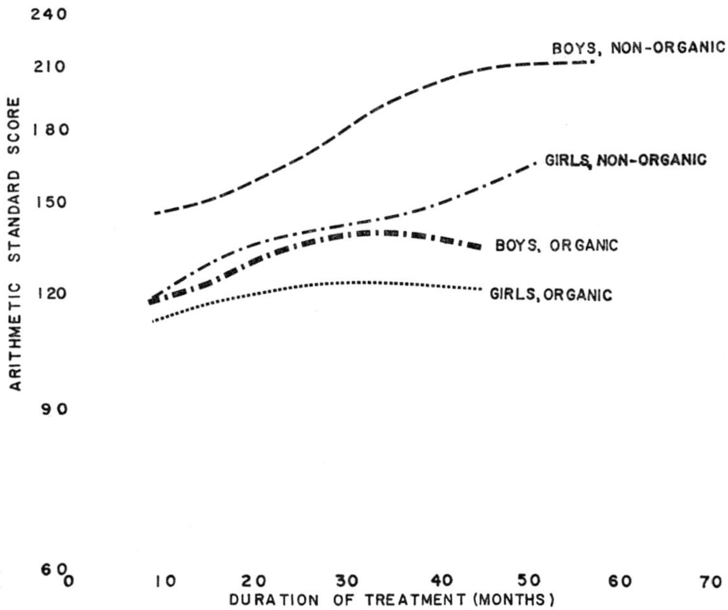

FIG. 4.—Arithmetic achievement of "organic" and "nonorganic" schizophrenic children: by median standard scores of boys and girls at 6 month intervals of residential treatment. (Curve smoothed by 18 month moving averages. A score of 105 was assigned as the test score when a child could not attain any score on the test. If the child never attained a score on any of the tests he was completely excluded from the data.)

4. "Organic" girls—Their curve rises at a steady rate until about 33 months of treatment and then a learning plateau is reached.

The curves of arithmetic achievement by age (fig. 3) are similar to the reading curves. Thus the curve of the "nonorganic" boys begins above that of the standardization population at 79 months, then dips toward the normal curve, with an upturn at 105 months so as to be superior thereafter to the normal standardization population. The curve of the "nonorganic" girls starts below that of the standardization population and rises at a normal rate so as to maintain its inferior position relative to the normal population throughout. The "organic" boys curve begins at a level equivalent to that of the standardization population but over-all shows little increment so as to end below the curve of the "nonorganic" girls. The lowest curve of all is that of the "organic" girls. This curve shows little increment and becomes increasingly divorced from that of the standardization population.

Again as in reading, the surest picture of growth in arithmetic skill with treatment is to be found in the curves of arithmetic achievement against duration of treatment. The curves of growth in arithmetic begin after the children have had 9 months of treatment. As in reading, some degree of improvement is to be found in all the subclusters. The arithmetic curves may be ranked in order of altitude as follows:

1. "Nonorganic" boys—This curve starts at the highest level and maintains its superiority.
2. "Nonorganic" girls—This curve starts at a lower level than that of the "nonorganic" boys and remains there. Unlike reading, there is only a suggestive trend toward approximating the curve of the "nonorganic" boys.
3. "Organic" boys—The curve rises to a peak at 33 months of treatment and then declines very slightly, so as to suggest a plateau.
4. "Organic" girls—Here too, a peak is reached after 33 months of treatment with a subsequent plateau.

Relationships among the curves are comparable in both reading and arithmetic. The "nonorganic" boys tend to be equal to or superior to the standardization population in educational skills at all points in time. All the other schizophrenic children, including "nonorganic" girls are inferior to the standardization population. However, the reading curve of the "nonorganic" girls appears to be approaching those of the normative population and the "nonorganic" boys. Of significance is the finding that the rates of increment of boys and girls in the "nonorganic" subcluster are comparable to that of the norming group in both reading and arithmetic. The "organic" boys and girls do show a response to schooling but their rate of growth is perceptibly less than that of the "nonorganic" and standardization groups. (As previously noted, the six totally uneducable children were all in the "organic" subclusters. Their exclusion from the present analysis acted to reduce differences between the "organic" children and the other schizophrenic children as well as the standardization population.) The more interesting observation, perhaps, is that these "organic" children do show an early gratifying response to education, presumably as their symptoms are ameliorated by treatment. However, they seem to reach an early peak of attainment and to stop learning prematurely. This phenomenon would seem to reflect the subnormal intellectual potentiality of a high percentage of children in the "organic" subcluster. The leveling of the educational curves begins approximately after 2½ years of treatment.

A very major advantage of longitudinal analysis is that it enables one to observe individual variations in growth. The individual curves can be characterized with ease and reliability. Table 1 describes the individual curves in reading by reference to two variables—first by initial level in comparison to normal, as defined by curve altitude, and then by rate of change in comparison to normal, as defined by curve

TABLE 1.—Reading Achievement Curves of 'Organic' and 'Nonorganic' Schizophrenic Children: by Number of Children

	Organic		Nonorganic	
Initial Attainment and Rate of Growth	*Boys*	*Girls*	*Boys*	*Girls*
I. *No Attainment Throughout Treatment*	4	2	0	0
II. *Initial Attainment Below Normal*				
1. Rate below normal	6	3	0	0
2. Rate normal	3	1	0	0
3. Rate above normal	3	0	4	4
III. *Initial Attainment Normal*				
1. Rate below normal	0	0	0	0
2. Rate normal	0	0	2	0
3. Rate above normal	0	0	1	0
IV. *Initial Attainment Above Normal*				
1. Rate below normal	0	0	0	0
2. Rate normal	3	0	1	0
3. Rate above normal	0	0	0	0
Total	19	6	8	4

slope. (The results in arithmetic are so similar that they need not be reproduced.)

The children in the "nonorganic" subcluster of schizophrenic children are clearly superior to the children of the "organic" subcluster. All the "nonorganic" children ultimately attain either normal or above normal levels of reading. Eight of the "nonorganic" children, 67 per cent of the total, start below the standardization population and eventually reach or exceed the normal children by rapid and above average rate of improvement.

Only the "organic" subcluster contains children who show below normal rates of improvement. Indeed these children constitute a majority (60 per cent) of the "organic" subcluster. Included in this group are the six children (24 per cent of the "organic" subcluster) who show no attainment throughout treatment. Nevertheless, it is

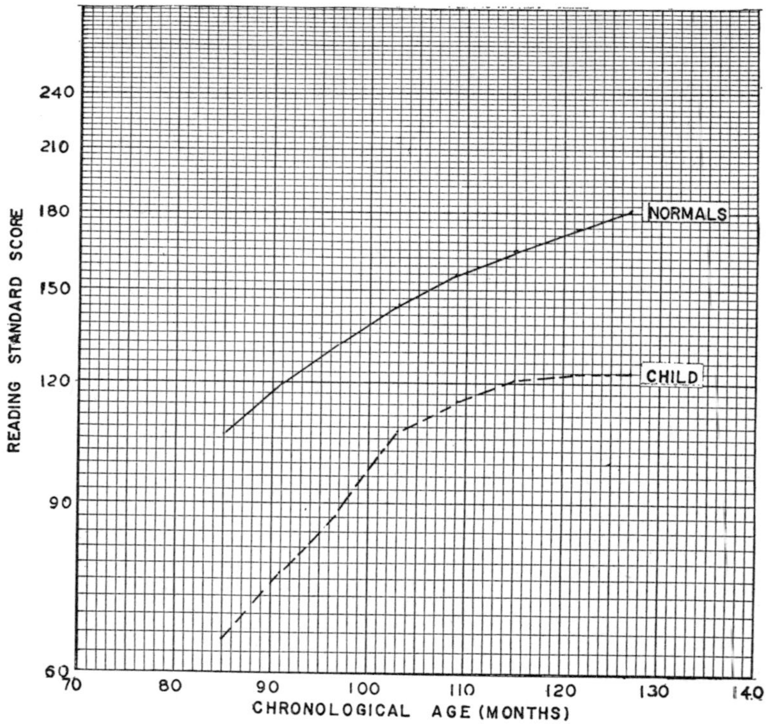

FIG. 5.—Reading achievement of schizophrenic child with initial achievement below normal and increment rate below normal: by standard score at 6 month intervals of age. (Curve smoothed by 18 months moving averages.)

noteworthy that the bulk of the "organic" children show some degree of educational response in reading (76 per cent of the "organic" subcluster). Ten of the "organic" children (40 per cent of the "organic" subcluster) show normal or above normal rates of improvement and six of these children (24 per cent of the "organic sub-cluster) actually reach or exceed normal levels of reading attainment.

An important and revealing subgroup among the "organic" children are 7 children (28 per cent of the "organic" subcluster) who start below normal and, while included in the "rate below normal" category, improve in a unique fashion, (see fig. 5). These children show characteristic stepwise curves rather than curves indicative of a regular rate of improvement. In this form of increment there is at first little or no improvement for a varying number of months after admission

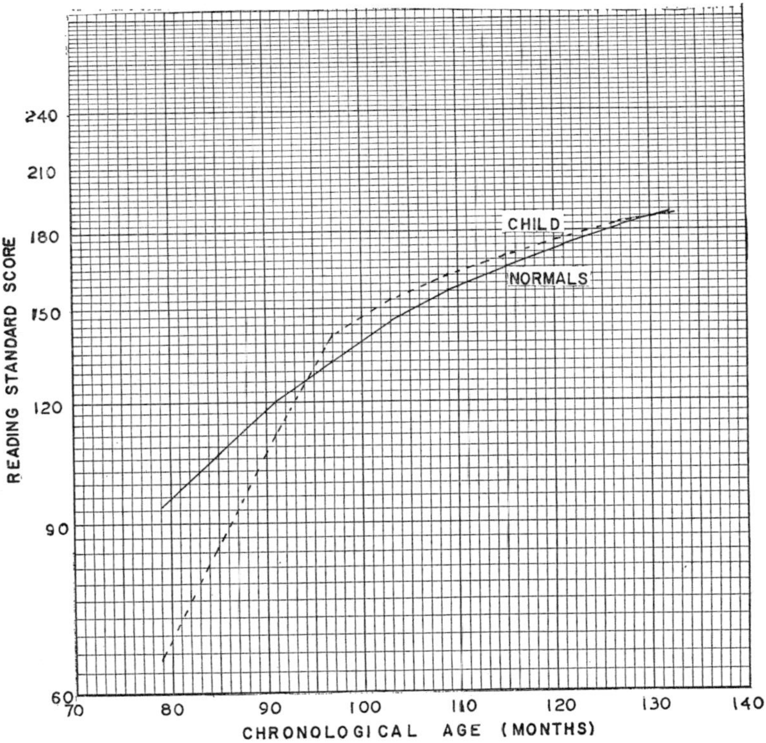

FIG. 6.—Reading achievement of a schizophrenic child with initial achievement below normal and increment rate normal: by standard score at 6 month intervals of age. (Curve smoothed by 18 month moving averages.)

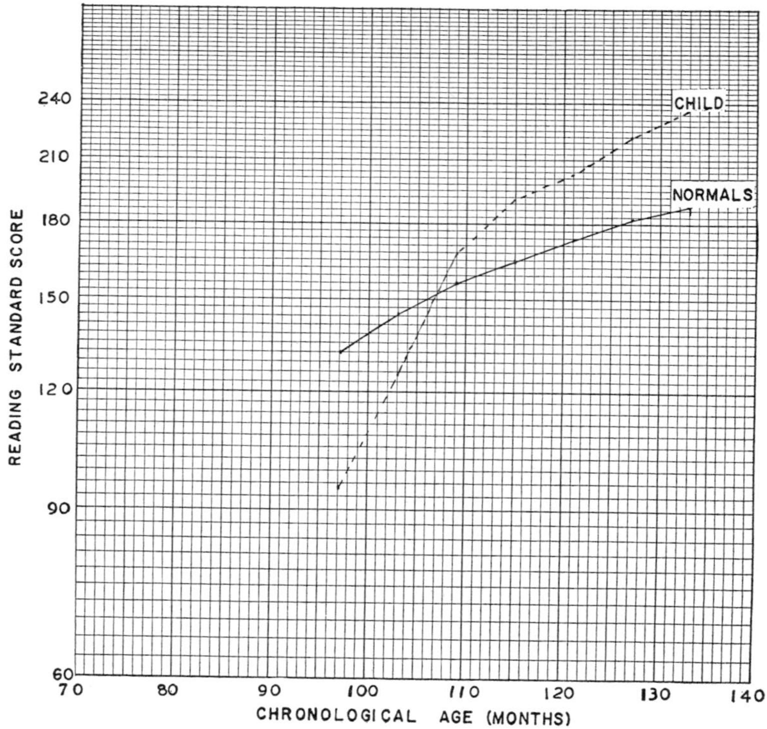

FIG. 7.—Reading achievement of a schizophrenic child with initial achievement below normal and increment rate above normal: by standard score at 6 month intervals of age. (Curve smoothed by 18 month moving averages.)

to the Center.* Then a sudden rapid rise in achievement occurs up to a peak that is still below the normal. This rise, in turn, is followed by a premature levelling off of the reading curve in a manner indicative of an arrest in further learning. The beginning point of improvement occurs when the children are at a median age of 101 months, and at an average of 18 months following the initiation of psychiatric treatment. Study of their treatment records indicates that the outstanding psychotic symptoms of the children are improved before the educational improvement occurs. The children have been able to develop object relationships and to engage with the Center personnel. They show a broader range of interest and pleasure; and they become accessible to visual

*The use of moving averages makes this phase of the curve less apparent in figure 5.

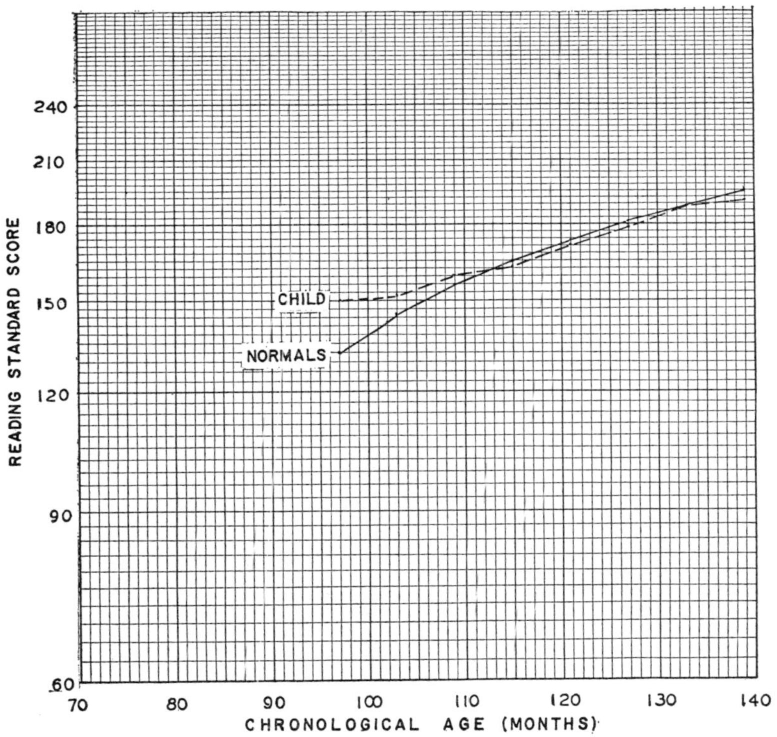

FIG. 8.—Reading achievement of a schizophrenic child with initial achievement normal and increment rate normal: by standard score at 6 months intervals of age. (Curve smoothed by 18 month moving averages.)

and auditory experiences. At this point, there is a burst of learning and the basic mechanical skills are rapidly achieved. When comprehension and conceptualization become more important for further progress, however, the learning slows down and the curve eventually reaches a plateau. This is true in reading when the test stresses reading comprehension; and similar curves are noted in arithmetic testing at the point where weight is given to arithmetic reasoning in addition to fundamentals. It may be inferred that at this phase of the learning plateau the children have been relieved of their psychotic symptomatology and are now reflecting the cognitive limitations secondary to cerebral dysfunction.

A child's rate and level of learning are normally related to his intellectual brightness. For example, one expects the child who is normal or superior in intelligence to progress at a more rapid rate and to reach higher levels in reading and arithmetic than the child who is defective in intelligence. This needs to be considered in the present analysis since a previous investigation of schizophrenic children at the Ittleson Center has demonstrated that the "nonorganic" schizophrenic children are superior to the "organic" schizophrenic children in intellectual functioning.[1] In the present study, too, the "nonorganic" children are significantly superior to the "organic" schizophrenic children in cognitive capacity. All the children at the Center have been administered the Wechsler Intelligence Scale for Children (WISC) on admission and annually thereafter on their birthdays while in treatment. An analysis of the children's WISC full IQs in

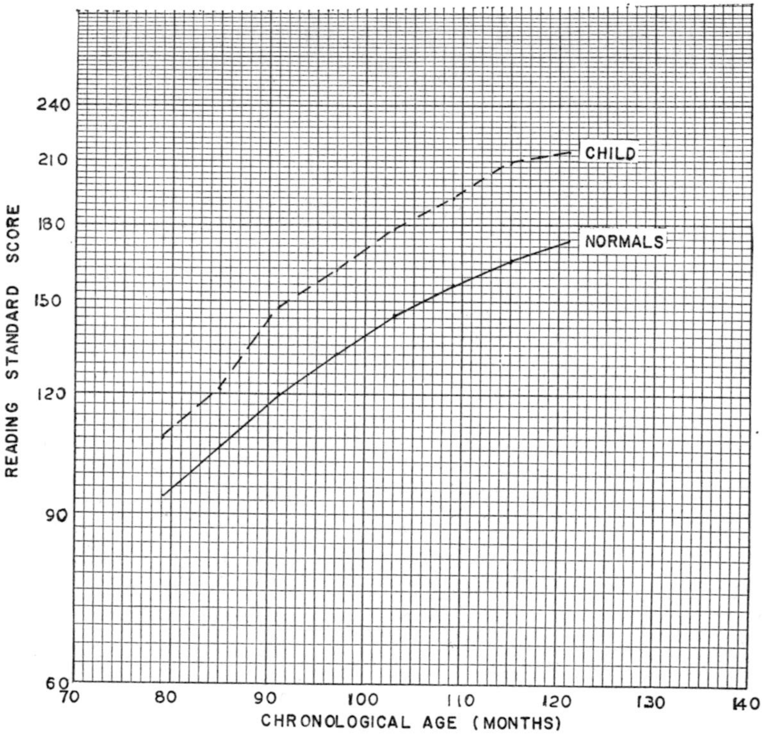

FIG. 9.—Reading achievement of a schizophrenic child with initial achievement normal and increment rate above normal: by standard score at 6 month intervals of age. (Curve smoothed by 18 months moving averages.)

the first testing* reveals that 5 of the 37 children in the present study showed such extreme incapacity that an IQ could not even be assigned. All five were boys in the "organic" group. If these children are excluded the mean full IQ of the "nonorganic" group is 96.9 ± 17.1 and that of the "organic" group is 69.9 ± 17.8. (These mean IQs differ significantly at the .01 level.) It is probable that a most important contributing factor in the differences in learning ability of the "organic" and "nonorganic" schizophrenic children (and possibly of the boys and girls) is the difference in intellectual potentiality.

Evidence in support of this likelihood is to be found in a more

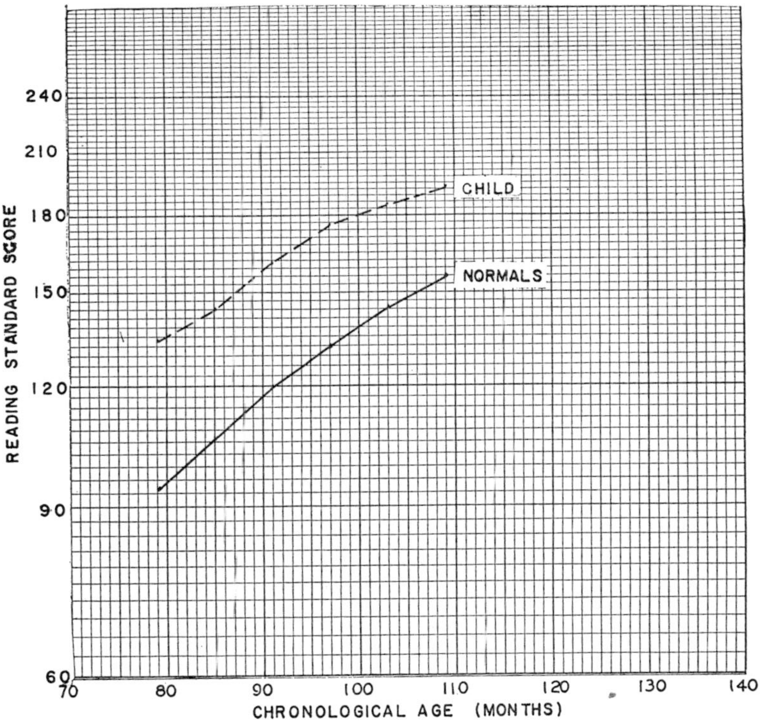

FIG. 10.—Reading achievement of a schizophrenic child with initial achievement above normal and increment rate normal: by standard score at 6 month intervals of age. (Curve smoothed by 18 months moving average.)

*Improvement in IQ occurred and will be summarized elsewhere. The first testing was employed in this study because of an interest in early prediction of educability.

detailed analysis of the educational curves of the boys within the "organic" subcluster, when the children are grouped according to intelligence level. (The other subgroups are too small to permit a similar analysis.) The children may be divided into four subgroups in order of intellectual functioning; that is, children with IQs of 90 and above, children with IQs between 75 and 89, children with IQs below 75, and, finally children with such extremely low functioning that IQs on the Wechsler Scale are unattainable. Figure 11 presents the reading curves for each of these subgroups. (The arithmetic findings are comparable.) The results are distinct and consistent. It is clear that the hierarchial ordering of the learning curves by altitude and rate of increment is in complete accord with the hierarchial ordering of the children by level of intellectual functioning. Thus the learning curves are arranged in order from most superior to most inferior as follows: children with IQs of 90 and above, those with IQs 75-89, those with IQs below 75 and finally the unscorable children.

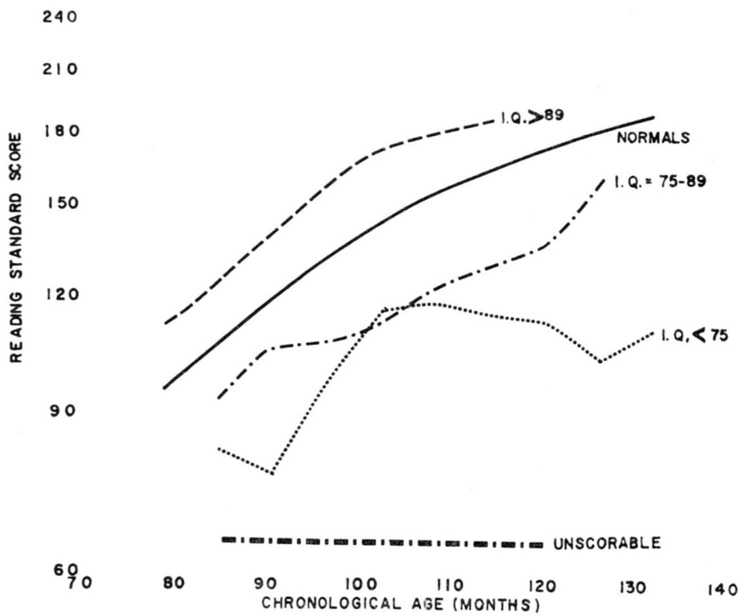

FIG. 11.—Reading achievement of boys at varying levels of intelligence quotient in organic subcluster of schizophrenic children: by median scores at 6 month intervals of age. (Curve smoothed by 18 months moving averages. A score of 65 was assigned as the test score when a child could not attain any score on the test. Intelligence groupings were made on the basis of the Full Intelligence Quotient of the Wechsler Intelligence Scales for Children.)

The curve of children with normal IQs (90 and over) is above that of the normal standardization population in altitude and shows a normal rate of increment. The curve of the children with IQs between 75 and 89 is below that of the standardization population. However, it is impressive that these children, too, show a steady and normal rate of increment in the age interval studied, i.e., between 79 and 130 months (6½ to 11 years). Children with IQs below 75 show a rise to a peak at about 103 to 110 months (8½ to 9 years) when a learning plateau is reached. As already mentioned, these are the children whose learning potentiality is restricted by intellectual incapacity once their emotional disabilities have been alleviated. Finally the children whose intellectual limitations are so extreme that an IQ score in the Wechsler Intelligence Scale for Children is not attainable are quite uneducable, at least as far as measured by the tests and during the period of time they are under treatment at the Center.*

These results support our contention that the learning differences between the "organic" and "nonorganic" subclusters and possibly, between the boys and girls may be explained in large measure by the differences in intellectual competence. Indeed the learning curves of the boys with WISC IQ above 90 in the "organic" subcluster are not distinguishable from the curves of the boys in the "nonorganic" subcluster.

This study should encourage a spirit of optimism in regard to the educability of schizophrenic children. It must be understood that the bulk of the children in the present study arrived at the Center without any educational accomplishments. Almost all had been considered unmanageable and, more often than not, uneducable by the schools in the community. It can be said emphatically that these most severely disordered children can adapt and respond to a special school regimen such as we have been able to organize at the Ittleson Center.†

---

*It must be understood that intellectual appraisal at the Center is very carefully done, involves repeated observations, sometimes as many as 12 or 15, and sensitivity to the emotional status of the child. Most typically, the absence of an IQ score represents a capacity level below the lowest standards of the Wechsler Intelligence Scales for Children. Scores are obtainable in infant scales but are not reported here.

†There is nothing mysterious about the school climate in a psychiatric treatment or hospital center. This climate can and ought to be delineated for application to community schools which could then conceivably absorb a good many of the children on a day basis. An intermediate experiment of this type is being explored in an experimental day treatment program at the Ittleson Center being run cooperatively with the New York State Department of Mental Hygiene for the same type of child who was previously treated in residence.

Within this therapeutically focussed school atmosphere, they are able to learn many important skills, among them reading and arithmetic. Thus, of 37 schizophrenic children treated in residence at the Ittleson Center in the past 3 years, improvements in reading and arithmetic skills have been noted in all but six children, that is, in 84 per cent of the entire group. Eventually almost half the children (49 per cent) actually attain normal levels.

Further information emerges when the total schizophrenic group is subdivided on the basis of neurological study into one subcluster of children with evidence of neurological aberration (the "organic" group) and another subcluster of children with no evidence of neurological aberration (the "nonorganic" group). All the "nonorganic" children in the present study ultimately show at least normal attainment. Indeed, most of them (83 per cent) reach above normal levels. Most striking among their learning curves while in psychiatric treatment are those that demonstrate bursts of learning, that is rates of increment in learning that are far more accelerated than that of the normal standardization population (see fig. 7).*

The children whose achievements remain so low that they are unscorable on our tests are in the "organic" subcluster. These children are the most impaired in general cognitive function and show the lowest capacity in a test of intelligence (the Wechsler Intelligence Scale for Children). It must be understood that, although they remain unscorable in our tests of schooling, it is not true that there has been no progress at all clinically or, even more specifically, in the perceptual and behavioral attributes that are encompassed in the term "reading readiness." Nor is it certain how long one must wait before an upturn in learning curve will occur or before deciding no learning of educational skills is to be expected.

The "organic" subcluster contains another group of children who show an initial delay in learning during a period when they are improving clinically and in general adaptive capacity. When they do attain a suitable threshold of ego competence, there is a rapid rise in reading and arithmetic skills to a peak which represents the limits of their capacity and a leveling off of learning below that of normal children. It is inferred that in these children whose brains have presumably been damaged cerebral deficits limit the learning potentiality of the children. They constitute about 28 per cent of the

*One wonders what the learning curves of normal children could be if they were given the small class groups and special educational attention given the schizophrenic children in the therapeutic environment of the Ittleson Center.

"organic" subcluster. Typically, they are much improved clinically after several years of residential treatment. That is, they have relinquished their bizarre symptoms, show a capacity for relationship, give definite evidence of appropriate response to pain and pleasure, attend to visual and auditory stimulation and are less frightened. Now they appear more like intellectually slow children. Their return to the community is quite feasible provided an educational plan suitable for the intellectually slow child can be effected.

Analysis of the attainments of one of the schizophrenic subgroups, the "organic" boys confirms the significance of capacity per se in determining the educational progress of the schizophrenic child. Even assuming brain damage, the extent of learning will reflect the amount of brain potential remaining. Prediction of therapeutic progress and assay of potential for change obviously needs to be based on an estimate of the child's ego capacity as well as of his motivational organization.

Psychiatric treatment centers engaging in intensive treatment of children are particularly apt settings for longitudinal study of individual children. The present investigation is the first of a series of group evaluations of schizophrenic children, in which the focus is on longitudinal trends in individual schizophrenic children. These investigations are prospective and anticipatory in design. In other words, utilizing guidelines from clinical, therapeutic, and experimental investigations with schizophrenic children, a conceptual model has been constructed, as the basis for observation and study of selected aspects of behavior in a group of schizophrenic children as they grow under therapeutic surveillance. The changes in the children undoubtedly represent age determined maturational growth as such but would also seem to reflect the impact of comprehensive psychiatric treatment as the latter is embodied in residential treatment. The initial efforts of the Center staff to summarize growth trends have brought a number of issues into relief. In concluding this report attention will be directed to some of these methodologic issue in the evaluation of change in schizophrenic children and the research decisions they require. More specifically, what is a representative sampling of schizophrenic children? Is representativeness improved by increasing the size of the sample? Is it more profitable to view childhood schizophrenia as a single disorder or as a multiplicity of disorders? Finally, what are some of the unique technical advantages of longitudinal analysis over cross-sectional study of independent samples in the evaluation of changes in schizophrenic children?

The suggestion has already been made that selectivity of sample is inevitable in any study of schizophrenic children and a truly randomized group is virtually impossible to achieve. This implies that each experimental sample of schizophrenic children may vary for arbitrary and accidental reasons such as community pressures and specific admission criteria. Proper evaluative investigation requires a vigilant and detailed alertness to the special character of the sample under consideration. Cognizance has already been taken of the selective nature of the sampling in the present study. As noted, these are children who have been admitted to a residential treatment center at early school age (6 to 7 years). In screening applications to the Center of schizophrenic children we have noted that the younger pre-school applicants have shown a higher relative incidence of children with neurological aberrations. To illustrate the selective nature of the present sample further, the Ittleson Center children are all children with fathers and mothers living together. The life experiences of such children are presumably different from the experiences of schizophrenic children who come from broken homes.

The size of the experimental sample in the present study is small, and we are accumulating data to increase the number of subjects. Yet, when the nature of the sampling is unknown, it may not be assumed that increasing the size of the group being evaluated necessarily improves its representativeness. In the present study, therefore, it seemed preferable to study a small group in great detail over time in order to delineate the subgroups under consideration with care and precision. In so doing, subgroups were created which are homogeneous in regard to some parameters considered significant. Because of the group homogeneity, curve trends emerge which differentiate the groups even when they are very small. (Some of the points on the curves in the present study are derived from as few as two children.) In addition, these curve trends from such small groups take on added significance since they are in accord with the expectations and predictions based on clinical and therapeutic experience.

The very distinct differences in learning curves among the subgroups in the present study would emphasize sharply the limitations of an evaluative study of schizophrenic children which does not account for the specific method of sampling of the children in the study. For example, present data would suggest that one might expect normal or above normal progress in educational skills in about 100 per cent of schizophrenic children treated in a center comparable to the Ittleson Center, provided the children demonstrate at least normal intellectual functioning at the outset. Limiting admissions to a treatment center to children with admission IQs that are average or above will thus produce treatment outcomes that are not comparable to those institutions which admit children at all levels of cognitive organization.

Of course, to analyze the sample, a fundamental conceptual decision has to be made. Are schizophrenic children to be treated as a group with a unitary disorder? If so, one needs merely to increase the size of the experimental group to increase the representativeness of the findings. Or should the children rather be treated as belonging to a group containing diverse disorders? We have preferred the latter concept and have referred to the scientific disadvantage in studying children with a multiplicity of disorders in combination and presuming that the children are comparable and suffering from a unitary disorder.[1] The hazard in so joining diverse disorders is evident from the finding in the present investigation which demonstrates differences in learning curves among two subclusters that have been defined, that is the "organic" and "nonorganic." It is obvious that in any study evaluating the educability of schizophrenics the results will reflect the incidence and proportion of children in the two categories as well as the further subdivision within these subclusters. It is safe to presume that limiting the schizophrenic group to children in the "nonorganic" group with above average IQs will most certainly assure excellent response to schooling, while "organic" children functioning at severely retarded levels will do poorly. If one assumes clinical progress accompanies school progress, as it is reasonable to do, one can anticipate treatment results in general by selection of children with respect to psychodynamic features and cognitive competence.

It has been our practical experience that dynamic observation of schizophrenic children in circumstances of intensive individualized treatment is essential to assure a proper analysis of the sample. Even in the case of schizophrenic children with brain damage, the diagnosis itself and the specific role played by cerebral limitations in his total psychodynamic organization is oftimes best understood after a period of psychotherapy. While such an intensively probing approach avoids the hazard of investigative triviality and improves knowledge of the sample, it ordinarily also means the slow accumulation of data for only a small sample. The chief disadvantage of a small longitudinal sample is the difficulty in achieving subgroups. This disadvantage is overcome in part by the improved homogeneity of the samples resulting from detailed study of the children. Intensive longitudinal study of children offers an additional vehicle for improving confidence in the data, namely that of longitudinal analysis.

In the present study each point on a curve is usually the average of a small number of children. Yet the reliability of the differences between these averages based on longitudinal data is much greater than would be obtained from the comparison of averages from independent samples. In addition, the reliability of the entire curve is related to the total number of scores rather than the number of scores entering into the average of any single point in time.

In summary, the educability of 37 schizophrenic children in residential psychiatric treatment has been evaluated by an analysis of their reading and arithmetic attainments. The approach to evaluation has been via the method of longitudinal analysis based on a study of changes of individual children over time. As a group, the children have shown an impressive and encouraging response to schooling in a therapeutic atmosphere, although the majority had been deemed uneducable while in the community. Individual variants in learning among the children have been described and their relationships to a number of factors, including presence or absence of cerebral dysfunction, level of intellectual functioning, and sex of child, have been noted. In evaluation of change in schizophrenic children, stress has been placed on careful delineation of subgroups and a theoretic model based on a concept of group heterogeneity and multiple etiologies. Finally, it has been implied that an approach to evaluation of change which is based on continuous intensive study of individual children and a detailed knowledge of the experimental sample is best achieved in an intimate therapeutic atmosphere.

REFERENCES

1. Goldfarb, W.: Childhood Schizophrenia. Cambridge, Harvard University Press, 1961.
2. —: Families of Schizophrenic Children in Mental Retardation. Ed. Kolb, L. C. Masland, R. L. and Cooke. R. E. Eds.) Vol. 39. Research Publications of Association for Research in Nervous and Mental Diseases. Baltimore, Williams & Williams Co., 1962.
3. Meyers, D. and —: Psychiatric appraisals of parents and siblings of schizophrenic children. Am. J. Psychiat. *118:* 902-915, 1962.
4. Metropolitan Achievement Tests Manual. New York, World Book Company, 1948.

16

EVALUATION OF PATIENTS FOLLOWING TREATMENT IN GENERAL HOSPITAL OUTPATIENT CLINICS

by JAMES P. CATTELL, M.D.* and EUGENE FORSTER, M.D.†

EVALUATION OF THE PSYCHIATRIC TREATMENT of outpatient department patients is complicated by several issues. This cannot be satisfactorily accomplished through a study of the patient's chart because of the variety of personnel involved and the usual lack of a systematic method of recording. A given patient usually has been examined and treated by several different psychiatric residents, supervised medical students and attending psychiatrists. The levels of skill and clinical orientation of these personnel vary. Their notes, written in the patient's chart, reflect their training and experience and may be uninformative or even contradictory.

A technique of more direct evaluation of the patient in a systematic manner is desirable. Nevertheless, this evaluation must involve a minimum of time and effort since both are precious in an OPD. Printed information sheets are convenient in that the questions to be answered by the evaluator are explicit. Items are underlined, briefly filled in, and numerically rated. The information sheet done by the clinic staff member, who initially examines the patient, establishes a base line. Filling out information sheets at any later stage of treatment or follow-up allows for immediate comparison with this base line. Differences in orientation and skill of observers are minimized by this approach. Hence, cross-sectional evaluations of a given patient, made by several members of the clinic staff at different times, can be compared. On the other hand, systematic comparison of the same patient's chart notes and summaries written by these same staff members is impossible.

---

*Ass't. Clin. Prof. of Psychiat., College of P & S, Columbia University; Ass't. Attd. Psychiat., Presbyterian Hospital.

†Instr. in Psychiat., College of P & S, Columbia University; Ass't. Attd. Psychiat., Vanderbilt Clinic.

Meaningful construction of such sheets requires a frame of reference. Evaluation of psychiatric treatment is impossible unless psychiatric disorders are conceptualized as disorders of adaptation. All symptoms of such disorders must be studied in their complex interrelationships with adaptive strivings, successes, and failures. Freud's discovery that all symptoms are manifestations of abortive defenses against anxiety is crucial to this frame of reference. The other working hypothesis is that an individual is prone to develop and perpetuate anxiety insofar as functional organismic integrity and pleasure economy are impaired. This is derived from the studies of Sandor Rado and Kurt Goldstein.

In accord with this frame of reference, the information sheets should enable one to distinguish whether or not there has been integrative growth, supportive maintenance, spontaneous remission or merely a shift in dominant symptomatology. Such distinctions must be based on evaluations of each area of adaptive functioning. Vague generalizations, such as "the patient seems to be functioning better," are misleading and valueless for statistical studies.

The environmental vicissitudes must also be evaluated as to their contribution to the patient's progress in the treatment, his lack of progress or the exacerbation of his symptomatology. The same considerations are involved after the termination of treatment. Has the patient consciously or unconsciously utilized these vicissitudes in facilitating or sabotaging his adaptation? The specific nature of the vicissitudes and the area of functioning involved are significant. Distinctions can then be made between fortuitous vicissitudes and those consciously or unconsciously activated by the patient.

Quantitative scales should be used to rate the individual areas of functioning and to rate the results of treatment. These are obviously necessary for statistical study of groups of patients. They sharpen the evaluation of the individual patient, especially in cross-sectional comparisons. Skill of the observer and subjective factors are variables in the use of a rating scale. Concise definition of the scales keeps these variables at a minimum. Without such scales, evaluation is anecdotal and statistics are meaningless.

Since these information sheets are for the evaluation of treatment in the OPD, how shall we evaluate our controls? One approach would be the evaluation of a random number of patients applying for outpatient clinic treatment, using the same information sheets. Following evaluation, these patients are left to their own resources and re-evaluated at some future date. Simple as it may seem, such a technique is invalid and impractical. Psychiatric evaluation cannot be separated from psychiatric treatment. The evaluation itself may have a therapeutic effect, placebo or otherwise. Control cases may present acute emergencies which must be treated. Such patients would be removed from the control group, which makes for a selective rather than a random group. The control cases would often maintain OPD contacts with other departments of the general hospital. Such contact, at least for the patient, would imply continued contact with the psychiatric OPD. Many of the patients would not be available for re-evaluation months or years later. Thus, the use of control groups would create many more problems than it would resolve.

The practical solution is to make the patient his own control. Psychopathology arises from a long-standing impairment of functioning

REFERRAL SOURCE:
DATE:

PSYCHIATRIC CLINIC INFORMATION SHEET
(underline terms that apply and print in data)

NAME ______________________________ UNIT # __________
Last First Initial

ADDRESS ______________________________ TEL: Home __________ Bus.

MARITAL STATUS S M W D Sep. SEX M F AGE ______

RACE ______________ OCCUPATION ______________

PRESENTING COMPLAINTS (in pt's own words - note duration and previous Rx)

PREVIOUS HISTORY OF EMOTIONAL ILLNESS: (dates, symptoms, treatment)

FAMILY HISTORY OF EMOTIONAL ILLNESS: (note relationship to pt., dx, Rx)

PERSONALITY ORGANIZATION AND FUNCTIONING PRIOR TO ILLNESS (rate each area with following scale: Good - 1; Fair - 2; Poor - 3) domestic ( ), social ( ), occupational ( ), sexual ( ), emotional ( ), intellectual ( ), sensory-motor ( ), autonomic ( ).

FIG. 1.

and gratification. Evaluation of the area and degree of impairment in a given patient establishes a base line for the evaluation of treatment. Each patient's history provides the control for that patient, if the adaptational frame of reference is used. This does not solve all the methodological problems but it comes closer to such a solution. It also makes evaluation and control studies compatible with the optimal clinical functioning of outpatient clinic psychiatrists.

Having discussed some general considerations, we turn to the actual structure and use of psychiatric information sheets.

The evaluation is made on a printed form: Psychiatric Clinic Information Sheet (fig. 1). The clinic secretary fills in the statistical data in the first section. This is done as soon as the patient is admitted to the OPD, and the sheet is immediately presented to the staff member who is to provide the initial evaluation of the patient.

The staff member then completes the next eight sections of the sheet during the diagnostic work-up of the patient. Filling in these sections is necessary for completion of the work-up. The headings of these sections are: Presenting Complaints, Previous History of Emotional Illness, Family History of Emotional Illness, Personality Organization and Functioning Prior to Illness, Symptom Constellation, Precipitating Factors, Diagnostic Impression, and Medical Diagnosis.

Presenting Complaints are recorded in the patient's own words. Duration and previous psychiatric treatments are noted.

Previous History of Emotional Illness is recorded in terms of dates, symptoms, and treatment.

Family History of Emotional Illness is recorded by listing the relationship to the patient, the diagnosis, and the psychiatric treatment of the relative.

Personality Organization and Function Prior to Illness consists of the following categories to be rated: domestic, social, occupational, sexual, emotional, intellectual, sensory-motor, and autonomic. Each category is separately rated with a (1) to (3) rating: (1) = Good; (2) = Fair; (3) = Poor. A rating (1) implies absence of symptoms, effective functioning and gratification; (2) implies the presence of symptoms, moderately effective functioning and diminished gratification; (3) implies domination by symptoms, incapacitation of functioning and no gratification. This section is of crucial importance in establishing the base line of functioning that will serve as the control for all future evaluation of the patient. Using these categories results in a detailed analysis of all phases of ego functioning.

Symptom Constellation (fig. 2) is an organized list of psychiatric symptoms. The evaluator underlines all those observed in the patient. Also to be filled in, if present, the specific types of drug dependence, sexual deviation, psychosomatic symptom, antisocial behavior, and symptoms of organic cerebral impairment. The list includes all significant psychiatric symptoms. In choosing from among these, the probability that all symptoms will be listed is much greater.

Precipitating Factors calls for the specific stress and when it was experienced. The areas of stress are the same as those used in Personality Organization and Functioning Prior to Illness. This eliminates vague and equivocal listings of alleged stresses.

Diagnostic Impression is a listing of the psychiatric diagnosis using the American Psychiatric Association classification. In addition, the diagnosis of Pseudoneurotic Schizophrenia is used when indicated.

Medical Diagnosis is listed. This is obtained from other clinics the patient has been attending or from a medical work-up done as part of the psychiatric evaluation.

Following the last diagnostic interview the staff member fills in the first line of the Record Clinic Treatment (fig. 3). This notes the number of visits, dates, recommendations, and name of the evaluator.

The remainder of the Record of Clinic Treatment is filled in by those who treat the patient. Types of treatment are noted under the heading of Recommendations. Social Service contact and hospitalization during clinic contact are tabulated in this section.

At the time of patient's discharge from the clinic, the staff member is given another copy of the information sheet. Ignoring the first four sections, he fills in the section: Personality Organization and Func-

PSYCHIATRIC CLINIC INFORMATION SHEET

SYMPTOM CONSTELLATION (as observed by psychiatrist - underline those which apply): Anxiety, depression, self-derogation, doubting, obsession, compulsion, phobia, conversion, dissociation, hysterical dramatizing, hypochondriasis, fatigue, depersonalization or unreality, sensitiveness, illusions, suspiciousness, no pleasure in living, subjective confusion, ideas of reference, loosening of associations, concrete thinking, inappropriate or flat affect, withdrawal, inability to concentrate, delusions (persecutory, grandiose, somatic), hallucinations (auditory, visual, other ______________), drug dependence (alcohol, other ________________), sexual deviation (____________________), psychosomatic (________________________), anti-social behavior (__________ ____________________), symptoms of organic cerebral impairment (__________ ____)

PRECIPITATING FACTORS: (Note specific stress and when it occurred: domestic, social, occupational, sexual, emotional, intellectual, sensory-motor and autonomic) ____

____

____

DIAGNOSTIC IMPRESSION (use American Psychiatric Association classification)

____

____

____

MEDICAL DIAGNOSIS: ____

____

FIG. 2.

tioning (fig. 1). The rating scale is used to provide a picture of adaptive functioning at the termination of treatment. Following this he goes on to Symptom Constellation (fig. 2) and underlines those symptoms present. Precipitating Factors is also filled in, but now it is in terms of environmental vicissitudes that occurred during the treatment, rather than those which led to the onset of illness. These factors may have had positive or negative effects on the treatment. The nature of the vicissitude is categorized as above. Then Discharge is filled out (fig. 3), giving date of discharge and destination of the patient. Final Diagnosis is filled in and Condition on Discharge is indicated by underlining one of six possibilities: Recovered, much improved, moderately improved, slightly improved, unimproved, worse. These possibilities warrant detailed consideration.

Each category is defined by specific criteria. Recovered implies the absence of symptoms and adequate functioning in all areas of behavior. Much improved implies the presence of a few symptoms of mild intensity and moderately adequate functioning in all areas or adequate in most areas and poor in a few. Moderately improved implies the presence of a moderate number of symptoms of moderate

PSYCHIATRIC CLINIC INFORMATION SHEET

RECORD OF CLINIC TREATMENT

Type of Treatment	No. of Visits	Dates From To	Recommendations	Evaluation or Rx by
Diagnostic Evaluation				
Treatment				
Treatment				
Treatment				
Hospitalization				
Social Service				

Discharge: Date ____________ Destination ____________________

Final Diagnosis: ____________________________________

Condition on Discharge: Recovered, Improved (Much, Moderately, Slightly),
(underline one) Unimproved, Worse

FIG. 3.

intensity and moderately adequate functioning in some areas or poor in most areas and adequate in a few. Slightly improved implies slight decrease in number and intensity of symptoms and essentially poor functioning in all areas. Unimproved and worse are self-explanatory.

This rating system emphasizes the relationships between symptoms and the various areas of personality functioning. It is obvious, using this system, to determine which patients have experienced personality growth. There is little chance of confusing this with symptomatic shifts or weathering of an acute emotional storm with no personality change. Results are not naively classified as successful or unsuccessful. Types and degrees of success are more carefully classified. Also, the rating at time of discharge serves as a base line for follow-up evaluations.

Follow-up evaluations are recorded on the same type of information sheet. The entire sheet is filled out and appended to the previous information sheets. Filling out these information sheets should take up no more than 5 minutes.

Comparison of the information sheets completed at various phases of contact with the patient immediately highlights a wealth of clinical data. Evaluation of treatment is concise, thorough, and consistent. From these information sheets data can be transposed onto large tabulation sheets or, preferably, punch cards. Statistical studies are facilitated.

In conclusion, the use of information sheets affords the best possibility of evaluation studies of patients treated in the psychiatric outpatient clinic of a general hospital. The sheets described make for descriptive accuracy and dynamic evaluation. Furthermore, their use is compatible with normal clinic functioning.

17

THE EVALUATION OF PATIENTS FOLLOWING TREATMENT IN A STATE HOSPITAL

by HENRY BRILL, M.D.* and ROBERT E. PATTON†

LOGICALLY ONE WOULD EXPECT that an evaluation of treatment in state mental hospitals would require as a first step a comparison of the results of such care or treatment with the outcomes in other settings. Actually, hospital treatment evaluation has been limited almost entirely to studies which compare the outcome of various kinds of treatment in a hospital setting against each other or against hospital treatment which has been standardized in a specific fashion.

While the problems of mental hospital evaluation include the problems of psychiatric evaluation generally they also have special aspects of their own and they have attracted particular attention for many reasons, among which one may list:

1. The bulk of published work on somatic therapy is and has been done in state mental hospitals or their equivalent and the status of the evaluation of these treatments is largely controlled by the status of hospital evaluation.
2. The speed of psychiatric advance, or the lack of such advance, has been linked in the minds of many scientists and in the opinion of the informed general public to scientific inadequacies in psychiatry generally and one of the focal points of recent criticism has been with regard to the scientific defects of evaluation of treatments in these hospitals.
3. Finally there has been a recent trend toward a re-examination of the mental hospital itself as a therapeutic influence and adequate evaluation now becomes a matter of urgent practical significance.

Great dissatisfaction has been expressed with such evaluations of hospital situated treatment as do exist, and the criticisms tend to revolve about one or more of the following issues:

A. In all aspects of the treatment process value judgments play a crucial role and since these judgments are arrived at by an essentially intuitive process

*Deputy Commissioner.
†Director of Statistical Services, New York State Department of Mental Hygiene.

they are open to the criticism that they are too much based on whim and bias which vary from one observer to another in random fashion and even in the same observer from one time to another.

B. The almost complete lack of objective elements underlying such intuitive judgments in psychiatry.

C. Criticisms become most outspoken when such clinical judgments achieve the status of published papers and seek to become the basis of general claims for the value of any given method of treatment.

Schwartz, for example, quoted in "Action for Mental Health" states: "We have reported on some recent trends in the care and treatment of outpatients, inpatients, and expatients. The practitioners who are developing the various new programs believe in them . . . However, we know that this is a field where fads and fancies flourish. Hardly a year passes without some new claim . . . the early promises of each of these discoveries are uniformly unfulfilled . . . We have observed the lack of definitive research findings with regard to any of these new programs. Hunches, guesses, and uncontrolled observations are the major sources of information on their operations and degrees of effectiveness."

Eysenck speaks in the same vein: "Psychosurgery has been based on a set of observations of dubious validity and on a tenuous rationale . . ." Speaking of drug research he says: "The data are too divergent to permit of any useful kind of summary . . . Few results have been found which stood up to replication of experiments, and few findings have achieved the status of facts on which future works may build. The reasons for this sorry state of affairs are obvious. Enthusiasm in research is no compensation for lack of competence, and few workers in the field have had the requisite training in psychological research methodology, statistical knowledge, biochemical expertise and general physiological knowledge . . . to avoid quite elementary errors."

It is interesting that Beckman, well known for his work in the field of general pharmacology, finds a somewhat different basis for criticism. Speaking of some tranquilizing drug trials, he says: "It is altogether too naive to believe that the stipulations were of necessity carried out merely because they were made. My plea is for sophistication rather than quantitation . . ." He is concerned essentially about the uncontrolled variables of interpretation and execution inherent in a multi-hospital study and points specifically to the "lowlier personnel . . . who actually did the work . . ."

These are but three samples from a large literature of criticism which has sprung up in the last few years, all bearing on work of the mental hospitals.

In the face of all this attention the question naturally arises, "Why indeed when we compare psychiatry with science generally or medicine and general pharmacology specifically has there been a lag in the development of scientifically validated work in the field?" Space will not permit a full review of the contrast between the nature of psychiatric problems and those in general science or in other branches of medicine. We shall attempt only a brief description of some of the problems relating to hospitals and how they have developed.

Evaluation by the Hospital Builders—Historical Note

In this connection it may be of some interest to return for a moment to the arguments and logic of the hospital builders of the nineteenth century to see perhaps how far we have advanced since then. The great wave of mental hospital building of the last century was motivated by the firm and general belief that separation from home and family and from accustomed associations was essential and that the mental hospital offered much for the treatment of a very large number of cases of mental illness. This separation was regularly described as one of the important elements of the "moral treatment" of the time.

Kirkbride in his "Hospitals for the Insane" (1880) summarizes this position: ". . . general experience seems to show that a very large proportion of all the insane are treated more effectively and far more economically among strangers and in well-managed institutions specially provided for their treatment than at their own homes and surrounded by their families and by familiar scenes and associations."

"Much as has been said in commendation of 'home treatment' and 'family treatment' it is not to be forgotten that these are commonly tried and fail before the idea of removing a patient to an institution is seriously discussed. The great danger in unduly protracting these efforts at home is that the best period for successful hospital treatment is lost and that what was recent in its character, becomes chronic with all the diminished chances for recovery . . ."

"The history of 'home' treatment before the establishment of hospitals is one of the saddest records of inhumanity and cruelty to be found anywhere. It was the discovery of this state of things and the plain unvarnished recital of what was found by benevolent women and men that led to the establishment of most of the state and government hospitals for the insane . . .

"Very often this simple change from home to an institution seems to be of itself sufficient to secure the beginning of convalescence and not infrequently the improvement in behavior and conversation is from the first most remarkable." Thus spoke Kirkbride, an often quoted authority of that day.

In his classical "Dictionary of Psychological Medicine" (Churchill, 1892, London) Hack Tuke states under "General or Moral Treatment:" "The primary object is to separate the patient as thoroughly as possible from his old surroundings. . . . shut him off from all objects with which he has formed, or is likely to form morbid mental associations. We find from experience that the sight of home surroundings perpetually recalls home cares and duties and that the enormous mass of associations connecting the patient with relations and immediate friends renders it difficult for him to procure mental tranquility in their midst."

Pinel is quoted by Galt as saying: "Experience has taught that the insane are scarcely ever cured in the bosom of their families. In Bethlehem Hospital on the admission of a patient they give his family the power of visiting him only once a week. . . . It is universally observed that the insane are scarcely ever restored under the immediate direction of their friends and neighbors. Their visits even augment the patient's excitement . . . many lunatics who were furious and intractable at home are calm and docile in a hospital."

Galt also quotes Bell as follows: "Moral treatment comprehends . . . (four points, the first of which is) . . .

1. The experience of all ages and all countries coincides as to its importance so that the general statement is fully warranted that patients in an institution usually recover, while those treated at home generally do not."

It was based on a well-accepted general theory—that of the association of ideas. The logic was that the pathological ideas were associated with home and familiar surroundings and that a change to new surroundings would break the associations. The idea was never validated, however, and neither was its opposite.

The judgment of these nineteenth century psychiatrists is subject to another valid criticism. It was the product of experience with uncontrolled mental illness in the community and led to a sweeping and urgent demand for large-scale early hospitalization as a preventive measure. There never was any attempt to secure a valid and quantitative comparison of the course of mental illness in hospital and in the community. At this distance in time it is apparent that even the most vivid criticisms of an existing situation constitute a very uncertain basis for precipitate flight into an alternate one with no better proof than rhetoric. Yet we cannot be too critical because some of the most heated discussions now taking place on this same question 50 and 100 years later still have this same basis; even now we do not possess the base lines which were then lacking and which led to decisions which are now criticized.

The early mental hospitals went through a phase of therapeutic optimism which is well known now as the Cult of Curability. The Happy Statistics reached their zenith in the 1850's, but it was not until the end of the century that the pendulum of professional opinion had swung to the opposite extreme in a phase of therapeutic nihilism from which we have not yet fully recovered, an opinion summarized in the phrase "once insane always insane." In the meanwhile, statistical sophistication advanced considerably over the decades but evaluation of clinical procedures still remained essentially intuitive.

The Somatic Therapies—Evaluation Still Controversial

When insulin therapy was introduced into this country, the first monograph by Sakel contained an introduction dated 1935 and written by the then Director of the University Clinic of Vienna: "The first cases that I saw, demonstrated to me that it (insulin treatment) surpassed by far any other treatment of schizophrenia at present available. It was clear to me that the remissions in these cases were not merely accidental but were directly caused by the the treatment itself. When the treatment was then tried on a large series of patients we had a percentage of practical results which were two or three times better than the most optimistic statistics for spontaneous remissions in schizophrenia."

It is perhaps worthy of note that more than 25 years have now gone by and thousands of patients have since been treated by this technique, yet our evaluation of insulin therapy has advanced relatively little and we still have no generally accepted outcome tables on "the spontaneous remissions" or any other kind.

Nor has the case been much better with any of the somatic therapies which have followed. The sequence has always been the same. Most of this work has been done in state mental hospitals and their equivalent here and abroad, a range of therapeutic utility has been clinically identified and the treatments applied in progressively larger numbers of cases until now some 60 per cent of all hospital cases are usually found under somatic treatment, yet critical surveys of the literature have repeatedly arrived at sweeping condemnation of lack of scientific evaluation and probable lack of therapeutic effect.

Other Psychiatric Therapies no Better Measured

What has been said about the somatic therapies is equally true of the milieu therapies, the complex process once known as moral treatment which, incidentally, meant nothing more than "general" or "environmental" treatment as contrasted with the "medical" treatments then known. Psychotherapy, as we now know it, had not been developed through moral treatment involved some rudiments of psychotherapy. It is true of the psychotherapies, individual as well as group, and their many modifications and it applies also to many elements of treatment which have recently come into prominence, such as hospital size and location. Sometimes this is misunderstood to mean that we have no knowledge in these fields, but this is not necessarily true. There are many levels of validation and many important decisions are made partly on an intuitive level which is still far better than random action. This is the field of professional judgment and its operational validity as well exemplified in business, political and military life and even in medicine, but the level is not that of a scientific method, and every experience we have points to the desirability of advancing as far and as rapidly as possible from intuitive judgments toward more objective ones. To say that the treatments are not scientifically proved is not the equivalent of saying they are scientifically disproved.

The Barriers to Evaluation—in Ourselves—Our Methods

The barriers lie in ourselves, as has been pointed out by many critics, and in our limitations. They lie also in our methods which perhaps are only a reflection of the skills which we can bring to bear on this problem. By definition better men could be expected to get better results but they lie also in the material and it would be a mistake to underestimate the difficulties in the material.

Problems with the Data

Essentially these difficulties can be divided into two classes, first the existence of multiple uncontrolled variables of environment and of patients and second, the subjectivity of mental illness and of judgments regarding it.

The scientific method demands techniques for control of variables whether these be direct as in a laboratory or indirect by statistical devices. When one reviews the classes of variables in hospital treatment of psychoses it becomes clear that each offers its own serious problems of definition, let alone control.

The Universe of Therapeutic Variables

It is extremely difficult to determine what in the complex environment of the patient constitutes therapy. This is known to vary from one patient to another and from one time to another. Much of the decisive work of therapy takes place on a subjective level and depends on personal relationships and individual responses to specific elements in the environment and their symbolic and experiental values. In case series of sufficient size such variables may cancel out, but, on the other hand, there are subtle group dynamics which may well play a significant role in large aggregations, and such variations may be as cumulative as small vibrations at a critical and harmonic frequency.

Anti-Therapy, Negative Components Unmeasured and Even Unidentified

After exploring all the possible significant therapeutic elements in a situation it then becomes necessary to consider the existence of antitherapeutic elements. It might seem that all these items represent a quibbling about details which are quantitatively unimportant and which, in any event, would tend to be canceled out in any large series of cases carried over a reasonable period of time. Unfortunately, this is difficult to prove and it is precisely such components in the therapeutic environment which have been seized upon by various critics of hospital and home care at different periods of history. Suggestive therapeutics have been invoked again and again to account for the changes following somatic therapies and the enthusiasm of staff has been given credit for various treatment effects, as has the extra attention which such patients have been thought to receive. Is it not reasonable to assume that opposite effects may result from opposite conditions?

The State Mental Hospital as a Therapeutic Modality

Perhaps one of the most challenging issues of recent years has been the question raised about the state mental hospital itself as a therapeutic modality. In America the issues seem to hinge about the size of the mental hospitals and their location but abroad, especially in France and England, where the 1,000 bed hospital is the rule and location a lesser problem, the question of mental hospitals is no less active. In Britain we hear of a move to reduce the number of mental hospitals by half with no particular mention about size or location.

No problem is more urgent today than the evaluation of the mental hospital in the mental health program. We must determine if we can whether hospitalization is as good as Pinel and Kirkbride thought or as bad as some twentieth century writers claim. This means measuring more than *how* good or *how* bad they are. We must know what kinds of hospitals, what aspects of their operation and what kinds of illness are really involved in positive and negative values.

We have, then, an imposing list of what it is to be evaluated and in any given hospital they are all present in a composition that is so complex that it seems to defy the imagination to analyze it. Can we really hope to evaluate a complex situation of this kind? Some of the differences may be small enough in effect to be disregarded, statistical measures will give some estimate of others, but a very large number remain to be identified as well as evaluated.

Other Environmental Variables

When we move outside of the subjective and often decisive realm of therapeutics and come to the objective and measurable characteristics we find here, too, a degree of complexity which is far from analyzed. Staffing ratios, for instance, tell nothing about staff competence; existence of the so-called adjunctive treatments give no inkling about the extent of their utilization nor about the skill with which they are coordinated and applied according to special needs. Even in such a deceptively simple problem as financing we find a degree of complexity which goes beyond that found in most basic laboratory work or even in many internal medical problems.

Financing

Financing has often been accepted as an important element in the therapeutic formula, and figure 1 shows the annual gross per capita dollar range among our own hospitals. All are standard New York State mental hospitals under one fiscal management, yet the fact stands out that there is a considerable variability within this closely knit system which applies similar criteria throughout, yet the highest per capita cost is some 50 per cent above that of the lowest.

At this point we must go further and ask how much the range of per capita cost truly reflects a range of services and how much it reflects the cost of delivering services under different operating conditions. This represents a problem in cost accounting hardly less complex than that of evaluation of many of the imponderables involved in the psychotherapeutic components. A recent VA study by Jenkins et al. brought out this point quite clearly.

Variation of Institutional Population

The formal characteristics of the population of institutions varies markedly from one place to another and from one time to another. This is a factor of considerable importance to us inasmuch as it is involved in all comparisons of hospital functions across a span of time or of geography; in addition, it is one type of variability that may be expressed in exact and objective form rather than descriptively, and may perhaps be some indicator of the range to be found in the other parameters which have not yet been reduced to quantitative terms.

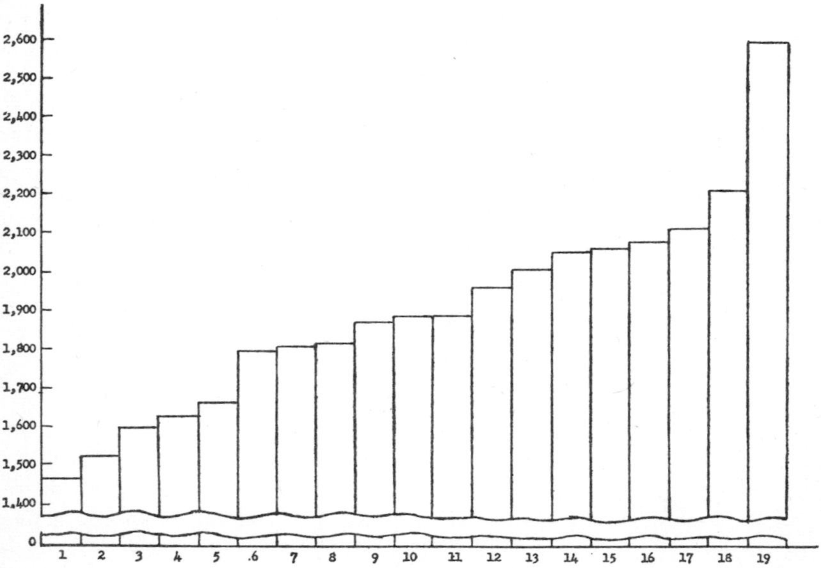

FIG. 1.—1960 per capita expenditures in the 19 New York State Mental Hospitals.

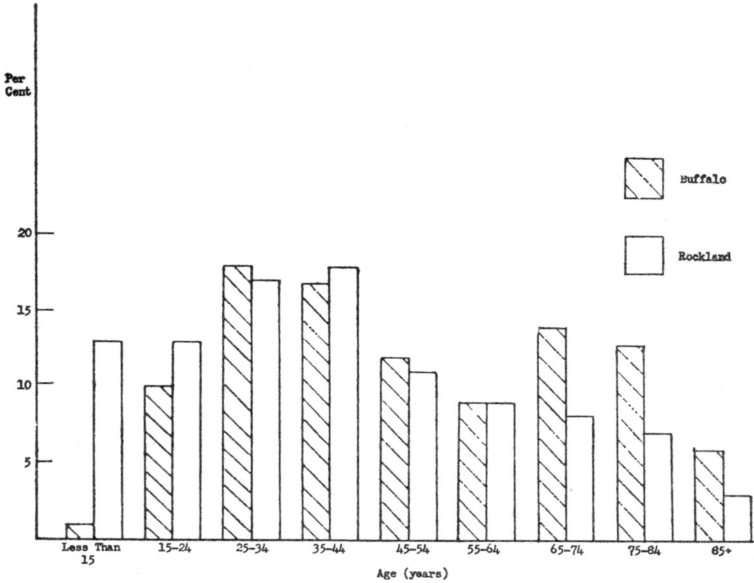

FIG. 2.—Percentage distribution of 1961 admissions by age to Buffalo and Rockland State Hospitals.

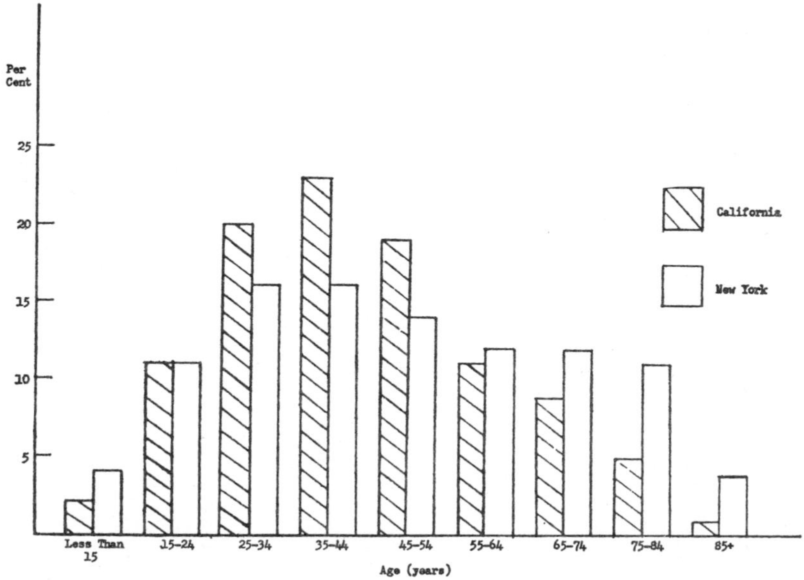

FIG. 3.—Percentage distribution of 1959 admissions by age to California and New York State Mental Hospital systems.

A factor which is of acknowledged importance in the outcome of mental hospital admissions is that of age. Prognosis is less favorable in the very young and very limited in the aged. A comparison of admissions at Buffalo State Hospital with those at Rockland State Hospital (fig. 2) shows how wide may be the range of variation in one hospital system. In this care the difference is due in part to the existence of special facilities at each institution, yet informal local differences of service occur everywhere and clearly influence the types of patients admitted to various hospitals.

Admission policies and historical backgrounds also play a role. A comparison of admissions in New York and California shows that the California group has an excess of the 25-54 year cases, while the New York group shows an excess at both extremes of life (fig. 3). Another comparison of the two states (fig. 4) is even more striking. The preponderance of California cases falls into the group of less than one year's duration of hospital life. The New York group, on the other hand, shows a very marked preponderance of cases at the other end of the scale with well over 25 per cent in the over 20 year group. This is at least in part attributable to the fact that the base

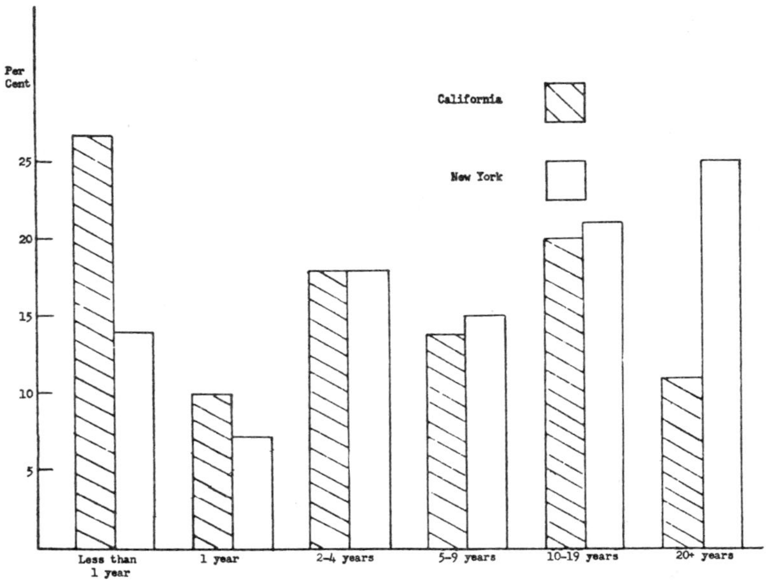

FIG. 4.—Percentage distribution of resident patients in 1959 by time since admission in California and New York State Mental Hospital systems.

population in California was much smaller than that of New York before 1940. The large New York group was accumulating during a period before the modern therapies were available. Any comparisons between over-all figures for the two states must take into account their different proportions of long-term cases as well as the possibility of an administrative policy which keeps California admissions of the very old to a lower level. For example, the possibility of future rapid decreases of mental hospital population is influenced by this distribution. However, a full comparison would have to take into account such questions as the proportion of new migrants from other areas, the proportion of negro to white and a relatively complex analysis of the other characteristics of the base population, of the mental hospital population, and the various administrative policies governing the movement of hospital population.

Diagnosis is another population characteristic which is still considered to be of importance, though perhaps less so than at one time. Here again one may see a large variation even between two of the New York State mental hospitals (fig. 5). The considerable number

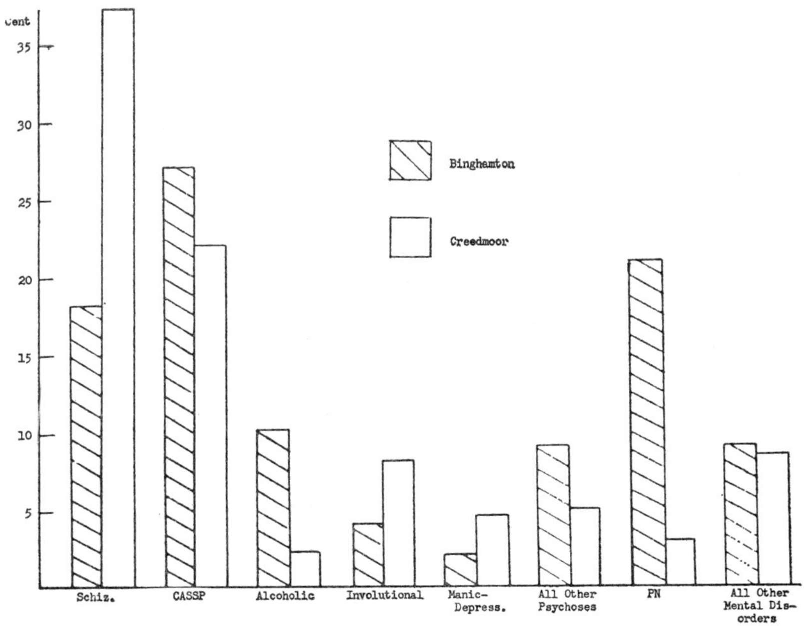

Fig. 5.—Percentage distribution of 1961 admissions by mental disorders to Binghamton and Creedmoor State Hospitals.

of cases of psychoneurosis diagnosed at Binghamton would agree well with the fact that this hospital serves the total mental hospital needs of a community and may reflect differences in local custom as compared with other hospitals. This is further supported by the relatively high proportion of alcoholics. At least if one were to compare the two institutions it would be necessary to consider these factors carefully. Nor can one be sure of diagnostic continuity within one hospital as has been pointed out by Kraepelin and many others. This variation is to be seen at Pilgrim (fig. 6) over a 20 year life-span with a sharp increase in schizophrenia and a decrease of all other psychoses (which includes paresis and epilepsy as well as encephalitis lethargica). Such variations over time can be regularly demonstrated and they reflect many factors, some of them identified and others not. Diagnostic variation is known to be very large from state to state and comparisons among various countries are almost without value if based on diagnosis.

Finally we come to the most important single fact with respect to prognosis, namely, the previous duration of mental hospital life. Here

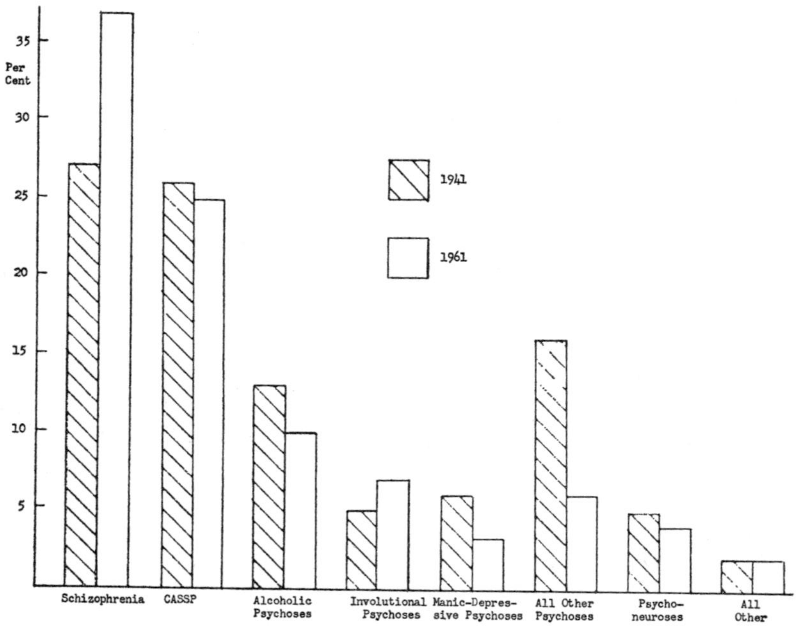

FIG. 6.—Percentage distribution of 1941 and 1961 admissions by mental disorder to Pilgrim State Hospital.

the spread between the two extremes of the department's hospitals is striking. At Manhattan State Hospital (fig. 7) less than a third of the patients are in hospital for more than 10 years, at Willard the proportion is almost twice that high. On the other hand, the patients with a duration of less than 2 years are percentage-wise twice as frequent in Manhattan as in Willard. The implications of such a variation of population distribution are obvious for any evaluation of hospital treatment.

Chronicity of Target Symptoms Contrasted with Chronicity of Patient

While it may be safely assumed that in cases of long hospital duration the patients' symptoms are sufficiently chronic to represent a serious therapeutic problem, the authors believe that it is incorrect to project this type of reasoning to newly admitted cases even though the history clearly reveals that some schizophrenic symptomatology had its onset long before; new symptoms which have arisen in the course of a long-standing schizophrenic state have a satisfactory prognosis under treatment and should not constitute a reason for removing a patient from a test group.

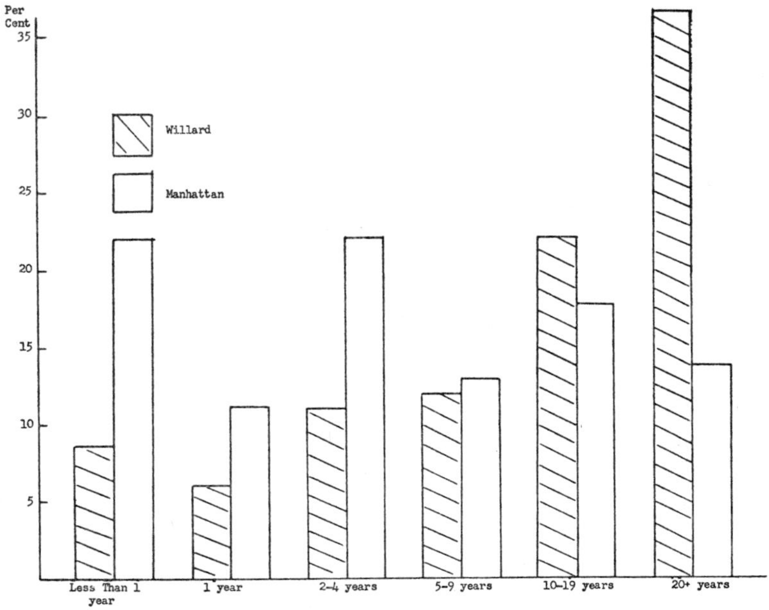

FIG. 7.—Percentage distribution of resident patients in 1961 by time since admission in Willard and Manhattan State Hospitals.

The variability of clinical material is not encompassed by these lists of characteristics. Many others come to mind, for instance, the degree of activity or inactivity of symptoms, the response of the patient to his symptomatology and the attitude of those in his surroundings, elusive but important personality characteristics which determine his capacity to adjust to his disability, and finally undefined factors, such as innate healing tendency or lack of it. All these problems may be statistically controlled by randomization, yet there is reason to believe that they can and have played an unrecognized role in the published results of many authors. At least the conditions of the work certainly allowed for biased selection toward the null hypothesis or toward a positive finding.

The Subjective Nature of Mental Disorder—A Problem in Evaluation

Finally we must consider the fact that psychiatric disorder is essentially a subjective experience of very complex nature. It is true that the more severe disorders have correlates in behavior which are often relatively reliable indicators, yet in the long run the opinion of the patient, his family and associates and of professional personnel must still remain data of quite another magnitude than the opinions of a physical scientist as to the titration point of a chemical reaction or a vernier measurement on a scale.

When one thinks of the great difficulty and elaborate precautions which must be taken in connection with the evaluation of such a simple psychic experience as ordinary pain, it would seem that evaluation of mental disorder is probably more subject to variability of interpretation and must suffer a corresponding loss of reliability, even under optimum conditions. One cannot help wondering how much reliability is lost under less than optimal conditions.

For most purposes it is sufficient to assume that social tolerance of symptoms represents a relatively objective cutting point and this is certainly true with respect to the more gross findings but it is precisely in the areas where ordinary inspection is inadequate that we need some more reliable indicator. At the present time active work is being carried out to devise more objective ways of inquiry about the patient, yet in the last analysis one must still return to the fact that we are only measuring opinions, those of the patient and his associates as well as the professional personnel involved, and this is a far cry from "the weighing, counting and measuring" of ponderable quantities. We cannot decry such work; it is of the utmost value, but it lies well within the area of the social sciences and well outside of the areas of the physical sciences and of physical medicine and these are the areas with which the most distressing comparisons of progress have been made.

We may, of course, depend on such operational correlates as work capacity, formal behavior and social capacity, and these have great practical value, yet we know that they bear only an incomplete relation to the patient's psychic state. The psychic state, the behavior and the environment are so intertwined and there is so much feedback involved among them that the only escape from complexity appears to be a statistical one and then we find that the limitations of time and of geography play a role if we wish to make comparison involving either dimension.

Finally it must be admitted that present approaches tend to deemphasize the importance of psychotic content. This tendency is partly a reaction against a previous overemphasis of delusions and hallucinations and partly has resulted from the greater interest in the dynamic aspects of mental life as well as the sociological interest in behavior. Yet it must be admitted that delusions and hallucinations are still among the most distinctive and decisive diagnostic characteristics of the schizophrenias and it remains to be seen how far the response to therapy can be accurately estimated without becoming involved with the problem of quantitation of these nonquantitative subjective elements of the illness.

Long-term Evaluation—Almost Untouched

In view of the difficulties which have already been outlined it is not surprising that most studies have been confined to short-term follow-up and that there is relatively little literature available with respect to the relationship between any one of the major modalities of treatment and the long-term result. Some work has been done on insulin therapy and it is believed that over the long run the condition of patients so treated tends to approximate that of others; long-term follow-up has also been done in psychosurgery but we still lack an adequate picture of the natural course of the various illnesses independent of any intervention and this deprives us of any possibility of measurement of any treatment regime against such base lines either for the long or short course. We are thus reduced to short-term studies which look like comparisons of various individual modalities but always represent various combinations of treatment methods and environmental adjuncts, and it is always with combined circumstances rather than with simple individual interventions that we must deal.

Conclusion

These problems are described not as an insuperable barrier to further progress but rather in the spirit of frank recognition of the difficulties which we face. These are being overcome by the discovery of new parameters of measurement, new techniques of investigation and originality of research, and advances are taking place. It is doubtful whether we would today accept a new method of therapy with the simple recommendation which brought insulin into such wide attention, and more and more we find a steady increase of the requirements of proof for all programs and all treatments which come up for consideration. There has never been a time when there was so much from which to choose and while we still do not have methods of selection which approximate those of more advanced fields of scientific endeavor we do have methods which are steadily improving. It would be an error of judgment to attribute to them more validly than they have actually demonstrated in our own field of work, yet they cannot be written off as unrealistic flights of academic fancy. In the last analysis, their value will depend on the judgment with which they are applied.

18

THE EVALUATION OF GERIATRIC PATIENTS FOLLOWING TREATMENT

by ALVIN I. GOLDFARB, M.D.*

"In talking they forget the common appellation of things, and the names of persons, even of those who are their nearest friends and relations. For the same reason, they never can amuse themselves with reading, because their memory will not serve to carry them from the beginning of a sentence to the end." *Jonathan Swift on the Struldbrugs*

GERIATRIC PSYCHIATRY deals with a heterogeneous group of patients. They vary in age, physical health, socioeconomic status and psychiatric condition. The psychiatric conditions of the aged include almost all of those commonly seen in younger groups. To these are added acute and chronic brain syndrome associated with the systemic, metabolic and deteriorative disorders common to old age. The psychiatric treatment of the aged ranges from psychotherapy through pharmacological and physical methods to complete supervision and custodial care. Good treatment usually includes a combination of techniques. Even when physical or pharmacological methods take precedence the relationship of therapist to patient may have great therapeutic value.

Aged persons with mental disorder who now most urgently concern the community and the psychiatrist can be subdivided into two groups; those who have brain syndrome with or without associated disease, and those with no, or minimal brain syndrome who have disorders in thinking or of affect. The preponderant affective disorder is depression and paranoid ideation is the most commonly observed thinking or "content" disorder. Depressive reactions and paranoid trends or behavior are also common in patients who have brain syndrome. For

---

*Consultant on Services for the Aged, New York State Department of Mental Hygiene, Queens Village, New York.

The author wishes to acknowledge his gratitude and indebtedness to the entire staff of the Office on Special Services for the Aged and especially to Mrs. Helen Turner, Assistant to the Consultant, for their patient and skillful assistance in the preparation of this paper and for the many investigative, statistical and clinical feats upon which it is based.

combinations of physical, mental and economic reasons many of these patients may require supervision or custodial care as well as general medical care, assistance in regulation of their time in occupation or recreation, and rehabilitative forms of education and re-education. Special attempts may be made to establish the controlled, continued, purposeful relationship in a physician-patient, or physician-group, experience we call psychotherapy. In addition, the families of aged persons with mental disorder often need help both on account of their relationship to the patient and because of their reaction to his illness. Counsel, socioeconomic or other assistance to the family of the person involves personal relationships which may be psychotherapeutic or psychonoxious for the patient or family.

Estimation of the usefulness of any attempts to modify the disorder depends upon accurate initial measurement or description of the patient's condition and notation of any change which occurs, with or without formal treatment, after a period of time. It is often difficult to determine what aspect or element of treatment effects change of measurable items. Obviously, it is important to know the "natural" course of a disorder if we are to evaluate the effects of factors introduced to modify it, and we should be prepared to measure specific changes in the components of a syndrome rather than global impressions of improvement or cure. The notation of change in specific items of behavior can lead to identification of useful therapeutic procedures and the recognition of those characteristics of an individual that are predictive of a favorable or unfavorable course, useful in the evaluation of treatment.

In this paper some of the problems of describing individual characteristics and measurement of specific items of functioning are briefly discussed. This is followed by a description of several methods of recording or testing mental and physical functional status in the aged which appear to be of predictive value and consequently of help in the evaluation of treatment. The remarks on the evaluation of change in geriatric patients with disorders of affect is based upon clinical experience. The tests and methods for the measurement and evaluation of brain syndrome described are based upon a review of data obtained from examination and follow up of more than 1,250 persons 65 years of age or over on first admission to old age homes, nursing homes and state hospitals conducted by the Office of the Consultant on Psychiatric Services for the Aged of the Department of Mental Hygiene of New York State. The persons followed constitute a representative sample of such institutionalized persons in New York City in 1957-58.[1] It is expected that follow-up will yield information about the course of similar types of patients in different settings, and of dissimilar persons in similar settings, to serve as a basis for the evaluation of care offered to aged persons.

Problems of Measurement

Definition of the Patient Group

For statistical purposes it is necessary to have a clear definition of the group studied. Lack of care in definition can lead to misleading comparisons of dissimilar aged patients considered similar merely because of chronological age or place of residence. Aged persons in psychiatric hospitals who developed mental illness in youth or middle age, or who had repeated exacerbations of mental disorder before chronological old age, differ from persons who first come to psychiatric attention in their old age. They should not be admixed with aged first admissions to mental hospitals. The natural course and prognosis of illness in the two groups appears to be different. Physical illness and impaired physical functional status are more common in the latter group who, furthermore, are often in a state of new and rapidly progressing social or economic change. They are usually first seen at a time of crisis which involves the family or community, in contrast to those who have aged in the hospital whose place in society has already "closed in" and disappeared.

Definition of Change Observed—Goals

Closely allied to defining the group is the definition of goals: what is considered success for one group may be called failure in another. In terms of goal the patient who has aged in the hospital should not be equated with first admissions in old age. The goals of treatment for those who became ill early in life and have remained chronically ill, for those who became ill in middle or late middle age, and for those in whom mental disorders come to attention late in life, may differ widely.

For example, a schizophrenic patient who has aged in the hospital may respond remarkably well to humane care, milieu and group therapy; he may become a well disciplined and manageable—although possibly erratic, untidy and socially detached—candidate for well supervised nonhospital care. Therapeutic efforts may also greatly increase socialization in such persons who, although surrounded by others, have been allowed to remain isolated because of fear, inertia, passivity, pessimism or ignorance on the part of attending personnel. Such results might be regarded as upgrading. Similarily, a goal might be taken to empty a state hospital of many of the aged schizophrenic patients by sending them to nonpsychiatric institutions for equivalent custodial care. Their tolerance of such transfer is not necessarily a measure of improvement. Parenthetically it should be noted that such a move does not necessarily indicate that improved care will be offered; it may merely indicate that a financial burden is being passed from one agency to another. In any case, the goal in the treatment of the long-term schizophrenic patient may merely be improvement with respect to management problems and capacity for self-care together with change in social behavior.

In contrast, the middle-aged or "young" aged patient who develops, or in whom affective disorder emerges as of medicosocial importance, may be highly responsive to psychiatric treatment and for him the goal may be complete restoration to the previous level of function. The truly "aged" patient may be a candidate for help toward greater comfort and manageability and adjustment to an institutional or home situation suitable to his impaired status. In his case there may be little or no emphasis on productivity and meaningful community resocialization but major emphasis upon physical well-being, relative self-reliance and institutional adjustment.

The classification of patients and the determination of goals of treatment so essential for the evaluation of treatment is beset by many problems. Some of these are mentioned to suggest areas in which clarification or change of procedures are indicated.

Psychiatric Classification

A psychiatric diagnosis made by a competent examiner should be useful for predictive purposes. However, traditional nosology is of limited value as a base line for measurements of change. For example, the categories "psychosis with cerebral arteriosclerosis" and "senile psychosis of presbyophrenic type" do not lend themselves to evaluation of improvement, stabilization, or no improvement, unless particular components of the disorder are enumerated. This requires that there be measures of specific items or components of a disorder.

Also, "traditional" diagnostic terms are untrustworthy because of different fashions of diagnosis in different institutions. The term "cerebral arteriosclerosis" is often used as a wastebasket category into which all aged patients with acquired dementia of questionable aetiology can be dumped. The co-existence of so-called "cerebral arteriosclerosis" and "senile deterioration" is often ignored as though these conditions were mutually exclusive. Furthermore, confusion arises from the fact that aged persons admitted to psychiatric hospitals are considered to be psychotic, while equally ill persons with the same or different behavioral manifestations, that are environmentally more tolerable, are not regarded as "psychotic." This is a subtle invasion of medical attitudes by quasilegal concepts of "insanity," and making psychiatric diagnosis in terms of social norms or judgements rather than in terms of suffering, efficiency of function and the realization of potential for performance.

Present diagnostic nomenclature does not provide for the frequent coincidence of acute and chronic brain syndrome. When acute brain syndrome is hidden in the diagnosis of "senile psychosis, delirious and confused," or under the heading of chronic brain syndrome, the recovery from the acute brain syndrome component of the disorder is often mistaken for change in degree of the chronic brain syndrome. Moreover, a clear-cut definition of how these disorders can be categorized as mild, moderate or severe, or in a way which would facilitate measuring change is lacking.

Psychological Testing

Psychological tests generally give limited, or no information, useful for the evaluation of treatment. The projective techniques in particular tend to become structured interviews which yield impressions rather than useful ratings or comparisons, or remain highly structured, detailed and pseudoprecise instruments which are cumbersome and untrustworthy. Hopkins and Roth[2] found that a number of standard psychometric examinations do not adequately differentiate "functional" from "organic" disorders. Unless psychological examination findings are reported in terms of specific performance which can be retested they are not helpful. Experience in reviewing charts of patients in the Hospital and Home for Aged and Infirm Hebrews of New York* who had had psychological and psychiatric examinations from 1 day to 10 years before, suggests that our present system of testing, and of recording data, provides little information of use in evaluation of the effect of therapy upon mental functioning. Organicity is presumed

*This institution is now known as the Jewish Home and Hospital for the Aged.

present in the absence of substantiating data, degree of disorder is not precisely stated or is remarked upon impressionistically and without supporting data.

Rating by Personnel

The use of ratings of patient behavior or performance by attendant, nursing, or administrative personnel is of doubtful value for the measurement of change and the evaluation of treatment. Ratings can be used best in the form of basic data which then need interpretation and conversion into rating scales by sociopsychological observers. In our pilot phase of the study of the characteristics of institutionalized aged persons in New York City[3] we obtained ratings, by both interview and questionnaire, of the patient's memory, orientation and behavior from personnel in the various institutions surveyed. There were wide variations in how the same patient was rated by different personnel. This was not necessarily a reflection of difference in patient-staff relations, or time of observation; the calibre and training of persons in similar positions and their interest and accuracy as observers and reporters differed widely. Many did not understand the questions asked, many were scarcely acquainted with their patients, others seemed to try to give the answers they thought were expected or desired. There was evidence of lack of understanding of the meaning of simple terms, of patients' behavior, and of how to elicit or interpret signs. Self-defensive falsification seemed common; ratings often appeared to be influenced by needs for self-aggrandizement or by economic motives. There was wide disagreement between the ratings of some personnel and the findings of our examining staff. For example, in one institution patients who were rated by its staff as being oriented and with no memory loss were actually found to be disoriented and with marked memory deficits. In one nursing home the chief nurse told an examiner that there were no "mentals" in her nursing home and no problems of management or behavior, that she would not tolerate such patients in her home because it was illegal, while she was affectionately restraining a gibbering, incontinent old lady and the investigating physician's sleeve was being pulled by an aimless, restless, incomprehensible muttering aged male.

Also, ratings even by conscientious and well-trained personnel are influenced by their type of training and even their personality. A study at the Home for Aged and Infirm Hebrews of New York of the patients referred to the psychiatrist revealed that social workers complained about patients' interpersonal friction, resident physicians referred patients with psychiatric diagnoses, and the nurses and administrators referred patients in terms of the management problems they presented.[4] In actuality they all referred patients with much the same psychiatric and behavioral disorders but with different complaints about them.

Furthermore, personnel on all levels may disagree with the patient as to what needs change or improvement. Improvement in mental functional impairment which leads to a decrease in physical disability and an increase in physical activity may pose administrative problems. Rehabilitation potential may remain unrecognized or ignored because of fixed notions about the kind of care the institution should provide and the type of patient it should treat. Administrators', physicians', nurses' and social workers' goals in therapy are by no means identical although we would like to believe so; the rating of patients may be influenced by the different aims of different disciplines unless they meet, discuss and agree on definitions.

To both understand and instruct personnel who care for the aged we have been experimenting with methods for evaluating personnel.* In this we have used the Modified F-scale, a test which may reveal authoritarian as opposed to democratic authoritative attitudes;[5] an attitude scale devised by Oberleder[6] to reveal prejudiced, stereotyped, notions about aging and the aged, and a multiple choice questionnaire (Goldfarb) which appears to reveal bias or mistaken notions about aged ill persons in even highly sophisticated persons such as physicians.

Regression as a Measure of Status or Change

It has been advocated, directly and by implication, that the degree of "regression" can be used to both describe and to explain the status of a mentally ill aged person. Alteration with respect to regression or regressive behavior would then be a measure of improvement or deterioration.

However, as used at present the term "regression" appears to be more a lay blanket term than a scientific concept. Even when used to denote one of several concepts—as return to a prior level of psychosexual development and libidinal cathexis, as abandonment of developed or acquired ego functions, or as the use of early developed defenses against anxiety—this term lacks precision unless properly qualified. The lay use of the term regression to describe and explain away

*Descriptions of these questionnaires and methods of the survey of institutionalized aged patients can be obtained from the author.

incontinence or slovenliness of complex aetiology as a return to the pleasures of infancy, is unwarranted.

The concept of regression can possibly be helpful when it is clearly defined to mean that the aged patient may make use of a developing deficit as a means of protest, or to signal distress, despair or helplessness, and that the defect or disorder may become integrated with the pattern of behavior. Because this tendency to integrate symptoms of physical illness and impairment into the personality as a mode of communication and to solve an interpersonal conflict is actually either repair, growth, compensatory action, or an attempt at problem-solving by flight or withdrawal—alone or in combination—its efficiency or adaptive value and its details should not be obscured by a blanket term.

The characteristics of an established dependency relationship, the exploitive behavior which is recognizable as the behavior of weak persons with stronger ones, can be likened or compared to the behavior of children with parental figures. However, such behavior need by no means necessarily be identical with or exactly recapitulate earlier patterns, nor need it remain the same unless circumstances favor that it become repetitive. The notation of behavior as stereotyped, oversimplified, or directly manipulative of personal relationships, rather than in terms of regression, may be useful for the evaluation of change.

Discharge, Transfer and Mortality as Measures of Change

As mentioned above, discussion of the aged schizophrenic patient's discharge or transfer cannot be accepted at face value as indicating either improvement or worsening of condition. Moves are frequently influenced by administrative policy and personnel or community expectations and tolerance. Persons transferred from old age homes to psychiatric hospitals, for example, may be less severely ill from a medical point of view than others who remain. Persons with affective disorder and relatively good prognosis, or persons with mild brain syndrome who are overreacting to their situation, may be disturbing to staff and be sent out, while the quiet and well-behaved but severely depressed or severely mentally impaired may be permitted to stay. However, the record of discharge and transfers of large numbers of persons over a sufficiently long period of time will probably reveal useful data about the natural course of disorders in the aged. Data on the mortality of patients, for example, suggests that patient groups in different institutions vary in their outlook for life, and therefore in their characteristics, thus influencing the selection of institution for care.

Figure 1 indicates that the death rate of the younger group of persons in nursing homes is comparable to that of the oldest in old age homes, and the death rate of the youngest in state hospitals is comparable to that of the oldest in nursing homes.[7]

The fact that these groups are about 20 years apart in chronological age suggests that there are marked health differences in the groups, in the effect of the characteristics which lead to institutional care, upon their capacity to survive, in the treatment they receive, or all these factors. For such data to be useful the physical functional state, the mental functional state, as well as general psychiatric classification, age, sex and institutional residence, must be known. More, because patients who develop disorder in old age are prone to be admitted at a time of crisis, the death rate of newly admitted patients may be very high. This is illustrated by the cumulative mortality rate of a small cohort of persons first admitted at the age of 65 or over to a state hospital.[8] This provides a base line for a comparison with patients who find their way to other facilities for care and must be evaluated with an understanding that some, but not all, of these persons are transfers from "screening hospitals" where there is also a high initial mortality.

In figure 2 the death rate of persons first admitted to a state hospital in old age is plotted. The sex difference is clearly seen here.

In the following section some methods of noting and recording the physical and mental status of aged persons so as to discover characteristics predictive of course, other factors being equal, will be described. The identification of characteristics predictive of course under known

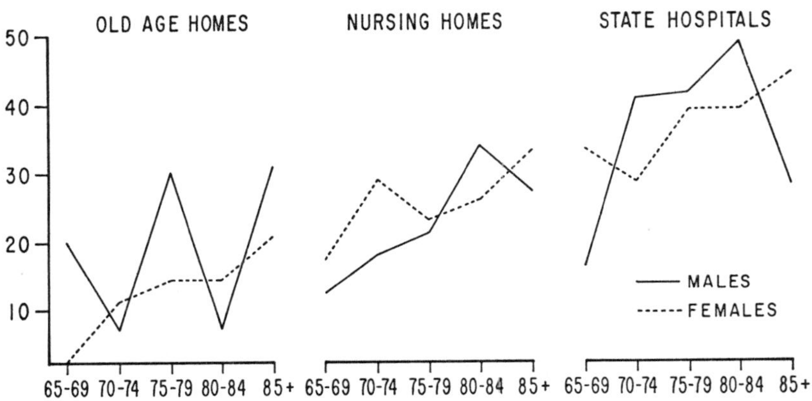

FIG. 1.—Deaths within 1 year of aged persons in specific age groups and institutions.

circumstances may be of use in the evaluation of the effect of factors introduced to modify the course of the disorder. This course can be measured—as noted above—in terms of change in classification, of behavior as variously noted, in terms of discharge as required or found feasible (up or downgrading) and in terms of longevity.

The likelihood that the mortality of these persons is a matter of individual status rather than of the effect of the institution or of transfer is shown by an examination of the relationship of physical infirmity, as judged by a physician, to death rate (fig. 3).[9]

SUGGESTED METHODS OF MEASUREMENT

Definition of the Aged Patient

The aged state is the result of decline in the capacity to meet specific demands. The age of 65 years can be taken as the chronological period at which, in our society, all persons begin to manifest a degree of decline. Serious psychiatric disorder clearly in evidence before old

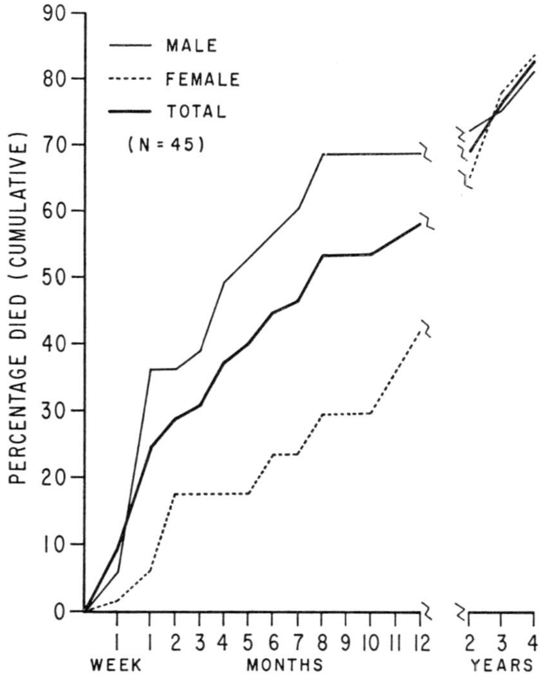

FIG. 2.—Time of death after examination.

age, here arbitrarily defined as 65 years old and over, probably should not be regarded as a geriatric condition although it may deserve special consideration as it influences or is complicated by aging. This is particularly true for chronic or recurrent psychoneuroses, character disorders, or the so-called psychophysiologic disorders of onset before old age. Some of these disorders may tend to exert influences upon personality which counter the tendency of aging, through impairment and decline of ability, to promote behavior similar to that of old age.

Defining a younger chronological age, say the 60th year, as the time of onset of old age means inclusion of a large group of so-called late developing schizophrenias, melancholias or depressions, and hypomanic disorders. Relatively few of these disorders are associated with or complicated by evolving signs of brain damage. In general the affective disorders in this age group have a good prognosis. I believe that successful treatment of such patients, if indiscriminately included in reports about "geriatric" patients, may be misleading as to what can be expected in the type of illness seen in the preponderant number of those who develop mental disorder after 64 years of age. Evaluation of treatment in persons in their 60's consequently is chiefly a matter of notation of improvement with respect to mood and content.

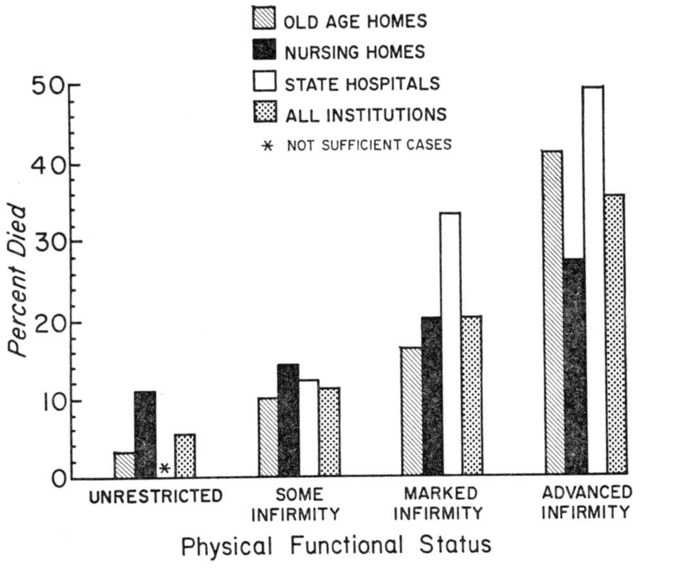

FIG. 3.—Physical functional status and death rate 1 year after examination.

The Aged Psychiatric Patient

At the present time the mental disorder which constitutes the greatest public health problem in the older age group is brain syndrome of any aetiology and severity, in association with many types of neurotic, psychotic or character disorders. Of first admissions in old age to mental hospitals, over 90 per cent of the aged patients with mental disorders who pass through metropolitan hospitals, at least 80 per cent of aged persons in old age homes and nursing homes,[10] and from 10 to 20 per cent of aged persons in the community,[11] are persons with chronic brain syndrome. The aged mentally ill who do not have a significant degree of brain syndrome usually have lost other resources for use in adaptation in their later years, which has resulted in the elaboration of syndromes based upon fear of helplessness, severity of functional loss, anger, and anxiety.

We can postulate or recognize a level of performance which a society, or the aged themselves, may expect of them. This level may be high for some activities and low for others, depending upon the type of society, its needs of the time, and the attitudes and norms of function of its aged. Required or accepted levels of achievement for most social functioning may be so low that illness and decline with aging may be accepted as "normal" until there is very great impairment. The less demanding, the more tolerant and the better organized a society is for automatically adjusting to or absorbing the weak and ill the less likely

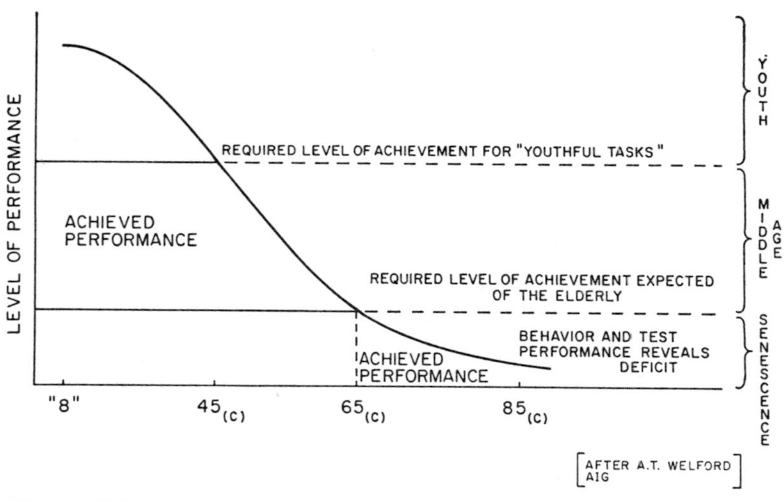

FIG. 4.—Relation of required level of achievement and level of performance.

is it that incapacity will call attention to itself as a difficult social problem.

However, for any society there is a quantitative point at which loss of self-orienting ability and memory renders the individual ineffective, even for routine tasks, and in need of assistance. It is this conversion of quantitative loss into qualitative change as a member of society, as it is reflected in and influences behavior, whose onset we strive to predict and the extent of which we wish to measure. This concept is diagrammatically shown in figure 4, suggested by Welford.[12]

To the alteration of behavior and of capacity to function which results in social incapacity we give a special name—brain syndrome.

Brain Syndrome

In discussing brain syndrome we must recognize that there is a difference between acute brain syndrome and chronic brain syndrome. We should keep in mind that chronic brain syndrome may be punctuated by episodes of acute brain syndrome. Thus, chronic brain syndrome may appear to wax and wane in intensity, on account of difference in the degree of acute brain syndrome present.

Brain Syndrome

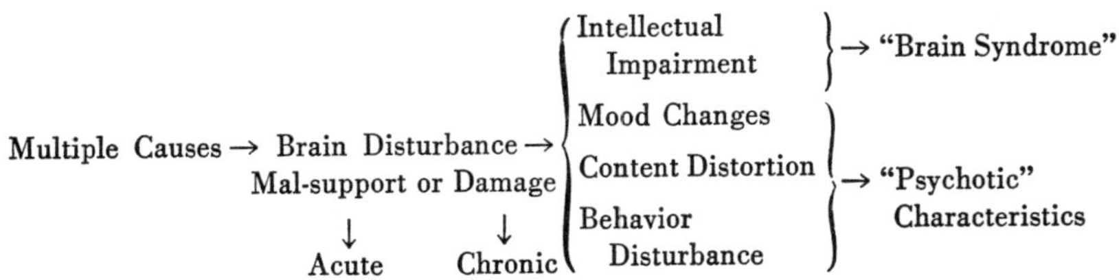

Fig. 5

Brain syndrome is complicated by changes in mood, content and behavior. The true measure of brain syndrome is probably the measurable intellectual deficit. Figure 5 is designed to illustrate that brain dysfunction either due to cerebral malsupport or on account of brain damage can be considered responsible for measurable intellectual deficit and some alteration in affect, thinking and the overt patterning of behavior. Obviously the premorbid personality may influence the patterning in which intellectual deficit will show itself as well as what deficits will first be most apparent. Well educated persons, well drilled in certain matters, may suffer considerable loss in these areas without their being obvious or even easily measurable. Affect, thought, and patterns of behavior, similarly, will in the event of brain damage differ from person to person, depending upon the amount and type of drilling in social and emotional responsivity. Persons in whom the intellectual deficit is most clearly obvious and who respond affectively to this, and whose thought and behavior are disorganized on this account, tend to be regarded as brain syndrome patients, whereas those whose premorbid personality more clearly contributes to affect and content as well as behavior tend to be noted as brain syndrome with psychosis. It is worth noting, therefore that a person with severe brain damage is more likely to be considered as "pure brain syndrome" or as "without psychoses," whereas persons with lesser degrees of brain dysfunction to whose behavior previous personality can make greater contributions may be regarded as "with psychoses." In line with this it is therefore to be expected that because the degree of brain syndrome is related to both physical functional status and chronological age, that individuals in the oldest age group and with the greatest impairment of physical functional status would be most likely to show least "psychoses," and conversely more persons "with psychoses" will be found in the relatively physically healthier and chronologically younger persons.

Specific Methods of Evaluation

Before discussing what is probably the most important problem in the aged group—methods of evaluating changes in the status of persons with brain syndrome—evaluation of persons with affective disorders will be briefly discussed.

Disorders of Affect

In the main, criteria for improvement in disorders of affect in the aged are the same as for younger persons. Notations of restoration to previous norms of sleep, appetite and bowel function are of special importance because these are matters about which the patient, nursing personnel or the physician can make relatively objective determinations. Just as in younger persons, in depressive reactions of the aged the patient is drowsy and falls asleep in the evening, wakes before bedtime, falls asleep without any trouble and then tends to wake in the early morning hours. Sleep is yearned for, it is looked forward to and the patient may retreat to bed during the day. On waking in the early morning there may be rumination and feelings of anxiety, worry and "heaviness." In the aged there is commonly no "worry" but rather feelings of malaise, restlessness, and "empty" concern over the depressed feelings and a drive to feel well. Improvement can be measured by tendency to wake later until it finally occurs at the previous customary time, by decreasing drowsiness in the evening, and elimination of evening naps; by decreased eagerness and yearning for evening or night and the relief that comes with the unconsciousness of sleep. The lifting of depression is also signalled for some by the return of dreaming which during the depth of the depression is reported as entirely absent.

Restoration of appetite to the previous norm is also an indicator of recovery. The usual pattern with depression is anorexia. As depression lifts, first, food, which was repellant or repulsive, can be better tolerated; people who could not eat became able to do so "because they know they should." Later, they begin to feel a little interest in the food, begin to feel hunger, and lastly, appetite returns. Accompanying this there tends to be a restoration of weight which was lost with the anxiety, depression, and anorexia. In a significant proportion of depressed aged persons there is bulemia, and preoccupation with food; as their depression lifts the compulsive overeating tends to decrease. As might be expected, the individual then eats in a less driven manner but with more enjoyment, and consequently may even become capable of following a regime helpful for the loss of the excess weight.

Bowel function is usually reduced with depression and constipation may be severe. As the depression lifts, previously "regular" persons recover their good habits of bowel function. A number of depressed persons have persistent or intermittent diarrhea. As with constipation, with lifting of the depression this tends to improve spontaneously.

The reports of subjective sadness or its equivalent in terms of "malaise," somatic discomfort or inertia, also offer an index of change. With improvement, these decrease toward the end of the day, and then decrease earlier with the passing days as recovery takes place, so that before relatively complete recovery it is only the early morning hours that are bad. The patient may describe the subjective sensations of depression in the morning simply as "heaviness" which tends to disappear or lessen after dressing or breakfast. With the decrease in subjective sensations there is also decrease in psychomotor retardation or in its equivalent—agitation. When a depression is communicated solely in terms of somatic complaints, which is very frequent in the aged, it is these complaints which are said to be worse in the morning and tend to decrease in their intensity as the day wears on.

Decrease in rumination of a paranoid nature also occurs as the depression lightens, but does not follow the same pattern as reports of depressed feelings. In fact, with decreasing depression "attacks" of a paranoid type upon a mate or attendants may increase markedly. Thus the quiet, meek, unobtrusive or clinging depressed patient may be preferred by family or staff to the angry, accusing, complaining, aged patient seemingly free of depression. Alternating expression of depressed feelings of this type is common. Feelings of jealousy for all persons around "who are not so sick" is also common and may be expressed in irritable querulous fashion. This increase in irritability and querulousness may indicate improvement or worsening of depression. In many, paranoid ideation and expression of paranoid ideas may become more marked as the depression lifts. Thus, they will appear with greatest force toward the end of the day at first, finally taking more of the day and eventually, especially if the person moves into a hypomanic or manic state, they become glaringly obvious. They may take the form of attacks upon the environment. They may be somatically expressed in terms of great suffering with implicit or explicit accusations about the neglect or the faults of others, or, as is most often the case, they will take the form of accusing and obvious diatribes and remarks about mates, children or relatives and friends. In the case of institutionalized persons such accusations invariably include members of the nursing and attending staff. Such paranoid ruminations or conversation is often complicated by paranoid behavior in the recovery stage. Many patients do not move from this stage of high nuisance value into relative normality, except to return to depressive reaction. Thus the improvement of depressed patients often converts a meek, mild, ingratiating or retarded, docile, manageable individual into a vociferous, annoying, accusing, and troublesome individual.

Somewhat similar to the diurnal variations are changes in the week. For some individuals such as housewives, the week-ends, if they mean a burden of involvement with otherwise absent family, or the absence of individuals they especially turn to, may be the worst. For some workers, such as teachers, for whom the week-end means relief from tasks which emphasize their poor concentration, week-ends may be best.

Improvement in concentration with concomitant capacity to do things, the ability for which is lost with depression, are useful measures. Ability to tend to the conversation of others, to follow radio or TV programs, to read with understanding, in that order and with increasing degree, improve with the lifting of depression. The capacity to concentrate upon tasks follows upon increase of capacity to receive and process communications. From the ability to do merely simple manual work of a mechanical and stereotyped nature the person becomes able to do tasks of increasing complexity. Eventually, appetite for pursuits of various types returns and initiative, previously strikingly absent, is restored to its former levels.

In general, symptomatic and behavior changes do not mean that the condition or process of affective disorder has been permanently arrested. Relapse or recurrence is common. This is true where the treatment has been solely or predominantly psychotherapeutic, pharmacologic, electro-convulsant or inclusive of environmental change or education.

One of the problems of measuring disorganized behavior in the presence of brain syndrome is that symptomatic repetitious, stereotyped, monotonous and usually inefficient behavior—rigidity of functioning based on a loss of resources—cannot be easily distinguished from repetitive behavior of intact individuals under conditions of purposeful "high drive" toward a single object and goal. In our study, methods of measuring purpose-driven from stereotyped repetitive behavior in the presence of chronic brain syndrome still remain to be tested. Nevertheless, techniques used for evaluating the functional level irrespective of cause are a useful and necessary first step in measurement.

Suggested Measures of Evaluation of "Organic" Syndromes

Brain Syndrome

The measures of brain syndrome we have used are selected items of uniform physical and mental status examinations administered by internists, psychiatrists and psychologists in a specified manner. Some of the tests and methods used for the purpose of measuring change could be related to the introduction of specific programs or methods of care in specific institutions. It is my hope that they will be used in testing the effectiveness of care in special units already operating or to be developed in New York State.

All the instruments we have used have shortcomings as individual measures. However, used together as a battery they have been found helpful in delineating the status of patients in our initial examinations, and in the objective evaluation of the effects of treatment or custodial programs for the aged ill. Measures such as these may have other uses.

When a patient's disorientation or intellectual deficit is carefully rated by standardized tests we may be able to demonstrate its relationship to neuropathological or electroencephalographic change. This will improve our diagnostic and prognostic skills by permitting more accurate evaluation of the degree to which behavior disturbance is contingent upon personality factors as contrasted to the disorganizing effects of brain damage or cerebral malsupport.

Psychiatric Examination

The psychiatric examination was used as a validation of our briefer instruments and to yield ratings of disturbed behavior in terms of psychiatrists' opinion of the patients' needs. Diagnostic classification could be expected to yield only limited information as to the patient's suffering or comfort, the problem of management posed, or the eligibility for or desirability of hospitalization. However, these items could be asked for directly or inferred from "forced" fulfillment of a schedule of psychiatric judgments about specific type of treatment needed, opinion as to "certifiability," the desirability of hospitalization, and problems of management. Such information was requested in addition to descriptive and etiologic diagnostic statements. The schedule used to obtain this information, the "Psychiatric Examination Form," will be found in Appendix B.

The results suggest that the degree of chronic brain syndrome present can be as accurately evaluated for purposes of comparison and follow-up by means of a brief direct questionnaire as by a complicated psychiatric interview or special psychometric techniques. In general, psychiatrists are on safe ground in evaluating the severity of chronic brain syndrome gauged by the patient's state of orientation for time, place and person.

The Mental Status Questionnaire

For speed, simplicity and ease of maintaining a standard in classification of chronic brain syndrome as none or "mild," "moderate" and "severe," 10 questions[13] were selected from a total test of battery of 31 drawn partly from standard mental status examination procedures and partly from special studies of altered behavior with cerebral dysfunction.[14] These questions were chosen as a measuring device because replies were easily checked for accuracy, there was least probability that they would measure other functions than those noted in the "test areas," they were simple to grasp, and they covered a very considerable spread of the intellectual functioning to be tested—disorientation for time and place, memory recent or remote, or both, and general information or "intellectual capacity." Omitted are tests of orientation for person, and of ability to learn, to reason, to calculate or judge. Table 1 presents this abbreviated test.

Tests of orientation are generally reliable and tend to discriminate between disorders of affect and brain damage. An instrument of this type, despite its seeming simplicity and skeletal brevity, is accurate for estimating brain syndrome in the aged group. This was demonstrated by cross correlation with the results of psychiatric examination in our study.

TABLE 1.—Mental Status Questionnaire—"Special Ten"*

Question	Presumed Test Area
1. Where are we now?	Place
2. Where is this place (located)?	Place
3. What is today's date-day of month?	Time
4. What month is it?	Time
5. What year is it?	Time
6. How old are you?	Memory-recent or remote
7. What is your birthday?	Memory-recent or remote
8. What year were you born?	Memory-remote
9. Who is president of the U.S.?	General information-memory
10. Who was president before him?	General information-memory

*Modified from Mental Status by Kahn, Pollack and Goldfarb.

Theoretically a psychiatrist's mental status should yield a more accurate and reliable assay of the degree of chronic brain syndrome present. However, psychiatrists are found to agree less well with each other than did the mental status questionnaire with the most skillful and experienced psychiatrist in the examination team. Also, psychologists in their use of the mental status questionnaire agreed better with each other than did psychiatrists, in their estimates of the same persons or of population samples.

The mental status questionnaire when scored in terms of number of errors made correlates well with psychiatric estimates of degree of brain syndrome, as shown in table 2 below.

TABLE 2.—Rating of Mental Functional Impairment by Mental Status Questionnaire

No. of errors	Presumed Mental Status
0 - 2	Chronic brain syndrome absent or mild
3 - 8	Chronic brain syndrome moderate
9 - 10	Chronic brain syndrome severe
Nontestable	Chronic brain syndrome severe*

*In the not uncooperative person without deafness or insuperable language barrier.

This, of course, is as should be expected because the questionnaire is a standardization of the items generally used in arriving at the psychiatric judgment.

The brief mental status questionnaire can be used with persons who are blind, bedridden, incontinent, disoriented, physically handicapped, and easily fatigued, as well as with healthy ambulatory persons, in contrast to tests which depend upon response to visual stimuli, or which demand drawing, copying, protracted attention or lengthy reply. This test may, however, appear to be less revealing of mental impairment in persons of high educational, occupational, and social background who have well-developed habits of remaining oriented for time and place. This effect probably accounts for the inverse relationship of years of education and number of errors that we do indeed find; however, I do not believe this is an invalidating defect of this or any other test for chronic brain syndrome. Rather, I feel that this helps us to define chronic brain syndrome as a condition in which brain damage is a necessary but not sufficient cause. Chronic brain syndrome as a diagnostic category then can be regarded as requiring deficits of orientation, in the absence of which the emergence of maladaptive symptoms of the syndrome would be minimal. Clinically, one not infrequently sees good orientation for time and place among better educated or more literate persons when a subtle degree of disorientation for persons has become manifest. Under such circumstances emotional disturbance may also arise and complicate the disorder. In such persons if there is no depression or anxiety with the loss of memory, the brain damage may not seriously interfere with individual social adjustment. In them we can only suspect early chronic brain syndrome and are confronted by a need for more delicate and precise tests for brain damage.

It should be noted that the mental status questionnaire can do more than evaluate the degree of brain syndrome. It can provide information about behavioral patterns. Patterns of evasion, defensiveness, hostility and confabulation are discernible when the mental status questionnaire is properly annotated and interpretively reviewed. Misnaming of place or mistakes about time can yield considerable information about the emotional state and adaptational striving of the person.

The Face-Hand Test

The face-hand test is a brief, simple procedure of double, simultaneous stimulation, first described by Fink, Green and Bender as a diagnostic test for brain damage[15] in which errors of response are reliably associated with brain damage in adults. The subject sits facing the examiner, hands resting on knees. He is touched or brushed simultaneously on one cheek and the dorsum of one hand, usually in a specified order, although the order need not be strictly adhered to.[16] Table 3 presents the order of stimulation.

TABLE 3.—Order of Stimulation Used in Face-Hand Test*

1.	Right cheek—left hand
2.	Left cheek—right hand
3.	Right cheek—right hand
4.	Left cheek—left hand
5.	Right cheek—left hand
6.	Right hand—left hand
7.	Right cheek—left hand
8.	Left cheek—right hand
9.	Right cheek—right hand
10.	Left cheek—left hand

*As modified from Bender, Fink and Green by Kahn and Pollack.

A patient who learns to report correctly consistently—verbally or by sign—when he is touched within the space of 10 trials is "negative;" those who report one place touched, omitting the other, or who localize one of the touches incorrectly on themselves or on the examiner, are "positive." The test is done first with the patient's eyes closed, and if he makes errors it is repeated with eyes open. It is of interest that when incorrect replies are made with eyes closed there is only infrequently improvement with eyes open. The test is very highly correlated with brain syndrome as measured by the mental status questionnaire, and as determined by psychiatric impression. It is somewhat less reliable in alert, well-educated persons and persons with depression, agitation or hypomania, than is the mental status questionnaire. The fact that the patient may respond to this test correctly, although a cursorily done mental status suggests severe chronic brain syndrome, should influence the examiner toward hopefulness about affecting functional ability despite impairment. Decrease of any affective disorder present may reveal more resources and adaptability than the history or the present mental status otherwise suggests.

Operational Definition of Chronic Brain Syndrome

In terms of the foregoing, chronic brain syndrome can be defined as that point at which the deficit in function of a person with brain damage emerges as disruptive of the personality for the individual, for society, or both. It probably emerges first as a loss of resources to which the person reacts or which he attempts to integrate into his personality; at a later point of progression it becomes manifest as "maladjustment." Our tests appear to be "positive" at this point; and

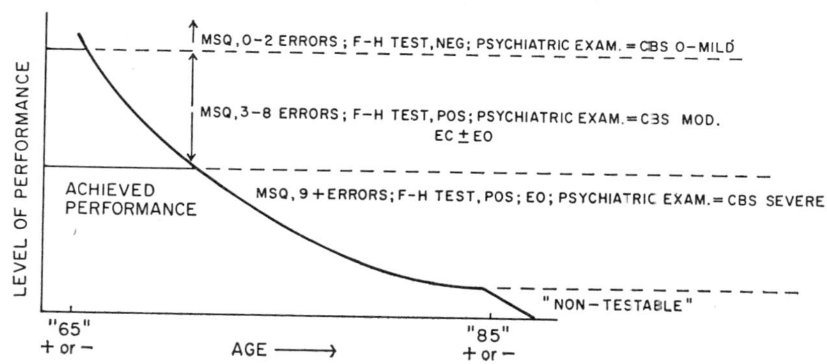

Fig. 6.—Relation of level of performance for age group and mental status questionnaire errors.

if they are then negative other diagnostic considerations should be considered as more likely than brain syndrome.

These remarks can be illustrated as an operational concept by referring back to the next scheme, suggested by Welford's diagram.[17]

TABLE 4.—Grading of Physical Function Status on the Basis of Internist's History and Physical Examination*

Degree of Incapacity		
0 to Mild	#1.	"Unrestricted Physical Capacity." No organic disease which seriously limits activity, e.g., moderate osteoarthritis, mild congestive failure, mild angina and hypertension alone are not considered limiting. These patients can live alone, travel alone and take care of their own needs. Even if also mentally ill they require little personal physical care.
	#2.	"Restricted Activity—Moderate." A limiting infirmity such as heart failure or osteoarthritis which is severe but does not confine to bed, e.g., blindness, infirmity, amputation, malnutrition, mild debilitation in association with slow growing malignant neoplasms or blood dyscrasia. The infirmities are usually progressive. These persons can take care of their own needs with supervision and assistance, are in need of intermittent or continuous medical care, usually if also mentally ill they need a protective environment.
Moderate	#3.	"Restricted Activity—Marked." Moderate to marked infirmity, associated with advanced age or the presence of disease which severely limits physical ability, e.g., Parkinson's disease, paralysis, severe osteoarthritis, advanced peripheral vascular disease, severe malnutrition and debility due to neoplasm or chronic infections in the terminal stages. These persons require constant help and cannot live alone.
Severe	#4.	"Restricted Activity Complete." Advanced infirmity much as above but with more limitation of mobility and complete dependence upon crutches, wheelchair, cane or etc., e.g., advanced infirmity of old age, crippling osteoarthritis, advanced debilitation of malignant disease, "senility." These persons require a competent devoted family or attendants. When mentally ill they are commonly totally bedridden and require complete nursing care.

*As modified from Zeman by Gerber and Goldfarb.

Physical Examination

A major psychiatric problem in the aged is the conversion of the bedridden, incontinent, physically dependent person in need of close supervision and nursing care into a relatively self-sufficient individual in need of less careful supervision through the improvement of mental status and motivation. There is also considerable evidence which suggests that improvement of physical status tends to carry with it improvement of mental status.[18] We have consequently been interested in determining the physical rehabilitation potential which may exist in an individual or groups of institutionalized persons. This task is complicated by the necessity for evaluating to what extent physical functional impairment is complicated by mental status to yield "disability." The data of the standard medical examination are difficult to process and evaluate. However, when the physician was asked to convert the results of his history and examination into a rating of physical functional status despite some shortcomings, a useful item was obtained.

The conversion of his examination data into an impression which could be graded was facilitated and controlled by the provision of guiding definitions shown in table 4.

With these definitions the physician could record an impression of the patient which was then categorized as "mild," "moderate," or "severe," as shown in table 5 below.

TABLE 5.—Physical Functional Status: Physician's Estimate of Degree of Incapacity

Estimated Incapacity	Presumed Physical Activity Level Possible	Rating
No incapacity	Unrestricted physical capacity	
Slight incapacity	Restricted physical capacity	1
Marked incapacity	Markedly restricted physical capacity	2
Severe incapacity	Severely restricted physical capacity	
Bedridden	Completely restricted physical capacity	3

A review of these gradations reveals the physician's estimate of physical functional capacity will to some degree almost unavoidably be contaminated by the patient's mental status.[19] The effect of mental impairment on physical functioning undoubtedly influences the physician in his "diagnosis." This does not militate, on account of circularity, against cross-correlation of this measure of physical functional status with mental status when we desire to demonstrate the reciprocal influence of mental and functional conditions.

When the physician's estimate of functional degree of physical incapacity is cross-correlated with the psychiatrist's estimate of mental functional status of chronic brain syndrome mild, moderate or severe, a close relationship of physical to mental status is revealed. Table 6 shows the per cent of persons of our sample in each category.

TABLE 6.—The Relationship of Physical Functional Status to Mental Status by Type of Institution—Percentages

Rating of	Old Age Home Residents				Nursing Home Residents				State Hospital Residents			
Physical Functional Status	Total	Mental Status			Total	Mental Status			Total	Total Status		
		1	2	3		1	2	3		1	2	3
1	49	63	38	13	23	32	20	13	23	34	31	16
2	36	29	46	46	35	34	35	35	39	34	46	36
3	15	7	16	42	42	34	44	51	38	31	23	48
Total	100	99	100	101	100	100	99	99	100	99	100	100

It can be seen that in each of the three types of institution that the proportion of persons with moderate to severe mental impairment rises as the physical limitation increases.

The physician's grading of function can be useful in comparing individuals and groups to eath other, and to themselves after intervals. A similar method from which this was developed, has been found useful in the Home for Aged and Infirm Hebrews*[20] where "down-grading" and "up-grading" of the patient occurs with time and is relevant to their transfer from one type of facility of the Home to another.

This rating of functional status is not valid for measuring impairment as opposed to disability, or as an index of rehabilitation potential. The physician's estimate of physical disability almost certainly includes the patient's limitation on account of impaired mental status which decreases his use of remaining physical resources. Observation of ambulatory status (table 7), or rating the capacity of self-care (table 8), are similarly contaminated. To ascertain the contribution to disability made by possibly remediable mental disorder, a clear measure of physical impairment alone is required.

The problem of tautology or circularity posed by the fact that an estimate of physical functioning is contaminated by recognized or

*Now Jewish Home and Hospital for the Aged.

unrecognized impaired mental status which limits physical functioning, dictates that we find a way of measuring actual physical impairment rather than disability.

Measuring Disability, Impairment, and Rehabilitation Potential

The failure of these tests to reveal actual impairment or rehabilitation potential is to be expected because disability is a compound of physical impairment, ignorance, lack of incentive and utilization of illness. Our data when cross-correlated show there is a close relationship to each other of mental status as determined by the psychologist on the mental status questionnaire, and limitation of activity, or physical functional status, as measured by (1) the physician's estimate, (2) the tests of physical independence, or (3) notation of ambulatory status. An actual test of available capacity for executive action, however, (table 9) does not exactly parallel these three.

Therefore, as might be expected, it does *not* exactly parallel mental functional impairment as measured by our mental status questionnaire or the psychiatric examination. This 10-item test of motor task performance may prove to be of assistance, when used with one of the other tests of physical function and the mental status questionnaire, in defining the physical rehabilitation potential, because it reveals neuromuscular power. The difference between capacity and functioning level may be ascribed to need for instruction, to absence of motivation, or the presence of inhibiting fear or anger. In evaluation of the patient, a review of the agreements and discrepancies in these tests can indicate how much was done or remains to be done in treatment.

Evaluation of Needs or of Effect of Treatment by Means of Physical-Mental Functional Ratio

We have discussed a number of ways to obtain over-all scores for both physical and mental functioning levels of individuals and groups

TABLE 7.—Ambulatory Status (Rating from observation on direct examination)

Ambulatory:	Patients who are classed as ambulatory can walk around by themselves.
Semi-ambulatory:	Those who can move around with the support of another person or by themselves in a wheelchair.
Bedfast:	Those patients are classed as bedfast who either remain constantly in bed or in a chair without any self-mobility.

TABLE 8.—6 Point Scale of Physical Independence*

The patient's function is rated on a series of six items.
Instructions: Check appropriate response for each item listed below.

	Rating	Yes	No	Comment	Degree of Impairment
1. Bathes independently	1	( )	( )		1
2. Dresses and washes independently	2	( )	( )		
3. Gets about on foot or wheelchair unassisted room to room	3	( )	( )		2
4. Gets in and out of bed with little or no assistance	4	( )	( )		
5. Incontinent by day	5	( )	( )		3
6. Bedfast (unless lifted bodily)	6	( )	( )		

*Devised by Dobrin, Gerber and Goldfarb.

TABLE 9.—10 Point Scale of Physical Performance*

Instructions: Patient is requested to perform 10 tasks.
Check appropriate response for each item.

Item	Yes	No	Comments
1. Lifts left heel 2 inches off bed	( )	( )	
2. Lifts right heel 2 inches off bed	( )	( )	
3. Lifts extended legs† together 2 inches off bed (heels)	( )	( )	
4. Sits up	( )	( )	
5. Gets out of bed	( )	( )	
6. Walks about or uses wheelchair‡	( )	( )	
7. Uses handkerchief	( )	( )	
8. Makes combing or brushing motions	( )	( )	
9. Opens and closes button at waist level	( )	( )	
10. Holds both hands palms up for 4-5 seconds	( )	( )	

*Devised by Goldfarb.

†Definition of "extended leg" is extension to the limits of the patient's capacity.

‡"Uses wheelchair" denotes can move from place to place in it under own power.

which reflect severity of impairment. If physical and mental functioning are disparate, the disparity is interpreted as an indication of something unexpected in their functioning, since we have found that in general physical and mental functioning are related and parallel. If tests of mental status are used as the base line for predicting total level of physical and mental functioning, and the level of physical function is poorer than the mental status would suggest, the ratio of physical to mental functioning may be informative about the individual and reflect his need for treatment or the effect of a treatment program upon him. Such ratios when used for groups in institutions may suggest how the individuals were selected by the institution, or how they have been treated or neglected.[21] For example, if the physical functional status rating of an individual or of a group is used as the numerator and the mental functional status rating as the denominator of a fraction, a derived quotient less than one would indicate probable optimal physical status of the individual or group. This would in all probability reflect good care; the converse, a quotient greater than one, might be indicative of considerable room for improvement in physical functioning and reflect poor care. Ratios which indicate equal physical and mental impairment would, of course, not be free of suspicion that matters could be improved. For evaluation after time or treatment, conversion of examination findings into this form would yield data about functioning which could be more easily processed, reviewed and integrated than verbal impressions or qualitative descriptions of changes.

Evaluating Comparable Degrees of Specific Incapacities

The most detailed or wide-ranging analyses generally descend or fit into a three-point scale. The three grades of severity as used by us for rating degrees of impairment can be correlated with graded estimates of depression or other disorders, such as those suggested by Ebaugh[22] and others; and they can also be compared to our own physical-mental functional ratio described. The scoring of 1, 2, and 3 makes possible the formation of total scores from 1 to 3 by simple addition, and division by the number of tests used. Two or more of the indices of physical functioning can be combined and the derived score can be combined with, compared, or contrasted to one or a combination of ratings of mental functional status. In table 10 the tests referred to are listed to show their comparability and suggest how they may be used as a battery.

Total Score for Individual

Seven tests used on our total sample population for measurement of various aspects of functioning are placed together in one table to show how each can be used to yield a rating of "mild," "moderate," or "severe," and a total score for the individual.[23]

TABLE 10.—Seven Techniques for Evaluating Comparable Degrees of Incapacity

Test Used	Examiner	Judgment made	Degree of Incapacity 0 to Mild	Moderate	Severe
Psychiatric exam.	Psychiatrist	Brain syndrome	0 to Mild	Moderate	Severe
Mental Status Questionnaire	Psychologist Psychiatrist Internist	Intellectual defect	0 to 2 errors	3 to 8 errors	9 to 10 errors
Face-Hand Test	Any of above	Brain syndrome	All correct	Pos. eyes closed only	Pos. eyes open
Physical exam.	Internist	Physical functional status	1 to 2	3	4
Ambulatory status	Any of above	Ambulatory status	Ambulatory	Semi-ambulatory	Bed-ridden
"6 Point Scale"	Any of above	Physical independence	Can bathe & wash self 1	Mobile 2	Bed-ridden 3
"10 Point Scale"	Any of above	Motor performance	No impair.	1 to 5	6 to 10
Total degree of incapacity scored as:			1	2	3

These tests can be useful as individual measures, as discussed above. From further study we hope to work out a combined functional index which will include all the aspects measured and a standard of functioning for older persons.

These investigations in measuring the extent of brain syndrome have also given opportunity to review the basis for diagnosis of brain syndrome and to suggest a new type of classification system (see Appendix A).

Summary

Geriatric psychiatry deals with a heterogeneous group of patients. Their psychiatric treatment ranges from psychotherapy to complete supervision and custodial care. The largest group which now urgently concerns the community and the psychiatrist consists of persons who are disabled to a degree which requires varying degrees of supervision and custody. Such means of care almost invariably include psychotherapeutic or psychonoxious relationships, medication, and general medical care in addition to the provision of food and shelter.

Estimates of the usefulness of psychiatric treatment depends upon the accuracy with which we can measure or describe the disorder, the degree or intensity with which it is present, and the amount of change which occurs over a period of time both with or without formal treatment. Obviously it is important to know the so-called natural course of the medical disorder if we are to properly evaluate the effects of any modifying factors we introduce.

Our present nosology is not helpful in giving us clear information about prognosis. Such terms as cerebral arteriosclerosis and senile deterioration, whether qualified with a description of psychiatric behavior and indications as to degree or intensity, are at best only slightly helpful and at times may even be misleading. We need to know whether the aged person is disoriented, whether he is disturbed or disturbing—whether he is physically impaired or disabled, to what extent, and how much care he appears to need. Inclusion of more specific etiologic or behavioral descriptive information may also provide information about specific needs for care. Change in any of the components of the disorder may indicate the effect of care. All of the tests we have used and can recommend have limitations. The tests of physical impairment are limited by the fact that impaired mental status decreases the use of remaining physical resources either clearly or subtly. The tests of mental status are limited in that emotional overreaction may exaggerate or disguise impairment of function related to cerebral damage while, conversely, the presence of brain syndrome may obscure affective disorder and interfere with its recognition.

The methods described, when used as a battery, appear to minimize the likelihood of errors in the estimation of the importance of brain dysfunction or physical impairment. They are, therefore, likely to be helpful in the objective evaluation of the effects of treatment and of custodial programs for the aged ill. It is also likely that we may be better able to demonstrate a relationship between disorientation or intellectual deficit and neuropathology or electroencephalographic changes if individuals are carefully rated by standardized tests or tests of this type, although it is doubtful that we will be able to demonstrate a direct uncomplicated relationship between disturbed or disturbing behavior, or disorders of affect or content, and neuropathology.

REFERENCES

1. Goldfarb, A. I.: Current trends in the management of the psychiatrically ill aged. *In* P. H. Hoch and J. Zubin (eds.) Psychopathology of Aging. New York, Grune and Stratton, 1961, pp. 248-265.
2. Hopkins, B. and Roth, M.: Psychological test performance in patients over 60. II. Paraphrenia, arteriosclerotic psychosis and acute confusion. J. Ment. Sci. *99:* 451-63, 1953.
3. Goldfarb, A. I.: Progress report on services for the aged from the Office of the Consultant on Services for the Aged. New York State Dept. of Mental Hygiene, January 1962 (Dittoed).
4. —: Psychiatry in a Home for the Aged: a seven-year follow-up of fifty-nine patients. Paper presented at the May 1958 meeting of the American Psychiatric Association.
5. Gallagher, E. B., Levinson, D. J. and Erlich, I.: Some sociopsychological characteristics of patients and their relevance for psychiatric treatment. *In* Greenblatt, M. Glencoe, Ill., Free Press, 1957, pp. 357-379.
6. Oberleder, M.: Attitudes related to adjustment in a home for the aged. *In* Kaplan, Jerome and Aldridge, Gerald (eds.) Social Welfare of the Aging. New York, Columbia University Press, 1962 pp. 25-33.
7. Goldfarb, A. I.: Progress Report op. cit.
8. Karp, E., Pollack, M. and Goldfarb, A. I.: Mental status and mortality: a four year study of elderly psychiatric patients. Paper presented at the Downstate Interhospital Conference, New York City, March 27, 1962.
9. Goldfarb, A. I.: Relationship of mortality to selected characteristics of metropolitan institutionalized aged persons. Paper presented at Sixth International Congress of Gerontology, Copenhagen August 11-16, 1963.
10. —: Summarization of activities for the year 1958. Report to Dr. P. H. Hoch, Commissioner of Mental Hygiene New York State, 1959 (Mimeographed).
11. —: Mental health of aged persons in a Housing Project. *In* New York State Conference on Aging *Proceedings* New York, 1963, pp. 11-16.
12. Welford, A. T.: Aging and Human Skill. London, Oxford University Press, 1958.
13. Goldfarb, A. I., Kahn, R. L., Pollack, M. and Peck, A.: Brief objective measures for the determination of mental status in the aged. Am. J. Psychiat. *117:* 326-338, 1960.
14. Weinstein, E. A. and Kahn, R. L.: Denial of Illness: Symbolic and Physiological aspects. Springfield, Ill., Charles C Thomas, 1955.
15. Fink, M. Green, A. and Bender, M. B.: The face-hand test as a diagnostic sign of organic mental syndrome. *Neurology 2:* 46, 1952.

16. Goldfarb, Kahn and Pollack: *op. cit.*
17. Welford: *op. cit.*
18. Pollack, M., Kahn, R. L., Gerber, I. and Goldfarb, A. I.: The relationship of mental and physical status of institutionalized aged persons. Am. J. Psychiat. *117:* 120-24, 1960.
19. Ibid.
20. Zeman, F. D.: The functional capacity of the aged: its estimation and practical importance. J. Mt. Sinai Hosp. *14:* 721-728, 1947.
21. Kahn, R. L. and Goldfarb, A. I.: Criteria for the evaluation of excess disability in the aged and the quality of institutional care. Paper presented at Downstate Interhospital Conference, New York City, March 1962.
22. Ebaugh, F. G.: Mental illness, reversible and irreversible. J. A. M. Assoc. *171:* 377-80, 1959.
23. Goldfarb, A. I.: Progress report. *op. cit.*
24. Vital Statistics of the United States, 1959, vol. 2, table No. 77A, page 202. Deaths by Suicide, by age, color and sex.

Acknowledgments

The sampling procedures were planned and supervised by Julius A. Jahn, Ph.D. Examinations upon which these findings are based were conducted by Kenneth Altshuler, M.D., Morton Aronson, M.D., Martin Barad, M.D., Arthur Peck, M.D., Vincent Squilla, M.D., Robert Shapiro, M.D., psychiatric examinations; Robert L. Kahn, Ph.D., Max Pollack, Ph.D., Arno Gruen, Ph.D., Robert Wolk, Ph.D., Eric Karp, psychological examinations; Isadore E. Gerber, M.D., with the assistance of Daniel B. Kushner, M.D., Martin Silbersweig, M.D., Alvin S. Teirstein, M.D., physical examinations. Coordination of the location follow-up study was done by Siroon Shahinian, Ph.D. Compilation of these data were supervised by Sydney Feldman, statistician, with the assistance of George Kaplan, Bennett Prieto, Ferdinand Fiore and Leonard D. Nierenberg. Dr. Goldfarb was assisted in the review of psychiatric data by Mayer Fisch, M.D., staff research psychiatrist. Project coordinator, Helen Turner, M.S., assistant to the Consultant on Psychiatric Services for the Aged. The secretarial staff who assisted in this work were Pearl Band, Veronica C. Crowley and Carmella Lauricella.

Appendix A

Recommended Criteria for Diagnosis of Brain Syndrome

The following suggestions are made to assist in the diagnosis and classification of aged patients.

For the diagnosis of *brain syndrome,* the following characteristics should be noted as present:

1. Disorientation for time, for place, or for person.
2. Evidence of impaired immediate recall.
3. Deficits of recent and remote memory.
4. Weakening of intellectual functions as indicated by difficulty and errors in doing simple calculations or in recalling simple items of general information.
5. Defects of grasp and comprehension: These may be discernible as difficulty

in retaining, and reacting to, questions or commands. They may also emerge as a faulty reaction to the situation or the interpersonal transaction, revealing that it is not understood. This can be briefly called situational disorientation.

6. A reliable history, from the patient or other sources, of episodic, intermittent, or persistent occurrences of the above.

These signs, in the absence of stupor, coma, catatonia, excitement, complete deafness, marked language difficulty, or other factors which make examination impossible, or its results questionable, are diagnostic of brain syndrome. The first five factors mentioned above should be present on examination. In chronic brain syndrome one of these deficits is rarely found without the others, although some may be less marked than others. If only one or several of the signs are found, one may suspect developing brain syndrome. The diagnosis is probably best made only when all are found to be present, in some, even though slight degree.

In addition to, and supporting the above, may be considered such clues as emotional ability, focal neurological signs (including aphasias, agnosias, and apraxias), slovenliness or poor habits, poor judgment not clearly related to emotional disturbance, and apathy. When these signs appear to be irreversible and related to brain damage rather than brain dysfunction of a reversible or transient nature the condition is termed chronic.

Acute brain syndrome is similar but is a transient and potentially reversible condition. It is usually related to a febrile, debilitating or exhausting illness; there is usually evidence of dehydration or malnutrition. However, in the aged, fever, tachycardia, leukocytosis, or obvious physical signs may be absent with acute illness. This may lead to the mistaken presumptive diagnosis of chronic brain syndrome. Blood chemistry, glucose or nonprotein nitrogen, physical examination, anemia, nutritional history or the history of drug ingestion, are often clues to the acute nature of the disorder. With acute brain syndrome all the signs of brain syndrome are not necessarily present simultaneously. There is usually fluctuation in degree of disorientation, misinterpretations, and there are occasionally hallucinatory phenomena. At times the disorder may be quiet; at other times it is characterized by restlessness, obvious "helpless" confusion with bewilderment and puzzlement, or by a tendency to wander, both physically and verbally. In some cases it can attract attention to underlying or developing illness as an exaggeration of pre-existing chronic brain syndrome, signs of which may or may not have been previously noted.

In almost all cases, the existence of acute brain syndrome in the aged may be taken as presumptive evidence of the simultaneous presence of developing chronic brain syndrome. Attacks of acute brain syndrome often contribute to a step-like progression of the more chronic form. In each person who has an episode of acute brain syndrome attempts should be made to determine whether chronic brain syndrome is present.

The Differentiation of "Cerebral Arteriosclerosis" from "Senile Brain Disease" or "Senile Deterioration" in the Development of Chronic Brain Syndrome

The term "cerebral arteriosclerosis" is best used as qualifying a type of chronic brain syndrome when the disorder appears to be the result of diffuse brain damage related to acutely and episodically focal brain damage. The most frequent cause of focal brain damage is cerebral thrombosis or carotid artery occlusion. Vasospastic episodes, anemia and anoxemia of the brain, hypotensive crisis in hypertensive persons, or in persons with myocardial infarction or cardiac failure, may be responsible for brain damage. So-called "small strokes" may actually occur, but the claim that they are frequent is questioned by some clinicians. Episodes of hypertensive encephalopathy may leave areas of focal damage. Cerebral hemorrhage is rarely a cause of chronic brain syndrome because few persons survive after such an event.

Diffuse brain damage appears to be necessary for the emergence of signs of chronic brain syndrome. Single episodes of cerebral thrombosis, hemorrhage, or embolism appear to give rise to signs of focal rather than diffuse damage unless there is cardiovascular, pulmonary, or other systemic disease which contributes to generalized cerebral damage through influence upon blood supply or metabolism. The effects of expanding intracranial lesions, when cerebral intracranial pressure is high and decompensation is occurring, or when the lesions are multiple, may be mistaken for "cerebral arteriosclerosis" in aged persons. The concept of functional neuronal mass may be helpful—brain syndrome can be considered to have emerged when neuronal mass has been decreased to a critical point. Patients can evidence many strokes before the emergence of brain syndrome, despite signs pointing to foci of brain damage.

Cerebral arteriosclerosis may slowly and chronically impair cerebral circulation and lead to loss of functional tissue. Because brain damage under such circumstances cannot clinically be differentiated from loss due to other causes, for the diagnosis of cerebral arteriosclerosis to be made there should be evidence of cerebral infarction—focal neurological signs or a history of stroke, whether large or small, mild or severe. Although the age of the patient cannot be considered a diagnostic sign, at the time of the first stroke he is usually less than 65 years. There may be a history of several such episodes in a patient with brain syndrome.

The patient with cerebral arteriosclerosis is usually aware of loss of physical and mental powers and reacts to his losses with feelings of depression. Depression is a common reaction to severe and threatening illness of any kind. It is especially notable in those whose personal integrity is threatened by the effects of brain damage. Attempts to repair, ward off, or defend oneself against the threat of disintegration are occasionally abetted by *anosognosia.* This is the term applied to brain damage in which the patient "does not know and knows not, that he knows not." Under such circumstances even gross physical defects such as hemiparesis may not be attended to, admitted to, or cannot come to awareness.

Senile brain changes are presumed to have been operative as etiological factors in the production of chronic brain syndrome when there are no focal neurological signs present on examination and when there is no history of stroke. This disorder is usually noted to begin after, rarely before, the age of 65 years; it is more common after the age of 70 and becomes almost universal in the ninth decade. It is often insidious in onset; its progression may be introduced by vaguely defined emotional disorders or by clear-cut depression. When diffuse brain damage develops slowly and environmental circumstances are supportive or there is a minimum of stress the individual may be able to compensate for them or make adjustments with little alteration or character and relatively little emotional upset. Good early education, high occupational and economic status and the early acquisition of socially acceptable patterns of action tend to "protect" against the emergence of troublesome behavior. There may be excellent preservation of function, especially on a social level, despite severe brain syndrome, and social behavior may be so well preserved as to mask severe memory deficit and disorientation.

Chronic Brain Syndrome with Psychosis

The diagnosis of brain syndrome may be qualified by the phrase "with psychosis" and the type of psychosis then specified, in the case of persons whose behavior is seriously disturbed or disturbing in ways determined *by more than disorientation and memory defect.*

The psychotic reactions most commonly seen with chronic brain syndrome are paranoid states and depressions with or without agitation. Involutional types of depressions, with guilt feelings, self-depreciation, with expressions of unworthiness, rumination over old faults or sins, with exacerbation of hostile thoughts about relatives and friends, as well as true suicidal thoughts or attempts, rarely occur in conjunction with CBS. It is almost as though a severely brain-damaged person does not have sufficient resources for the elaboration of so complex a psychological system. Nevertheless, with illness and pain, especially in males, suicide is not rare even in the presence of brain syndrome.[24] True depressions in aged persons may be erroneously diagnosed as chronic brain syndrome with affective disturbance; this is particularly so if the attendant psychomotor retardation, preoccupation, poor concentration, and the patient's insistence that he is deficient or defective, are not recognized as emotionally determined.

The old clinical subtypes of senile psychosis tend to overlap with chronic and acute brain syndrome as follows:

a. *Delirious and Confused:* Synonymous with delirium. This is an acute brain syndrome occurring in a patient with chronic brain syndrome. Most of these persons, if not all, are physically ill, or have metabolic disturbance due to dehydration, malnutrition, trauma, or exhaustion.
b. *The Depressed and Agitated:* Depressed persons with emotional agitation or restlessness ascribable to their disorientation and to anxiety.
c. *The Paranoid:* The persons who with chronic brain syndrome show angry, hostile, fault-finding, complaining behavior, some of which is discernible as poorly organized delusional thought and bizarre, self-aggrandizing phantasies, often about persecution.
d. *Simple Deterioration:* A term usually denoting relatively uncomplicated cases of memory loss with little or no affective reaction and little behavioral disorder, other than wandering, nocturnal restlessness and the effects of disorientation and gross memory defect.
e. *Presbyophrenia:* Literally, "old mind," is the term usually applied to those persons in whom confabulatory trends are prominent and who appear to retain superficially good social habits despite sweeping memory defects. Among them are those who seek out the rocker, enjoy sitting in the sun, and cheerfully greet the doctor or nurse each day.

APPENDIX B

PSYCHIATRIC EXAMINATION FORM

Institution ______________________ Examiner ______________

Date of Exam. ______________

Subject ______________________ Institution Code ______________

Subj. Study No. ______________

Check or fill in the appropriate item or items in each of the sections below:

A. "Organic" Reactions
"Organic" Aspects

1. Brain syndrome Mild Mod. Sev.
(a)______acute
(b)______chronic
(c)______unspecif.
(d)______none

2. *Due to:*
(a)______None
(b)______senile brain changes
(c)______cereb. arteriosclerosis
(d)______________________

3. With psychosis: ______Yes______No
Mild Mod. Sev.
(a)______depressed
(b)______depr. & agit.
(c)______paranoid
(d)__________

Prominent Signs of A or B:
None __________

B. "Organic" Reactions
Psychotic Aspects Yes___No___
(a)___Psychosis with cereb. art
(b)___senile psychosis
___simple deterioration
___delirious and confused
___depressed and agitated
___paranoid
___presbyophrenic
(c)___schizophrenic
(d)___manic depr. psycho.
___M___D
(e)___involutional psychosis
(f)______________________

Presence of:	Defects of:	*Time*	*Place*	*Person*	*Situation*
(a)__neurological signs	(l)__orientation for				
(b)__confabulation	(j)__grasp & compre.				
(c)__emotional liability	(k)__memory-remote				
(d)__depression	(l)__memory-recent				
(e)__agitation	(m)__calculation				
(f)__paranoid trends	(n)__gen. information				
(g)__hallucinations	(o)__judgment				
(h)__delusions					

C. "Non-organic" Conditions:
None ________________

1. Psychosis:
(a)__schizophrenia
(b)__man-dep-psychosis __M__D
(c)__invol. psychosis

2. Nonpsychotic Conditions:
(a)__psychoneurosis
(b)__psychophysiologic reactions
(c)__personality disorders

D. Physical Status Observed:
(a)__no significant disorder
(b)__infirm
(c)__disabled__motor__sensory
(d)__acutely ill
(e)__chronically ill

E. Prognosis for Life:
(a)__less than 3 months
(b)__from 3 months to 1 year
(c)__more than 1 year

F. Severity of behavioral disorder:
("management problem" aspect)
(a)__none
(b)__mild
(c)__moderate
(d)__severe

G. Certifiability:
(a)__certifiable
(b)__not certifiable

H. Psychiatric hospitalization:
(a)__desirable
(b)__not desirable

I. Type of treatment needed:	Either Anc. or Primary
(a)__Psychiatric	
1__ind.psych.rx.	______
2__milieu psychother.	______
3__group psychother.	______
4__apprec.of Pd.fac.	______
5__drugs	______
6__phys. procedure	______
(b)__Medical rx.	______
(c)__Medical-Nursing rx.	______
(d)__Custodial care	______
(e)__Supervisory care	______
(f)__Social Asst.	______
(g)__other	______

Discussion

by DEAN J. CLYDE, PH.D.*

IN LISTENING TO THE SPEAKERS, and indeed to those throughout the meeting, I have discerned two themes which have recurred like the themes in a symphony, repeated again and again, each time with variations. I would like to discuss these two themes and show how they are related to each other.

The first theme is this: there are many factors involved in evaluating psychiatric treatment. These factors interact in complicated ways, and in order to come to grips with psychiatric problems we cannot study one factor at a time, ignoring its relationship with other factors.

The second theme has been bluntly stated by some speakers and politely implied by others. Many of you have expressed dissatisfaction with the statistical methods which are often used for evaluating psychiatric treatment.

I agree with these two points. We have been using oversimplified mathematical models to describe complicated patterns of relationships. Percentages, t ratios and chi square are examples of simple statistics which usually do not do justice to the richness of our observations and concepts.

Are there statistical methods which consider a number of factors together which are interacting in complicated ways? Yes, and they are not new. During the 1930's R. A. Fisher and Harold Hotelling published numerous articles on the subject of what came to be called multivariate analysis. Although they developed the theory, it was not feasible to apply their techniques to any real problems except the most simple ones because of the extensive computations required. For example, Fisher's discriminant function is impossible to carry out on a desk calculator with the number of variables we often encounter in psychiatric research. Fortunately the electrical engineers have solved this problem for us. It is now easy and economical to apply multivariate statistical procedures to our data with the help of modern computing equipment.

Let me illustrate with a problem from the nine-hospital collabora-

*The George Washington University.

tive study of phenothiazines sponsored by the National Institute of Mental Health. Given 23 different measures of each patient's behavior, how do we best describe the effects drugs are producing? Considering all the interrelationships of 23 measures—which were consistent with each other, which were going in opposite directions, which were unrelated to each other—what is the simplest and clearest description of drug effects? The aim of statistics is to simplify a mass of data but not to oversimplify it.

As Jonathan O. Cole said, "Fisher's discriminant function identified certain key measures among the 23 which summarized drug effects. Three of the most clear-cut were the nurses' ratings of behavior on the ward, the doctors' ratings of apathy and retardation, and the patients' self-ratings of aggressiveness. Drugs improved ward behavior and reduced apathy and aggressiveness."

As we all know, it is possible to be swamped with too much information. Some of the 23 measures used in the nine-hospital study were redundant and duplicated other information. The discriminant function showed that in order to describe drug effects simply and clearly it would be better to pay no attention to those redundant measures. They added no new information, only noise. It is as if a patient had described his symptoms to a physician accurately, enabling a diagnosis to be made, and then added, "And besides, doctor, I feel sick." His final statement could be perfectly true, but might add nothing to clarify the diagnosis. Multivariate statistical methods can detect such unneeded information in our experiments.

Too often as a result of our statistical manipulations we lose sight of the individual patient. Averages and percentages may conceal as much as they reveal. The discriminant function computations in the nine-hospital study led us back to patients' individual reactions to the drugs. A few patients who were in the drug-treated group reacted exactly like those in the placebo group, and these patients were clearly identified. It had not been apparent from examination of their individual scores, but their pattern of response was like those on placebo. Why? Perhaps they were not taking the drug after all, or perhaps their disorder was different from those who responded to the drug. A close individual study of these idiosyncratic patients is indicated. The statistical procedure alerted us to the fact that some patients did not respond typically.

After discriminant function has separated the drug responders in a study from the nonresponders, it can be used to search for predictors of response. If we have a variety of observations of the patients before treatment started, discriminant function will show us whether some pattern of those observations would have predicted drug response better than chance. We have not tried this step in the nine-hospital study yet, but we will when all the data are in.

I have used discriminant function as an example of a statistical procedure, but, of course, this does not mean that it is the only mathematical model available for evaluating the results of psychiatric treatment. If you are studying a multivariate problem, and most of us are, I suggest you consult a statistician, because he may have a procedure in his bag of tricks which will help to clarify the answers to your questions. He can probably assist you a lot more now than he could 10 years ago.

APPENDIX

Membership of American Psychopathological Association

Theodora M. Abel, Ph.D.
Palisades
Rockland County, New York

David Abrahamsen, M.D.
1035 Fifth Avenue
New York 28, New York

Nathan Ackerman, M.D.
43 East 78th Street
New York 21, New York

Alexandra Adler, M.D.
30 Park Avenue
New York 16, New York

Leslie R. Angus, M.D.
1120 East Market Street
Danville, Pennsylvania

Silvano Arieti, M.D.
22 East 72nd Street
New York 21, New York

Walter W. Baker, M.D.
Assoc. Prof. of Psychopharmacology
Medical College of Philadelphia
1025 Walnut Street
Philadelphia 7, Pennsylvania

Paul Bergman, M.D.
Clinical Center
Room 2W 238
National Institute of Mental Health
Bethesda 14, Maryland

H. Waldo Bird, M.D.
1313 East Ann Street
Ann Arbor, Michigan

Eugene Brady, M.D.
University of Maryland
School of Medicine
Baltimore, Maryland

Henry Brill, M.D.
Pilgrim State Hospital
W. Brentwood, L.I., New York

Albert Browne-Mayers, M.D.
55 East 86th Street
New York 28, New York

Ernest W. Burgess, Ph.D.
University of Chicago
1225 East 60th Street
Chicago 37, Illinois

Dale C. Cameron, M.D.
Assistant Superintendent
Saint Elizabeths Hospital
Washington 20, D. C.

Douglas G. Campbell, M.D.
490 Post Street
San Francisco 2, California

Eric T. Carlson, M.D.
60 Sutton Place, South
New York 22, New York

James P. Cattell, M.D.
880 Fifth Avenue
New York 21, New York

Robert Clark, M.D.
Friends Hospital
Roosevelt Blvd. & Adams Avenue
Philadelphia 24, Pennsylvania

John A. Clausen, Ph.D.
1963 Yosemite Road
Berkeley 7, California

Robert A. Cohen, M.D.
4514 Dorset Avenue
Chevy Chase 15, Maryland

Oskar Dietheim, M.D.
New York Hospital
525 East 68th Street
New York 21, New York

Roy M. Dorcus, Ph.D.
University of California
Los Angeles 24, California

Leon Eisenberg, M.D.
2610 Whitney Avenue
Baltimore, Maryland

William W. Elgin, M.D.
Sheppard & Enoch Pratt Hospital
Towson 4, Maryland
or
P.O. Box 6815
Towson 4, Maryland

Joel Elkes, M.D.
9902 Cedar Lane
Bethesda, Maryland

Raymond Feldman, M.D.
9900 Old Spring Road
Kensington, Maryland

Robert H. Felix, M.D.
National Institute of Mental Health
U. S. Public Health Service
Bethesda 14, Maryland

Max Fink, M.D.
Department of Experimental Psychiatry
Hillside Hospital
Glen Oaks, L. I., New York

Barbara Fish, M.D.
70 East 10th Street
New York 3, New York

Arthur N. Foxe, M.D.
9 East 67th Street
New York 21, New York

Richard L. Frank, M.D.
15 East 91st Street
New York 28, New York

John Frosch, M.D.
1 Gracie Terrace
New York 21, New York

Daniel H. Funkenstein, M.D.
74 Fenwood Road
Boston 14, Massachusetts

Murray Glusman, M.D.
50 East 72nd Street
New York 21, New York

William Goldfarb, M.D.
530 West End Avenue
New York 24, New York

Jacques Gottlieb, M.D.
Lafayette Clinic
951 East Lafayette
Detroit 7, Michigan

Ernest M. Gruenberg, M.D.
722 West 168th Street
New York 32, New York

Volta R. Hall, M.D.
412 Beacon Street
Boston 15, Massachusetts

A. Irving Hallowell, Ph.D.
Box 14, Bennet Hall
University of Pennsylvania
Philadelphia, Pennsylvania

David A. Hamburg, M.D.
National Institute of Mental Health
Building 10, Room 3N 212
Bethesda 14, Maryland

Irving B. Harrison, M.D.
142 Garth Road
Scarsdale, New York

Lynwood Heaver, M.D.
61 Irving Place
New York 3, New York

Morris Herman, M.D.
30 East 40th Street
New York 16, New York

Donald M. Hamilton, M.D.
121 Westchester Avenue
White Plains, New York

Bernard Holland, M.D.
Emory University
P.O. Box 459
Atlanta 22, Georgia

William A. Horwitz, M.D.
722 West 168th Street
New York 32, New York

Joseph Hughes, M.D.
111 North 49th Street
Philadelphia 39, Pennsylvania

Lissy Jarvik, M.D., Ph.D.
722 West 168th Street
New York 32, New York

George A. Jervis, M.D., Ph.D.
Letchworth Village
Research Department
Thiells, Rockland County, New York

Lothar B. Kalinowsky, M.D.
115 East 82nd Street
New York 28, New York

Franz J. Kallmann, M.D.
722 West 168th Street
New York 32, New York

William Raymond Keeler, M.D.
484 Avenue Road
Toronto 7, Ontario, Canada

Edward J. Kempf, M.D.
Wading River
Long Island, New York

Isabelle V. Kendig, Ph.D.
Sandy Spring, Maryland

Seymour S. Kety, M.D.
National Institute of Mental Health
National Institutes of Health
Bethesda 14, Maryland

Vojtech Adalbert Kral, M.D.
4145 Blueridge Crescent
Montreal 25, Canada

Morton Kramer, Sc.D.
9612 Sutherland Road
Silver Spring, Maryland

Emma Layman, Ph.D.
Department of Psychiatry
Children's Hospital
2125 - 13th Street, N.W.
Washington 9, D. C.

Zigmond M. Lebensohn, M.D.
1712 Rhode Island Avenue, N.W.
Washington 6, D. C.

Heinz E. Lehmann, M.D.
6603 LaSalle Boulevard
Montreal, Quebec, Canada

Alexander H. Leighton, M.D.
Payne Whitney Clinic
525 East 68th Street
New York, New York

David M. Levy, M.D.
47 East 77th Street
New York 21, New York

William T. Lhamon, M.D.
Baylor University
College of Medicine
1 Blalock Circle
Houston 25, Texas

W. T. Liberson, M.D., Ph.D.
Chief, Physical Education
and Rehabilitation Service
V.A. Hospital
P.O. Box 28
Hines, Illinois

Howard S. Liddell, Ph.D.
Department of Psychology
Cornell University
Ithaca, New York

Ogden R. Lindsley, Ph.D.
Behavior Research Lab.
Harvard Medical School
Metropolitan State Hospital
Waltham 54, Massachusetts

Hans Lowenbach, M.D.
Duke University Medical Center
Durham, North Carolina

Sidney Malitz, M.D.
722 West 168th Street
New York 32, New York

Benjamin Malzberg, Ph.D.
Research Foundation for
Mental Hygiene, Inc.
240 State Street
Albany 1, New York

Paul Meehl, Ph.D.
Box 390
University Hospitals
Minneapolis 14, Minnesota

John A. P. Millet, M.D.
25 East 92nd Street
New York 28, New York

Robert S. Morrow, Ph.D.
16 Pietro Place
Dobbs Ferry, New York

Leon Moses, M.D.
19 East 74th Street
New York 21, New York

Hobart Mowrer, M.D.
445 Gregory Hall
University of Illinois
Urbana, Illinois

J. Martin Myers, Jr., M.D.
Institute of Pennsylvania Hospital
111 North 49th Street
Philadelphia 39, Pennsylvania

Leo P. O'Donnell, M.D.
Harlem Valley Hospital
Wingdale, New York

Joseph B. Parker, Jr., M.D.
University of Kentucky
Medical Center
Lexington, Kentucky

Benjamin Pasamanick, M.D.
Columbus Psychiatric Institute
and Hospital, OSO Health Center
Columbus 10, Ohio

Grosvenor B. Pearson, M.D.
550 Grant Street
Pittsburgh 19, Pennsylvania

Harris B. Peck, M.D.
11 East 68th Street
New York 21, New York

Harry H. Pennes, M.D.
611 West 239th Street
Bronx 63, New York

Zygmont A. Piotrowski, Ph.D.
1025 Walnut Street
Philadelphia 7, Pennsylvania

Phillip Polatin, M.D.
4667 Delafield Avenue
New York 71, New York

Sandor Rado, M.D.
235 East 73rd Street
New York 21, New York

John Rainer, M.D.
110 East 87th Street
New York, New York

Fritz Redl, M.D.
20001 Warrington Drive
Detroit 21, Michigan

F. C. Redlich, M.D.
333 Cedar Street
New Haven 11, Connecticut

David McK. Rioch, M.D.
4607 Dorset Avenue
Chevy Chase 15, Maryland

Janet Mackenzie Rioch, M.D.
220 Central Park, South
New York 19, New York

Margaret Rioch, M.D.
4607 Dorset Avenue
Chevy Chase 15, Maryland

Fred V. Rockwell, M.D.
Grasslands Hospital
Valhalla, New York

Howard P. Rome, M.D.
Mayo Clinic
Rochester, Minnesota

Mathew Ross, M.D.
Medical Director
American Psychiatric Association
1700 Eighteenth Street, N.W.
Washington 9, D. C.

Theodore Rothman, M.D.
415 North Camden Drive
Beverly Hills, California

G. Wilson Schaffer, Ph.D.
Johns Hopkins University
Baltimore 18, Maryland

Isidore W. Scherer, Ph.D.
Veterans Administration Hospital
Northampton, Massachusetts

Charles Shagass, M.D.
The Psychopathic Hospital
State University of Iowa
500 Newton Road
Iowa City, Iowa

Rene A. Spitz, M.D.
45 South Ash Street
Denver 22, Colorado

Edward J. Stainbrook, M.D.
509 Prospect Boulevard
Pasadena, California

Gregory Stragnell, M.D.
388 Homewood Road
Los Angeles 49, California

Joseph G. Sutton, M.D.
5 Roosevelt Street
Montclair, New Jersey

Hans C. Syz, M.D.
The Lifwynne Foundation
Westport, Connecticut

Harry A. Teitelbaum, M.D.
1801 Eutaw Place
Baltimore 17, Maryland

Charles B. Thompson, M.D.
The Lifwynne Foundation
52 South Morningside Drive
Westport, Connecticut

Harvey J. Tompkins, M.D.
157 Chapel Road
Manhasset, L. I., New York

Heinrich B. Waelsch, M.D.
722 West 168th Street
New York 32, New York

Raymond W. Waggoner, M.D.
University Hospital
1313 East Ann Street
Ann Arbor, Michigan

James Hardin Wall, M.D.
121 Westchester Avenue
White Plains, New York

David Wechsler, Ph.D.
Bellevue Hospital
New York, New York

Edith Weigert, M.D.
12 Oxford Street
Chevy Chase 15, Maryland

Edwin A. Weinstein, M.D.
7101 Pyle Road
Bethesda 14, Maryland

Livingston Welch, Ph.D.
Hunter College
695 Park Avenue
New York 21, New York

Frederick L. Weniger, M.D.
3811 O'Hara Street
Pittsburgh 13, Pennsylvania

Louis J. West, M.D.
University of Oklahoma
Medical Center
800 N.E. 13th Street
Oklahoma City 4, Oklahoma

Robert W. White, Ph.D.
Department of Social Relations
Harvard University
Cambridge, Massachusetts

John C. Whitehorn, M.D.
210 Northfield Place
Baltimore 10, Maryland

William Preston Wilson, M.D.
Duke University
Medical Center
Durham, North Carolina

Cecil L. Wittson, M.D.
9651 North 29th Street
Omaha 12, Nebraska

Lewis R. Wolberg, M.D.
55 East 86th Street
New York 28, New York

Past and Present Officers of the American Psychopathological Association

Presidents

1912	Adolf Meyer
1913	James T. Putnam
1914	Alfred R. Allen
1915	Alfred R. Allen
1916	Adolf Meyer
1917	Adolf Meyer
1918	Smith Ely Jelliffe
1921	William A. White
1922	John T. MacCurdy
1923	L. Pierce Clark
1924	L. Pierce Clark
1925	Albert M. Barrett
1927	Sanger Brown II
1928	Ross McC. Chapman
1929	Ross McC. Chapman
1930	William Healy
1931	William Healy
1932	J. Ramsay Hunt
1933	Edward J. Kempf
1934	Edward J. Kempf
1935	Nolan D. C. Lewis
1936	Nolan D. C. Lewis
1937	Nolan D. C. Lewis
1938	Samuel W. Hamilton
1939	Abraham Myerson
1940	Douglas A. Thom
1941	Roscoe W. Hall
1942	Roscoe W. Hall
1943	Frederick L. Wells
1944	Frederick L. Wells
1945	Bernard Glueck
1946	Robert P. Knight
1947	Frederick L. Wells
1948	Donald J. MacPherson
1949	Paul Hoch
1950	William B. Terhune
1951	Lauren H. Smith
1952	Joseph Zubin
1953	Clarence P. Oberndorf
1954	David McK. Rioch
1955	Merrill Moore
1956	Oskar Diethelm
1957	Howard S. Liddell
1958	Leslie B. Hohman
1959	Harry C. Solomon
1960	David Wechsler
1961	William Horsley Gantt
1962	Lauretta Bender

Vice-Presidents

1924	William Healy George H. Kirby
1925	J. Ramsay Hunt Sidney L. Schwab
1927	Ross McC. Chapman Edward J. Kempf
1928	Edward J. Kempf E. Stanley Abbott
1929	Edward J. Kempf E. Stanley Abbott
1930	J. Ramsay Hunt Herman N. Adler
1931	J. Ramsay Hunt Herman N. Adler
1933	Albert M. Barrett Trigant Burrow
1934	Albert M. Barrett Trigant Burrow
1935	J. Ramsay Hunt Smith Ely Jelliffe
1936	J. Ramsay Hunt Smith Ely Jelliffe
1937	Samuel W. Hamilton Ray G. Hoskins

Vice-Presidents

1938 Lydiard H. Horton
Hans Syz
1939 Roscoe W. Hall
Douglass A. Thom
1940 George S. Sprague
Bernard Glueck
1941 Frederick L. Wells
Lowell S. Selling
1943 Frederick L. Wells
Lowell S. Selling
1944 Lowell S. Selling
Flanders Dunbar
1945 Thomas V. Moore
Robert P. Knight
1946 Paul H. Hoch
Thos. A. C. Rennie
1947 William C. Menninger
Ruth Benedict
1948 Ruth Benedict
Lauren H. Smith
1949 Arthur N. Foxe
Norman Cameron
1950 Harry M. Murdock
William S. Taylor
1951 Harry M. Murdock
Lauretta Bender
1952 William Horowitz
S. Bernard Wortis
1953 David McK. Rioch
Merrill Moore
Howard S. Liddell
1955 Oskar Diethelm
Howard S. Liddell
1956 Leslie B. Hohman
1957 David Wechsler
1958 David Wechsler
1959 Clara Thompson
1960 Theodora M. Abel
1961 Donald M. Hamilton
1962 Jerome D. Frank

Secretaries

1921 H. W. Frink
1922-1926 Sanger Brown, II
1927-1929 Martin W. Peck
1930-1939 L. Eugene Emerson
1940-1948 Merrill Moore
1944-1951 Samuel W. Hamilton
1952-1960 Donald M. Hamilton
1961-1962 Fritz A. Freyhan

Treasurers

1924-1942 William C. Garvin
1943-1951 Joseph Zubin
1952-1962 Bernard C. Glueck, Jr.

Honorary Members

Brock G. Chisholm, M.D.
Seawood, West Coast Road
R.R. 2, Victoria
British Columbia, Canada

Thomas Verner Moore, Ph.D., M.D.
Carthusian Foundation in America, Inc.
Sky Farm
Whitingham, Vermont

Aubrey J. Lewis, M.D.
The Maudsley Hospital
Denmark Hill, S.E. 5
London, England

Life Members

Leo Alexander, M.D.
433 Marlboro Street
Boston 15, Massachusetts

Edward B. Allen, M.D.
21 Greenridge Avenue
White Plains, New York

George S. Amsden, M.D.
Acworth, New Hampshire

Irma Bache, M.D.
1 East 368
Pentagon Building
Washington 25, D. C.

Daniel Blain, M.D.
1320 K Street
Sacramento 14, California

A. Louise Brush, M.D.
55 East 86th Street
New York 28, New York

Dexter M. Bullard, Sr., M.D.
M.E.A., 500 West Montgomery Avenue
Rockville, Maryland

Carl D. Camp, M.D.
304 South State Street
Ann Arbor, Michigan

Edward J. Carroll, M.D.
121 University Place
Pittsburgh 13, Pennsylvania

Hollis E. Clow, M.D.
121 Westchester Avenue
White Plains, New York

John M. Dorsey, M.D.
Wayne St. University
Detroit 2, Michigan

Milton H. Erickson, M.D.
32 West Cypress Street
Phoenix, Arizona

Bernard Glueck, Sr., M.D.
University of North Carolina
Box 1020
Chapel Hill, North Carolina

Leslie B. Hohman, M.D.
Duke Medical School
Durham, North Carolina

William A. Hunt, Ph.D.
Northwestern University
Evanston, Illinois

Abram Kardiner, M.D.
1100 Park Avenue
New York, New York

Solomon Katzenelbogen, M.D.
9305 Parkhill Terrace
Bethesda 14, Maryland

Richard D. Kepner, M.D.
P.O. Box 3119
Honolulu 2, Hawaii

Lawrence C. Kolb, M.D.
6645 32nd Street
Washington, D.C.

Nolan D. C. Lewis, M.D.
5 Rivercrest Road
New York 71, New York

Donald J. MacPherson, M.D.
270 Commonwealth Avenue
Boston 16, Massachusetts

Charles A. McDonald, M.D.
106 Waterman Street
Providence 6, Rhode Island

Edwin E. McNiel, M.D.
3875 Wilshire Boulevard
Los Angeles 5, California

Edward E. Mayer, M.D.
5601 Forbes Street
Pittsburgh 17, Pennsylvania

William C. Menninger, M.D.
Menninger Foundation
Topeka, Kansas

Harry M. Murdock, M.D.
Sheppard and Enoch Pratt Hospital
Towson 4, Maryland

Henry A. Murray, Ph.D., M.D.
48 Mount Auburn Street
Cambridge, Massachusetts

Raymond L. Osborne, M.D.
140 East 54th Street
New York 22, New York

Winfred Overholser, M.D.
St. Elizabeths Hospital
Washington 20, D. C.

Hyman L. Rachlin, M.D.
35 Park Avenue
New York 16, New York

William S. Sadler, M.D.
533 Diversey Parkway
Chicago, Illinois

David Shakow, Ph.D.
912 South Wood Street
Chicago, Illinois

Alexander Simon, M.D.
Langley Porter Clinic
San Francisco, California

John L. Smalldon, M.D.
104 Pleasant Street
Concord, New Hampshire

George W. Smeltz, M.D.
Marlborough-Blenheim Hotel
Atlantic City, New Jersey

Lauren H. Smith, M.D.
111 North 49th Street
Philadelphia, Pennsylvania

Harry C. Solomon, M.D.
74 Fenwood Road
Boston, Massachusetts

Charles W. Stephenson
South Hero, Vermont

William S. Taylor, Ph.D.
55 Dryads Green
Northampton, Massachusetts

William B. Terhune, M.D.
Silver Hill Foundation
Box 1114
New Canaan, Connecticut

Kenneth J. Tillotson, M.D.
1265 Beacon Street
Brookline, Massachusetts

Vladimir G. Urse, M.D.
Cook County Hospital
Polk and Wood Streets
Chicago 12, Illinois

Roy McL. Van Wart, M.D.
10431 Bellagio Road
Los Angeles 24, California

George A. Waterman, M.D.
200 Beacon Street
Boston, Massachusetts

Frederic Lyman Wells, Ph.D.
19 Bowdoin Street
Newton Highlands 61, Massachusetts

Louis Wender, M.D.
59 East 79th Street
New York 21, New York

Cornelius C. Wholey, M.D.
University of Pittsburgh
Medical School
Pittsburgh, Pennsylvania

George B. Wilbur, M.D.
Cove Road
South Dennis, Massachusetts

S. Bernard Wortis, M.D.
410 East 57th Street
New York 22, New York

INDEX